FINANCIAL INSTITUTIONS AND SERVICES

THE BANK SECRECY ACT AND ANTI-MONEY LAUNDERING EXAMINATION MANUAL

FINANCIAL INSTITUTIONS AND SERVICES

Additional books in this series can be found on Nova's website at:

https://www.novapublishers.com/catalog/index.php?cPath=23_29&seriesp=
Financial+Institutions+and+Services

Additional E-books in this series can be found on Nova's website at:

https://www.novapublishers.com/catalog/index.php?cPath=23_29&seriespe=
Financial+Institutions+and+Services

FINANCIAL INSTITUTIONS AND SERVICES

THE BANK SECRECY ACT AND ANTI-MONEY LAUNDERING EXAMINATION MANUAL

ANNE LEUTER
EDITOR

Nova
Nova Science Publishers, Inc.
New York

For permission to use material from this book please contact us:
Telephone 631-231-7269; Fax 631-231-8175
Web Site: http://www.novapublishers.com

NOTICE TO THE READER

LIBRARY OF CONGRESS CATALOGING-IN-PUBLICATION DATA
The Bank Secrecy Act and anti-money laundering examination manual / editor, Anne Leuter.
p. cm.
Includes index.
ISBN 978-1-60876-162-3 (hbk.)
1. United States. Bank Secrecy Act. 2. Banks and banking--Records and correspondence--Law and legislation--United States. 3. Confidential communications--Banking--United States. 4. Money laundering--United States. I. Leuter, Anne.
KF1030.R3B328 2010
346.73'082--dc22
2010013757

Published by Nova Science Publishers, Inc. ✢ New York

CONTENTS

PREFACE

This book provides an overview of The Bank Secrecy Act (BSA) and the Anti-Money Laundering Manual (AML) which is intended to safeguard the U.S. financial system and the financial institutions that make up that system from the abuses of financial crime, including money laundering, terrorist financing, and other illicit financial transactions. Money laundering and terrorist financing are financial crimes with potentially devastating social and financial effects. The BSA was designed to help identify the source, volume, and movement of currency and other monetary instruments transported or transmitted into or out of the U.S. or deposited in financial institutions.

This is an edited, reformatted and augmented edition of a Federal Financial Institutions Examination Council publication, dated July 28, 2006 and edited by Anne Leuter.

In: The Bank Secrecy Act and Anti-Money Laundering... ISBN: 978-1-60876-162-3
Editor: Anne Leuter

Chapter 1

INTRODUCTION

This Federal Financial Institutions Examination Council (FFIEC) Bank Secrecy Act (BSA) /Anti-Money Laundering (AML) Examination Manual provides guidance to examiners for carrying out BSA/AML and Office of Foreign Assets Control (OFAC) examinations. An effective BSA/AML compliance program requires sound risk management; therefore, the manual also provides guidance on identifying and controlling risks associated with money laundering and terrorist financing. The manual contains an overview of BSA/AML compliance program requirements, BSA/AML risks and risk management expectations, industry sound practices, and examination procedures. The development of this manual was a collaborative effort of the federal banking agencies[1] and the Financial Crimes Enforcement Network (FinCEN), a bureau of the U.S. Department of the Treasury, to ensure consistency in the application of the BSA/AML requirements. In addition, OFAC assisted in the development of the sections of the manual that relate to OFAC reviews. Refer to Appendices A ("BSA Laws and Regulations"), B ("BSA/AML Directives"), and C ("BSA/AML References") for guidance.

STRUCTURE OF MANUAL

In order to effectively apply resources and ensure compliance with BSA requirements, the manual is structured to allow examiners to tailor the BSA/AML examination scope and procedures to the specific risk profile of the banking organization. The manual consists of the following sections:

- Introduction.
- Core Examination Overview and Procedures for Assessing the BSA/AML Compliance Program.
- Core Examination Overview and Procedures for Regulatory Requirements and Related Topics.
- Expanded Examination Overview and Procedures for an Enterprise-Wide Compliance Program and Other Structures.

- Expanded Examination Overview and Procedures for Products and Services.
- Expanded Examination Overview and Procedures for Persons and Entities.
- Appendices.

The core and expanded overview sections provide narrative guidance and background information on each topic; each overview is followed by examination procedures. The "Core Examination Overview and Procedures for Assessing the BSA/AML Compliance Program" and the "Core Examination Overview and Procedures for Regulatory Requirements and Related Topics" (core) sections serve as a platform for the BSA/AML examination and, for the most part, address legal and regulatory requirements of the BSA/AML compliance program. The "Scoping and Planning" and the "BSA/AML Risk Assessment" sections help the examiner develop an appropriate examination plan based on the risk profile of the bank. There may be instances where a topic is covered in both the core and expanded sections (e.g., funds transfers and foreign correspondent banking). In such instances, the core overview and examination procedures address the BSA requirements while the expanded overview and examination procedures address the AML risks of the specific activity.

At a minimum, examiners should use the following examination procedures included within the "Core Examination Overview and Procedures for Assessing the BSA/AML Compliance Program" section of this manual to ensure that the bank has an adequate BSA/AML compliance program commensurate with its risk profile:

- Scoping and Planning (refer to pages 15 to 17).
- BSA/AML Risk Assessment (refer to page 27).
- BSA/AML Compliance Program (refer to pages 34 to 39).
- Developing Conclusions and Finalizing the Examination (refer to pages 41 to 44).

While OFAC regulations are not part of the BSA, the core sections include overview and examination procedures for examining a bank's policies, procedures, and processes for ensuring compliance with OFAC sanctions. As part of the scoping and planning procedures, examiners must review the bank's OFAC risk assessment and independent testing to determine the extent to which a review of the bank's OFAC program should be conducted during the examination. Refer to core examination procedures, "Office of Foreign Assets Control," pages 144 to 146, for further guidance.

The expanded sections address specific lines of business, products, customers, or entities that may present unique challenges and exposures for which banks should institute appropriate policies, procedures, and processes. Absent appropriate controls, these lines of business, products, customers, or entities could elevate BSA/AML risks. In addition, the expanded section provides guidance on enterprise-wide BSA/AML risk management.

Not all of the core and expanded examination procedures will likely be applicable to every banking organization. The specific examination procedures that will need to be performed depend on the BSA/AML risk profile of the banking organization, the quality and quantity of independent testing, the financial institution's history of BSA/AML compliance, and other relevant factors.

BACKGROUND

In 1970, Congress passed the Currency and Foreign Transactions Reporting Act commonly known as the "Bank Secrecy Act,"[2] which established requirements for recordkeeping and reporting by private individuals, banks,[3] and other financial institutions. The BSA was designed to help identify the source, volume, and movement of currency and other monetary instruments transported or transmitted into or out of the United States or deposited in financial institutions. The statute sought to achieve that objective by requiring individuals, banks, and other financial institutions to file currency reports with the U.S. Department of the Treasury (U.S. Treasury), properly identify persons conducting transactions, and maintain a paper trail by keeping appropriate records of financial transactions. These records enable law enforcement and regulatory agencies to pursue investigations of criminal, tax, and regulatory violations, if warranted, and provide evidence useful in prosecuting money laundering and other financial crimes.

The Money Laundering Control Act of 1986 augmented the B SA's effectiveness by the interrelated sections 8(s) and 21 to the Federal Deposit Insurance Act (FDI Act), which sections apply equally to banks of all charters.[4] The Money Laundering Control Act of 1986 precludes circumvention of the BSA requirements by imposing criminal liability on a person or financial institution that knowingly assists in the laundering of money, or that structures transactions to avoid reporting them. The 1986 statute directed banks to establish and maintain procedures reasonably designed to ensure and monitor compliance with the reporting and recordkeeping requirements of the BSA. As a result, on January 27, 1987, all federal banking agencies issued essentially similar regulations requiring banks to develop programs for BSA compliance.

The 1992 Annunzio–Wylie Anti-Money Laundering Act strengthened the sanctions for BSA violations and the role of the U.S. Treasury. Two years later, Congress passed the Money Laundering Suppression Act of 1994 (MLSA), which further addressed the U.S. Treasury's role in combating money laundering.

In April 1996, a Suspicious Activity Report (SAR) was developed to be used by all banking organizations in the United States. A banking organization is required to file a SAR whenever it detects a known or suspected criminal violation of federal law or a suspicious transaction related to money laundering activity or a violation of the BSA.

In response to the September 11, 2001, terrorist attacks, Congress passed the Uniting and Strengthening America by Providing Appropriate Tools Required to Intercept and Obstruct Terrorism Act of 2001 (Patriot Act). Title III of the Patriot Act is the International Money Laundering Abatement and Anti-Terrorist Financing Act of 2001. The Patriot Act is arguably the single most significant AML law that Congress has enacted since the BSA itself. Among other things, the Patriot Act criminalized the financing of terrorism and augmented the existing BSA framework by strengthening customer identification procedures; prohibiting financial institutions from engaging in business with foreign shell banks; requiring financial institutions to have due diligence procedures and, in some cases, enhanced due diligence procedures for foreign correspondent and private banking accounts; and improving information sharing between financial institutions and the U.S. government. The Patriot Act and its implementing regulations also:

- Expanded the AML program requirements to all financial institutions.[5] Refer to Appendix D ("Statutory Definition of Financial Institution") for further clarification.
- Increased the civil and criminal penalties for money laundering.
- Provided the Secretary of the Treasury with the authority to impose "special measures" on jurisdictions, institutions, or transactions that are of "primary money-laundering concern."
- Facilitated records access and required banks to respond to regulatory requests for information within 120 hours.
- Required federal banking agencies to consider a bank's AML record when reviewing bank mergers, acquisitions, and other applications for business combinations.

Role of Government Agencies in the BSA

Certain government agencies play a critical role in implementing BSA regulations, developing examination guidance, ensuring compliance with the BSA, and enforcing the BSA. These agencies include the U.S. Treasury, FinCEN, and the federal banking agencies (Board of Governors of the Federal Reserve System, Federal Deposit Insurance Corporation, National Credit Union Administration, Office of the Comptroller of the Currency, and Office of Thrift Supervision). Internationally there are various multilateral government bodies that support the fight against money laundering and terrorist financing. Refer to Appendix E ("International Organizations") for additional information.

U.S. Treasury

The BSA authorizes the Secretary of the Treasury to require financial institutions to establish AML programs, file certain reports, and keep certain records of transactions. Certain BSA provisions have been extended to cover not only traditional depository institutions, such as banks, savings associations, and credit unions, but also non-bank financial institutions, such as money services businesses, casinos, brokers/dealers in securities, futures commission merchants, mutual funds, insurance companies, and operators of credit card systems.

FinCEN

FinCEN, a bureau of the U.S. Treasury, is the delegated administrator of the BSA. In this capacity, FinCEN issues regulations and interpretive guidance, provides outreach to regulated industries, supports the examination functions performed by federal banking agencies, and pursues civil enforcement actions when warranted. FinCEN relies on the federal banking agencies to examine banks within their respective jurisdictions for compliance with the BSA. FinCEN's other significant responsibilities include providing investigative case support to law enforcement, identifying and communicating financial crime trends and patterns, and fostering international cooperation with its counterparts worldwide.

Federal Banking Agencies

The federal banking agencies are responsible for the oversight of the various banking entities operating in the United States, including foreign branch offices of U.S. banks. The federal banking agencies are charged with chartering (National Credit Union Administration, Office of the Comptroller of the Currency, and Office of Thrift Supervision), insuring (Federal Deposit Insurance Corporation and National Credit Union Administration), regulating, and supervising banks.[6] 12 USC 1818(s)(2) requires that the appropriate federal banking agency include a review of the BSA compliance program at each examination of an insured depository institution. The federal banking agencies may use their authority, as granted under section 8 of the FDI Act, to enforce compliance with appropriate banking rules and regulations, including compliance with the BSA.

The federal banking agencies require each bank under their supervision to establish and maintain a BSA compliance program.[7] In accordance with the Patriot Act, FinCEN's regulations require certain financial institutions to establish an AML compliance program that guards against money laundering and terrorist financing and ensures compliance with the BSA and its implementing regulations. When the Patriot Act was passed, banks under the supervision of a federal banking agency were already required by law to establish and maintain a BSA compliance program that, among other things, requires the bank to identify and report suspicious activity promptly. For this reason, 31 CFR 103.120 states that a bank regulated by a federal banking agency is deemed to have satisfied the AML program requirements of the Patriot Act if the bank develops and maintains a BSA compliance program that complies with the regulation of its federal functional regulator[8] governing such programs. This manual will refer to the BSA compliance program requirements for each federal banking agency as the "BSA/AML compliance program."

Banks should take reasonable and prudent steps to combat money laundering and terrorist financing and to minimize their vulnerability to the risk associated with such activities. Some banking organizations have damaged their reputations and have been required to pay civil money penalties for failing to implement adequate controls within their organization resulting in noncompliance with the BSA. In addition, due to the AML assessment required as part of the application process, BSA/AML concerns can have an impact on the bank's strategic plan. For this reason, the federal banking agencies' and FinCEN's commitment to provide guidance that assists banks in complying with the BSA remains a high supervisory priority.

The federal banking agencies work to ensure that the organizations they supervise understand the importance of having an effective BSA/AML compliance program in place. Management must be vigilant in this area, especially as business grows and new products and services are introduced. An evaluation of the bank's BSA/AML compliance program and its compliance with the regulatory requirements of the BSA has been an integral part of the supervision process for years. Refer to Appendix A ("BSA Laws and Regulations") for further information.

As part of a strong BSA/AML compliance program, the federal banking agencies seek to ensure that a bank has policies, procedures, and processes to identify and report suspicious transactions to law enforcement. The agencies' supervisory processes assess whether banks have established the appropriate policies, procedures, and processes based on their BSA/AML risk to identify and report suspicious activity and that they provide sufficient detail in reports to law enforcement agencies to make the reports useful for investigating suspicious transactions that are reported. Refer to Appendices B ("BSA/AML Directives") and C ("BSA/AML References") for guidance.

OFAC

OFAC administers and enforces economic and trade sanctions based on U.S. foreign policy and national security goals against targeted foreign countries, terrorists, international narcotics traffickers, and those engaged in activities related to the proliferation of weapons of mass destruction. OFAC acts under the President's wartime and national emergency powers, as well as under authority granted by specific legislation, to impose controls on transactions and freeze assets under U.S. jurisdiction. Many of the sanctions are based on United Nations and other international mandates, are multilateral in scope, and involve close cooperation with allied governments.

OFAC requirements are separate and distinct from the BSA, but both OFAC and the BSA share a common national security goal. For this reason, many financial institutions view compliance with OFAC sanctions as related to BSA compliance obligations; supervisory examination for BSA compliance is logically connected to the examination of a financial institution's compliance with OFAC sanctions. Refer to the core overview and examination procedures, "Office of Foreign Assets Control," pages 135 and 144, respectively, for guidance.

Money Laundering and Terrorist Financing

The BSA is intended to safeguard the U.S. financial system and the financial institutions that make up that system from the abuses of financial crime, including money laundering, terrorist financing, and other illicit financial transactions. Money laundering and terrorist financing are financial crimes with potentially devastating social and financial effects. From the profits of the narcotics trafficker to the assets looted from government coffers by dishonest foreign officials, criminal proceeds have the power to corrupt and ultimately destabilize communities or entire economies. Terrorist networks are able to facilitate their activities if they have financial means and access to the financial system. In both money laundering and terrorist financing, criminals can exploit loopholes and other weaknesses in the legitimate financial system to launder criminal proceeds, finance terrorism, or conduct other illegal activities, and, ultimately, hide the actual purpose of their activity.

Banking organizations must develop, implement, and maintain effective AML programs that address the ever-changing strategies of money launderers and terrorists who attempt to gain access to the U.S. financial system. A sound BSA/AML compliance program is critical in deterring and preventing these types of activities at, or through, banks and other financial institutions. Refer to Appendix F ("Money Laundering and Terrorist Financing Red Flags") for examples of suspicious activities that may indicate money laundering or terrorist financing.

Money Laundering

Money laundering is the criminal practice of processing ill-gotten gains, or "dirty" money, through a series of transactions; in this way the funds are "cleaned" so that they appear to be proceeds from legal activities. Money laundering generally does not involve currency at every stage of the laundering process. Although money laundering is a diverse and often complex process, it basically involves three independent steps that can occur simultaneously:

Placement

The first and most vulnerable stage of laundering money is placement. The goal is to introduce the unlawful proceeds into the financial system without attracting the attention of financial institutions or law enforcement. Placement techniques include structuring currency deposits in amounts to evade reporting requirements or commingling currency deposits of legal and illegal enterprises. An example may include: dividing large amounts of currency into less-conspicuous smaller sums that are deposited directly into a bank account, depositing a refund check from a canceled vacation package or insurance policy, or purchasing a series of monetary instruments (e.g., cashier's checks or money orders) that are then collected and deposited into accounts at another location or financial institution. Refer to Appendix G ("Structuring") for additional guidance.

Layering

The second stage of the money laundering process is layering, which involves moving funds around the financial system, often in a complex series of transactions to create confusion and complicate the paper trail. Examples of layering include exchanging monetary instruments for larger or smaller amounts, or wiring or transferring funds to and through numerous accounts in one or more financial institutions.

Integration

The ultimate goal of the money laundering process is integration. Once the funds are in the financial system and insulated through the layering stage, the integration stage is used to create the appearance of legality through additional transactions. These transactions further shield the criminal from a recorded connection to the funds by providing a plausible explanation for the source of the funds. Examples include the purchase and resale of real estate, investment securities, foreign trusts, or other assets.

Terrorist Financing

The motivation behind terrorist financing is ideological as opposed to profit-seeking, which is generally the motivation for most crimes associated with money laundering. Terrorism is intended to intimidate a population or to compel a government or an international organization to do or abstain from doing any specific act through the threat of violence. An effective financial infrastructure is critical to terrorist operations. Terrorist groups develop sources of funding that are relatively mobile to ensure that funds can be used to obtain material and other logistical items needed to commit terrorist acts. Thus, money laundering is often a vital component of terrorist financing.

Terrorists generally finance their activities through both unlawful and legitimate sources. Unlawful activities, such as extortion, kidnapping, and narcotics trafficking, have been found to be a major source of funding. Other observed activities include smuggling, fraud, theft, robbery, identity theft, use of conflict diamonds,[9] and improper use of charitable or relief funds. In the last case, donors may have no knowledge that their donations have been diverted to support terrorist causes.

Other legitimate sources have also been found to provide terrorist organizations with funding; these legitimate funding sources are a key difference between terrorist financiers and traditional criminal organizations. In addition to charitable donations, legitimate sources include foreign government sponsors, business ownership, and personal employment.

Although the motivation differs between traditional money launderers and terrorist financiers, the actual methods used to fund terrorist operations can be the same as or similar to those methods used by other criminals that launder funds. For example, terrorist financiers use currency smuggling, structured deposits or withdrawals from bank accounts; purchases of various types of monetary instruments; credit, debit, or stored value cards; and funds transfers. There is also evidence that some forms of informal banking (e.g., "hawala"[10]) have played a role in moving terrorist funds. Transactions through hawalas are difficult to detect given the lack of documentation, their size, and the nature of the transactions involved. Funding for terrorist attacks does not always require large sums of money, and the associated transactions may not be complex.

Criminal Penalties for Money Laundering, Terrorist Financing, and Violations of the BSA

Penalties for money laundering and terrorist financing can be severe. A person convicted of money laundering can face up to 20 years in prison and a fine of up to $500,000.[11] Any property involved in a transaction or traceable to the proceeds of the criminal activity, including property such as loan collateral, personal property, and, under certain conditions, entire bank accounts (even if some of the money in the account is legitimate), may be subject to forfeiture. Pursuant to various statutes, banks and individuals may incur criminal and civil liability for violating AML and terrorist financing laws. For instance, pursuant to 18 USC 1956 and 1957, the Department of Justice may bring criminal actions for money laundering that may include criminal fines, imprisonment, and forfeiture actions.[12] In addition, banks risk losing their charters, and bank employees risk being removed and barred from banking.

Moreover, there are criminal penalties for willful violations of the BSA and its implementing regulations under 31 USC 5322 and for structuring transactions to evade BSA reporting requirements under 31 USC 5324(d). For example, a person, including a bank employee, willfully violating the BSA or its implementing regulations is subject to a criminal fine of up to $250,000 or five years in prison, or both.[13] A person who commits such a violation while violating another U.S. law, or engaging in a pattern of criminal activity, is subject to a fine of up to $500,000 or ten years in prison, or both.[14] A bank that violates certain BSA provisions, including 31 USC 5318(i) or (j), or special measures imposed under

31 USC 531 8A, faces criminal money penalties up to the greater of $1 million or twice the value of the transaction.[15]

Civil Penalties for Violations of the BSA

Pursuant to 12 USC 1818(i) and 31 USC 5321, the federal banking agencies and FinCEN, respectively, can bring civil money penalty actions for violations of the BSA. Moreover, in addition to criminal and civil money penalty actions taken against them, individuals may be removed from banking pursuant to 12 USC 181 8(e)(2) for a violation of the AML laws under Title 31 of the U.S. Code, as long as the violation was not inadvertent or unintentional. All of these actions are publicly available.

End Notes

[1] The five federal banking agencies that are members of the FFIEC are the Board of Governors of the Federal Reserve System, Federal Deposit Insurance Corporation, National Credit Union Administration, Office of the Comptroller of the Currency, and Office of Thrift Supervision.

[2] 31 USC 5311 *et seq.*, 12 USC 1829b, and 1951 – 1959. See also 12 USC 1818(s) (federally insured depository institutions) and 12 USC 1786(q) (federally insured credit unions).

[3] Under the BSA, as implemented by 31 CFR 103.11, the term "bank" includes each agent, agency, branch or office within the United States of commercial banks, savings and loan associations, thrift institutions, credit unions, and foreign banks.

[4] 12 USC 1 818(s) and 1829(b), respectively.

[5] The Patriot Act expanded the AML program requirement to all financial institutions as that term is defined in 31 USC 53 12(a)(2). However, as of the publication of this manual, only certain types of financial institutions are subject to final rules implementing the AML program requirements of 31 USC 531 8(h)(1) as established by the Patriot Act. Those financial institutions that are not currently subject to a final AML program rule are temporarily exempted from the Patriot Act requirements to establish an AML program, as set forth in 31 CFR 103.170.

[6] The Board of Governors of the Federal Reserve System, Federal Deposit Insurance Corporation, and Office of Thrift Supervision may collaborate with state banking agencies on the examination, oversight, and enforcement of BSA/AML for state-chartered banks.

[7] See 12 CFR 208.63, 12 CFR 211.5(m) and 12 CFR 211.24(j) (Board of Governors of the Federal Reserve System); 12 CFR 326.8 (Federal Deposit Insurance Corporation); 12 CFR 748.2 (National Credit Union Administration); 12 CFR 21.21 (Office of the Comptroller of the Currency); and 12 CFR 563.177 (Office of Thrift Supervision).

[8] Federal functional regulator means: Board of Governors of the Federal Reserve System; Federal Deposit Insurance Corporation; National Credit Union Administration; Office of the Comptroller of the Currency; Office of Thrift Supervision; Securities and Exchange Commission; or Commodity Futures Trading Commission.

[9] Conflict diamonds originate from areas controlled by forces or factions opposed to legitimate and internationally recognized governments and are used to fund military action in opposition to those governments, or in contravention of the decisions of the United Nations Security Council (www.un.org).

[10] "Hawala" refers to one specific type of informal value transfer system. FinCEN describes hawala as "a method of monetary value transmission that is used in some parts of the world to conduct remittances, most often by persons who seek to legitimately send money to family members in their home country. It has also been noted that hawala, and other such systems, are possibly being used as conduits for terrorist financing or other illegal activity." For additional information and guidance on hawalas and FinCEN's report to Congress in accordance with section 359 of the Patriot Act refer to FinCEN's web site: www.fincen.gov.

[11] 18 USC 1956.

[12] 18 USC 981 and 982.

[13] 31 USC 5322(a).

[14] *Id.*

[15] Id.

In: The Bank Secrecy Act and Anti-Money Laundering... ISBN: 978-1-60876-162-3
Editor: Anne Leuter

Chapter 2

CORE EXAMINATION OVERVIEW AND PROCEDURES FOR ASSESSING THE BSA/AML COMPLIANCE PROGRAM

SCOPING AND PLANNING — OVERVIEW

Objective. *Identify the bank's BSA/AML risks, develop the examination scope, and document the plan. This process includes determining examination staffing needs and technical expertise, and selecting examination procedures to be completed.*

The BSA/AML examination is intended to assess the effectiveness of the bank's BSA/AML compliance program and the bank's compliance with the regulatory requirements pertaining to the BSA, including a review of risk management practices.

Whenever possible, the scoping and planning process should be completed before entering the bank. During this process, it may be helpful to discuss BSA/AML matters with bank management, including the BSA compliance officer, either in person or by telephone. The scoping and planning process generally begins with an analysis of:

- Off-site monitoring information.
- Prior examination reports and workpapers.
- Request letter items completed by bank management. Refer to Appendix H ("Request Letter Items") for additional information.
- The bank's BSA/AML risk assessment.
- BSA-reporting databases (e.g., Currency and Banking Retrieval System (CBRS) and Currency and Banking Query System (CBQS)).
- Independent reviews or audits.

Review of the Bank's BSA/AML Risk Assessment

The scoping and planning process should be guided by the examiner's review of the bank's BSA/AML risk assessment. Information gained from the examiner's review of the risk assessment will assist the scoping and planning process as well as the evaluation of the adequacy of the BSA/AML compliance program. If the bank has not developed a risk assessment, this fact should be discussed with management. For the purposes of the examination, whenever the bank has not completed a risk assessment, or the risk assessment is inadequate, the examiner must complete a risk assessment. Refer to the core overview section, "BSA/AML Risk Assessment," page 18, for guidance on developing a BSA/AML risk assessment. Evaluating the BSA/AML risk assessment is part of scoping and planning the examination, and the inclusion of a section on risk assessment in the manual does not mean the two processes are separate. Rather, risk assessment has been given its own section to emphasize its importance in the examination process and in the bank's design of effective risk-based controls.

Independent Testing

As part of the scoping and planning process, examiners should obtain and evaluate the supporting documents of the independent testing (audit)[1] of the bank's BSA/AML compliance program. The scope and quality of the audit may provide examiners with a sense of particular risks in the bank, how these risks are being managed and controlled, and the status of compliance with the BSA. The independent testing scope and workpapers can assist examiners in understanding the audit coverage and the quality and quantity of transaction testing. This knowledge will assist the examiner in determining the examination scope, identifying areas requiring greater (or lesser) scrutiny, and identifying when expanded examination procedures may be necessary.

Examination Plan

At a minimum, examiners should conduct the examination procedures included in the following sections of this manual to ensure that the bank has an adequate BSA/AML compliance program commensurate with its risk profile:

- Scoping and Planning (refer to pages 15 to 17).
- BSA/AML Risk Assessment (refer to page 27).
- BSA/AML Compliance Program (refer to pages 34 to 39).
- Developing Conclusions and Finalizing the Examination (refer to pages 41 to 44).

The "Core Examination Overview and Procedures for Regulatory Requirements and Related Topics" section includes an overview and examination procedures for examining a bank's policies, procedures, and processes to ensure compliance with OFAC sanctions. As part of the scoping and planning procedures, examiners must review the bank's OFAC risk assessment and independent testing to determine the extent to which a review of the bank's OFAC program should be conducted during the examination. Refer to core overview and examination procedures, "Office of Foreign Assets Control," pages 135 to 146, for further guidance.

The examiner should develop and document an initial examination plan commensurate with the overall BSA/AML risk profile of the bank. This plan may change during the examination as a result of on-site findings, and any changes to the plan should likewise be documented. The examiner should prepare a request letter to the bank. Suggested request letter items are detailed in Appendix H ("Request Letter Items"). On the basis of the risk profile, quality of audit, previous examination findings, and initial examination work, examiners should complete additional core and expanded examination procedures, as appropriate. The examiner must include an evaluation of the BSA/AML compliance program within the supervisory plan or cycle. At larger, more complex banking organizations, examiners may complete various types of examinations throughout the supervisory plan or cycle to assess BSA/AML compliance. These reviews may focus on one or more business lines (e.g., private banking, trade financing, or foreign correspondent banking relationships), based upon the banking organization's risk assessment and recent audit and examination findings.

Transaction Testing

Examiners perform transaction testing to evaluate the adequacy of the bank's compliance with regulatory requirements, determine the effectiveness of its policies, procedures, and processes, and evaluate suspicious activity monitoring systems. Transaction testing is an important factor in forming conclusions about the integrity of the bank's overall controls and risk management processes. Transaction testing must be performed at each examination and should be risk-based. Transaction testing can be performed either through conducting the transaction testing procedures within the independent testing (audit) section (refer to the core examination procedures, "BSA/AML Compliance Program," page 34, for further guidance) or completing the transaction testing procedures contained elsewhere within the core or expanded sections.

The extent of transaction testing and activities conducted is based on various factors including the examiner's judgment of risks, controls, and the adequacy of the independent testing. Once on-site, the scope of the transaction testing can be expanded to address any issues or concerns identified during the examination. Examiners should document their decision regarding the extent of transaction testing to conduct, the activities for which it is to be performed, and the rationale for any changes to the scope of transaction testing that occur during the examination.

Information Available from BSA-Reporting Databases

Examination planning should also include an analysis of the Suspicious Activity Reports (SARs), Currency Transaction Reports (CTRs), and CTR exemptions that the bank has filed. SARs, CTRs, and CTR exemptions may be downloaded from or obtained directly on-line from the BSA-reporting databases (e.g., CBRS and CBQS). Each federal banking agency has staff authorized to obtain this data from the BSA-reporting database. When requesting searches from the BSA-reporting database, the examiner should contact the appropriate person (or persons), within his or her agency, sufficiently in advance of the examination start date in order to obtain the requested information. When a bank has recently purchased or merged with another bank, the examiner should obtain SARs, CTRs, and CTR exemptions data on the acquired bank, as well.

Downloaded information can be displayed on an electronic spreadsheet, which contains all of the data included on the original document filed by the bank as well as the Internal Revenue Service (IRS) Document Control Number (DCN), and the date the document was entered into the BSA-reporting database. Downloaded information may be important to the examination, as it will help examiners:

- Identify high-volume currency customers.
- Assist in selecting accounts for transaction testing.
- Identify the number and characteristics of SARs filed.
- Identify the number and nature of exemptions.

Examination Procedures

Scoping and Planning

Objective. *Identify the bank's BSA/AML risks, develop the examination scope, and document the plan. This process includes determining examination staffing needs and technical expertise, and selecting examination procedures to be completed.*

To facilitate the examiner's understanding of the bank's risk profile and to adequately establish the scope of the BSA/AML examination, the examiner should complete the following steps, in conjunction with the review of the bank's BSA/AML risk assessment:

1. Review prior examination or inspection reports, related workpapers, and management's responses to previously identified BSA violations, deficiencies, and recommendations. Discuss, as necessary, with the person(s) responsible for ongoing supervision of the bank or with the prior examiner in charge (EIC) any additional information or ongoing concerns that are not documented in the correspondence. Consider reviewing news articles concerning or pertaining to the bank or its management.
2. Review the prior examination workpapers to identify the specific BSA/AML examination procedures completed, obtain BSA contact information, identify the report titles and formats the bank uses to detect unusual activity, identify previously noted high-risk banking operations, and review recommendations for the next examination.
3. As appropriate, contact bank management, including the BSA compliance officer, to discuss the following:
    - BSA/AML compliance program.
    - BSA/AML management structure.
    - BSA/AML risk assessment.

- Suspicious activity monitoring and reporting systems.
- Level and extent of automated BSA/AML systems.

For the above topics, refer to the appropriate overview and examination procedures sections in the manual for guidance.

4. Send the request letter to the bank. Review the request letter documents provided by the bank. Refer to Appendix H ("Request Letter Items").
5. Read correspondence between the bank and its primary regulators, if not already completed by the examiner in charge, or other dedicated examination personnel. The examiner should become familiar with the following, as applicable:
   - Outstanding, approved, or denied applications.
   - Change of control documents, when applicable.
   - Approvals of new directors or senior management, when applicable.
   - Details of meetings with bank management.
   - Other significant activity affecting the bank or its management.
6. Review correspondence that the bank or the primary regulators have received from, or sent to, outside regulatory and law enforcement agencies relating to BSA/AML compliance. Communications, particularly those received from FinCEN, and the Internal Revenue Service (IRS) Detroit Computing Center may document matters relevant to the examination, such as the following:
   - Filing errors for Suspicious Activity Reports (SARs), Currency Transaction Reports (CTRs), and CTR exemptions.
   - Civil money penalties issued by or in process from FinCEN.
   - Law enforcement subpoenas or seizures.
   - Notification of mandatory account closures of non-cooperative foreign customers holding correspondent accounts as directed by the Secretary of the Treasury or the U.S. Attorney General.
7. Review SARs, CTRs, and CTR exemption information obtained from downloads from the BSA-reporting database. The number of SARs, CTRs, and CTR exemptions filed should be obtained for a defined time period, as determined by the examiner. Consider the following information, and analyze the data for unusual patterns, such as:
   - Volume of activity, and whether it is commensurate with the customer's occupation or type of business.
   - Number and dollar volume of transactions involving high-risk customers.
   - Volume of CTRs in relation to the volume of exemptions (i.e., whether additional exemptions resulted in significant decreases in CTR filings).
   - Volume of SARs and CTRs in relation to the bank's size, asset or deposit growth, and geographic location.

   The federal banking agencies do not have targeted volumes or "quotas" for SAR and CTR filings for a given bank size or geographic location. Examiners should not criticize a bank solely because the number of SARs or CTRs filed is lower than SARs or CTRs filed by "peer" banks. However, as part of the examination, examiners must review significant changes in the volume or nature of SARs and CTRs filed and assess potential reasons for these changes.

8. Review internal or external audit reports and workpapers for BSA/AML compliance, as necessary, to determine the comprehensiveness and quality of audits, findings, and management responses and corrective action. A review of the independent audit's scope, procedures, and qualifications will provide valuable information on the adequacy of the BSA/AML compliance program.
9. While OFAC regulations are not part of the BSA, evaluation of OFAC compliance is frequently included in BSA/AML examinations. It is not the federal banking agencies' primary role to identify OFAC violations, but rather to evaluate the sufficiency of a bank's implementation of policies, procedures, and processes to ensure compliance with OFAC laws and regulations. To facilitate the examiner's understanding of the bank's risk profile and to adequately establish the scope of the OFAC examination, the examiner should complete the following steps:
   - Review the bank's OFAC risk assessment. The risk assessment should consider the various types of products, services, customers, transactions, and geographic locations in which the bank is engaged, including those that are processed by, through, or to the bank to identify potential OFAC exposure.
   - Review the bank's independent testing of its OFAC program.
   - Review correspondence received from OFAC and, as needed, the civil penalties area on OFAC's web site to determine whether the bank had any warning letters, fines, or penalties imposed by OFAC since the most recent examination.
   - Review correspondence between the bank and OFAC (e.g., periodic reporting of prohibited transactions and, if applicable, annual OFAC reports on blocked property).

   In addition to the above, at larger, more complex banking organizations, examiners may complete various types of examinations throughout the supervisory plan or cycle to assess OFAC compliance. These reviews may focus on one or more business lines.
10. On the basis of the above examination procedures, in conjunction with the review of the bank's BSA/AML risk assessment, develop an initial examination plan. The examiner should adequately document the plan, as well as any changes to the plan that occur during the examination. The scoping and planning process should ensure that the examiner is aware of the bank's BSA/AML compliance program, OFAC program, compliance history, and risk profile (products, services, customers, and geographic locations).

As necessary, additional core and expanded examination procedures may be completed. While the examination plan may change at any time as a result of on-site findings, the initial risk assessment will enable the examiner to establish a reasonable scope for the BSA/AML review. For the examination process to be successful, examiners must maintain open communication with the bank's management and discuss relevant concerns as they arise.

BSA/AML Risk Assessment — Overview

Objective. *Assess the BSA/AML risk profile of the bank and evaluate the adequacy of the bank's BSA/AML risk assessment process.*

Evaluating the BSA/AML risk assessment should be part of scoping and planning the examination, and the inclusion of a section on risk assessment in the manual does not mean the two processes are separate. Rather, risk assessment has been given its own section to emphasize its importance in the examination process and in the bank's design of effective risk-based controls.

The same risk management principles that the bank uses in traditional operational areas should be applied to assessing and managing BSA/AML risk. A well-developed risk assessment will assist in identifying the bank's BSA/AML risk profile. Understanding the risk profile enables the bank to apply appropriate risk management processes to the BSA/AML compliance program to mitigate risk. This risk assessment process enables management to better identify and mitigate gaps in the bank's controls. The risk assessment should provide a comprehensive analysis of the BSA/AML risks in a concise and organized presentation, and should be shared and communicated with all business lines across the bank, board of directors, management, and appropriate staff; as such, it is a sound practice that the risk assessment be reduced to writing. There are many effective methods and formats used in completing a BSA/AML risk assessment; therefore, examiners should not advocate a particular method or format. Whatever format the bank chooses to use for its risk assessment, it should be easily understood by all appropriate parties.

The development of the BSA/AML risk assessment generally involves two steps: first, identify the specific risk categories (i.e., products, services, customers, entities, and geographic locations) unique to the bank; and second, conduct a more detailed analysis of the data identified to better assess the risk within these categories. In reviewing the risk assessment, the examiner should determine whether management has considered all products, services, customers, and geographic locations, and whether management's detailed analysis within these specific risk categories was adequate. If the bank has not developed a risk assessment, this fact should be discussed with management. For the purposes of the examination, whenever the bank has not completed a risk assessment, or the risk assessment is inadequate, the examiner must complete a risk assessment based on available information.[2]

Evaluating the Bank's BSA/AML Risk Assessment

An examiner must review the bank's BSA/AML compliance program with sufficient knowledge of the bank's BSA/AML risks in order to determine whether the program is adequate and provides the controls necessary to mitigate risks. For example, during the examination scoping and planning process, the examiner may initially determine that the bank has a high-risk profile, but during the examination, the examiner may determine that the bank's BSA/AML compliance program adequately mitigates these risks. Alternatively, the examiner may initially determine that the bank has a low or moderate risk profile; however, during the examination, the examiner may determine that the bank's BSA/AML compliance program does not adequately mitigate these risks.

In evaluating the risk assessment, an examiner should not necessarily take any single indicator as determinative of the existence of a lower or higher BSA/AML risk. The assessment of risk factors is bank-specific, and a conclusion regarding the risk profile should be based on a consideration of all pertinent information. Banks may determine that some factors should be weighed more heavily than others. For example, the number of funds transfers is certainly one factor to be considered in assessing risk; however, in order to effectively identify and weigh the risks, the examiner should look at other factors associated with those funds transfers, such as whether they are international or domestic, the dollar amounts involved, and the nature of the customer relationships.

Identification of Specific Risk Categories

The first step of the risk assessment process is to identify the specific products, services, customers, entities, and geographic locations unique to the bank. Although attempts to launder money, finance terrorism, or conduct other illegal activities through a bank can emanate from many different sources, certain products, services, customers, and geographic locations may be more vulnerable or have been historically abused by money launderers and criminals. Depending on the specific characteristics of the particular product, service, or customer, the risks are not always the same. Various factors, such as the number and volume of transactions, geographic locations, and nature of the customer relationships, should be considered when the bank prepares its risk assessment. The differences in the way a bank interacts with the customer (face-to-face contact versus electronic banking) also should be considered. Because of these factors, risks will vary from one bank to another. In reviewing the bank's risk assessment, examiners should determine whether management has developed an accurate risk assessment that identifies the significant risks to the bank.

The expanded sections in this manual provide guidance and discussions on specific lines of business, products, and customers that may present unique challenges and exposures for which banks may need to institute appropriate policies, procedures, and processes. Absent appropriate controls, these lines of business, products, or customers could elevate aggregate BSA/AML risks. The examiner should expect the bank's ongoing risk assessment process to address the varying degrees of risk associated with its products, services, customers and geographic locations, as applicable.

Products and Services

Certain products and services offered by banks may pose a higher risk of money laundering or terrorist financing depending on the nature of the specific product or service offered. Such products and services may facilitate a higher degree of anonymity, or involve the handling of high volumes of currency or currency equivalents. Some of these products and services are listed below, but the list is not all inclusive:

- Electronic funds payment services — electronic cash (e.g., stored value and payroll cards), funds transfers (domestic and international), payable upon proper identification (PUPID) transactions, third-party payment processors, remittance

activity, automated clearing house (ACH) transactions, and automated teller machines (ATMs).
- Electronic banking.
- Private banking (domestic and international).
- Trust and asset management services.
- Monetary instruments.[3]
- Foreign correspondent accounts (e.g., pouch activity, payable through accounts (PTAs), and U.S. dollar drafts).
- Trade finance (letters of credit).
- Special use or concentration accounts.
- Lending activities, particularly loans secured by cash collateral and marketable securities.
- Nondeposit account services (e.g., nondeposit investment products and insurance).

The expanded sections of the manual provide guidance and discussion on specific products and services detailed above.

Customers and Entities

Although any type of account is potentially vulnerable to money laundering or terrorist financing, by the nature of their business,[4] occupation, or anticipated transaction activity, certain customers and entities may pose specific risks. At this stage of the risk assessment process, it is essential that banks exercise judgment and neither define nor treat all members of a specific category of customer as posing the same level of risk. In assessing customer risk, banks should consider other variables, such as services sought and geographic locations. The expanded sections of the manual provide guidance and discussion on specific customers and entities that are detailed below:

- Foreign financial institutions, including banks and foreign money services providers (e.g., casas de cambio, currency exchanges, and money transmitters).
- Non-bank financial institutions (e.g., money services businesses; casinos and card clubs; brokers/dealers in securities; and dealers in precious metals, stones, or jewels).
- Senior foreign political figures and their immediate family members and close associates (collectively known as politically exposed persons (PEPs)).[5]
- Nonresident alien (NRA)[6] and accounts of foreign individuals.
- Foreign corporations and domestic business entities, particularly offshore corporations (such as domestic shell companies and Private Investment Companies (PICs) and international business corporations (IBCs))[7] located in high-risk geographic locations.
- Deposit brokers, particularly foreign deposit brokers.
- Cash-intensive businesses (e.g., convenience stores, restaurants, retail stores, liquor stores, cigarette distributors, privately owned ATMs, vending machine operators, and parking garages).
- Non-governmental organizations and charities (foreign and domestic).
- Professional service providers (e.g., attorneys, accountants, doctors, or real estate brokers).

Geographic Locations

Identifying geographic locations that may pose a higher risk is essential to a bank's BSA/AML compliance program. U.S. banks should understand and evaluate the specific risks associated with doing business in, opening accounts for customers from, or facilitating transactions involving certain geographic locations. However, geographic risk alone does not necessarily determine a customer's or transaction's risk level, either positively or negatively.

High-risk geographic locations can be either international or domestic. International high-risk geographic locations generally include:

- Countries subject to OFAC sanctions, including state sponsors of terrorism. [8]
- Countries identified as supporting international terrorism under section 6(j) of the Export Administration Act of 1979, as determined by the Secretary of State.[9]
- Jurisdictions determined to be "of primary money laundering concern" by the Secretary of the Treasury, and jurisdictions subject to special measures imposed by the Secretary of the Treasury, through FinCEN, pursuant to section 311 of the Patriot Act.[10]
- Jurisdictions or countries identified as non-cooperative by the Financial Action Task Force on Money Laundering (FATF).[11]
- Major money laundering countries and jurisdictions identified in the U.S. Department of State's annual International Narcotics Control Strategy Report (INCSR), in particular, countries which are identified as jurisdictions of primary concern.[12]
- Offshore financial centers (OFCs) as identified by the U.S. Department of State.[13]
- Other countries identified by the bank as high-risk because of its prior experiences or other factors (e.g., legal considerations, or allegations of official corruption).

Domestic high-risk geographic locations may include, but are not limited to, banking offices doing business within, or having customers located within, a U.S. Government–designated high-risk geographic location. Domestic high-risk geographic locations include:

- High Intensity Drug Trafficking Areas (HIDTAs).[14]
- High Intensity Financial Crime Areas (HIFCAs).[15]

Analysis of Specific Risk Categories

The second step of the risk assessment process entails a more detailed analysis of the data obtained during the identification stage in order to more accurately assess BSA/AML risk. This step involves evaluating data pertaining to the bank's activities (e.g., number of: domestic and international funds transfers; private banking customers; foreign correspondent accounts; PTAs; and domestic and international geographic locations of the bank's business area and customer transactions) in relation to Customer Identification Program (CIP) and customer due diligence (CDD) information. The level and sophistication of analysis may vary by bank. The detailed analysis is important because within any type of product or category of customer there will be accountholders that pose varying levels of risk.

This step in the risk assessment process gives management a better understanding of the bank's risk profile in order to develop the appropriate policies, procedures, and processes to mitigate the overall risk. Specifically, the analysis of the data pertaining to the bank's activities should consider, as appropriate, the following factors:

- Purpose of the account.
- Actual or anticipated activity in the account.
- Nature of the customer's business.
- Customer's location.
- Types of products and services used by the customer.

The value of a two-step risk assessment process is illustrated in the following example. The data collected in the first step of the risk assessment process reflects that a bank sends out 100 international funds transfers per day. Further analysis may show that approximately 90 percent of the funds transfers are recurring well-documented transactions for long-term customers. On the other hand, the analysis may show that 90 percent of these transfers are non-recurring or are for noncustomers. While the numbers are the same for these two examples, the overall risks are different.

As illustrated above, the bank's CIP and CDD information take on important roles in this process. Refer to the core overview sections, "Customer Identification Program" and "Customer Due Diligence" found pages 45 and 56, respectively, for additional guidance.

Developing the Bank's BSA/AML Compliance Program Based Upon its Risk Assessment

Management should structure the bank's BSA/AML compliance program to adequately address its risk profile, as identified by the risk assessment. Management should understand the bank's BSA/AML risk exposure and develop the appropriate policies, procedures, and processes to monitor and control BSA/AML risks. For example, the bank's monitoring systems to identify, research, and report suspicious activity should be risk-based, with particular emphasis on high-risk products, services, customers, and geographic locations as identified by the bank's BSA/AML risk assessment.

Independent testing (audit) should review the bank's risk assessment for reasonableness. Additionally, management should consider the staffing resources and the level of training necessary to promote adherence with these policies, procedures, and processes. For those banks that assume a higher risk BSA/AML profile, management should provide a more robust program that specifically monitors and controls the higher risks that management and the board have accepted. Refer to Appendix I ("Risk Assessment Link to the BSA/AML Compliance Program") for a chart depicting the risk assessment's link to the BSA/AML compliance program.

Enterprise-Wide BSA/AML Risk Assessment

Holding companies or lead financial institutions that implement an enterprise-wide BSA/AML compliance program should assess risk both individually within business lines and on a consolidated basis across all activities and legal entities. To avoid having an outdated understanding of the BSA/AML risk exposures, the holding company or lead financial institution should continually reassess the organization's BSA/AML risks and communicate with business units, functions, and legal entities. The identification of a BSA/AML risk or deficiency in one area of business may indicate concerns elsewhere in the organization, which management should identify and control. Refer to the expanded overview section, "Enterprise-Wide BSA/AML Compliance Program," page 147, for additional guidance.

Bank's Updating of the Risk Assessment

An effective BSA/AML compliance program controls risks associated with the bank's products, services, customers, and geographic locations; therefore, an effective risk assessment should be an ongoing process, not a one-time exercise. Management should update its risk assessment to identify changes in the bank's risk profile, as necessary (e.g., when new products and services are introduced, existing products and services change, high-risk customers open and close accounts, or the bank expands through mergers and acquisitions). Even in the absence of such changes, it is a sound practice for banks to periodically reassess their BSA/AML risks at least every 12 to 18 months.

Examiner Development of a BSA/AML Risk Assessment

In some situations, banks may not have performed or completed an adequate BSA/AML risk assessment and examiners must complete one based on available information. When doing so, examiners do not have to use any particular format. In such instances, documented workpapers should include the bank's risk assessment, the deficiencies noted in the bank's risk assessment, and the examiner-prepared risk assessment.

Examiners should ensure that they have a general understanding of the bank's BSA/AML risks and, at a minimum, document these risks within the examination scoping process. This section provides some general guidance that examiners can use when they are required to complete a BSA/AML risk assessment. In addition, examiners may share this information with bankers to develop or improve their own BSA/AML risk assessment.

The risk assessment developed by examiners generally will not be as comprehensive as one developed by a bank. However, similar to what is expected in a bank's risk assessment, examiners should obtain information on the bank's products, services, customers, and geographic locations to determine the volume and trend for potentially higher risk areas. This process can begin with an analysis of:

- BSA-reporting database information (e.g., Currency and Banking Retrieval System (CBRS) and Currency and Banking Query System (CBQS)).
- Prior examination or inspection reports and workpapers.
- Response to request letter items.
- Discussions with bank management and appropriate regulatory agency personnel.
- Reports of Condition and Income (Call Report) and Uniform Bank Performance Report (UBPR).

Examiners should complete this analysis by reviewing the level and trend of information pertaining to banking activities identified, for example:

- Funds transfers.
- Private banking.
- Monetary instrument sales.
- Foreign correspondent accounts and PTAs.
- Branch locations.
- Domestic and international geographic locations of the bank's business area.

This information should be evaluated relative to such factors as the bank's total asset size, customer base, products, services, and geographic locations. Examiners should exercise caution if comparing information between banks and use their experience and insight when performing this analysis. Specifically, examiners should avoid comparing the number of Suspicious Activity Reports (SARs) filed by a bank to those filed by another bank in the same geographic location. Examiners can and should use their knowledge of the risks associated with products, services, customers, and geographic locations to help them determine the bank's BSA/AML risk profile. Examiners may refer to Appendix J ("Quantity of Risk Matrix") when completing this evaluation.

After identifying potential high-risk operations, examiners should form a preliminary BSA/AML risk profile of the bank. The preliminary risk profile will provide the examiner with the basis for the initial BSA/AML examination scope and the ability to determine the adequacy of the bank's BSA/AML compliance program. Banks may have an appetite for high-risk activities, but these risks should be appropriately mitigated by an effective BSA/AML compliance program tailored to those specific risks.

The examiner should develop an initial examination scoping and planning document commensurate with the preliminary BSA/AML risk profile. As necessary, the examiner should identify additional examination procedures beyond the minimum procedures that must be completed during the examination. While the initial scope may change during the examination, the preliminary risk profile will enable the examiner to establish a reasonable scope for the BSA/AML review.

Examiner Determination of the Bank's BSA/AML Aggregate Risk Profile

The examiner, during the "Developing Conclusions and Finalizing the Examination" phase of the BSA/AML examination, should assess whether the controls of the bank's BSA/AML compliance program are appropriate to manage and mitigate its BSA/AML risks. Through this process the examiner should determine an aggregate risk profile for the bank. This aggregate risk profile should take into consideration the risk assessment developed either by the bank or by the examiner and should factor in the adequacy of the BSA/AML compliance program. Examiners should determine whether the bank's BSA/AML compliance program is adequate to appropriately mitigate the BSA/AML risks, based on the risk assessment. The existence of BSA/AML risk within the aggregate risk profile should not be criticized as long as the bank's BSA/AML compliance program adequately identifies, measures, monitors, and controls this risk as part of a deliberate risk strategy. When the risks are not appropriately controlled, examiners must communicate to management and the board of directors the need to mitigate BSA/AML risk. Examiners should document deficiencies as directed in the core examination procedures, "Developing Conclusions and Finalizing the Examination," page 41.

EXAMINATION PROCEDURES

BSA/AML Risk Assessment

Objective. *Assess the BSA/AML risk profile of the bank and evaluate the adequacy of the bank's BSA/AML risk assessment process.*

1. Review the bank's BSA/AML risk assessment. Determine whether the bank has included all risk areas, including any new products, services, or targeted customers and geographic locations. Determine whether the bank's process for periodically reviewing and updating its BSA/AML risk assessment is adequate.
2 If the bank has not developed a risk assessment, or if the risk assessment is inadequate, the examiner must complete a risk assessment.
3 Examiners should document and discuss the bank's BSA/AML risk profile and any identified deficiencies in the bank's BSA/AML risk assessment process with bank management.

BSA/AML COMPLIANCE PROGRAM — OVERVIEW

Objective. *Assess the adequacy of the bank's BSA/AML compliance program. Determine whether the bank has developed, administered, and maintained an effective program for compliance with the BSA and all of its implementing regulations.*

Review of the bank's written policies, procedures, and processes is a first step in determining the overall adequacy of the BSA/AML compliance program. The completion of applicable core and, if warranted, expanded examination procedures is necessary to support the overall conclusions regarding the adequacy of the BSA/AML compliance program. Examination findings should be discussed with the bank's management, and significant findings must be included in the report of examination.

The BSA/AML compliance program[16] must be written, approved by the board of directors,[17] and noted in the board minutes. A bank must have a BSA/AML compliance program commensurate with its respective BSA/AML risk profile. Refer to the core overview section, "BSA/AML Risk Assessment," page 18, for additional guidance on developing a BSA/AML risk assessment. Refer to Appendix I ("Risk Assessment Link to the BSA/AML Compliance Program") for a chart depicting the risk assessment's link to the BSA/AML compliance program. Furthermore, the program must be fully implemented and reasonably designed to meet the BSA requirements. Policy statements alone are not sufficient; practices must coincide with the bank's written policies, procedures, and processes. The BSA/AML compliance program must provide for the following minimum requirements:

- A system of internal controls to ensure ongoing compliance.
- Independent testing of BSA/AML compliance.
- Designate an individual or individuals responsible for managing BSA compliance (BSA compliance officer).
- Training for appropriate personnel.

In addition, a Customer Identification Program (CIP) must be included as part of the BSA/AML compliance program. Refer to the core overview section, "Customer Identification Program," page 45, for additional guidance.

Internal Controls

The board of directors, acting through senior management, is ultimately responsible for ensuring that the bank maintains an effective BSA/AML internal control structure, including suspicious activity monitoring and reporting. The board of directors and management should create a culture of compliance to ensure staff adherence to the bank's BSA/AML policies, procedures, and processes. Internal controls are the bank's policies, procedures, and processes designed to limit and control risks and to achieve compliance with the BSA. The level of sophistication of the internal controls should be commensurate with the size, structure, risks, and complexity of the bank. Large complex banks are more likely to implement departmental internal controls for BSA/AML compliance. Departmental internal controls typically address risks and compliance requirements unique to a particular line of business or department and are part of a comprehensive BSA/AML compliance program.

Internal controls should:

- Identify banking operations (products, services, customers, and geographic locations) more vulnerable to abuse by money launderers and criminals; provide for periodic updates to the bank's risk profile; and provide for a BSA/AML compliance program tailored to manage risks.
- Inform the board of directors, or a committee thereof, and senior management, of compliance initiatives, identified compliance deficiencies, and corrective action taken, and notify directors and senior management of Suspicious Activity Reports (SARs) filed.[18]
- Identify a person or persons responsible for BSA/AML compliance.
- Provide for program continuity despite changes in management or employee composition or structure.
- Meet all regulatory recordkeeping and reporting requirements, meet recommendations for BSA/AML compliance, and provide for timely updates in response to changes in regulations.[19]
- Implement risk-based customer due diligence (CDD) policies, procedures, and processes.

- Identify reportable transactions and accurately file all required reports including SARs, Currency Transaction Reports (CTRs), and CTR exemptions. (Banks should consider centralizing the review and report-filing functions within the banking organization.)
- Provide sufficient controls and systems for filing CTRs and CTR exemptions.
- Provide sufficient controls and monitoring systems for timely detection and reporting of suspicious activity.
- Provide for adequate supervision of employees that handle currency transactions, complete reports, grant exemptions, monitor for suspicious activity, or engage in any other activity covered by the BSA and its implementing regulations.
- Incorporate BSA compliance into the job descriptions and performance evaluations of appropriate personnel.

The above list is not designed to be all-inclusive and should be tailored to reflect the bank's BSA/AML risk profile. Additional policy guidance for specific risk areas is provided in the expanded sections of this manual.

Independent Testing

Independent testing (audit) should be conducted by the internal audit department, outside auditors, consultants, or other qualified independent parties. While the frequency of audit is not specifically defined in any statute, a sound practice is for the bank to conduct independent testing generally every 12 to 18 months, commensurate with the BSA/AML risk profile of the bank. Banks that do not employ outside auditors or consultants or have internal audit departments may comply with this requirement by using qualified persons who are not involved in the function being tested. The persons conducting the BSA/AML testing should report directly to the board of directors or to a designated board committee comprised primarily or completely of outside directors.

Those persons responsible for conducting an objective independent evaluation of the written BSA/AML compliance program should perform testing for specific compliance with the BSA, and evaluate pertinent management information systems (MIS). The audit should be risk based[20] and evaluate the quality of risk management for all banking operations, departments, and subsidiaries. Risk-based audit programs will vary depending on the bank's size, complexity, scope of activities, risk profile, quality of control functions, geographic diversity, and use of technology. An effective risk-based auditing program will cover all of the bank's activities. The frequency and depth of each activity's audit will vary according to the activity's risk assessment. Risk-based auditing enables the board of directors and auditors to use the bank's risk assessment to focus the audit scope on the areas of greatest concern. The testing should assist the board of directors and management in identifying areas of weakness or areas where there is a need for enhancements or stronger controls.

Independent testing should, at a minimum, include:

- An evaluation of the overall integrity and effectiveness of the BSA/AML compliance program, including policies, procedures, and processes.

- A review of the bank's risk assessment for reasonableness given the bank's risk profile (products, services, customers, and geographic locations).
- Appropriate risk-based transaction testing to verify the bank's adherence to the BSA recordkeeping and reporting requirements (e.g., CIP, SARs, CTRs and CTR exemptions, and information sharing requests).
- An evaluation of management's efforts to resolve violations and deficiencies noted in previous audits and regulatory examinations, including progress in addressing outstanding supervisory actions, if applicable.
- A review of staff training for adequacy, accuracy, and completeness.
- A review of the effectiveness of the suspicious activity monitoring systems (manual, automated, or a combination) used for BSA/AML compliance. Related reports may include, but are not limited to:
  - Suspicious activity monitoring reports.
  - Large currency aggregation reports.
  - Monetary instrument records.
  - Funds transfer records.
  - Nonsufficient funds (NSF) reports.
  - Large balance fluctuation reports.
  - Account relationship reports.
- An assessment of the overall process for identifying and reporting suspicious activity, including a review of filed or prepared SARs to determine their accuracy, timeliness, completeness, and effectiveness of the bank's policy.

Auditors should document the audit scope, procedures performed, transaction testing completed, and findings of the review. All audit documentation and workpapers should be available for examiner review. Any violations, policy or procedures exceptions, or other deficiencies noted during the audit should be included in an audit report and reported to the board of directors or a designated committee in a timely manner. The board or designated committee and the audit staff should track audit deficiencies and document corrective actions.

BSA Compliance Officer

The bank's board of directors must designate a qualified individual to serve as the BSA compliance officer.[21] The BSA compliance officer is responsible for coordinating and monitoring day-to-day BSA/AML compliance. The BSA compliance officer is also charged with managing all aspects of the BSA/AML compliance program and with managing the bank's adherence to the BSA and its implementing regulations; however, the board of directors is ultimately responsible for the bank's BSA/AML compliance.

While the title of the individual responsible for overall BSA/AML compliance is not important, his or her level of authority and responsibility within the bank is critical. The BSA compliance officer may delegate BSA/AML duties to other employees, but the officer should be responsible for overall BSA/AML compliance. The board of directors is responsible for ensuring that the BSA compliance officer has sufficient authority and resources (monetary, physical, and personnel) to administer an effective BSA/AML compliance program based on the bank's risk profile.

The BSA compliance officer should be fully knowledgeable of the BSA and all related regulations. The BSA compliance officer should also understand the bank's products, services, customers, and geographic locations, and the potential money laundering and terrorist financing risks associated with those activities. The appointment of a BSA compliance officer is not sufficient to meet the regulatory requirement if that person does not have the expertise, authority, or time to satisfactorily complete the job.

The line of communication should allow the BSA compliance officer to regularly apprise the board of directors and senior management of ongoing compliance with the BSA. Pertinent BSA-related information, including the reporting of SARs filed with FinCEN, should be reported to the board of directors or an appropriate board committee so that these individuals can make informed decisions about overall BSA/AML compliance. The BSA compliance officer is responsible for carrying out the direction of the board and ensuring that employees adhere to the bank's BSA/AML policies, procedures, and processes.

Training

Banks must ensure that appropriate personnel are trained in applicable aspects of the BSA. Training should include regulatory requirements and the bank's internal BSA/AML policies, procedures, and processes. At a minimum, the bank's training program must provide training for all personnel whose duties require knowledge of the BSA. The training should be tailored to the person's specific responsibilities. In addition, an overview of the BSA/AML requirements typically should be given to new staff during employee orientation. Training should encompass information related to applicable business lines, such as trust services, international, and private banking. The BSA compliance officer should receive periodic training that is relevant and appropriate given changes to regulatory requirements as well as the activities and overall BSA/AML risk profile of the bank.

The board of directors and senior management should be informed of changes and new developments in the BSA, its implementing regulations and directives, and the federal banking agencies' regulations. While the board of directors may not require the same degree of training as banking operations personnel, they need to understand the importance of BSA/AML regulatory requirements, the ramifications of noncompliance, and the risks posed to the bank. Without a general understanding of the BSA, the board of directors cannot adequately provide BSA/AML oversight; approve BSA/AML policies, procedures, and processes; or provide sufficient BSA/AML resources.

Training should be ongoing and incorporate current developments and changes to the BSA and any related regulations. Changes to internal policies, procedures, processes, and monitoring systems should also be covered during training. The program should reinforce the importance that the board and senior management place on the bank's compliance with the BSA and ensure that all employees understand their role in maintaining an effective BSA/AML compliance program.

Examples of money laundering activity and suspicious activity monitoring and reporting can and should be tailored to each individual audience. For example, training for tellers should focus on examples involving large currency transactions or other suspicious activities; training for the loan department should provide examples involving money laundering through lending arrangements.

Banks should document their training programs. Training and testing materials, the dates of training sessions, and attendance records should be maintained by the bank and be available for examiner review.

EXAMINATION PROCEDURES

BSA/AML Compliance Program

Objective. *Assess the adequacy of the bank's BSA/AML compliance program. Determine whether the bank has developed, administered, and maintained an effective program for compliance with the BSA and all of its implementing regulations.*

1. Review the bank's board approved[22] written BSA/AML compliance program[23] to ensure it contains the following required elements:
   - A system of internal controls to ensure ongoing compliance.
   - Independent testing of BSA compliance.
   - A specifically designated person or persons responsible for managing BSA compliance (BSA compliance officer).
   - Training for appropriate personnel.

   A bank must have a BSA/AML compliance program commensurate with its respective BSA/AML risk profile. In addition, a Customer Identification Program (CIP) must be included as part of the BSA/AML compliance program.
2. Assess whether the board of directors and senior management receive adequate reports on BSA/AML compliance.

Risk Assessment Link to the BSA/AML Compliance Program

3. On the basis of examination procedures completed in the scoping and planning process, including the review of the risk assessment, determine whether the bank has adequately identified the risk within its banking operations (products, services, customers, and geographic locations) and incorporated the risk into the BSA/AML compliance program. Refer to Appendix I ("Risk Assessment Link to the BSA/AML Compliance Program") when performing this analysis.

Internal Controls

4. Determine whether the BSA/AML compliance program includes policies, procedures, and processes that:

- Identify high-risk banking operations (products, services, customers, and geographic locations); provide for periodic updates to the bank's risk profile; and provide for a BSA/AML compliance program tailored to manage risks.
- Inform the board of directors, or a committee thereof, and senior management, of compliance initiatives, identified compliance deficiencies, Suspicious Activity Reports (SARs) filed,[24] and corrective action taken.
- Identify a person or persons responsible for BSA/AML compliance.
- Provide for program continuity despite changes in management or employee composition or structure.
- Meet all regulatory requirements, meet recommendations for BSA/AML compliance, and provide for timely updates to implement changes in regulations.
- Implement risk-based customer due diligence (CDD) policies, procedures, and processes.
- Identify reportable transactions and accurately file all required reports, including SARs, Currency Transaction Reports (CTRs), and CTR exemptions. (Banks should consider centralizing the review and report-filing functions within the banking organization.)
- Provide for dual controls and the segregation of duties. Employees that complete the reporting forms (e.g., SARs, CTRs, and CTR exemptions) should not also be responsible for filing the reports or granting the exemptions.
- Provide sufficient controls and monitoring systems for the timely detection and reporting of suspicious activity.
- Provide for adequate supervision of employees that handle currency transactions, complete reports, grant exemptions, monitor for suspicious activity, or engage in any other activity covered by the BSA and its implementing regulations.
- Train employees to be fully aware of their responsibilities under the BSA regulations and internal policy guidelines.
- Incorporate BSA compliance into job descriptions and performance evaluations of appropriate personnel.

Independent Testing

5. Determine whether the BSA/AML testing (audit) is independent (e.g., performed by a person (or persons) not involved with the bank's BSA/AML compliance staff) and whether persons conducting the testing report directly to the board of directors or to a designated board committee comprised primarily or completely of outside directors.
6. Evaluate the qualifications of the person (or persons) performing the independent testing to assess whether the bank can rely upon the findings and conclusions.
7. Validate the auditor's reports and workpapers to determine whether the bank's independent testing is comprehensive, accurate, adequate, and timely. The independent audit should address the following:
   - The overall integrity and effectiveness of the BSA/AML compliance program, including policies, procedures, and processes.
   - BSA/AML risk assessment.

- BSA reporting and recordkeeping requirements.
- Customer Identification Program (CIP) implementation.
- The adequacy of CDD policies, procedures, and processes and whether they comply with internal requirements.
- Personnel adherence to the bank's BSA/AML policies, procedures, and processes.
- Appropriate transaction testing, with particular emphasis on high-risk operations (products, service, customers, and geographic locations).
- Training adequacy, including its comprehensiveness, accuracy of materials, the training schedule, and attendance tracking.
- The integrity and accuracy of management information systems (MIS) used in the BSA/AML compliance program (e.g., MIS includes reports used to identify large currency transactions, aggregate daily currency transactions, funds transfer transactions, and monetary instrument sales transactions).

8. If an automated system is not used to identify or aggregate large transactions, determine whether the audit or independent review includes a sample test check of tellers' cash proof sheets, tapes, or other documentation to determine whether large currency transactions are accurately identified and reported.
9. Determine whether the audit's review of suspicious activity *monitoring* systems includes an evaluation of the system's ability to identify unusual activity. Ensure through a validation of the auditor's reports and workpapers that the bank's independent testing:
   - Reviews policies, procedures, and processes for suspicious activity monitoring.
   - Evaluates the system's methodology for establishing and applying expected activity or filtering criteria.
   - Evaluates the system's ability to generate monitoring reports.
   - Determines whether the system filtering criteria are reasonable.
10. Determine whether the audit's review of suspicious activity *reporting* systems includes an evaluation of the research and referral of unusual activity. Ensure through a validation of the auditor's reports and workpapers that the bank's independent testing includes a review of policies, procedures, and processes for referring unusual activity from all business lines (e.g., legal, private banking, foreign correspondent banking) to the personnel or department responsible for evaluating unusual activity.
11. Determine whether audit reviews the effectiveness of the bank's policy for reviewing accounts that generate multiple SAR filings.
12. Determine whether audit tracks previously identified deficiencies and verifies that they are corrected by management.
13. Review the audit scope, procedures, and workpapers to determine adequacy of the audit based on the following:
    - Overall audit coverage and frequency in relation to the risk profile of the bank.
    - Board reporting and supervision of, and its responsiveness to, audit findings.
    - Adequacy of transaction testing, particularly for high-risk banking operations and suspicious activity monitoring systems.

- Competency of the auditors or independent reviewers regarding BSA/AML requirements.

BSA Compliance Officer

14. Determine whether the board of directors has designated a person or persons responsible for the overall BSA/AML compliance program. Determine whether the BSA compliance officer has the necessary authority and resources to effectively execute all duties.
15. Assess the competency of the BSA compliance officer and his or her staff, as necessary. Determine whether the BSA compliance area is sufficiently staffed for the bank's overall risk level (based on products, services, customers, and geographic locations), size, and BSA/AML compliance needs. In addition, ensure that no conflict of interest exists and that staff is given adequate time to execute all duties.

Training

16. Determine whether the following elements are adequately addressed in the training program and materials:
    - The importance the board of directors and senior management place on ongoing education, training, and compliance.
    - Employee accountability for ensuring BSA compliance.
    - Comprehensiveness of training, considering specific risks of individual business lines.
    - Training of personnel from all applicable areas of the bank.[25]
    - Frequency of training.
    - Documentation of attendance records and training materials.
    - Coverage of bank policies, procedures, processes, and new rules and regulations.
    - Coverage of different forms of money laundering and terrorist financing as it relates to identification and examples of suspicious activity.
    - Penalties for noncompliance with internal policies and regulatory requirements.
17. As appropriate, conduct discussions with employees (e.g., tellers, funds transfer personnel, internal auditors, and loan personnel) to assess their knowledge of BSA/AML policies and regulatory requirements.

Transaction Testing

Transaction testing must include, at a minimum, either examination procedures detailed below (independent testing) or transaction testing procedures selected from within the core or expanded sections. While some transaction testing is required, examiners have the discretion to decide what testing to conduct. Examiners should document their decision regarding the extent of transaction testing to conduct and the activities where it is to be performed, as well as the rationale for any changes to the scope of transaction testing that occur during the examination.

Independent Testing

18. Select a judgmental sample that includes transactions other than those tested by the independent auditor and determine whether independent testing:
    - Is comprehensive, adequate, and timely.
    - Has reviewed the accuracy of MIS used in the BSA/AML compliance program.
    - Has reviewed suspicious activity monitoring systems to include the identification of unusual activity.
    - Has reviewed whether suspicious activity reporting systems include the research and referral of unusual activity.

Preliminary Evaluation

After the examiner has completed the review of all four required elements of the bank's BSA/AML compliance program, the examiner should document a preliminary evaluation of the bank's program. At this point, the examiner should revisit the initial examination plan, in order to determine whether any strengths or weaknesses identified during the review of the institution's BSA/AML compliance program warrant adjustments to the initial planned scope. Keep in mind, the examiner may complete the core examination procedures, "Office of Foreign Assets Control," page 144. The examiner should document and support any changes to the examination scope, then proceed to the applicable core and, if warranted, expanded examination procedures. If there are no changes to the examination scope, the examiner should proceed to the core examination procedures, "Developing Conclusions and Finalizing the Examination," page 41.

DEVELOPING CONCLUSIONS AND FINALIZING THE EXAMINATION — OVERVIEW

Objective. *Formulate conclusions, communicate findings to management, prepare report comments, develop an appropriate supervisory response, and close the examination.*

In the final phase of the BSA/AML examination, the examiner should assemble all findings from the examination procedures completed. From those findings, the examiner should develop and document conclusions about the BSA/AML compliance program's adequacy, discuss preliminary conclusions with bank management, present these conclusions in a written format for inclusion in the report of examination, and determine and document what regulatory response, if any, is appropriate.

In formulating a written conclusion, the examiner does not need to discuss every procedure performed during the examination. During discussions with management about examination conclusions, examiners should include discussions of both strengths and weaknesses of the bank's BSA/AML compliance. Examiners should document all relevant determinations and conclusions.

EXAMINATION PROCEDURES

Developing Conclusions and Finalizing the Examination

Objective. *Formulate conclusions, communicate findings to management, prepare report comments, develop an appropriate supervisory response, and close the examination.*

Formulating Conclusions

1. Accumulate all pertinent findings from the BSA/AML examination procedures performed. Evaluate the thoroughness and reliability of any risk assessment conducted by the bank. Determine whether the following requirements are met:
    - The BSA/AML compliance program is effectively monitored and supervised in relation to the bank's risk profile as determined by the risk assessment. The examiner should ascertain if the BSA/AML compliance program is effective in mitigating the bank's overall risk.
    - The board of directors and senior management are aware of BSA/AML regulatory requirements, effectively oversee BSA/AML compliance, and commit, as necessary, to corrective actions (e.g., audit and regulatory examinations).
    - BSA/AML policies, procedures, and processes are adequate to ensure compliance with applicable laws and regulations and appropriately address high-risk operations (products, services, customers, and geographic locations).
    - Internal controls ensure compliance with the BSA and provide sufficient risk management, especially for high-risk operations (products, services, customers, and geographic locations).
    - Independent testing (audit) is appropriate and adequately tests for compliance with required laws, regulations, and policies.
    - The designated person responsible for coordinating and monitoring day-to-day compliance is competent and has the necessary resources.
    - Personnel are sufficiently trained to adhere to legal, regulatory, and policy requirements.
    - Information and communication policies, procedures, and processes are adequate and accurate.

All relevant determinations should be documented and explained.

2. Determine the underlying cause of policy, procedure, or process deficiencies, if identified. These deficiencies can be the result of a number of factors, including, but not limited to, the following:

- Management has not assessed, or has not accurately assessed, the bank's BSA/AML risks.
- Management is unaware of relevant issues.
- Management is unwilling to create or enhance policies, procedures, and processes.
- Management or employees disregard established policies, procedures, and processes.
- Management or employees are unaware of or misunderstand regulatory requirements, policies, procedures, or processes.
- High-risk operations (products, services, customers, and geographic locations) have grown faster than the capabilities of the BSA/AML compliance program.
- Changes in internal policies, procedures, and processes are poorly communicated.

3. Determine whether deficiencies or violations were previously identified by management or audit or were only identified as a result of this examination.
4. Develop findings and conclusions and discuss them with the examiner in charge (EIC) or examiner responsible for reviewing the bank's overall BSA/AML compliance.
5. Identify actions needed to correct outstanding deficiencies or violations, as appropriate, including the possibility of, among other things, requiring the bank to conduct more detailed risk assessments or taking formal enforcement action.
6. Discuss findings with management and obtain a commitment for improvements or corrective action, if needed.

Preparing the BSA/AML Comments for the Report of Examination

7. Develop a conclusion regarding the adequacy of the bank's BSA/AML compliance program. Discuss the effectiveness of each of these elements of the bank's BSA/AML compliance program. Indicate whether the BSA/AML compliance program meets all the regulatory requirements by providing the following:
   - A system of internal controls.
   - Independent testing for compliance.
   - A specific person to coordinate and monitor the BSA/AML compliance program.
   - Training of appropriate personnel.

   The BSA/AML compliance program must also include a written Customer Identification Program (CIP) appropriate for the bank's size, location, and type of business.

   The examiner should ensure that workpapers are prepared in sufficient detail to support issues discussed in the report of examination (ROE). The examiner does not need to provide a written comment on every one of the following items 8 through 15. Written comments should cover only areas or subjects pertinent to the examiner's findings and conclusions. All significant findings must be included in the ROE. To the extent that the following items are discussed in the workpapers, but not the ROE, the examiner should ensure that the workpapers thoroughly and adequately document each review, as well as any other aspect of the bank's BSA/AML compliance program that merits attention, but may not rise to the level of being included in the ROE. As applicable, the examiner should prepare a discussion of the following items.

8. Describe whether the bank's polices and procedures for law enforcement requests for information under section 314(a) of the Patriot Act (31 CFR 103.100) meet regulatory requirements.
9. If the bank maintains any foreign correspondent or private banking accounts for non-U.S. persons, describe whether the bank's due diligence policies, procedures, and processes meet regulatory requirements under section 312 of the Patriot Act (31 CFR 103.176 and 103.178).
10. Describe the board of directors' and senior managements' commitment to BSA/AML compliance. Consider whether management has the following:
    - A strong BSA/AML compliance program fully supported by the board of directors.
    - A requirement that the board of directors and senior management are kept informed of BSA/AML compliance efforts, audit reports, any compliance failures, and the status of corrective actions.
11. Describe whether the bank's policies, procedures, and processes for SAR filings meet the regulatory requirements and are effective.
12. Describe whether the bank's policies, procedures, and processes for large currency transactions meet the requirements of 31 CFR 103.22 and are effective.
13. If applicable, describe whether the bank's policies, procedures, and processes for Currency Transaction Report (CTR) exemptions meet regulatory reporting requirements, appropriately grant exemptions, and use the correct forms.
14. Describe whether the bank's funds transfer policies, procedures, and processes meet the requirements of 31 CFR 103.33(e) and (g). Briefly discuss whether the policies, procedures, and processes include effective internal controls (e.g., separation of duties, proper authorization for sending and receiving, and posting to accounts), and provide a means to monitor transfers for CTR reporting purposes.
15. Describe the bank's recordkeeping policies, procedures, and processes. Indicate whether they meet the requirements of 31 CFR 103.

Preparing an Appropriate Supervisory Response

16. Identify violations and assess the severity of those violations. As appropriate, record violations in internal databases or the ROE.
17. On the basis of overall findings and conclusions, confer with the EIC to formulate appropriate ratings.
18. As appropriate, develop recommendations for supervisory actions by conferring with the EIC, supervisory management, and legal staff.
19. Organize and reference workpapers.

End Notes

[1] The federal banking agencies' reference to "audit" does not confer an expectation that the required independent testing must be performed by a specifically designated auditor, whether internal or external. However, the person performing the independent testing must not be involved in any part of the bank's BSA/AML compliance program. The findings should be reported directly to the board of directors or an audit committee composed primarily or completely of outside directors.

[2] Refer to "Examiner Development of a BSA/AML Risk Assessment," page 25, for guidance.

[3] Monetary instruments in this context include official bank checks, cashier's checks, money orders, and traveler's checks. Refer to the expanded overview section, "Purchase and Sale of Monetary Instruments," page 208, for further discussion on risk factors and risk mitigation regarding monetary instruments.

[4] Banks may wish to use the North American Industry Classification System (NAICS) codes to assist in classifying business customers by industry type. Refer to www.census.gov/epcd/www/naics.html for additional information.

[5] Refer to core overview, "Private Banking Due Diligence Program (Non-U.S. Persons)," page 118, and expanded overview, "Politically Exposed Persons," page 261, for additional guidance.

[6] NRA accounts may be identified by obtaining a list of financial institution customers who filed W-8s. Additional information can be found at www.irs.gov/formspubs.

[7] For explanations of PICs and IBCs and additional guidance refer to expanded overview, "Business Entities (Domestic and Foreign)," page 284.

[8] A list of such countries, jurisdictions, and governments is available on OFAC's web site: www.treas.gov/ofac.

[9] A list of the countries supporting international terrorism appears in the U.S. Department of State's annual "Country Reports on Terrorism." This chapter is available on the U.S. Department of State's web site for its Counterterrorism Office: www.state.gov/s/ct/.

[10] Notices of proposed rulemaking and final rules accompanying the determination "of primary money laundering concern," and imposition of a special measure (or measures) pursuant to section 311 of the Patriot Act are available on the FinCEN web site: www.fincen.gov/reg_section311.html.

[11] A current list of countries designated by FATF as non-cooperative countries and territories (NCCT) is available on the FATF web site: www.fatf-gafi.org.

[12] The INCSR, including the lists of high-risk money laundering countries and jurisdictions, may be accessed on the U.S. Department of State's Bureau of International Narcotics and Law Enforcement Affairs web page www.state.gov/p/inl/rls/nrcrpt/

[13] OFCs offer a variety of financial products and services. Typically, they are jurisdictions that have relatively large numbers of financial institutions engaged primarily in business with nonresidents. OFCs are generally known to provide some or all of the following services: low or zero taxation; limited financial regulation; and banking secrecy and anonymity. Some OFCs offer the ability to form and maintain a variety of legal entities such as IBCs, "exempt" companies, trusts, investment funds, and insurance companies. To maintain the anonymity of the true beneficial owner of these entities, many are formed with nominee directors, officeholders, and shareholders. These financial institutions may have little or no physical presence in a given OFC, and the activity may be limited to the booking of the transaction. For additional information, including assessments of OFCs, see www.imf.org/external/ns/cs.aspx?id=55.

[14] The Anti-Drug Abuse Act of 1988 and The Office of National Drug Control Policy (ONDCP) Reauthorization Act of 1998 authorized the Director of ONDCP to designate areas within the United States that exhibit serious drug trafficking problems and harmfully impact other areas of the country as HIDTAs. The HIDTA Program provides additional federal resources to those areas to help eliminate or reduce drug trafficking and its harmful consequences. A listing of these areas can be found at www.whitehousedrugpolicy.gov.

[15] HIFCAs were first announced in the 1999 National Money Laundering Strategy and were conceived in the Money Laundering and Financial Crimes Strategy Act of 1998 as a means of concentrating law enforcement efforts at the federal, state, and local levels in high intensity money laundering zones. A listing of these areas can be found at www.fincen.gov/hifcaregions.html.

[16] The Board of Governors of the Federal Reserve System requires Edge and agreement corporations and U.S. branches, agencies, and other offices of foreign banks supervised by the Federal Reserve to establish and maintain procedures reasonably designed to ensure and monitor compliance with the BSA and related regulations (see Regulation K, 12 CFR 211 .5(m)(1) and 12 CFR 211 .24(j)(1)). In addition, since the BSA does not apply extraterritorially, foreign offices of domestic banks are expected to have policies, procedures, and processes in place to protect against risks of money laundering and terrorist financing (12 CFR 21 1.24(j)(1) and 12 CFR 326.8).

[17] The Board of Governors of the Federal Reserve System, the Federal Deposit Insurance Corporation, and the Office of the Comptroller of the Currency, each require the U.S. branches, agencies, and representative offices of the foreign banks they supervise operating in the United States to develop written BSA compliance programs that are approved by their respective bank's board of directors and noted in the minutes, or that are

approved by delegees acting under the express authority of their respective bank's board of directors to approve the BSA compliance programs.

[18] Credit unions do not have a regulatory requirement to notify the board of directors of SAR filings, although many take this action as a matter of sound practice. On June 22, 2006, the NCUA Board issued a proposed revision to 12 CFR 748 to require such action (71 *Federal Register* 36720).

[19] Refer to Appendix P ("BSA Record Retention Requirements") for guidance.

[20] Refer to Appendix I ("Quantity of Risk Matrix") for guidance.

[21] The bank must designate one or more persons to coordinate and monitor day-to-day compliance. This requirement is detailed in the federal banking agencies' BSA compliance program regulations: 12 CFR 208.63, 12 CFR 211.5(m), and 12 CFR 211.24(j) (Board of Governors of the Federal Reserve System); 12 CFR 326.8 (Federal Deposit Insurance Corporation); 12 CFR 748.2 (National Credit Union Administration); 12 CFR 21.21 (Office of the Comptroller of the Currency); and 12 CFR 563.177 (Office of Thrift Supervision).

[22] The Board of Governors of the Federal Reserve System, the Federal Deposit Insurance Corporation, and the Office of the Comptroller of the Currency each require the U.S. branches, agencies, and representative offices of the foreign banks they supervise operating in the United States to develop written BSA compliance programs that are approved by their respective bank's board of directors and noted in the minutes, or that are approved by delegees acting under the express authority of their respective bank's board of directors to approve the BSA compliance programs.

[23] The Board of Governors of the Federal Reserve System requires Edge and agreement corporations and U.S. branches, agencies, and other offices of foreign banks supervised by the Federal Reserve to establish and maintain procedures reasonably designed to ensure and monitor compliance with the BSA and related regulations (see Regulation K, 12 CFR 211 .5(m)(1) and 12 CFR 211 .24(j)(1)). In addition, since the BSA does not apply extraterritorially, foreign offices of domestic banks are expected to have policies, procedures, and processes in place to protect against risks of money laundering and terrorist financing (12 CFR 21 1.24(j)(1) and 12 CFR 326.8).

[24] Credit unions do not have a regulatory requirement to notify the board of directors of SAR filings, although many take this action as a sound practice. On June 22, 2006, the NCUA Board issued a proposed revision to 12 CFR 748 to require such action (71 *Federal Register* 36720).

[25] As part of this element, determine whether the bank conducts adequate training for any agents who are responsible for conducting CIP or other BSA-related functions on behalf of the bank.

In: The Bank Secrecy Act and Anti-Money Laundering... ISBN: 978-1-60876-162-3
Editor: Anne Leuter

Chapter 3

CORE EXAMINATION OVERVIEW AND PROCEDURES FOR REGULATORY REQUIREMENTS AND RELATED TOPICS

CUSTOMER IDENTIFICATION PROGRAM — OVERVIEW

Objective. *Assess the bank's compliance with the statutory and regulatory requirements for the Customer Identification Program (CIP).*

All banks must have a written CIP.[1] The CIP rule implements section 326 of the Patriot Act and requires each bank to implement a written CIP that is appropriate for its size and type of business and that includes certain minimum requirements. The CIP must be incorporated into the bank's BSA/AML compliance program, which is subject to approval by the bank's board of directors.[2] The implementation of a CIP by subsidiaries of banks is appropriate as a matter of safety and soundness and protection from reputational risks. Domestic subsidiaries (other than functionally regulated subsidiaries subject to separate CIP rules) of banks should comply with the CIP rule that applies to the parent bank when opening an account within the meaning of 31 CFR 103.121.[3]

The CIP is intended to enable the bank to form a reasonable belief that it knows the true identity of each customer. The CIP must include account opening procedures that specify the identifying information that will be obtained from each customer. It must also include reasonable and practical risk-based procedures for verifying the identity of each customer. Banks should conduct a risk assessment of their customer base and product offerings, and in determining the risks, consider:

- The types of accounts offered by the bank.
- The bank's methods of opening accounts.
- The types of identifying information available.

- The bank's size, location, and customer base, including types of products and services used by customers in different geographic locations.

Pursuant to the CIP rule, an "account" is a formal banking relationship to provide or engage in services, dealings, or other financial transactions, and includes a deposit account, a transaction or asset account, a credit account, or another extension of credit. An account also includes a relationship established to provide a safe deposit box or other safekeeping services or to provide cash management, custodian, or trust services.

An account does not include:

- Products or services for which a formal banking relationship is not established with a person, such as check cashing, funds transfer, or the sale of a check or money order.
- Any account that the bank acquires. This may include single or multiple accounts as a result of a purchase of assets, acquisition, merger, or assumption of liabilities.
- Accounts opened to participate in an employee benefit plan established under the Employee Retirement Income Security Act of 1974.

The CIP rule applies to a "customer." A customer is a "person" (an individual, a corporation, partnership, a trust, an estate, or any other entity recognized as a legal person) who opens a new account, an individual who opens a new account for another individual who lacks legal capacity, and an individual who opens a new account for an entity that is not a legal person (e.g., a civic club). A customer does not include a person who does not receive banking services, such as a person whose loan application is denied.[4] The definition of "customer" also does not include an existing customer as long as the bank has a reasonable belief that it knows the customer's true identity.[5] Excluded from the definition of customer are federally regulated banks, banks regulated by a state bank regulator, governmental entities, and publicly traded companies (as described in 31 CFR 103 .22(d)(2)(ii) through (iv)).

Customer Information Required

The CIP must contain account-opening procedures detailing the identifying information that must be obtained from each customer.[6] At a minimum, the bank must obtain the following identifying information from each customer before opening the account:[7]

- Name.
- Date of birth, for individuals.
- Address.[8]
- Identification number.[9]

Based on its risk assessment, a bank may require identifying information in addition to the items above for certain customers or product lines.

Customer Verification

The CIP must contain risk-based procedures for verifying the identity of the customer within a reasonable period of time after the account is opened. The verification procedures must use "the information obtained in accordance with [31 CFR 103.121] paragraph (b)(2)(i)," namely the identifying information obtained by the bank. A bank need not establish the accuracy of every element of identifying information obtained, but it must verify enough information to form a reasonable belief that it knows the true identity of the customer. The bank's procedures must describe when it will use documents, nondocumentary methods, or a combination of both.

Verification through Documents

A bank using documentary methods to verify a customer's identity must have procedures that set forth the minimum acceptable documentation. The CIP rule gives examples of types of documents that have long been considered primary sources of identification. The rule reflects the federal banking agencies' expectations that banks will review an unexpired government-issued form of identification from most customers. This identification must provide evidence of a customer's nationality or residence and bear a photograph or similar safeguard; examples include a driver's license or passport. However, other forms of identification may be used if they enable the bank to form a reasonable belief that it knows the true identity of the customer. Nonetheless, given the availability of counterfeit and fraudulently obtained documents, a bank is encouraged to review more than a single document to ensure that it has a reasonable belief that it knows the customer's true identity.

For a "person" other than an individual (such as a corporation, partnership, or trust), the bank should obtain documents showing the legal existence of the entity, such as certified articles of incorporation, an unexpired government-issued business license, a partnership agreement, or a trust instrument.

Verification through Nondocumentary Methods

Banks are not required to use nondocumentary methods to verify a customer's identity. However, a bank using nondocumentary methods to verify a customer's identity must have procedures that set forth the methods the bank will use. Nondocumentary methods may include contacting a customer; independently verifying the customer's identity through the comparison of information provided by the customer with information obtained from a consumer reporting agency, public database, or other source; checking references with other financial institutions; and obtaining a financial statement. The bank's nondocumentary procedures must also address the following situations: An individual is unable to present an unexpired government-issued identification document that bears a photograph or similar safeguard; the bank is not familiar with the documents presented; the account is opened without obtaining documents (e.g., the bank obtains the required information from the customer with the intent to verify it); the customer opens the account without appearing in person; or the bank is otherwise presented with circumstances that increase the risk that it will be unable to verify the true identity of a customer through documents.

Additional Verification for Certain Customers

The CIP must address situations where, based on its risk assessment of a new account opened by a customer that is not an individual, the bank will obtain information about individuals with authority or control over such accounts, including signatories, in order to verify the customer's identity. This verification method applies only when the bank cannot verify the customer's true identity using documentary or nondocumentary methods. For example, a bank may need to obtain information about and verify the identity of a sole proprietor or the principals in a partnership when the bank cannot otherwise satisfactorily identify the sole proprietorship or the partnership.

Lack of Verification

The CIP must also have procedures for circumstances in which the bank cannot form a reasonable belief that it knows the true identity of the customer. These procedures should describe:

- Circumstances in which the bank should not open an account.
- The terms under which a customer may use an account while the bank attempts to verify the customer's identity.
- When the bank should close an account, after attempts to verify a customer's identity have failed.
- When the bank should file a SAR in accordance with applicable law and regulation.

Recordkeeping Requirements and Retention

A bank's CIP must include recordkeeping procedures. At a minimum, the bank must retain the identifying information (name, address, date of birth for an individual, TIN, and any other information required by the CIP) obtained at account opening for a period of five years after the account is closed.[10] For credit cards, the retention period is five years after the account closes or becomes dormant.

The bank must also keep a description of the following for five years after the record was made:

- Any document that was relied on to verify identity, noting the type of document, the identification number, the place of issuance, and, if any, the date of issuance and expiration date.
- The method and the results of any measures undertaken to verify identity.
- The results of any substantive discrepancy discovered when verifying identity.

Comparison with Government Lists

The CIP must include procedures for determining whether the customer appears on any federal government list of known or suspected terrorists or terrorist organizations.[11] Banks will be contacted by the U.S. Treasury in consultation with their federal banking agency when a list is issued. At such time, banks must compare customer names against the list within a reasonable time of account opening or earlier, if required by the government, and they must follow any directives that accompany the list.

Adequate Customer Notice

The CIP must include procedures for providing customers with adequate notice that the bank is requesting information to verify their identities. The notice must generally describe the bank's identification requirements and be provided in a manner that is reasonably designed to allow a customer to view it or otherwise receive the notice before the account is opened. Examples include posting the notice in the lobby, on a web site, or within loan application documents. Sample language is provided in the regulation:

> IMPORTANT INFORMATION ABOUT PROCEDURES FOR OPENING A NEW ACCOUNT — To help the government fight the funding of terrorism and money laundering activities, federal law requires all financial institutions to obtain, verify, and record information that identifies each person who opens an account. What this means for you: When you open an account, we will ask for your name, address, date of birth, and other information that will allow us to identify you. We may also ask to see your driver's license or other identifying documents.

Reliance on Another Financial Institution

A bank is permitted to rely on another financial institution (including an affiliate) to perform some or all of the elements of the CIP, if reliance is addressed in the CIP and the following criteria are met:

- The relied-upon financial institution is subject to a rule implementing the AML program requirements of 31 USC 5318(h) and is regulated by a federal functional regulator.[12]
- The customer has an account or is opening an account at the bank and at the other functionally regulated institution.
- Reliance is reasonable, under the circumstances.
- The other financial institution enters into a contract requiring it to certify annually to the bank that it has implemented its AML program, and that it will perform (or its agent will perform) the specified requirements of the bank's CIP.

Use of Third Parties

The CIP rule does not alter a bank's authority to use a third party, such as an agent or service provider, to perform services on its behalf. Therefore, a bank is permitted to arrange for a third party, such as a car dealer or mortgage broker, acting as its agent in connection with a loan, to verify the identity of its customer. The bank can also arrange for a third party to maintain its records. However, as with any other responsibility performed by a third party, the bank is ultimately responsible for that third party's compliance with the requirements of the bank's CIP. As a result, banks should establish adequate controls and review procedures for such relationships. This requirement contrasts with the reliance provision of the rule that permits the relied-upon party to take responsibility. Refer to "Reliance on Another Financial Institution" page 50.

Other Legal Requirements

Nothing in the CIP rule relieves a bank of its obligations under any provision of the BSA or other AML laws, rules, and regulations, particularly with respect to provisions concerning information that must be obtained, verified, or maintained in connection with any account or transaction.

The U.S. Treasury and the federal banking agencies have provided banks with Frequently Asked Questions (FAQs), which may be revised periodically. The FAQs and other related documents (e.g., the CIP rule) are available on FinCEN's and the federal banking agencies' web sites.

EXAMINATION PROCEDURES

Customer Identification Program

Objective. *Assess the bank's compliance with the statutory and regulatory requirements for the Customer Identification Program (CIP).*

1. Verify that the bank's policies, procedures, and processes include a comprehensive program for identifying customers who open an account after October 1, 2003. The written program must be included within the bank's BSA/AML compliance program and must include, at a minimum, policies, procedures, and processes for the following:
   - Identification of information required to be obtained (including name, address, taxpayer identification number (TIN), and date of birth, for individuals), and risk- based identity verification procedures (including procedures that address situations in which verification cannot be performed).
   - Procedures for complying with recordkeeping requirements.
   - Procedures for checking new accounts against prescribed government lists, if applicable.
   - Procedures for providing adequate customer notice.
   - Procedures covering the bank's reliance on another financial institution or a third party, if applicable.
   - Procedures for determining whether and when a Suspicious Activity Report (SAR) should be filed.

2. Determine whether the bank's CIP considers the types of accounts offered; methods of account opening; and the bank's size, location, and customer base.
3. Determine whether the bank's policy for opening new accounts for existing customers appears reasonable.
4. Review board minutes and verify that the board of directors approved the CIP, either separately or as part of the BSA/AML compliance program (31 CFR 103.121(b)(1)).
5. Evaluate the bank's audit and training programs to ensure that the CIP is adequately incorporated (31 CFR 103. 121(b)(1)).
6. Evaluate the bank's policies, procedures, and processes for verifying that all new accounts are checked against prescribed government lists for suspected terrorists or terrorist organizations on a timely basis, if such lists are issued (31 CFR 103.121(b)(4)).

Transaction Testing

7. On the basis of a risk assessment, prior examination reports, and a review of the bank's audit findings, select a sample of new accounts opened since the most recent examination to review for compliance with the bank's CIP. The sample should include a cross-section of accounts (e.g., consumers and businesses, loans and deposits, credit card relationships, and Internet accounts). The sample should also include the following:
   - Accounts opened for a customer that provides an application for a TIN or accounts opened with incomplete verification procedures.
   - New accounts opened using documentary methods and new accounts opened using nondocumentary methods.
   - Accounts identified as high risk by the bank or its regulator.[13]
   - Accounts opened by existing high-risk customers.
   - Accounts opened with exceptions.
   - Accounts opened by a third party (e.g., indirect loans).
8. From the previous sample of new accounts, determine whether the bank has performed the following procedures:
   - Opened the account in accordance with the requirements of the CIP (31 CFR 103.121(b)(1)).
   - Formed a reasonable belief as to the true identity of a customer, including a high- risk customer. (The bank should already have a reasonable belief as to the identity of an existing customer (31 CFR 103.121(b)(2)).)
   - Obtained from each customer, before opening the account, the identity information required by the CIP (31 CFR 103.121 (b)(2)(i)) (e.g., name, date of birth, address, and identification number).
   - Within a reasonable time after account opening, verified enough of the customer's identity information to form a reasonable belief as to the customer's true identity (31 CFR 103.121(b)(2)(ii)).
   - Appropriately resolved situations in which customer identity could not be reasonably established (31 CFR 103.121(b)(2)(iii)).

- Maintained a record of the identity information required by the CIP, the method used to verify identity, and verification results (including results of discrepancies) (31 CFR 103.121(b)(3)).
- Compared the customer's name against the list of known or suspected terrorists or terrorist organizations, if applicable (31 CFR 103.121 (b)(4)).
- Filed SARs, as appropriate.

9. Evaluate the level of CIP exceptions to determine whether the bank is effectively implementing its CIP. A bank's policy may not allow staff to make or approve CIP exceptions. However, a bank may exclude isolated, non-systemic errors (such as an insignificant number of data entry errors) from CIP requirements without compromising the effectiveness of its CIP (31 CFR 103.121(b)(1)).
10. On the basis of a risk assessment, prior examination reports, and a review of the bank's audit, select a sample of relationships with third parties the bank relies on to perform its CIP (or portions of its CIP), if applicable. If the bank is using the "reliance provision":
    - Determine whether the third party is a federally regulated institution subject to a final rule implementing the AML program requirements of 31 USC 5318(h).
    - Review the contract between the parties, annual certifications, and other information, such as the third party's CIP (31 CFR 103.121 (b)(6)).
    - Determine whether reliance is reasonable. The contract and certification will provide a standard means for a bank to demonstrate that it has satisfied the "reliance provision," unless the examiner has reason to believe that the bank's reliance is not reasonable (e.g., the third party has been subject to an enforcement action for AML or BSA deficiencies or violations).
11. If the bank is using an agent or service provider to perform elements of its CIP, determine whether the bank has established appropriate internal controls and review procedures to ensure that its CIP is being implemented for third-party agent or service-provider relationships (e.g., car dealerships).
12. Review the adequacy of the bank's customer notice and the timing of the notice's delivery (31 CFR 103.121(b)(5)).
13. Evaluate the bank's CIP record retention policy and ensure that it corresponds to the regulatory requirements to maintain certain records. The bank must retain the identity information obtained at account opening for five years after the account closes. The bank must also maintain a description of documents relied on, methods used to verify identity, and resolution of discrepancies for five years after the record is made (31 CFR 103.121(b)(3)(ii)).
14. On the basis of examination procedures completed, including transaction testing, form a conclusion about the ability of policies, procedures, and processes to meet regulatory requirements associated with CIP.

Customer Due Diligence — Overview

Objective. *Assess the appropriateness and comprehensiveness of the bank's customer due diligence (CDD) policies, procedures, and processes for obtaining customer information* *and assess the value of this information in detecting, monitoring, and reporting suspicious activity.*

The cornerstone of a strong BSA/AML compliance program is the adoption and implementation of comprehensive CDD policies, procedures, and processes for all customers, particularly those that present a high risk for money laundering and terrorist financing. The objective of CDD should be to enable the bank to predict with relative certainty the types of transactions in which a customer is likely to engage. These processes assist the bank in determining when transactions are potentially suspicious. The concept of CDD begins with verifying the customer's identity and assessing the risks associated with that customer. Processes should also include enhanced CDD for high- risk customers and ongoing due diligence of the customer base.

Effective CDD policies, procedures, and processes provide the critical framework that enables the bank to comply with regulatory requirements and to report suspicious activity. An illustration of this concept is provided in Appendix K ("Customer Risk Versus Due Diligence and Suspicious Activity Monitoring"). CDD policies, procedures, and processes are critical to the bank because they can aid in:

- Detecting and reporting unusual or suspicious transactions that potentially expose the bank to financial loss, increased expenses, or reputational risk.
- Avoiding criminal exposure from persons who use or attempt to use the bank's products and services for illicit purposes.
- Adhering to safe and sound banking practices.

Customer Due Diligence Guidance

BSA/AML policies, procedures, and processes should include CDD guidelines that:

- Are commensurate with the bank's BSA/AML risk profile, paying particular attention to high-risk customers.
- Contain a clear statement of management's overall expectations and establish specific staff responsibilities, including who is responsible for reviewing or approving changes to a customer's risk rating or profile, as applicable.
- Ensure that the bank possesses sufficient customer information to implement an effective suspicious activity monitoring system.
- Provide guidance for documenting analysis associated with the due diligence process, including guidance for resolving issues when insufficient or inaccurate information is obtained.
- Ensure the bank maintains current customer information.

Customer Risk

Management should have a thorough understanding of the money laundering or terrorist financing risks of the bank's customer base. Under this approach, the bank should obtain information at account opening sufficient to develop an understanding of normal and expected activity for the customer's occupation or business operations.

Much of the CDD information can be confirmed through an information-reporting agency, banking references (for larger accounts), correspondence and telephone conversations with the customer, and visits to the customer's place of business. Additional steps may include obtaining third-party references or researching public information (e.g., on the Internet or commercial databases).

CDD processes should include periodic risk-based monitoring of the customer relationship to determine whether there are substantive changes to the original CDD information (e.g., change in employment or business operations).

Enhanced Due Diligence for High-Risk Customers

Customers that pose high money laundering or terrorist financing risks present increased exposure to banks; due diligence policies, procedures, and processes should be enhanced as a result. Enhanced due diligence for high-risk customers is especially critical in understanding their anticipated transactions and implementing a suspicious activity monitoring system that reduces the bank's reputation, compliance, and transaction risks. High-risk customers and their transactions should be reviewed more closely at account opening and more frequently throughout the term of their relationship with the bank. Guidance for identifying high-risk customers may be found in the core overview section, "BSA/AML Risk Assessment," page 18.

The bank may determine that a customer poses a high risk because of the customer's business activity, ownership structure, anticipated or actual volume and types of transactions, including those transactions involving high-risk jurisdictions. If so, the bank should consider obtaining, both at account opening and throughout the relationship, the following information on the customer:

- Purpose of the account.
- Source of funds and wealth.
- Beneficial owners of the accounts, if applicable.
- Customer's (or beneficial owner's) occupation or type of business.
- Financial statements.
- Banking references.
- Domicile (where the business is organized).
- Proximity of the customer's residence, place of employment, or place of business to the bank.
- Description of the customer's primary trade area and whether international transactions are expected to be routine.
- Description of the business operations, the anticipated volume of currency and total sales, and a list of major customers and suppliers.
- Explanations for changes in account activity.

As due diligence is an ongoing process, a bank should take measures to ensure account profiles are current and monitoring should be risk-based. Banks should consider whether risk profiles should be adjusted or suspicious activity reported when the activity is inconsistent with the profile.

EXAMINATION PROCEDURES

Customer Due Diligence

Objective. *Assess the appropriateness and comprehensiveness of the bank's customer due diligence (CDD) policies, procedures, and processes for obtaining customer information and assess the value of this information in detecting, monitoring, and reporting suspicious activity.*

1. Determine whether the bank's CDD policies, procedures, and processes are commensurate with the bank's risk profile. Determine whether the bank has processes in place for obtaining information at account opening, in addition to ensuring current customer information is maintained.
2. Determine whether policies, procedures, and processes allow for changes to a customer's risk rating or profile. Determine who is responsible for reviewing or approving such changes.
3. Review the enhanced due diligence procedures and processes the bank uses to identify customers that may pose higher risk for money laundering or terrorist financing.
4. Determine whether the bank provides guidance for documenting analysis associated with the due diligence process, including guidance for resolving issues when insufficient information or inaccurate information is obtained.

Transaction Testing

5. On the basis of a risk assessment, prior examination reports, and a review of the bank's audit findings, sample CDD information for high-risk customers. Determine whether the bank collects appropriate information and effectively incorporates this information into the suspicious activity monitoring process. This sample can be performed when testing the bank's compliance with its policies, procedures, and processes as well as when reviewing transactions or accounts for possible suspicious activity.
6. On the basis of examination procedures completed, including transaction testing, form a conclusion about the adequacy of policies, procedures, and processes associated with CDD.

SUSPICIOUS ACTIVITY REPORTING — OVERVIEW

Objective. *Assess the bank's policies, procedures, and processes, and overall compliance with statutory and regulatory requirements for monitoring, detecting, and reporting suspicious activities.*

Suspicious activity reporting forms the cornerstone of the BSA reporting system. It is critical to the United States' ability to utilize financial information to combat terrorism, terrorist financing, money laundering, and other financial crimes. Within this system, FinCEN and the federal banking agencies recognize that, as a practical matter, it is not possible for a bank to detect and report all potentially illicit transactions that flow through the bank. Examiners should focus on evaluating a bank's policies, procedures, and processes to identify and research suspicious activity. However, as part of the examination process, examiners should review individual Suspicious Activity Report (SAR) filing decisions to determine the effectiveness of the suspicious activity monitoring and reporting process. Above all, examiners and banks should recognize that the quality of SAR data is paramount to the effective implementation of the suspicious activity reporting system.

Banks, bank holding companies, and their subsidiaries are required by federal regulations[14] to file a SAR with respect to:

- Criminal violations involving insider abuse in any amount.
- Criminal violations aggregating $5,000 or more when a suspect can be identified.
- Criminal violations aggregating $25,000 or more regardless of a potential suspect.
- Transactions conducted or attempted by, at, or through the bank (or an affiliate) and aggregating $5,000 or more, if the bank or affiliate knows, suspects, or has reason to suspect that the transaction:
  - May involve potential money laundering or other illegal activity (e.g., terrorism financing).
  - Is designed to evade the BSA or its implementing regulations.[15]
  - Has no business or apparent lawful purpose or is not the type of transaction that the particular customer would normally be expected to engage in, and the bank knows of no reasonable explanation for the transaction after examining the available facts, including the background and possible purpose of the transaction.

A transaction includes a deposit; a withdrawal; a transfer between accounts; an exchange of currency; an extension of credit; a purchase or sale of any stock, bond, certificate of deposit, or other monetary instrument or investment security; or any other payment, transfer, or delivery by, through, or to a bank.

Safe Harbor for Banks from Civil Liability for Suspicious Activity Reporting

Federal law (31 USC 531 8(g)(3)) provides protection from civil liability for all reports of suspicious transactions made to appropriate authorities, including supporting documentation, regardless of whether such reports are filed pursuant to the SAR instructions. Specifically, the law provides that a bank and its directors, officers, employees, and agents that make a disclosure to the appropriate authorities of any possible violation of law or regulation, including a disclosure in connection with the preparation of SARs, "shall not be liable to any person under any law or regulation of the United States, any constitution, law, or regulation of any State or political subdivision of any State, or under any contract or other legally enforceable agreement (including any arbitration agreement), for such disclosure or for any failure to provide notice of such disclosure to the person who is the subject of such disclosure or any other person identified in the disclosure." The safe harbor applies to SARs filed within the required reporting thresholds as well as to SARs filed voluntarily on any activity below the threshold.

Systems to Identify, Research, and Report Suspicious Activity

Policies, procedures, and processes should indicate the persons responsible for the identification, research, and reporting of suspicious activities. Appropriate policies, procedures, and processes should be in place to monitor and identify unusual activity. The level of monitoring should be dictated by the bank's assessment of risk, with particular emphasis on high-risk products, services, customers, and geographic locations. Monitoring systems typically include employee identification or referrals, manual systems, automated systems, or any combination. The bank should ensure adequate staff is assigned to the identification, research, and reporting of suspicious activities taking into account the bank's overall risk profile and the volume of transactions.

Upon identification of unusual activity, additional research is typically conducted. Customer due diligence (CDD) information will assist banks in evaluating if the unusual activity is considered suspicious. For additional information, refer to the core overview section, "Customer Due Diligence," page 56. After thorough research and analysis, decisions to file or not to file a SAR should be documented. If applicable, reviewing and understanding suspicious activity monitoring across the organizations' affiliates, business lines, and risk types (e.g., reputation, compliance, or transaction) may enhance a banking organizations' ability to detect suspicious activity and thus minimize the potential for financial losses, increased expenses, and reputational risk to the organization. Refer to the expanded overview section, "Enterprise-Wide BSA/AML Compliance Program," page 147, for further guidance.

Manual Transaction Monitoring

A manual transaction monitoring system consists of a review of various reports generated by the bank's management information systems (MIS) or vendor systems. Some banks' MIS are supplemented by vendor systems designed to identify reportable currency transactions and to maintain required funds transfer records. Many of these vendor systems include filtering models for identification of unusual activity. Examples of MIS reports include currency activity reports, funds transfer reports, monetary instrument sales reports, large item reports, significant balance change reports, and nonsufficient funds (NSF) reports. The process may involve review of daily reports, reports that cover a period of time (e.g., rolling 30-day reports, monthly reports), or a combination of both types of reports. The type and frequency of reviews and resulting reports used should be commensurate with the bank's BSA/AML risk profile and appropriately cover its high- risk products, services, customers, and geographic locations.

MIS or vendor system-generated reports typically use a discretionary dollar threshold. Thresholds selected by management for the production of transaction reports should enable management to detect unusual activity. Upon identification of unusual activity, assigned personnel should review CDD and other pertinent information to determine whether the activity is suspicious. Management should periodically evaluate the appropriateness of filtering criteria and thresholds used in the monitoring process. Each bank should evaluate and identify filtering criteria most appropriate for their bank. Typical manual transaction monitoring reports are as follows. In addition, the programming of the bank's monitoring systems should be independently reviewed for reasonable filtering criteria.

Currency activity reports

Most vendors offer reports that identify all currency activity or currency activity greater than $10,000. These reports assist bankers with filing Currency Transaction Reports (CTRs) and identifying suspicious currency activity. Most bank information service providers offer currency activity reports that can filter transactions using various parameters, for example:

- Currency activity including multiple transactions greater than $10,000.
- Currency activity (single and multiple transactions) below the $10,000 reporting requirement (e.g., between $7,000 and $10,000).
- Currency transactions involving multiple lower dollar transactions (e.g., $3,000) that over a period of time (e.g., 15 days) aggregate to a substantial sum of money (e.g., $30,000).
- Currency transactions aggregated by customer name, tax identification number, or customer information file number.

Such filtering reports, whether implemented through a purchased vendor software system or through requests from information service providers, will significantly enhance a bank's ability to identify and evaluate unusual currency transactions.

Funds transfer records

The BSA requires banks to maintain records of funds transfer in amounts of $3,000 and above. Periodic review of this information can assist banks in identifying patterns of unusual activity. A periodic review of the funds transfer records in banks with low funds transfer activity is usually sufficient to identify unusual activity. For banks with more significant funds transfer activity, use of spreadsheet or vendor software is an efficient way to review funds transfer activity for unusual patterns. Most vendor software systems include standard suspicious activity filter reports. These reports typically focus on identifying certain high-risk geographic locations and larger dollar funds transfer transactions for individuals and businesses. Each bank should establish its own filtering criteria for both individuals and businesses. Noncustomer funds transfer transactions and payable upon proper identification (PUPID) transactions should also be reviewed for unusual activity.

Monetary instrument records

Records for monetary instrument sales are required by the BSA. Such records can assist the bank in identifying possible currency structuring through the purchase of cashier's checks, official bank checks, money orders, or traveler's checks in amounts of $3,000 to $10,000. A periodic review of these records can also help identify frequent purchasers of monetary instruments and common payees.

Automated Account Monitoring

Automated account-monitoring systems typically use computer programs, developed in-house or purchased from vendors, to identify individual transactions, patterns of unusual activity, or deviations from expected activity. These systems can capture a wide range of account activity, such as deposits, withdrawals, funds transfers, automated clearing house (ACH) transactions, and automated teller machine (ATM) transactions, directly from the bank's core data processing system. Banks that are large, operate in many locations, or have a large volume of high-risk customers typically use automated account-monitoring systems.

Current types of automated systems include rule-based and intelligent systems. Rule-based systems detect unusual transactions that are outside of system-developed or management-established "rules." Such systems can consist of few or many rules, depending on the complexity of the in-house or vendor product. These rules are applied using a series of transaction filters or a rules engine. Rule-based automated systems are more sophisticated than the basic manual system, which only filters on one rule (e.g., transaction greater than $10,000). Rule-based automated monitoring systems can apply complex or multiple filters. For example, rule-based automated monitoring systems can apply first to all accounts, then to a subset or risk category of accounts (such as all customers with direct deposit or all restaurants). Rule-based monitoring systems can also filter individual customer-account profiles.

Intelligent systems are adaptive systems that can change their analysis over time on the basis of activity patterns, recent trends, changes in the customer base, and other relevant data. Intelligent systems review transactions in context with other transactions and the customer profile. In doing so, these systems increase their information database on the customer, account type, category, or business, as more transactions and data are stored in the system.

Understanding the filtering criteria of a software-based monitoring system is critical to assessing the effectiveness of automated account monitoring systems. System filtering criteria should be developed through a review of specific high-risk customers, products, and services. System filtering criteria, including specific profiles and rules, should be based on what is reasonable and expected for each type of customer. Monitoring customers purely on the basis of historical activity can be misleading if their activity is not actually consistent with similar types of customers. For example, a customer may have a historical transaction activity that is substantially different from what would normally be expected from that type of customer (e.g., a check-cashing business that deposits large sums of currency versus withdrawing currency to fund the cashing of checks).

The authority to establish or change expected activity profiles should be clearly defined and should generally require the approval of the BSA compliance officer or senior management. Controls should ensure limited access to the monitoring system. Management should document or be able to explain filtering criteria, thresholds used, and how both are appropriate for the bank's risks. Management should also periodically review the filtering criteria and thresholds established to ensure that they are still effective. In addition, the bank's programming methodology should be independently validated.

Identifying Underlying Crime

Banks are required to report suspicious activity that may involve money laundering, BSA violations, terrorist financing,[16] and certain other crimes above prescribed dollar thresholds. However, banks are not obligated to investigate or confirm the underlying crime (e.g., terrorist financing, money laundering, tax evasion, identity theft, and various types of fraud). Investigation is the responsibility of law enforcement. When evaluating suspicious activity and completing the SAR, banks should, to the best of their ability, identify the characteristics of the suspicious activity. Part III, section 35, of the SAR provides 20 different characteristics of suspicious activity. Although an "Other" category is available, the use of this category should be limited to situations that cannot be broadly identified within the 20 characteristics provided.

Law Enforcement Inquiries and Requests

Banks should establish policies, procedures, and processes for identifying subjects of law enforcement requests, monitoring the transaction activity of those subjects, identifying unusual or suspicious activity related to those subjects, and filing, as applicable, SARs related to those subjects. Law enforcement inquiries and requests can include grand jury subpoenas, National Security Letters (NSLs), and section 3 14(a) requests.[17]

Mere receipt of any law enforcement inquiry, does not, by itself, require the filing of a SAR by the bank. Nonetheless, a law enforcement inquiry may be relevant to a bank's overall risk assessment of its customers and accounts. For example, the receipt of a grand jury subpoena should cause a bank to review account activity for the relevant customer.[18] It is incumbent upon a bank to assess all of the information it knows about its customer, including the receipt of a law enforcement inquiry, in accordance with its risk-based BSA/AML compliance program. The bank should determine whether a SAR should be filed based on all customer information available.

National Security Letters

NSLs are written investigative demands that may be issued by the local Federal Bureau of Investigation (FBI) and other federal governmental authorities in counterintelligence and counterterrorism investigations to obtain the following:

- Telephone and electronic communications records from telephone companies and Internet service providers.[19]
- Information from credit bureaus.[20]
- Financial records from financial institutions.[21]

NSLs are highly confidential documents; as such, examiners will not review or sample specific NSLs.[22] Pursuant to 12 USC 3414(a)(3) and (5)(D), no bank, or officer, employee or agent of the institution, can disclose to any person that a government authority or the FBI has sought or obtained access to records through a Right to Financial Privacy Act NSL. Banks that receive NSLs must take appropriate measures to ensure the confidentiality of the letters and should have procedures in place for processing and maintaining the confidentiality of NSLs.

If a bank files a SAR after receiving a NSL, the SAR should not contain any reference to the receipt or existence of the NSL. The SAR should reference only those facts and activities that support a finding of unusual or suspicious transactions identified by the bank.

Questions regarding NSLs should be directed to the bank's local FBI field office. Contact information for the FBI field offices can be found at www.fbi.gov.

SAR Decision-Making Process

The bank should have policies, procedures, and processes for referring unusual activity from all business lines to the personnel or department responsible for evaluating unusual activity. The process should ensure that all applicable information (e.g., grand jury subpoenas, NSLs, or section 314(a) requests) is effectively evaluated.

The decision to file a SAR is an inherently subjective judgment. Examiners should focus on whether the bank has an effective SAR decision-making process, not individual SAR decisions. Examiners may review individual SAR decisions as a means to test the effectiveness of the SAR monitoring, reporting, and decision-making process. In those instances where the bank has an established SAR decision-making process, has followed existing policies, procedures, and processes, and has determined not to file a SAR, the bank should not be criticized for the failure to file a SAR unless the failure is significant or accompanied by evidence of bad faith.

Banks are encouraged to document SAR decisions. Thorough documentation provides a record of the SAR decision-making process, including final decisions not to file a SAR; however, due to the variety of systems used to identify, track, and report suspicious activity, as well as the fact that each suspicious activity reporting decision will be based on unique facts and circumstances, no single form of documentation is required when a bank makes a decision not to file.[23]

Timing of a SAR Filing

The SAR rules require that a SAR be filed no later than 30 calendar days from the date of the initial detection of facts that may constitute a basis for filing a SAR. If no suspect can be identified, the time period for filing a SAR is extended to 60 days. Organizations may need to review transaction or account activity for a customer to determine whether to file a SAR. The need for a review of customer activity or transactions does not necessarily indicate a need to file a SAR. The time period for filing a SAR starts when the organization, during its review or because of other factors, knows or has reason to suspect that the activity or transactions under review meet one or more of the definitions of suspicious activity.[24]

The phrase "initial detection" should not be interpreted as meaning the moment a transaction is highlighted for review. There are a variety of legitimate transactions that could raise a red flag simply because they are inconsistent with an accountholder's normal account activity. For example, a real estate investment (purchase or sale), the receipt of an inheritance, or a gift, may cause an account to have a significant credit or debit that would be inconsistent with typical account activity. The bank's automated account monitoring system or initial discovery of information, such as system-generated reports, may flag the transaction; however, this should not be considered initial detection of potential suspicious activity. [25]

Whenever possible, an expeditious review of the transaction or the account is recommended and can be of significant assistance to law enforcement. In any event, the review should be completed in a reasonable period of time. What constitutes a "reasonable period of time" will vary according to the facts and circumstances of the particular matter being reviewed and the effectiveness of the SAR monitoring, reporting, and decision-making process of each bank. The key factor is that a bank has established adequate procedures for reviewing and assessing facts and circumstances identified as potentially suspicious, and that those procedures are documented and followed. [26]

For violations requiring immediate attention, in addition to filing a timely SAR, a bank is required to immediately notify, by telephone, an "appropriate law enforcement authority" and, as necessary, the bank's primary regulator. An "appropriate law enforcement authority" would generally be the local office of the Internal Revenue Service Criminal Investigation Division or the FBI. Notifying law enforcement of a suspicious activity does not relieve a bank of its obligation to file a SAR.[27]

Notifying Board of Directors of SAR Filings

Banks are required by the SAR regulations of their federal banking agency to notify the board of directors or an appropriate board committee that SARs have been filed.[28] However, the regulations do not mandate a particular notification format and banks should have flexibility in structuring their format. Therefore, banks may, but are not required to, provide actual copies of SARs to the board of directors or a board committee. Alternatively, banks may opt to provide summaries, tables of SARs filed for specific violation types, or other forms of notification. Regardless of the notification format used by the bank, management should provide sufficient information on its SAR filings to the board of directors or an appropriate committee in order to fulfill its fiduciary duties.[29]

Sharing SARs with Head Offices and Controlling Companies

Interagency guidance clarifies that banking organizations may share SARs with head offices and controlling companies, whether located in the United States or abroad.[30] A controlling company as defined in the guidance includes:

- A bank holding company (BHC), as defined in section 2 of the BHC Act.
- A savings and loan holding company, as defined in section 10(a) of the Home Owners' Loan Act.
- A company having the power, directly or indirectly, to direct the management policies of an industrial loan company or a parent company or to vote 25 percent or more of any class of voting shares of an industrial loan company or parent company.

The guidance confirms that:

- A U.S. branch or agency of a foreign bank may disclose a SAR to its head office outside the United States.
- A U.S. bank may disclose a SAR to controlling companies whether domestic or foreign.

Banks should maintain appropriate arrangements to protect the confidentiality of SARs. The guidance does not address whether a bank may share a SAR with an affiliate other than a controlling company or head office. Therefore, banks should not share SARs with such affiliates. However, in order to manage risk across an organization, banks that file a SAR may disclose to entities within its organization the information underlying a SAR filing.

SAR Filing on Continuing Activity

One purpose of filing SARs is to identify violations or potential violations of law to the appropriate law enforcement authorities for criminal investigation. This objective is accomplished by the filing of a SAR that identifies the activity of concern. If this activity continues over a period of time, such information should be made known to law enforcement (and the federal banking agencies). FinCEN's guidelines suggest that banks should report continuing suspicious activity by filing a report at least every 90 days.[31] This practice will notify law enforcement of the continuing nature of the activity, as well as remind the bank that it should continue to review the suspicious activity to determine whether other actions may be appropriate, such as bank management determining that it is necessary to terminate a relationship with the customer or employee that is the subject of the filing.

The bank should develop policies, procedures, and processes indicating when to escalate issues or problems identified as the result of repeat SAR filings on accounts. The procedures should include:

- Review by senior management and legal staff (e.g., BSA compliance officer or SAR committee).
- Criteria for when analysis of the overall customer relationship is necessary.
- Criteria for when to close the account.
- Criteria for when to notify law enforcement, if applicable.

SAR Quality

Banks are required to file SAR forms that are complete, thorough, and timely. Banks should include all known suspect information on the SAR form, and the importance of the accuracy of this information cannot be overstated. Inaccurate information on the SAR form, or an incomplete or disorganized narrative, may make further analysis difficult, if not impossible. However, there may be legitimate reasons why certain information may not be provided in a SAR, such as when the filer does not have the information. A thorough and complete narrative may make the difference in whether the described conduct and its possible criminal nature are clearly understood by law enforcement. Because the SAR narrative section is the only area summarizing suspicious activity, the narrative section, as stated on the SAR form, is "critical." Thus, a failure to adequately describe the factors making a transaction or activity suspicious undermines the purpose of the SAR.

By their nature, SAR narratives are subjective, and examiners generally should not criticize the bank's interpretation of the facts. Nevertheless, banks should ensure that SAR narratives are complete, thoroughly describe the extent and nature of the suspicious activity, and are included within the SAR form (e.g., no attachments to the narrative section will be included within the BSA-reporting database). More specific guidance is available in Appendix L ("SAR Quality Guidance") to assist banks in writing, and assist examiners in evaluating, SAR narratives. In addition, comprehensive guidance is available from FinCEN ("Guidance on Preparing a Complete & Sufficient Suspicious Activity Report Narrative") at www.fincen.gov.

Prohibition of SAR Disclosure

No bank, and no director, officer, employee, or agent of a bank, that reports a suspicious transaction may notify any person involved in the transaction that the transaction has been reported. Thus, any person subpoenaed or otherwise requested to disclose a SAR or the information contained in a SAR, except when such disclosure is requested by FinCEN or an appropriate law enforcement or federal banking agency, shall decline to produce the SAR or to provide any information that would disclose that a SAR has been prepared or filed, citing 31 CFR 103.18(e) and 31 USC 5318(g)(2). FinCEN and the bank's federal banking agency should be notified of any such request and of the bank's response. Furthermore, FinCEN and the federal banking agencies take the position that banks' internal controls for the filing of SARs should minimize the risks of disclosure.

Record Retention

Banks must retain copies of SARs and supporting documentation for five years from the date of the report.

EXAMINATION PROCEDURES

Suspicious Activity Reporting

Objective. *Assess the bank's policies, procedures, and processes, and overall compliance with statutory and regulatory requirements for monitoring, detecting, and reporting suspicious activities.*

Review of Policies, Procedures, and Processes

1. Review the bank's policies, procedures, and processes for identifying, researching, and reporting suspicious activity. Determine whether they include the following:
   - Lines of communication for the referral of unusual activity to appropriate personnel.
   - Designation of individual(s) responsible for identifying, researching, and reporting suspicious activities.
   - Monitoring systems used to identify unusual activity.
   - Procedures to ensure the timely generation of, review of, and response to reports used to identify unusual activities.
   - Procedures for reviewing and evaluating the transaction activity of subjects included in law enforcement requests (e.g., grand jury subpoenas, section 3 14(a) requests, or National Security Letters (NSLs)) for suspicious activity. NSLs are highly confidential documents; as such, examiners will not review or sample specific NSLs. Instead, examiners should evaluate the policies, procedures, and processes for:
     Responding to NSLs.
     Evaluating the account of the target for suspicious activity.
     Filing Suspicious Activity Reports (SARs), if necessary.
     Handling account closures.
   - Procedures for documenting decisions not to file a SAR.
   - Procedures for considering closing accounts as a result of continuous suspicious activity.
   - Procedures for completing, filing, and retaining SARs and their supporting documentation.
   - Procedures for reporting SARs to the board of directors, or a committee thereof, and senior management.
   - Procedures for sharing SARs with head offices and controlling companies.

Evaluating Suspicious Activity Monitoring Systems

2. Review the bank's monitoring systems and how the system(s) fits into the bank's overall suspicious activity monitoring and reporting process. Complete the appropriate examination procedures that follow. When evaluating the effectiveness

of the bank's monitoring systems, examiners should consider the bank's overall risk profile (high-risk products, services, customers, and geographic locations), volume of transactions, and adequacy of staffing.

Manual Transaction Monitoring

3. Review the bank's transaction monitoring reports. Determine whether the reports capture all areas that pose money laundering and terrorist financing risks. Examples of these reports include: currency activity reports, funds transfer reports, monetary instrument sales reports, large item reports, significant balance change reports, nonsufficient funds (NSF) reports, and nonresident alien (NRA) reports.
4. Determine whether the bank's monitoring systems use reasonable filtering criteria whose programming has been independently verified. Determine whether the monitoring systems generate accurate reports at a reasonable frequency.

Automated Account Monitoring

5. Identify the types of customers, products, and services that are included within the automated account monitoring system.
6. Identify the system's methodology for establishing and applying expected activity or profile filtering criteria and for generating monitoring reports. Determine whether the system's filtering criteria are reasonable.
7. Determine whether the programming of the methodology has been independently validated.
8. Determine that controls ensure limited access to the monitoring system and sufficient oversight of assumption changes.

Evaluating the SAR Decision-Making Process

9. Evaluate the bank's policies, procedures, and processes for referring unusual activity from all business lines to the personnel or department responsible for evaluating unusual activity. The process should ensure that all applicable information (e.g., criminal subpoenas, NSLs, and section 314(a) requests) is effectively evaluated.
10. Determine whether policies, procedures, and processes require appropriate research when monitoring reports identify unusual activity.
11. Determine whether the bank's SAR decision process appropriately considers all available customer due diligence (CDD) information.

Transaction Testing

Evaluating SAR Quality

12. On the basis of a risk assessment, prior examination reports, and a review of the bank's audit findings, sample the SARs downloaded from the BSA reporting

database or the bank's internal SAR records. Review the quality of SAR data to assess the following:

- SARs contain accurate information.
- SAR narratives are complete and thorough, and clearly explain why the activity is suspicious.
- If SAR narratives from the BSA reporting database are blank or contain language, such as "see attached," ensure that the bank is not mailing attachments to the Internal Revenue Service (IRS) Detroit Computing Center. [32]

Testing the Suspicious Activity Monitoring System

Transaction testing of suspicious activity monitoring systems and reporting processes is intended to determine whether the bank's policies, procedures, and processes are adequate and effectively implemented. Examiners should document the factors they used to select samples and should maintain a list of the accounts sampled. The size and the sample should be based on the following:

- Weaknesses in the account monitoring systems.
- The bank's overall BSA/AML risk profile (e.g., number and type of high-risk products, services, customers, and geographic locations).
- The quality and extent of review by audit or independent parties.
- Prior examination findings.
- Recent mergers, acquisitions, or other significant organizational changes.
- Conclusions or questions from the review of the bank's SARs.

Refer to Appendix O ("Examiner Tools for Transaction Testing") for additional guidance.

13. On the basis of a risk assessment, prior examination reports, and a review of the bank's audit findings, sample specific customer accounts to review the following:
    - Suspicious activity monitoring reports.
    - CTR download information.
    - High-risk banking operations (products, services, customers, and geographic locations).
    - Customer activity.
    - Subpoenas received by the bank.
    - Decisions not to file a SAR.
14. For the customers selected previously, obtain the following information, if applicable:
    - Customer Identification Program (CIP) and account-opening documentation.
    - CDD documentation.
    - Two to three months of account statements covering the total customer relationship and showing all transactions.
    - Sample items posted against the account (e.g., copies of checks deposited and written, debit or credit tickets, and funds transfer beneficiaries and originators).
    - Other relevant information, such as loan files and correspondence.

15. Review the selected accounts for unusual activity. If the examiner identifies unusual activity, review customer information for indications that the activity is typical for the customer (i.e., the sort of activity in which the customer is normally expected to engage). When reviewing for unusual activity, consider the following:
    - For individual customers, whether the activity is consistent with CDD information (e.g., occupation, expected account activity, and sources of funds and wealth).
    - For business customers, whether the activity is consistent with CDD information (e.g., type of business, size, location, and target market).
16. Determine whether the manual or automated suspicious activity monitoring system detected the activity that the examiner identified as unusual.
17. For transactions identified as unusual, discuss the transactions with management. Determine whether the account officer demonstrates knowledge of the customer and the unusual transactions. After examining the available facts, determine whether management knows of a reasonable explanation for the transactions.
18. Determine whether the bank has failed to identify any reportable suspicious activity.
19. From the results of the sample, determine whether the manual or automated suspicious activity monitoring system effectively detects unusual or suspicious activity. Identify the underlying cause of any deficiencies in the monitoring systems (e.g., inappropriate filters, insufficient risk assessment, or inadequate decision-making).

Evaluating the SAR Decision-Making Process

20. On the basis of a risk assessment, prior examination reports, and a review of the bank's audit findings, select a sample of management's research decisions to determine the following:
    - Whether management decisions to file or not file a SAR are supported and reasonable.
    - Whether documentation is adequate.
    - Whether the decision process is completed and SARs are filed in a timely manner.
21. On the basis of examination procedures completed, including transaction testing, form a conclusion about the ability of policies, procedures, and processes to meet regulatory requirements associated with monitoring, detecting, and reporting suspicious activity.

Currency Transaction Reporting — Overview

Objective. *Assess the bank's compliance with statutory and regulatory requirements for the reporting of large currency transactions.*

A bank must file a Currency Transaction Report (CTR) (FinCEN Form 104) for each transaction in currency[33] (deposit, withdrawal, exchange, or other payment or transfer) of more than $10,000 by, through, or to the bank. Certain types of currency transactions need not be reported, such as those involving "exempt persons," a group which can include retail or commercial customers meeting specific criteria for exemption. Refer to the core overview section, "Currency Transaction Reporting Exemptions," page 80, for further guidance.

Aggregation of Currency Transactions

Multiple currency transactions totaling more than $10,000 during any one business day are treated as a single transaction if the bank has knowledge that they are by or on behalf of the same person. Transactions throughout the bank should be aggregated when determining multiple transactions. Types of currency transactions subject to reporting requirements individually or by aggregation include, but are not limited to, denomination exchanges, individual retirement accounts (IRAs), loan payments, automated teller machine (ATM) transactions, purchases of certificates of deposit, deposits and withdrawals, funds transfers paid for in currency, and monetary instrument purchases. Banks are strongly encouraged to develop systems necessary to aggregate currency transactions throughout the bank. Management should ensure that an adequate system is implemented that will appropriately report currency transactions subject to the BSA requirement.

Filing Time Frames and Record Retention Requirements

A completed CTR must be filed with FinCEN within 15 days after the date of the transaction (25 days if filed magnetically or electronically). The bank must retain copies of CTRs for five years from the date of the report (31 CFR 103.27(a)(3)).

CTR Backfiling

If a bank has failed to file CTRs on reportable transactions, the bank should begin filing CTRs and should contact the Internal Revenue Service (IRS) Detroit Computing Center[34] to request a determination on whether the backfiling of unreported transactions is necessary.

Examination Procedures

Currency Transaction Reporting

Objective. *Assess the bank's compliance with statutory and regulatory requirements for the reporting of large currency transactions.*

1. Determine whether the bank's policies, procedures, and processes adequately address the preparation, filing, and retention of Currency Transaction Reports (CTRs) (FinCEN Form 104).
2. Review correspondence that the bank has received from the IRS Detroit Computing Center relating to incorrect or incomplete CTRs (errors). Determine whether management has taken corrective action, when necessary.
3. Review the currency transaction system (e.g., how the bank identifies transactions applicable for the filing of a CTR). Determine whether the bank aggregates all or some currency transactions within the bank. Determine whether the bank aggregates transactions by taxpayer identification number (TIN), individual taxpayer identification number (ITIN), employer identification number (EIN), or customer information file (CIF) number. Also, evaluate how CTRs are filed on customers with missing TINs or EINs.

Transaction Testing

4. On the basis of a risk assessment, prior examination reports, and a review of the bank's audit findings, select a sample of filed CTRs (hard copy or from computer-generated filings) to determine whether:
   - CTRs are completed in accordance with FinCEN instructions.
   - CTRs are filed for large currency transactions identified by tellers' cash proof sheets, automated large currency transaction systems, or other types of aggregation systems that cover all relevant areas of the bank, unless an exemption exists for the customer.
   - CTRs are filed accurately and completely within 15 calendar days after the date of the transaction (25 days if filed magnetically or electronically).
   - The bank's independent testing confirms the integrity and accuracy of the management information systems (MIS) used for aggregating currency transactions. If not, the examiner should confirm the integrity and accuracy of the MIS. The examiner's review should confirm that tellers do not have the capability to override currency aggregation systems.
   - Discrepancies exist between the bank's records of CTRs and the CTRs reflected in the download from the BSA reporting databases.
   - The bank retains copies of CTRs for five years from the date of the report (31 CFR 103.27(a)(3)).
5. On the basis of examination procedures completed, including transaction testing, form a conclusion about the ability of policies, procedures, and processes to meet regulatory requirements associated with currency transaction reporting.

CURRENCY TRANSACTION REPORTING EXEMPTIONS — OVERVIEW

Objective. *Assess the bank's compliance with statutory and regulatory requirements for exemptions from the currency transaction reporting requirements.*

U.S. Treasury regulations have historically recognized that the routine reporting of some types of large currency transactions does not necessarily aid law enforcement authorities and may place unreasonable burdens on banks. Consequently, a bank may exempt certain types of customers from currency transaction reporting.

The Money Laundering Suppression Act of 1994 (MLSA) established a two-phase exemption process. Under Phase I exemptions, transactions in currency by banks, governmental departments or agencies, and public or listed companies and their subsidiaries are exempt from reporting. Under Phase II exemptions, transactions in currency by smaller businesses that meet specific criteria laid out in FinCEN's regulations may be exempted from reporting. To exempt a customer from CTR reporting, a bank must file a Designation of Exempt Person form (FinCEN Form 110).

Phase I CTR Exemptions (31 CFR 103.22(d)(2)(i)–(v))

FinCEN's rule identifies five categories of Phase I exempt persons:

- A bank, to the extent of its domestic operations.
- A federal, state, or local government agency or department.
- Any entity exercising governmental authority within the United States.
- Any entity (other than a bank) whose common stock is listed on the New York, American, or NASDAQ stock exchanges (with some exceptions).
- Any subsidiary (other than a bank) of any "listed entity" that is organized under U.S. law and at least 51 percent of whose common stock is owned by the listed entity.

Filing Time Frames

Banks must file a one-time Designation of Exempt Person form to exempt a Phase I entity from currency transaction reporting. The exemption of a Phase I entity covers all transactions in currency with the exempted entity, not only transactions in currency conducted through an account. The form must be filed with the Internal Revenue Service (IRS) within 30 days after the first transaction in currency that the bank wishes to exempt.

Annual Review

The information supporting each designation of a Phase I exempt person must be reviewed and verified by the bank at least once per year. Annual reports, stock quotes from newspapers, or other information, such as electronic media could be used to document the review.

Phase II CTR Exemptions (31 CFR 103.22(d)(2) (vi)–(vii))

A business that does not fall into any of the Phase I categories may still be exempted under the Phase II exemptions if it qualifies as either a "non-listed business" or as a "payroll customer."

Non-Listed Businesses

A "non-listed business" is defined as a commercial enterprise to the extent of its domestic operations and only with respect to transactions conducted through its exemptible accounts and that (i) has maintained a transaction account at the exempting bank for at least 12 months, (ii) frequently[35] engages in transactions in currency with the bank in excess of $10,000, and (iii) is incorporated or organized under the laws of the United States or a state, or is registered as and eligible to do business within the United States or a state.

Ineligible Businesses

Certain businesses are ineligible for treatment as an exempt non-listed business (31 CFR 103.22(d)(6)(viii)). An ineligible business is defined as a business engaged primarily in one or more of the following specified activities:

- Serving as a financial institution or as agents for a financial institution of any type.
- Purchasing or selling motor vehicles of any kind, vessels, aircraft, farm equipment, or mobile homes.
- Practicing law, accounting, or medicine.
- Auctioning of goods.
- Chartering or operation of ships, buses, or aircraft.
- Operating a pawn brokerage.
- Engaging in gaming of any kind (other than licensed pari-mutuel betting at race tracks).
- Engaging in investment advisory services or investment banking services.
- Operating a real estate brokerage.
- Operating in title insurance activities and real estate closings.
- Engaging in trade union activities.
- Engaging in any other activity that may, from time to time, be specified by FinCEN.

A business that engages in multiple business activities may qualify for an exemption as a non-listed business as long as no more than 50 percent of its gross revenues per year[36] are derived from one or more of the ineligible business activities listed in the rule.

Payroll Customers

A "payroll customer" is defined solely with respect to withdrawals for payroll purposes from existing exemptible accounts and as a person who: (i) has maintained a transaction account at the bank for at least 12 months; (ii) operates a firm that regularly withdraws more than $10,000 in order to pay its U.S. employees in currency; and (iii) is incorporated or organized under the laws of the United States or a state, or is registered as and is eligible to do business within the United States or a state.

Filing Time Frames

After a bank has decided to exempt a Phase II customer, the bank must file an initial Designation of Exempt Person form (FinCEN Form 110) within 30 days after the first customer transaction the bank wishes to exempt.

Annual Review

The information supporting each designation of a Phase II exempt person must be reviewed and verified by the bank at least once per year. The bank should document the annual review. Moreover, consistent with this annual review, a bank must review and verify at least once each year that management monitors these Phase II accounts for suspicious transactions.

Biennial Renewals

Additionally, for Phase II customers, the form must be refiled every two years, on or before March 15, as part of the biennial renewal process. Under the biennial renewal process applicable to Phase II customers, a bank must include the following information on the biennial renewal: (i) any change in control of the exempt person known to the bank (or for which the bank has reason to know) and (ii) a certification that the bank has applied its suspicious activity monitoring system to transactions in currency of the exempt person as necessary, but at least annually.

Safe Harbor for Failure to File CTRs

The rules (31 CFR 103.22(d)(8)) provide a safe harbor that a bank is not liable for the failure to file a CTR for a transaction in currency by an exempt person, unless the bank knowingly provides false or incomplete information or has reason to believe that the customer does not qualify as an exempt customer. In the absence of any specific knowledge or information indicating that a customer no longer meets the requirements of an exempt person, the bank is entitled to a safe harbor from civil penalties to the extent it continues to treat that customer as an exempt customer until the date of the customer's annual review.

Effect on Other Regulatory Requirements

The exemption procedures do not have any effect on the requirement that banks file SARs. For example, the fact that a customer is an exempt person has no effect on a bank's obligation to retain records of funds transfers by that person, or to retain records in connection with the sale of monetary instruments to that person.

If a bank has improperly exempted accounts, the examiner may require management to revoke the exemption. In any case, the bank should begin filing CTRs and should contact the Internal Revenue Service (IRS) Detroit Computing Center[37] to request a determination on whether the backfiling of unreported currency transactions is necessary.

Additional information about the currency transaction exemption process can be found on FinCEN's web site at www.fincen.gov.

Examination Procedures

Currency Transaction Reporting Exemptions

Objective. *Assess the bank's compliance with statutory and regulatory requirements for exemptions from the currency transaction reporting requirements.*

1. Determine whether the bank uses the Currency Transaction Report (CTR) exemption process. If yes, determine whether the policies, procedures, and processes for CTR exemptions are adequate.

Phase I Exemptions (31 CFR 103.22(d)(2)(i)–(v))

2. Determine whether the bank files the Designation of Exempt Person form (FinCEN Form 110) with the Internal Revenue Service (IRS) to exempt a customer from CTR reporting as defined in 31 CFR 103.22. The form should be filed within 30 days of the first reportable transaction that was exempted.
3. Assess whether ongoing and reasonable due diligence is performed, including required annual reviews to determine whether a customer remains eligible for designation as an exempt person under the regulatory requirements. Management should properly document exemption determinations (e.g., with stock quotes from newspapers and consolidated returns for the entity).

Phase II Exemptions (31 CFR 103.22(d)(2)(vi)–(vii))

Under the regulation, the definition of exempt persons includes "non-listed businesses" and "payroll customers" as defined in 31 CFR 103.22(d)(2)(vi)–(vii). Nevertheless, several businesses remain ineligible for exemption purposes; refer to 31 CFR 103.22(d)(6)(viii) and the "Currency Transaction Reporting Exemptions" core overview section of this manual.

4. Determine whether the bank files a FinCEN Form 110 with the IRS to exempt a customer, as identified by management, from CTR reporting.
5. Determine whether the bank maintains documentation to support that the "non-listed businesses" it has designated as exempt from CTR reporting do not receive more than 50 percent of gross revenue from ineligible business activities.
6. Assess whether ongoing and reasonable due diligence is performed, including required annual reviews, to determine whether a customer is eligible for designation as exempt from CTR reporting. Customers must meet the following requirements to be eligible for exemption under the regulation:
   - Have frequent[38] currency transactions in excess of $10,000 (withdrawals to pay domestic employees in currency in the case of a payroll customer).
   - Be incorporated or organized under the laws of the United States or a state, or registered as and eligible to do business within the United States or a state.

- Maintain a transaction account at the bank for at least 12 months.

7. Determine whether the bank's policies, procedures, and processes ensure that the FinCEN Form 110 is filed on or before March 15 of the second year from the date of the original filing and biennially thereafter (for 31 CFR 103.22(d)(2)(vi)–(vii) exemptions only). Ascertain whether filings include both a notification of any change in control relative to the exempt persons and a certification by the bank that it maintains a system for reporting suspicious activity.

Transaction Testing

8. On the basis of a risk assessment, prior examination reports, and a review of the bank's audit findings, select a sample of Designation of Exempt Person forms (FinCEN Form 110) from the bank to test compliance with the regulatory requirements (e.g., only eligible businesses are exempted, adequate supporting documentation is maintained, and biennial filings are timely).
9. On the basis of examination procedures completed, including transaction testing, form a conclusion about the ability of policies, procedures, and processes to meet regulatory requirements associated with currency transaction reporting exemptions.

Information Sharing — Overview

Objective. *Assess the financial institution's compliance with the statutory and regulatory requirements for the "Special Information Sharing Procedures to Deter Money Laundering and Terrorist Activity" (section 314 Information Requests).*

On September 26, 2002, final regulations (31 CFR 103.100 and 31 CFR 103.110) implementing section 314 of the Patriot Act became effective. The regulations established procedures for information sharing to deter money laundering and terrorist activity.

Information Sharing between Law Enforcement and Financial Institutions — Section 314(a) of the Patriot Act (31 CFR 103.100)

A federal law enforcement agency investigating terrorist activity or money laundering may request that FinCEN solicit, on its behalf, certain information from a financial institution or a group of financial institutions. The federal law enforcement agency must provide a written certification to FinCEN attesting that there is credible evidence of engagement or reasonably suspected engagement in terrorist activity or money laundering for each individual, entity, or organization about which the federal law enforcement agency is seeking information. The federal law enforcement agency also must provide specific identifiers, such as a date of birth and address, which would permit a financial institution to differentiate among common or similar names. Upon receiving a completed written certification from a federal law enforcement agency, FinCEN may require a financial institution to search its records to determine whether it maintains or has maintained accounts for, or has engaged in transactions with, any specified individual, entity, or organization.

Search Requirements

Upon receiving an information request,[39] a financial institution must conduct a one-time search of its records to identify accounts or transactions of a named suspect. Unless otherwise instructed by an information request, financial institutions must search their records for current accounts, accounts maintained during the preceding 12 months, and transactions conducted outside of an account by or on behalf of a named suspect during the preceding six months. The financial institution must search its records and report any positive matches to FinCEN within 14 days, unless otherwise specified in the information request.

In March 2005, FinCEN began posting section 314(a) subject lists through the 314(a) Secure Information Sharing System. Every two weeks, or more frequently if an emergency request is transmitted, the financial institution's designated point(s) of contact will receive notification from FinCEN that there are new postings to FinCEN's secure web site. The point of contact will be able to access the current section 314(a) subject list (and one prior) and download the files in various formats for searching. Financial institutions should report all positive matches via the Secure Information Sharing System. Those financial institutions choosing to receive the section 314(a) subject lists by facsimile will continue to receive the lists in that manner. For those financial institutions, positive matches should be indicated on the respective subject information form and faxed to FinCEN.[40]

FinCEN has provided financial institutions with General Instructions and Frequently Asked Questions (FAQs) relating to the section 314(a) process. Unless otherwise instructed by an information request, financial institutions must search the records specified in the General Instructions.[41] The General Instructions or FAQs are made available to the financial institutions on the 314(a) Secure Information Sharing System or by contacting FinCEN.[42]

If a financial institution identifies any account or transaction, it must report to FinCEN that it has a match. No details should be provided to FinCEN other than the fact that the financial institution has a match. A negative response is not required. A financial institution may provide the subject lists to a third-party service provider or vendor to perform or facilitate record searches as long as the institution takes the necessary steps, through the use of an agreement or procedures, to ensure that the third party safeguards and maintains the confidentiality of the information.

Use Restrictions and Confidentiality

Financial institutions should develop and implement comprehensive policies, procedures, and processes for responding to section 314(a) requests. The regulation restricts the use of the information provided in a section 3 14(a) request (31 CFR 103.100(b)(2)(iv)). A financial institution may only use the information to report the required information to FinCEN, to determine whether to establish or maintain an account or engage in a transaction, or to assist in BSA/AML compliance. While the section 314(a) list could be used to determine whether to establish or maintain an account, FinCEN strongly discourages financial institutions from using this as the sole factor in reaching a decision to do so unless the request specifically states otherwise. Unlike the OFAC lists, section 314(a) lists are not permanent "watch lists." In fact, section 314(a) lists generally relate to one-time inquiries and are not updated or corrected if an investigation is dropped, a prosecution is declined, or a subject is exonerated. Further, the names do not correspond to convicted or indicted persons; rather a 314(a) subject need only be "reasonably suspected" based on credible evidence of engaging in terrorist acts or money laundering. Moreover, FinCEN advises that inclusion on a section 314(a) list should not be the sole factor used to determine whether to file a Suspicious Activity Report (SAR). Financial institutions should establish a process for determining when and if a SAR should be filed. Refer to the core overview section, "Suspicious Activity Reporting," page 60, for additional guidance.

Actions taken pursuant to information provided in a request from FinCEN do not affect a financial institution's obligations to comply with all of the rules and regulations of OFAC nor do they affect a financial institution's obligations to respond to any legal process. Additionally, actions taken in response to a request do not relieve a financial institution of its obligation to file a SAR and immediately notify law enforcement, if necessary, in accordance with applicable laws and regulations.

A financial institution cannot disclose to any person, other than to FinCEN, the institution's primary banking regulator, or the federal law enforcement agency on whose behalf FinCEN is requesting information, the fact that FinCEN has requested or obtained information. A financial institution should designate one or more points of contact for receiving information requests. FinCEN has stated that an affiliated group of financial institutions may establish one point of contact to distribute the section 314(a) list to respond to requests. However, the section 314(a) lists cannot be shared with any foreign office, branch, or affiliate (unless the request specifically states otherwise), and the lists cannot be shared with affiliates, or subsidiaries of bank holding companies, if the affiliates or subsidiaries are not financial institutions as described in 31 USC 531 2(a)(2).

Each financial institution must maintain adequate procedures to protect the security and confidentiality of requests from FinCEN. The procedures to ensure confidentiality will be considered adequate if the financial institution applies procedures similar to those it has established to comply with section 501 of the Gramm–Leach–Bliley Act (15 USC 6801) for the protection of its customers' nonpublic personal information. Financial institutions may keep a log of all section 314(a) requests received and of any positive matches identified and reported to FinCEN.

Documentation

Additionally, documentation that all required searches were performed is essential. This may be accomplished by maintaining copies of the cover page of the request with a financial institution sign-off that the records were checked, the date of the search, and search results (e.g., positive or negative). For positive matches, copies of the form returned to FinCEN and the supporting documentation should be retained. For those institutions utilizing the web-based 314(a) Secure Information Sharing System, a Subject Response List can be printed for documentation purposes. The Subject Response List displays the total number of positive responses submitted to FinCEN for that transmission, the transmission date, the submitted date, and the tracking number and subject name that had the positive hit. If the financial institution elects to maintain copies of the section 314(a) requests, it should not be criticized for doing so, as long as it appropriately secures them and protects their confidentiality. Audits should include an evaluation of compliance with these guidelines within their scope.

FinCEN regularly updates a list of recent search transmissions, including information on the date of transmission, tracking number, and number of subjects listed in the transmission.[43] Bankers and examiners may review this list to verify that search requests have been received. Each bank should contact its primary federal regulator for guidance to ensure it obtains the section 314(a) list and for updating contact information.[44]

Voluntary Information Sharing — Section 314(b) of the Patriot Act (31 CFR 103.110)

Section 314(b) encourages financial institutions and associations of financial institutions located in the United States to share information in order to identify and report activities that may involve terrorist activity or money laundering. Section 314(b) also provides specific protection from civil liability. To avail itself of this statutory safe harbor from liability, a financial institution or an association must notify FinCEN of its intent to engage in information sharing and that it has established and will maintain adequate procedures to protect the security and confidentiality of the information. Failure to comply with the requirements of 31 CFR 103.110 will result in loss of safe harbor protection for information sharing and may result in a violation of privacy laws or other laws and regulations.

If a financial institution chooses to voluntarily participate in section 3 14(b), policies, procedures, and processes should be developed and implemented for sharing and receiving of information.

A notice to share information is effective for one year.[45] The financial institution should designate a point of contact for receiving and providing information. A financial institution should establish a process for sending and receiving information sharing requests. Additionally, a financial institution must take reasonable steps to verify that the other financial institution or association of financial institutions with which it intends to share information has also submitted the required notice to FinCEN. FinCEN provides participating financial institutions with access to a list of other participating financial institutions and their related contact information.

If a financial institution receives such information from another financial institution, it must also limit use of the information and maintain its security and confidentiality (31 CFR 103.110(b)(4)). Such information may be used only to identify and, where appropriate, report on money laundering and terrorist activities; to determine whether to establish or maintain an account; to engage in a transaction; or to assist in BSA compliance. The procedures to ensure confidentiality will be considered adequate if the financial institution applies procedures similar to the ones it has established to comply with section 501 of the Gramm–Leach–Bliley Act (15 USC 6801) for the protection of its customers' nonpublic personal information. The safe harbor does not extend to sharing of information across international borders. In addition, section 314(b) does not authorize a financial institution to share a SAR, nor does it permit the financial institution to disclose the existence or nonexistence of a SAR. If a financial institution shares information under section 314(b) about the subject of a prepared or filed SAR, the information shared should be limited to underlying transaction and customer information. A financial institution may use information obtained under section 314(b) to determine whether to file a SAR, but the intention to prepare or file a SAR cannot be shared with another financial institution. Financial institutions should establish a process for determining when and if a SAR should be filed.

Actions taken pursuant to information obtained through the voluntary information sharing process do not affect a financial institution's obligations to respond to any legal process. Additionally, actions taken in response to information obtained through the voluntary information sharing process do not relieve a financial institution of its obligation to file a SAR and to immediately notify law enforcement, if necessary, in accordance with all applicable laws and regulations.

EXAMINATION PROCEDURES

Information Sharing

Objective. *Assess the financial institution's compliance with the statutory and regulatory requirements for the "Special Information Sharing Procedures to Deter Money Laundering and Terrorist Activity" (section 314 Information Requests).*

Information Sharing between Law Enforcement and Financial Institutions (Section 3 14(a))

1. Verify that the financial institution is currently receiving section 314(a) requests from FinCEN or from an affiliated financial institution that serves as the subject financial institution's point of contact. If the financial institution is not receiving information requests or contact information changes, the financial institution should update its contact information with its primary regulator in accordance with the instructions at www.fincen.gov.
2. Verify that the financial institution has sufficient policies, procedures, and processes to document compliance; maintain sufficient internal controls; provide ongoing training; and independently test its compliance with 31 CFR 103.100, which implements section 314(a) of the Patriot Act. At a minimum, the procedures should accomplish the following:
   - Designate a point of contact for receiving information requests.
   - Ensure that the confidentiality of requested information is safeguarded.
   - Establish a process for responding to FinCEN's requests.
   - Establish a process for determining if and when a SAR should be filed.
3. Determine whether the search policies, procedures, and processes the financial institution uses to respond to section 314(a) requests are comprehensive and cover all records identified in the General Instructions for such requests. The General Instructions include searching accounts maintained by the named subject during the preceding 12 months and transactions conducted within the last six months. Financial institutions have 14 days from the transmission date of the request to respond to a section 314(a) Subject Information Form.

4. If the financial institution uses a third-party vendor to perform or facilitate searches, determine whether an agreement or procedures are in place to ensure confidentiality.
5. Review the financial institution's internal controls and determine whether its documentation to evidence compliance with section 314(a) requests is adequate. This documentation could include, for example the following:
   - Copies of section 314(a) requests.
   - A log that records the tracking numbers and includes a sign-off column.
   - Copies of the cover page of the requests, with a financial institution sign-off, that the records were checked, the date of the search, and search results (e.g., positive or negative).
   - For positive matches, copies of the form returned to FinCEN and the supporting documentation should be retained.

Voluntary Information Sharing (Section 314(b))

6. Determine whether the financial institution has decided to share information voluntarily. If so, verify that the financial institution has filed a notification form with FinCEN and provides an effective date for the sharing of information that is within the previous 12 months.
7. Verify that the financial institution has policies, procedures, and processes for sharing information and receiving shared information, as specified under 31 CFR 103.110, (which implements section 314(b) of the Patriot Act).
8. Financial institutions that choose to share information voluntarily should have policies, procedures, and processes to document compliance; maintain adequate internal controls; provide ongoing training; and independently test its compliance with 31 CFR 103.110. At a minimum, the procedures should:
   - Designate a point of contact for receiving and providing information.
   - Ensure the safeguarding and confidentiality of information received and information requested.
   - Establish a process for sending and responding to requests, including ensuring that other parties with whom the financial institution intends to share information (including affiliates) have filed the proper notice.
   - Establish procedures for determining whether and when a SAR should be filed.
9. If the financial institution is sharing information with other entities and is not following the procedures outlined in 31 CFR 103.110(b), notify the examiners reviewing the privacy rules.
10. Through a review of the financial institution's documentation (including account analysis) on a sample of the information shared and received, evaluate how the financial institution determined whether a Suspicious Activity Report (SAR) was warranted. The financial institution is not required to file SARs solely on the basis of information obtained through the voluntary information sharing process. In fact, the information obtained through the voluntary information sharing process may enable the financial institution to determine that no SAR is required for transactions that

may have initially appeared suspicious. The financial institution should have considered account activity in determining whether a SAR was warranted.

Transaction Testing

11. On the basis of a risk assessment, prior examination reports, and a review of the financial institution's audit findings, select a sample of positive matches or recent requests to determine whether the following requirements have been met:
    - The financial institution's policies, procedures, and processes enable it to search all of the records identified in the General Instructions for section 314(a) requests. Such processes may be electronic, manual, or both.
    - The financial institution searches appropriate records for each information request received. For positive matches:

      Verify that a response was provided to FinCEN within the designated time period (31 CFR 103.1 00(b)(2)(ii)).

      Review the financial institution's documentation (including account analysis) to evaluate how the financial institution determined whether a SAR was warranted. Financial institutions are not required to file SARs solely on the basis of a match with a named subject; instead, account activity should be considered in determining whether a SAR is warranted.
    - The financial institution uses information only in the manner and for the purposes allowed and keeps information secure and confidential (31 CFR 103.100(b)(2)(iv)). (This requirement can be verified through discussions with management.)
12. On the basis of examination procedures completed, including transaction testing, form a conclusion about the ability of policies, procedures, and processes to meet regulatory requirements associated with information sharing.

PURCHASE AND SALE OF MONETARY INSTRUMENTS RECORDKEEPING — OVERVIEW

Objective. *Assess the bank's compliance with statutory and regulatory requirements for the recording of information required for the purchase and sale of monetary instruments for currency in amounts between $3,000 and $10,000, inclusive. This section covers the regulatory requirements as set forth by the BSA. Refer to the expanded sections of this manual for additional discussions and procedures on specific money laundering risks for purchase and sale of monetary instruments activities.*

Banks sell a variety of monetary instruments (e.g., bank checks or drafts, including foreign drafts, money orders, cashier's checks, and traveler's checks) in exchange for currency. Purchasing these instruments in amounts of less than $10,000 is a common method used by money launderers to evade large currency transaction reporting requirements. Once converted from currency, criminals typically deposit these instruments in accounts with other banks to facilitate the movement of funds through the payment system. In many cases, the persons involved do not have an account with the bank from which the instruments are purchased.

Purchaser Verification

Under 31 CFR 103.29 banks are required to verify the identity of persons purchasing monetary instruments for currency in amounts between $3,000 and $10,000, inclusive, and to maintain records of all such sales.

Banks may either verify that the purchaser of monetary instruments is a deposit accountholder with identifying information on record with the bank, or a bank may verify the identity of the purchaser by viewing a form of identification that contains the customer's name and address and that the financial community accepts as a means of identification when cashing checks for noncustomers. The bank must obtain additional information for purchasers who do not have deposit accounts. The method used to verify the identity of the purchaser must be recorded.

Acceptable Identification

The U.S. Treasury's Administrative Ruling 92-1 provides guidance on how a bank can verify the identity of an elderly or disabled customer who does not possess the normally acceptable forms of identification. A bank may accept a Social Security, Medicare, or Medicaid card along with another form of documentation bearing the customer's name and address. Additional forms of documentation include a utility bill, a tax bill, or a voter registration card. The forms of alternate identification a bank decides to accept should be included in its formal policies, procedures, and processes.

Contemporaneous Purchases

Contemporaneous purchases of the same or different types of instruments totaling $3,000 or more must be treated as one purchase. Multiple purchases during one business day totaling $3,000 or more must be aggregated and treated as one purchase if the bank has knowledge that the purchases have occurred.

Indirect Currency Purchases of Monetary Instruments

Banks may implement a policy requiring customers who are deposit accountholders and who want to purchase monetary instruments in amounts between $3,000 and $10,000 with currency to first deposit the currency into their deposit accounts. Nothing within the BSA or its implementing regulations prohibits a bank from instituting such a policy.

However, FinCEN takes the position[46] that when a customer purchases a monetary instrument in amounts between $3,000 and $10,000 using currency that the customer first deposits into the customer's account, the transaction is still subject to the recordkeeping requirements of 31 CFR 103.29. This requirement applies whether the transaction is conducted in accordance with a bank's established policy or at the request of the customer. Generally, when a bank sells monetary instruments to deposit accountholders, the bank will already maintain most of the information required by 31 CFR 103.29 in the normal course of its business.

Recordkeeping and Retention Requirements

Under 31 CFR 103.29, a bank's records of sales must contain, at a minimum, the following information:

- If the purchaser **has a deposit account** with the bank:
  - Name of the purchaser.
  - Date of purchase.
  - Types of instruments purchased.
  - Serial numbers of each of the instruments purchased.
  - Dollar amounts of each of the instruments purchased in currency.
  - Specific identifying information, if applicable.[47]
- If the purchaser **does not have a deposit account** with the bank:
  - Name and address of the purchaser.
  - Social Security or alien identification number of the purchaser.
  - Date of birth of the purchaser.
  - Date of purchase.
  - Types of instruments purchased.
  - Serial numbers of each of the instruments purchased.
  - Dollar amounts of each of the instruments purchased.
  - Specific identifying information for verifying the purchaser's identity (e.g., state of issuance and number on driver's license).

If the purchaser cannot provide the required information at the time of the transaction or through the bank's own previously verified records, the transaction should be refused. The records of monetary instrument sales must be retained for five years and be available to the appropriate agencies upon request.

EXAMINATION PROCEDURES

Purchase and Sale of Monetary Instruments Recordkeeping

Objective. *Assess the bank's compliance with statutory and regulatory requirements for the recording of information required for the purchase and sale of monetary instruments for currency in amounts between $3,000 and $10,000, inclusive. This section covers the regulatory requirements as set forth by the BSA. Refer to the expanded sections of this manual for additional discussions and procedures on specific money laundering risks for purchase and sale of monetary instruments activities.*

1. Determine whether the bank maintains the required records (in a manual or an automated system) for sales of bank checks or drafts including foreign drafts, cashier's checks, money orders, and traveler's checks for currency in amounts between $3,000 and $10,000, inclusive, to purchasers who have deposit accounts with the bank.
2. Determine whether the bank's policies, procedures, and processes permit currency sales of monetary instruments to purchasers who do not have deposit accounts with the bank (nondepositors):
   - If so, determine whether the bank maintains the required records for sales of monetary instruments to nondepositors.
   - If not permitted, determine whether the bank allows sales on an exception basis.

Transaction Testing

3. On the basis of a risk assessment, prior examination reports, and a review of the bank's audit findings, select a sample of monetary instruments sold for currency in amounts between $3,000 and $10,000, inclusive, to determine whether the bank obtains, verifies, and retains the required records to ensure compliance with regulatory requirements.
4. On the basis of examination procedures completed, including transaction testing, form a conclusion about the ability of policies, procedures, and processes to meet regulatory requirements associated with the purchase and sale of monetary instruments.
5. On the basis of the previous conclusion and the risks associated with the bank's activity in this area, proceed to expanded examination procedures, if necessary.

FUNDS TRANSFERS RECORDKEEPING — OVERVIEW

Objective. *Assess the bank's compliance with statutory and regulatory requirements for funds transfers. This section covers the regulatory requirements as set forth in the BSA. Refer* *to the expanded sections of this manual for discussions and procedures regarding specific money laundering risks for funds transfer activities.*

Funds transfer systems enable the instantaneous transfer of funds, including both domestic and cross-border transfers. Consequently these systems can present an attractive method to disguise the source of funds derived from illegal activity. The BSA was amended by the Annunzio–Wylie Anti-Money Laundering Act of 1992 to authorize the U.S. Treasury and the Federal Reserve Board to prescribe regulations for domestic and international funds transfers.

In 1995, the U.S. Treasury and the Board of Governors of the Federal Reserve System issued a final rule on recordkeeping requirements concerning payment orders by banks (31 CFR 103.33). [48] The rule requires each bank involved in funds transfers[49] to collect and retain certain information in connection with funds transfers of $3,000 or more.[50] The information required to be collected and retained depends on the bank's role in the particular funds transfer (originator's bank, intermediary bank, or beneficiary's bank).[51] The requirements may also vary depending on whether an originator or beneficiary is an established customer of a bank and whether a payment order is made in person or otherwise.

Also in 1995, the U.S. Treasury issued a final rule that requires all financial institutions to include certain information in transmittal orders for funds transfers of $3,000 or more (31 CFR 103.33).[52] This requirement is commonly referred to as the "Travel Rule."

Responsibilities of Originator's Banks

Recordkeeping Requirements

For each payment order in the amount of $3,000 or more that a bank accepts as an originator's bank, the bank must obtain and retain the following records (31 CFR 103.33(e)(1)(i)):

- Name and address of the originator.
- Amount of the payment order.
- Date of the payment order.
- Any payment instructions.
- Identity of the beneficiary's institution.
- As many of the following items as are received with the payment order:
  - Name and address of the beneficiary.
  - Account number of the beneficiary.
  - Any other specific identifier of the beneficiary.

Additional Records for Non-Established Customers

If the originator is not an established customer of the bank, collect and retain the information listed above. In addition, the originator's bank must collect and retain other information, depending on whether the payment order is made in person.

Payment Orders Made in Person

If the payment order is made in person, the originator's bank must verify the identity of the person placing the payment order before it accepts the order. If it accepts the payment order, the originator's financial institution must obtain and retain the following records:

- Name and address of the person placing the order.
- Type of identification reviewed.
- Number of the identification document (e.g., driver's license).
- The person's taxpayer identification number (TIN) (e.g., Social Security number (SSN) or employer identification number (EIN)) or, if none, the alien identification number or passport number and country of issuance, or a notation in the record of the lack thereof. If the originator's bank has knowledge that the person placing the payment order is not the originator, the originator's bank must obtain and record the originator's TIN (e.g., SSN or EIN) or, if none, the alien identification number or passport number and country of issuance, or a notation of the lack thereof.

Payment Orders Not Made in Person

If a payment order is not made in person, the originator's bank must obtain and retain the following records:

- Name and address of the person placing the payment order.
- The person's TIN (e.g., SSN or EIN) or, if none, the alien identification number or passport number and country of issuance, or a notation in the record of the lack thereof, and a copy or record of the method of payment (e.g., check or credit card transaction) for the funds transfer. If the originator's bank has knowledge that the person placing the payment order is not the originator, the originator's bank must obtain and record the originator's TIN (e.g., SSN or EIN) or, if none, the alien identification number or passport number and country of issuance, or a notation of the lack thereof.

Retrievability

Information retained must be retrievable by reference to the name of the originator. When the originator is an established customer of the bank and has an account used for funds transfers, information retained must also be retrievable by account number (31 CFR 103.3 3(e)(4)). Records must be maintained for five years.

Travel Rule Requirement

For funds transmittals of $3,000 or more, the transmittor's financial institution must include the following information in the transmittal order at the time that a transmittal order is sent to a receiving financial institution (31 CFR 103.33 (g)(1)):

- Name of the transmittor, and, if the payment is ordered from an account, the account number of the transmittor.
- Address of the transmittor.
- Amount of the transmittal order.

- Date of the transmittal order.
- Identity of the recipient's financial institution.
- As many of the following items as are received with the transmittal order:
  - Name and address of the recipient.
  - Account number of the recipient.
  - Any other specific identifier of the recipient.
- Either the name and address or the numerical identifier of the transmittor's financial institution.

There are no recordkeeping requirements in the Travel Rule.

Responsibilities of Intermediary Institutions

Recordkeeping Requirements

For each payment order of $3,000 or more that a bank accepts as an intermediary bank, the bank must retain a record of the payment order.

Travel Rule Requirements

For funds transmittals of $3,000 or more, the intermediary financial institution must include the following information if received from the sender in a transmittal order at the time that order is sent to a receiving financial institution (31 CFR 103.33 (g)(2)):

- Name and account number of the transmittor.
- Address of the transmittor.
- Amount of the transmittal order.
- Date of the transmittal order.
- Identity of the recipient's financial institution.
- As many of the following items as are received with the transmittal order:
  - Name and address of the recipient.
  - Account number of the recipient.
  - Any other specific identifier of the recipient.
- Either the name and address or the numerical identifier of the transmittor's financial institution.

Intermediary financial institutions must pass on all of the information received from a transmittor's financial institution or the preceding financial institution, but they have no duty to obtain information not provided by the transmittor's financial institution or the preceding financial institution.

Responsibilities of Beneficiary's Banks

Recordkeeping Requirements

For each payment order of $3,000 or more that a bank accepts as a beneficiary's bank, the bank must retain a record of the payment order.

If the beneficiary is not an established customer of the bank, the beneficiary's institution must retain the following information for each payment order of $3,000 or more.

Proceeds Delivered in Person

If proceeds are delivered in person to the beneficiary or its representative or agent, the institution must verify the identity of the person receiving the proceeds and retain a record of the following:

- Name and address.
- The type of document reviewed.
- The number of the identification document.
- The person's TIN, or, if none, the alien identification number or passport number and country of issuance, or a notation in the record of the lack thereof.
- If the institution has knowledge that the person receiving the proceeds is not the beneficiary, the institution must obtain and retain a record of the beneficiary's name and address, as well as the beneficiary's identification.

Proceeds Not Delivered in Person

If proceeds are not delivered in person, the institution must retain a copy of the check or other instrument used to effect the payment, or the institution must record the information on the instrument. The institution must also record the name and address of the person to whom it was sent.

Retrievability

Information retained must be retrievable by reference to the name of the beneficiary. When the beneficiary is an established customer of the institution and has an account used for funds transfers, information retained must also be retrievable by account number (31 CFR 103.33(e)(4)).

There are no Travel Rule requirements for beneficiary banks.

Expiration of the Conditional Customer Information File Exception — Travel Rule

From 1998 to 2004, a conditional exception to the Travel Rule generally permitted banks to include a customer's coded name or pseudonym in a transmittal order, provided that the bank maintained the customer's full information in an automated customer information file (CIF). FinCEN revoked this exception, known as the "CIF exception," as of July 1, 2004. After that date institutions must use a customer's true name and address to comply with the Travel Rule. At this time, banks may still be examined where transactions subject to the CIF exception may be included in the examiner's sample for transaction testing.

Abbreviations and Addresses

Although the Travel Rule does not permit the use of coded names or pseudonyms, the rule does allow the use of abbreviated names, names reflecting different accounts of a corporation (e.g., XYZ Payroll Account), and trade and assumed names of a business ("doing business as") or the names of unincorporated divisions or departments of the business.

Customer Address

The term "address," as used in 31 CFR 103.33(g), is not defined. Previously issued guidance from FinCEN had been interpreted as not allowing the use of mailing addresses in a transmittal order when a street address is known to the transmittor's financial institution. However, in the November 28, 2003, *Federal Register* notice,[53] FinCEN issued a regulatory interpretation that states the Travel Rule should allow the use of mailing addresses, including post office boxes, in the transmittor address field of transmittal orders in certain circumstances.

The regulatory interpretation states that, for purposes of 31 CFR 103.33(g), the term "address" means either the transmittor's street address or the transmittor's address maintained in the financial institution's automated CIF (such as a mailing address including a post office box) as long as the institution maintains the transmittor's address[54] on file and the address information is retrievable upon request by law enforcement.

EXAMINATION PROCEDURES

Funds Transfers Recordkeeping

Objective. *Assess the bank's compliance with statutory and regulatory requirements for funds transfers. This section covers the regulatory requirements as set forth in the BSA. Refer to the expanded sections of this manual for discussions and procedures regarding specific money laundering risks for funds transfer activities.*

1. Verify that the bank obtains and maintains appropriate records for compliance with 31 CFR 103.33(e).
2. Verify that the bank transmits payment information as required by 31 CFR 103.33(g) (the "Travel Rule").
3. Verify that the bank files Currency Transaction Reports (CTRs) when currency is received or dispersed in a funds transfer that exceeds $10,000 (31 CFR 103.22).
4. If the bank sends or receives funds transfers to or from institutions in other countries, especially those with strict privacy and secrecy laws, assess whether the bank has policies, procedures, and processes to determine whether amounts, the frequency of the transfer, and countries of origin or destination are consistent with the nature of the business or occupation of the customer.

Transaction Testing

5. On the basis of a risk assessment, prior examination reports, and a review of the bank's audit findings, select a sample of funds transfers processed as an originator's bank, an intermediary bank, and a beneficiary's bank to ensure the institution collects, maintains, or transmits the required information, depending on the institution's role in the transfer.
6. On the basis of examination procedures completed, including transaction testing, form a conclusion about the ability of policies, procedures, and processes to meet regulatory requirements associated with funds transfers.
7. On the basis of the previous conclusion and the risks associated with the bank's activity in this area, proceed to expanded examination procedures, if necessary.

FOREIGN CORRESPONDENT ACCOUNT RECORDKEEPING AND DUE DILIGENCE — OVERVIEW

Objective. *Assess the bank's compliance with statutory and regulatory requirements for correspondent accounts for foreign shell banks, foreign correspondent account recordkeeping, and due diligence programs to detect and report money laundering and suspicious activity. Refer to the expanded sections of the manual for discussions and examination procedures regarding specific money laundering risks associated with foreign correspondent accounts.*

One of the central goals of the Patriot Act was to protect access to the U.S. financial system by requiring certain records and due diligence programs for foreign correspondent accounts. In addition, the Patriot Act prohibits accounts with foreign shell banks. Foreign correspondent accounts, as noted in past U.S. Senate investigative reports,[55] are a gateway into the U.S. financial system. This section of the manual covers the regulatory requirements established by sections 312, 313, and 319(b) of the Patriot Act and by the implementing regulations at 31 CFR 103.175, 103.176, 103.177, and 103.185. Additional discussions and procedures regarding specific money laundering risks for foreign correspondent banking activities, such as pouch activity, U.S. dollar drafts, and payable through accounts, are included in the expanded sections.

Foreign Shell Bank Prohibition and Foreign Correspondent Account Recordkeeping

On October 28, 2002, final regulations (31 CFR 103.177 and 103.185) implementing sections 313 and 319(b) of the Patriot Act became effective. The regulations implemented new provisions of the BSA that relate to foreign correspondent accounts.

For purposes of 31 CFR 103.177 and 103.185, a "correspondent account" is an account established by a bank for a foreign bank to receive deposits from, or to make payments or other disbursements on behalf of the foreign bank, or to handle other financial transactions related to the foreign bank. An "account" means any formal banking or business relationship established to provide regular services, dealings, and other financial transactions. It includes a demand deposit, savings deposit, or other transaction or asset account and a credit account or other extension of credit (31 CFR 103.175(d)). Accounts maintained by foreign banks for financial institutions covered by the rule are not "correspondent accounts" subject to this regulation. [56]

Under 31 CFR 103.177, a bank is prohibited from establishing, maintaining, administering, or managing a correspondent account in the United States for, or on behalf of, a foreign shell bank. A foreign shell bank is defined as a foreign bank without a physical presence in any country.[57] An exception, however, permits a bank to maintain a correspondent account for a foreign shell bank that is a regulated affiliate.[58] 31 CFR 103.177 also requires that a bank take reasonable steps to ensure that any correspondent account established, maintained, administered, or managed in the United States for a foreign bank is not being used by that foreign bank to provide banking services indirectly to foreign shell banks.

Certifications

A bank that maintains a correspondent account in the United States for a foreign bank must maintain records in the United States identifying the owners of each foreign bank.[59] A bank must also record the name and street address of a person who resides in the United States and who is authorized, and has agreed, to be an agent to accept service of legal process.[60] Under 31 CFR 103.185, a bank must produce these records within seven days upon receipt of a written request from a federal law enforcement officer.

The U.S. Treasury, working with the industry and federal banking and law enforcement agencies, developed a "certification process" to assist banks in complying with the recordkeeping provisions. This process includes certification and recertification forms. While banks are not required to use these forms, a bank will be "deemed to be in compliance" with the regulation if it obtains a completed certification form from the foreign financial institution and receives a recertification on or before the three-year anniversary of the execution of the initial or previous certification.[61]

Account Closure

The regulation also contains specific provisions as to when banks must obtain the required information or close correspondent accounts. Banks must obtain certifications (or recertifications) or otherwise obtain the required information within 30 calendar days after the date an account is established and at least once every three years thereafter. If the bank is unable to obtain the required information, it must close all correspondent accounts with the foreign bank within a commercially reasonable time.

Verification

A bank should review certifications for reasonableness and accuracy. If a bank at any time knows, suspects, or has reason to suspect that any information contained in a certification (or recertification), or that any other information it relied on is no longer correct, the bank must request that the foreign bank verify or correct such information, or the bank must take other appropriate measures to ascertain its accuracy. Therefore, banks should review certifications for potential problems that may warrant further review, such as use of post office boxes or forwarding addresses. If the bank has not obtained the necessary or corrected information within 90 days, it must close the account within a commercially reasonable time. During this time, the bank may not permit the foreign bank to establish any new financial positions or execute any transactions through the account, other than those transactions necessary to close the account. Also, a bank may not establish any other correspondent account for the foreign bank until it obtains the required information.

A bank must also retain the original of any document provided by a foreign bank, and retain the original or a copy of any document otherwise relied on for the purposes of the regulation, for at least five years after the date that the bank no longer maintains any correspondent account for the foreign bank.

Subpoenas

Under section 319(b) of the Patriot Act, the Secretary of the Treasury or the U.S. Attorney General may issue a subpoena or summons to any foreign bank that maintains a correspondent account in the United States to obtain records relating to that account, including records maintained abroad, or to obtain records relating to the deposit of funds into the foreign bank. If the foreign bank fails to comply with the subpoena or fails to initiate proceedings to contest that subpoena, the Secretary of the Treasury or the U.S. Attorney General (after consultations with each other) may, by written notice, direct a bank to terminate its relationship with a foreign correspondent bank. If a bank fails to terminate the correspondent relationship within ten days of receipt of notice, it could be subject to a civil money penalty of up to $10,000 per day until the correspondent relationship is terminated.

Requests for AML Records by Federal Regulator

Also, upon request by its federal regulator, a bank must provide or make available records related to AML compliance of the bank or one of its customers, within 120 hours from the time of the request (31 USC 5318(k) (2)).

Special Due Diligence Program for Foreign Correspondent Accounts

Section 312 of the Patriot Act added new subsection (i) to 31 USC 5318 of the BSA. This subsection requires each U.S. financial institution that establishes, maintains, administers, or manages a correspondent account in the United States for a foreign financial institution to take certain AML measures for such accounts. In addition, section 312 of the Patriot Act specifies additional standards for correspondent accounts maintained for certain foreign banks.

On January 4, 2006, FinCEN published a final regulation (31 CFR 103.176) implementing the due diligence provisions of 31 USC 5318(i)(1). FinCEN also published a Notice of Proposed Rulemaking on January 4, 2006, implementing 31 USC 531 8(i)(2), which focuses exclusively on enhanced due diligence measures for certain foreign banks. Until such time that a final rule is published, financial institutions that are not otherwise exempt must follow the enhanced due diligence requirements set forth in the statute.

General Due Diligence

31 CFR 103.176(a) requires banks to establish a due diligence program that includes appropriate, specific, risk-based, and, where necessary, enhanced policies, procedures, and controls that are reasonably designed to enable the bank to detect and report, on an ongoing basis, any known or suspected money laundering activity conducted through or involving any correspondent account established, maintained, administered, or managed by the bank in the United States for a foreign financial institution ("foreign correspondent account").[62]

Due diligence policies, procedures, and controls must include each of the following:

- Determining whether each such foreign correspondent account is subject to enhanced due diligence (refer to "Enhanced Due Diligence" below).
- Assessing the money laundering risks presented by each such foreign correspondent account.
- Applying risk-based procedures and controls to each such foreign correspondent account reasonably designed to detect and report known or suspected money laundering activity, including a periodic review of the correspondent account activity sufficient to determine consistency with information obtained about the type, purpose, and anticipated activity of the account.

Risk assessment of foreign financial institutions

A bank's general due diligence program must include policies, procedures, and processes to assess the risks posed by the bank's foreign financial institution customers. A bank's resources are most appropriately directed at those accounts that pose a more significant money laundering risk. The bank's due diligence program should provide for the risk assessment of foreign correspondent accounts considering all relevant factors, including, as appropriate:

- The nature of the foreign financial institution's business and the markets it serves.
- The type, purpose, and anticipated activity of the foreign correspondent account.
- The nature and duration of the bank's relationship with the foreign financial institution (and, if relevant, with any affiliate of the foreign financial institution).
- The AML and supervisory regime of the jurisdiction that issued the charter or license to the foreign financial institution and, to the extent that information regarding such jurisdiction is reasonably available, of the jurisdiction in which any company that is an owner of the foreign financial institution is incorporated or chartered.
- Information known or reasonably available to the bank about the foreign financial institution's AML record, including public information in standard industry guides, periodicals, and major publications.

Banks are not required to evaluate all of the above factors for every correspondent account.

Monitoring of foreign correspondent accounts

As part of ongoing due diligence, banks should periodically review their foreign correspondent accounts. Monitoring will not, in the ordinary situation, involve scrutiny of every transaction taking place within the account, but, instead, should involve a review of the account sufficient to ensure that the bank can determine whether the nature and volume of account activity is generally consistent with information regarding the purpose of the account and expected account activity and to ensure that the bank can adequately identify suspicious transactions.

An effective due diligence program will provide for a range of due diligence measures, based upon the bank's risk assessment of each foreign correspondent account. The starting point for an effective due diligence program, therefore, should be a stratification of the money laundering risk of each foreign correspondent account based on the bank's review of relevant risk factors (such as those identified above) to determine which accounts may require increased measures. The due diligence program should identify risk factors that would warrant the institution conducting additional scrutiny or increased monitoring of a particular account. As due diligence is an ongoing process, a bank should take measures to ensure account profiles are current and monitoring should be risk-based. Banks should consider whether risk profiles should be adjusted or suspicious activity reported when the activity is inconsistent with the profile.

Enhanced Due Diligence

Subsection 5318(i)(2) requires banks to establish enhanced due diligence policies and procedures when opening or maintaining a correspondent account in the United States requested or maintained by, or on behalf of, certain foreign banks operating under any one or more of the following:

- An offshore banking license.[63]
- A banking license issued by a foreign country that has been designated as non-cooperative with international AML principles or procedures by an intergovernmental group or organization of which the United States is a member, and with which designation the United States representative to the group or organization concurs.
- A banking license issued by a foreign country that has been designated by the Secretary of the Treasury as warranting special measures due to money laundering concerns.

If such an account is requested or maintained, subsections 5318(i)(2)(B)(i) through (iii) require the bank to establish enhanced due diligence policies, procedures, and controls to ensure that the bank takes reasonable steps to do each of the following:

- Ascertain, for any such foreign bank whose shares are not publicly traded, the identity of each of the owners of the foreign bank, and the nature and extent of the ownership interest of each such owner.[64]
- Conduct enhanced scrutiny of such account to guard against money laundering and to identify and report any suspicious transactions in accordance with SAR laws and regulations.
- Ascertain whether such foreign bank provides correspondent accounts to other foreign banks and, if so, to ascertain the identity of those foreign banks and conduct

due diligence, as appropriate under the requirements of subsection 531 8(i)(1) (i.e., the bank's general due diligence program).

On January 4, 2006, FinCEN published a second Notice of Proposed Rulemaking to implement the enhanced due diligence provisions of 31 USC 5318(i)(2). Until this rulemaking is finalized, the enhanced due diligence requirements of 31 USC 5318(i)(2) continue to apply to financial institutions that are not otherwise exempt.

In addition to those categories of foreign banks identified by statute (31 USC 5318(i)(2)(A)) as requiring enhanced due diligence, banks may find it appropriate to conduct additional due diligence measures on foreign financial institutions identified through application of the bank's general due diligence program as posing a high risk for money laundering. Such measures may include any or all of the elements of enhanced due diligence set forth in the statute (31 USC 5318(i)(2)(B)), as appropriate for the risks posed by the specific correspondent account.

Special Procedures When Due Diligence Cannot Be Performed

A bank's due diligence policies, procedures, and controls established pursuant to 31 CFR 103.176(a) must include special procedures, when appropriate due diligence cannot be performed with respect to a foreign correspondent account. These policies, procedures, and controls must include when the bank should do each of the following:

- Refuse to open the account.
- Suspend transaction activity.
- File a SAR.
- Close the account.

Applicability Dates

31 CFR 103.176 includes applicability dates for various components of the regulation. The requirements of the regulation shall apply to each foreign correspondent account established on or after July 5, 2006 (i.e., a bank's due diligence policies, procedures, and controls required by 31 CFR 103.176 must apply to all foreign correspondent accounts opened on or after July 5, 2006).

In addition, the requirements of 31 CFR 103.176 are retroactive to previously established accounts. However, banks have additional time to apply to existing accounts their due diligence policies, procedures, and controls established pursuant to 31 CFR 103.176. For correspondent accounts established prior to July 5, 2006, 31 CFR 103.176 provides that the requirements of the regulation are effective October 2, 2006 (i.e., by October 2, 2006, a bank must have concluded performing the due diligence policies, procedures, and controls designed pursuant to 31 CFR 103.176 to all correspondent accounts in existence before July 5, 2006).

EXAMINATION PROCEDURES

Foreign Correspondent Account Recordkeeping and Due Diligence

Objective. *Assess the bank's compliance with statutory and regulatory requirements for correspondent accounts for foreign shell banks, foreign correspondent account recordkeeping, and due diligence programs to detect and report money laundering and suspicious activity. Refer to the expanded sections of the manual for discussions and examination procedures regarding specific money laundering risks associated with foreign correspondent accounts.*

1. Determine whether the bank engages in foreign correspondent banking.

Foreign Shell Bank Prohibition and Foreign Correspondent Account Recordkeeping

2. If so, review the bank's policies, procedures, and processes. At a minimum, policies, procedures, and processes should accomplish the following:
   - Prohibit dealings with foreign shell banks and specify the responsible party for obtaining, updating, and managing certifications or information for foreign correspondent accounts.
   - Identify foreign correspondent accounts and address the sending, tracking, receiving, and reviewing of certification requests or requests for information.
   - Evaluate the quality of information received in responses to certification requests or requests for information.
   - Determine whether and when a Suspicious Activity Report (SAR) should be filed.
   - Maintain sufficient internal controls.
   - Provide for ongoing training.
   - Independently test the bank's compliance with 31 CFR 103.177.
3. Determine whether the bank has on file a current certification or current information (that would otherwise include the information contained within a certification) for each foreign correspondent account to determine whether the foreign correspondent is not a foreign shell bank (31 CFR 103.177(a)).
4. If the bank has foreign branches, determine whether the bank has taken reasonable steps to ensure that any correspondent accounts maintained for its foreign branches are not used to indirectly provide banking services to a foreign shell bank.

Special Due Diligence Program for Foreign Correspondent Accounts

5. Determine whether the bank has established a due diligence program that includes appropriate, specific, risk-based, and, where necessary, enhanced policies, procedures, and controls for correspondent accounts established, maintained,

administered, or managed in the United States for foreign financial institutions ("foreign correspondent account"). The due diligence program must be applied to each foreign correspondent account established on or after July 5, 2006. Verify that due diligence policies, procedures, and controls include:

- Determining whether any foreign correspondent account is subject to enhanced due diligence (31 CFR 103.176(a)(1)).
- Assessing the money laundering risks presented by the foreign correspondent account (31 CFR 103.176(a)(2)).
- Applying risk-based procedures and controls to each foreign correspondent account reasonably designed to detect and report known or suspected money laundering activity, including a periodic review of the correspondent account activity sufficient to determine consistency with information obtained about the type, purpose, and anticipated activity of the account (31 CFR 103.176(a)(3)).

6. Review the due diligence program's policies, procedures, and processes governing the BSA/AML risk assessment of foreign correspondent accounts (31 CFR 103.176(a)(2)). Verify that the bank's due diligence program considers the following factors, as appropriate, as criteria in the risk assessment:
   - The nature of the foreign financial institution's business and the markets it serves.
   - The type, purpose, and anticipated activity of the foreign correspondent account.
   - The nature and duration of the bank's relationship with the foreign financial institution and any of its affiliates.
   - The AML and supervisory regime of the jurisdiction that issued the charter or license to the foreign financial institution, and, to the extent that information regarding such jurisdiction is reasonably available, of the jurisdiction in which any company that is an owner of the foreign financial institution is incorporated or chartered.
   - Information known or reasonably available to the bank about the foreign financial institution's AML record.
7. Ensure the program is reasonably designed to:
   - Detect and report, on an ongoing basis, known or suspected money laundering activity.
   - Perform periodic reviews of correspondent account activity to determine consistency with the information obtained about the type, purpose, and anticipated activity of the account.
8. Verify that by October 2, 2006, the bank has completed applying the requirements of its due diligence program to correspondent accounts in existence prior to July 5, 2006.
9. For foreign banks subject to enhanced due diligence, evaluate the criteria that the U.S. bank uses to conduct enhanced scrutiny to guard against money laundering in any accounts held by such foreign banks.
10. Review the bank's policies, procedures, and processes for determining whether foreign correspondent banks subject to enhanced due diligence maintain correspondent accounts for other foreign banks, and, if so, determine whether the bank's policies, procedures, and processes include reasonable steps to ascertain the

identity of those foreign banks and conduct due diligence, as appropriate under the requirements of subsection 5318(i)(1) (i.e., the bank's general due diligence program).

11. Determine whether policies, procedures, and processes require the bank to identify each of the owners of a non-publicly traded foreign correspondent bank for which it opens or maintains an account that is subject to enhanced due diligence. For such accounts, evaluate the bank's policies, procedures, and processes to determine each owner's interest.

Transaction Testing

Foreign Shell Bank Prohibition and Foreign Correspondent Account Recordkeeping

12. On the basis of a risk assessment, prior examination reports, and a review of the bank's audit findings, select a sample of foreign bank accounts. From the sample selected determine the following:
    - Whether certifications and information on the accounts are complete and reasonable.
    - Whether the bank has adequate documentation to evidence that it does not maintain accounts for, or indirectly provide services to, foreign shell banks.
    - For account closures, whether closures were made within a reasonable time period and that the relationship was not re-established without sufficient reason.
    - Whether there are any federal law enforcement requests for information regarding foreign correspondent accounts. If so, ascertain that requests were met in a timely manner.
    - Whether the bank received any official notifications to close a foreign financial institution account.[65] If so, ascertain that the accounts were closed within ten business days.
    - Whether the bank retains, for five years from the date of account closure, the original of any document provided by a foreign financial institution, as well as the original or a copy of any document relied on in relation to any summons or subpoena of the foreign financial institution issued under 31 CFR 103.185.

Special Due Diligence Program for Foreign Correspondent Accounts

13. From a sample selected, determine whether the bank consistently follows its general due diligence policies, procedures, and processes for foreign correspondent accounts. It may be necessary to expand the sample to include correspondent accounts maintained for foreign financial institutions other than foreign banks (such as money transmitters or currency exchangers), as appropriate.
14. From the original sample, determine whether the bank has implemented enhanced due diligence procedures for higher risk foreign banks operating under:
    - An offshore banking license.
    - A banking license issued by a foreign country that has been designated as non-cooperative with international AML principles or procedures.

- A banking license issued by a foreign country that has been designated by the Secretary of the Treasury as warranting special measures due to AML concerns.

15. From a sample of accounts that are subject to enhanced due diligence, verify that the bank has taken reasonable steps, in accordance with the bank's policies, procedures, and processes, to:
    - Ascertain, for any such foreign bank whose shares are not publicly traded, the identity of each of the owners of the foreign bank, and the nature and extent of the ownership interest of each such owner.
    - Conduct enhanced scrutiny of any accounts held by such banks to guard against money laundering.
    - Ascertain whether such foreign bank provides correspondent accounts to other foreign banks and, if so, to ascertain the identity of those foreign banks and conduct due diligence, as appropriate.
16. On the basis of examination procedures completed, including transaction testing, form a conclusion about the adequacy of policies, procedures, and processes to meet regulatory requirements associated with foreign correspondent account recordkeeping and due diligence.
17. On the basis of the previous conclusion and the risks associated with the bank's activity in this area, proceed to expanded examination procedures, if necessary.

PRIVATE BANKING DUE DILIGENCE PROGRAM (NON-U.S. PERSONS) — OVERVIEW

Objective. *Assess the bank's compliance with the statutory and regulatory requirements to implement policies, procedures, and controls to detect and report money laundering and suspicious activity through private banking accounts established, administered, or maintained for non-U.S. persons. Refer to the expanded sections of the manual for discussions and examination procedures regarding specific money laundering risks associated with private banking.*

Private banking can be broadly defined as providing personalized financial services to wealthy clients. Section 312 of the Patriot Act added new subsection (i) to 31 USC 5318 of the BSA. This subsection requires each U.S. financial institution that establishes, maintains, administers, or manages a private banking account in the United States for a non-U.S. person to take certain AML measures with respect to these accounts. In particular, a bank must establish appropriate, specific, and, where necessary, enhanced due diligence policies, procedures, and controls that are reasonably designed to enable the bank to detect and report instances of money laundering through such accounts. In addition, section 312 mandates enhanced scrutiny to detect and, if appropriate, report transactions that may involve proceeds of foreign corruption for private banking accounts that are requested or maintained by or on behalf of a senior foreign political figure or the individual's immediate family and close associates. On January 4, 2006, FinCEN issued a final regulation (31 CFR 103.178) to implement the private banking requirements of 31 USC 5318(i).

The overview and examination procedures set forth in this section are intended to evaluate the bank's due diligence program concerning private banking accounts offered to non-U.S. persons. Additional procedures for specific risk areas of private banking are included in the expanded examination procedures, "Private Banking," page 249.

Private Banking Accounts

For purposes of 31 CFR 103.178, a "private banking account" is an account (or any combination of accounts) maintained at a bank that satisfies all three of the following criteria:

- Requires a minimum aggregate deposit of funds or other assets of not less than $1,000,000.
- Is established on behalf of or for the benefit of one or more non-U.S. persons who are direct or beneficial owners[66] of the account.
- Is assigned to, or is administered by, in whole or in part, an officer, employee, or agent of a bank acting as a liaison between a financial institution covered by the regulation and the direct or beneficial owner of the account.

With regard to the minimum deposit requirement, a "private banking account" is an account (or combination of accounts) that *requires* a minimum deposit of not less than $1,000,000. A bank may offer a wide range of services that are generically termed private banking, and even if certain (or any combination, or all) of the bank's private banking services do not *require* a minimum deposit of not less than $1,000,000, these relationships should be subject to a greater level of due diligence under the bank's risk- based BSA/AML compliance program but are not subject to 31 CFR 103.178. Refer to the expanded overview section, "Private Banking," page 243, for further guidance.

Due Diligence Program

A bank must establish and maintain a due diligence program that includes policies, procedures, and controls that are reasonably designed to detect and report any known or suspected money laundering or suspicious activity conducted through or involving any private banking account for a non-U.S. person that is established, maintained, administered, or managed in the United States by the bank. The due diligence program must ensure that, at a minimum, the bank takes reasonable steps to do each of the following:

- Ascertain the identity of all nominal and beneficial owners of a private banking account.
- Ascertain whether the nominal or beneficial owner of any private banking account is a senior foreign political figure.
- Ascertain the source(s) of funds deposited into a private banking account and the purpose and expected use of the account.
- Review the activity of the account to ensure that it is consistent with the information obtained about the client's source of funds, and with the stated purpose and expected use of the account, and to file a Suspicious Activity Report (SAR), as appropriate, to

report any known or suspected money laundering or suspicious activity conducted to, from, or through a private banking account.

Risk Assessment of Private Banking Accounts for Non-U.S. Persons

The nature and extent of due diligence conducted on private banking accounts for non-U.S. persons will likely vary for each client depending on the presence of potential risk factors. More extensive due diligence, for example, may be appropriate for new clients; clients who operate in, or whose funds are transmitted from or through, jurisdictions with weak AML controls; and clients whose lines of business are primarily currency-based (e.g., casinos or currency exchangers). Due diligence should also be commensurate with the size of the account. Accounts with relatively more deposits and assets should be subject to greater due diligence. In addition, if the bank at any time learns of information that casts doubt on previous information, further due diligence would be appropriate.

Ascertaining Source of Funds and Monitoring Account Activity

Banks that provide private banking services generally obtain considerable information about their clients, including the purpose for which the customer establishes the private banking account. This information can establish a baseline for account activity that will enable a bank to better detect suspicious activity and to assess situations where additional verification regarding the source of funds may be necessary. Banks are not expected, in the ordinary course of business, to verify the source of every deposit placed into every private banking account. However, banks should monitor deposits and transactions as necessary to ensure that activity is consistent with information that the bank has received about the client's source of funds and with the stated purpose and expected use of the account. Such monitoring will facilitate the identification of accounts that warrant additional scrutiny.

Enhanced Scrutiny of Private Banking Accounts for Senior Foreign Political Figures

For the purposes of private banking accounts under 31 CFR 103.175(r), the regulation defines the term "senior foreign political figure" to include one or more of the following:

- A current or former:
  - Senior official in the executive, legislative, administrative, military, or judicial branches of a foreign government (whether elected or not).
  - Senior official of a major foreign political party.
  - Senior executive of a foreign-government-owned commercial enterprise.[67]
- A corporation, business, or other entity that has been formed by, or for the benefit of, any such individual.
- An immediate family member (including spouses, parents, siblings, children, and a spouse's parents and siblings) of any such individual.
- A person who is widely and publicly known (or is actually known by the relevant bank) to be a close associate of such individual.

Senior foreign political figures as defined above are often referred to as "politically exposed persons" or PEPs. Refer to the expanded overview section, "Politically Exposed Persons," page 261, for additional guidance, in particular with respect to due diligence on accounts maintained for PEPs that do not meet the regulatory definition of "private banking account" set forth in 31 CFR 103.175(o).

For private banking accounts for which a senior foreign political figure is a nominal or beneficial owner, the bank's due diligence program must include enhanced scrutiny that is reasonably designed to detect and report transactions that may involve the proceeds of foreign corruption. The term "proceeds of foreign corruption" means any asset or property that is acquired by, through, or on behalf of a senior foreign political figure through misappropriation, theft, or embezzlement of public funds, the unlawful conversion of property of a foreign government, or through acts of bribery or extortion, and includes any other property into which any such assets have been transformed or converted.[68]

Enhanced scrutiny of private banking accounts for senior foreign political figures should be risk-based. Reasonable steps to perform enhanced scrutiny may include consulting publicly available information regarding the home country of the client, contacting branches of the U.S. bank operating in the home country of the client to obtain additional information about the client and the political environment, and conducting greater scrutiny of the client's employment history and sources of income. For example, funds transfers from a government account to the personal account of a government official with signature authority over the government account may raise a bank's suspicions of possible political corruption. In addition, if a bank's review of major news sources indicates that a client may be or is involved in political corruption, the bank should review the client's account for unusual activity.

Identifying Senior Foreign Political Figures

Banks are required to establish policies, procedures, and controls that include reasonable steps to ascertain the status of an individual as a senior foreign political figure. Procedures should require obtaining information regarding employment and other sources of income, and the bank should seek information directly from the client regarding possible senior foreign political figure status. The bank should also check references, as appropriate, to determine whether the individual holds or has previously held a senior political position or may be a close associate of a senior foreign political figure. In addition, the bank should make reasonable efforts to review public sources of information regarding the client.

Banks applying reasonable due diligence procedures in accordance with 31 CFR 103.178 may not be able to identify in every case individuals who qualify as senior foreign political figures, and, in particular, their close associates, and thus may not apply enhanced scrutiny to all such accounts. If the bank's program is reasonably designed to make this determination, and the bank administers this program effectively, then the bank should generally be able to detect, report, and take appropriate action when suspected money laundering is occurring with respect to these accounts, even in cases when the bank has not been able to identify the accountholder as a senior foreign political figure warranting enhanced scrutiny.

Special Procedures When Due Diligence Cannot Be Performed

A bank's due diligence policies, procedures, and controls established pursuant to 31 CFR 103.178(a) must include special procedures when appropriate due diligence cannot be performed. These special procedures must include when the bank should:

- Refuse to open the account.
- Suspend transaction activity.
- File a SAR.
- Close the account.

Applicability Dates

31 CFR 103.178 includes applicability dates for various components of the regulation. The requirements of the regulation shall apply to each private banking account established on or after July 5, 2006 (i.e., a bank's due diligence policies, procedures, and controls required by 31 CFR 103.178 must apply to all new accounts opened on or after July 5, 2006).

In addition, the requirements of 31 CFR 103.178 are retroactive to previously established accounts. However, banks have additional time to apply to existing accounts their due diligence policies, procedures, and controls established pursuant to 31 CFR 103.178. For existing private banking accounts established prior to July 5, 2006, 31 CFR 103.178 provides that the requirements of the regulation are effective October 2, 2006 (i.e., by October 2, 2006, a bank must have concluded applying the due diligence policies, procedures, and controls designed pursuant to 31 CFR 103.178 to all private banking accounts in existence before July 5, 2006). Until the due diligence requirements of 31 CFR 103.178 become applicable, the requirements of 31 USC 531 8(i)(3) shall continue to apply.

EXAMINATION PROCEDURES

Private Banking Due Diligence Program (Non-U.S. Persons)

Objective. *Assess the bank's compliance with the statutory and regulatory requirements to implement policies, procedures, and controls to detect and report money laundering and suspicious activity through private banking accounts established, administered, or maintained for non-U.S. persons. Refer to the expanded sections of the manual for discussions and examination procedures regarding specific money laundering risks associated with private banking.*

1. Determine whether the bank offers private banking accounts in accordance with the regulatory definition of a private banking account. A private banking account means an account (or any combination of accounts) maintained at a financial institution covered by the regulation that satisfies all three of the following criteria:

- Requires a minimum aggregate deposit of funds or other assets of not less than $1,000,000 (31 CFR 103.1 75(o)(1)).
- Is established on behalf of or for the benefit of one or more non-U.S. persons who are direct or beneficial owners of the account (31 CFR 103.175(o)(2)).
- Is assigned to, or is administered or managed by, in whole or in part, an officer, employee, or agent of the bank acting as a liaison between the bank and the direct or beneficial owner of the account (31 CFR 103.175(o)(3)).

The final rule reflects the statutory definition found in the Patriot Act. If an account satisfies the last two criteria in the definition of a private banking account as described above, but the institution does not require a minimum balance of $1,000,000, then the account does not qualify as a private banking account under this rule. However, the account is subject to the internal controls and risk-based due diligence included in the institution's general AML program.[69]

2. Determine whether the bank has implemented due diligence policies, procedures, and controls for private banking accounts established, maintained, administered, or managed in the United States by the bank for non-U.S. persons. The due diligence program must be applied to each private banking account established on or after July 5, 2006. Determine whether the policies, procedures, and controls are reasonably designed to detect and report any known or suspected money laundering or suspicious activity conducted through or involving any private banking account.
3. Review the bank's policies, procedures, and controls to assess whether the bank's due diligence program includes reasonable steps to:
   - Ascertain the identity of the nominal and beneficial owners of a private banking account (31 CFR 103.178(b)(1)).
   - Ascertain whether any nominal or beneficial owner of a private banking account is a senior foreign political figure (31 CFR 103.178(b)(2)).
   - Ascertain the source(s) of funds deposited into a private banking account and the purpose and expected use of the private banking account for non-U.S. persons (31 CFR 103.178(b)(3)).
   - Review the activity of the account to ensure that it is consistent with the information obtained about the client's source of funds and with the stated purpose and expected use of the account, as needed, to guard against money laundering and to report any known or suspected money laundering or suspicious activity conducted to, from, or through a private banking account for non-U.S. persons (31 CFR 103.178(b)(4)).
4. Review the bank's policies, procedures, and controls for performing enhanced scrutiny to assess whether they are reasonably designed to detect and report transactions that may involve the proceeds of foreign corruption[70] for which a senior foreign political figure[71] is a nominal or beneficial owner (31 CFR 103.178(c)(1)).
5. Verify that by October 2, 2006, the bank has completed applying the requirements of its due diligence program to private banking accounts in existence prior to July 5, 2006.

Transaction Testing

6. On the basis of a risk assessment, prior examination reports, and a review of the bank's audit findings, select a sample of customer files to determine whether the bank has ascertained the identity of the nominal and beneficial owners of, and the source of funds deposited into, private banking accounts for non-U.S. persons. From the sample selected determine the following:
   - Whether the bank's procedures comply with internal policies and statutory requirements.
   - Whether the bank has followed its procedures governing risk assessment of private banking accounts for non-U.S. persons.
   - Whether the bank performs enhanced scrutiny of private banking accounts for which senior foreign political figures are nominal or beneficial owners, consistent with its policy, regulatory guidance, and statutory requirements.
7. On the basis of examination procedures completed, including transaction testing, form a conclusion about the ability of policies, procedures, and processes to meet regulatory requirements associated with private banking due diligence programs.
8. On the basis of the previous conclusion and the risks associated with the bank's activity in this area, proceed to expanded examination procedures, if necessary.

Special Measures — Overview

Objective. *Assess the bank's compliance with statutory and regulatory requirements for special measures issued under section 311 of the Patriot Act.*

Section 311 of the Patriot Act added 31 USC 5318A to the BSA, which authorizes the Secretary of the Treasury to require domestic financial institutions and domestic financial agencies to take certain special measures against foreign jurisdictions, foreign financial institutions, classes of international transactions, or types of accounts of primary money laundering concern. Section 311 provides the Secretary of the Treasury with a range of options that can be adapted to target specific money laundering and terrorist financing concerns. Section 311 is implemented through various orders and regulations that are incorporated into 31 CFR 103.[72] As set forth in section 311, certain special measures may be imposed by an order without prior public notice and comment, but such orders must be of limited duration and must be issued together with a Notice of Proposed Rulemaking.

Section 311 establishes a process for the Secretary of the Treasury to follow, and identifies federal agencies to consult before the Secretary of the Treasury may conclude that a jurisdiction, financial institution, class of transactions, or type of account is of primary money laundering concern. The statute also provides similar procedures, including factors and consultation requirements, for selecting the specific special measures to be imposed against a jurisdiction, financial institution, class of transactions, or type of account that is of primary money laundering concern.

It is important to note that, while a jurisdiction, financial institution, class of transactions, or type of account may be designated of primary money laundering concern in an order issued together with a Notice of Proposed Rulemaking, special measures of unlimited duration can only be imposed by a final rule issued after notice and an opportunity for comment.

Types of Special Measures

The following five special measures can be imposed, either individually, jointly, or in any combination:

Recordkeeping and Reporting of Certain Financial Transactions

Under the first special measure, banks may be required to maintain records or to file reports, or both, concerning the aggregate amount of transactions or the specifics of each transaction with respect to a jurisdiction, financial institution, class of transactions, or type of account that is of primary money laundering concern. The statute contains minimum information requirements for these records and reports and permits the Secretary of the Treasury to impose additional information requirements.

Information Relating to Beneficial Ownership

Under the second special measure, banks may be required to take reasonable and practicable steps, as determined by the Secretary of the Treasury, to obtain and retain information concerning the beneficial ownership of any account opened or maintained in the United States by a foreign person (other than a foreign entity whose shares are subject to public reporting requirements or are listed and traded on a regulated exchange or trading market), or a representative of such foreign person, that involves a jurisdiction, financial institution, class of transactions, or type of account that is of primary money laundering concern.

Information Relating to Certain Payable through Accounts

Under the third special measure, banks that open or maintain a payable through account in the United States involving a jurisdiction, financial institution, class of transactions, or type of account that is of primary money laundering concern may be required (i) to identify each customer (and representative) who is permitted to use the account or whose transactions are routed through the account and (ii) to obtain information about each customer (and representative) that is substantially comparable to that which the bank obtains in the ordinary course of business with respect to its customers residing in the United States.[73]

Information Relating to Certain Correspondent Accounts

Under the fourth special measure, banks that open or maintain a correspondent account in the United States involving a jurisdiction, financial institution, class of transactions, or type of account that is of primary money laundering concern may be required to: (i) identify each customer (and representative) who is permitted to use the account or whose transactions are routed through the account; and (ii) obtain information about each such customer (and representative) that is substantially comparable to that which a United States depository institution obtains in the ordinary course of business with respect to its customers residing in the United States.[74]

Prohibitions or Conditions on Opening or Maintaining Certain Correspondent or Payable through Accounts

Under the fifth, and strongest, special measure, banks may be prohibited from opening or maintaining in the United States any correspondent account or payable through account for, or on behalf of, a foreign financial institution if the account involves a jurisdiction, financial institution, class of transactions, or type of account that is of primary money laundering concern. The imposition of this measure can prohibit U.S. banks from establishing, maintaining, administering, or managing in the United States a correspondent or payable through account for, or on behalf of, any financial institution from a specific foreign jurisdiction. This measure may also be applied to specific foreign financial institutions and their subsidiaries.

The regulations that implement these prohibitions may require banks to review their account records to determine whether they maintain no accounts directly for, or on behalf of, such entities. In addition to the direct prohibition, banks may also be:

- Prohibited from knowingly providing indirect access to the specific entities through its other banking relationships.
- Required to notify correspondent accountholders that they must not provide the specific entity with access to the account maintained at the U.S. bank.
- Required to take reasonable steps to identify any indirect use of its accounts by the specific entity.

Special Measures Guidance

Orders and regulations implementing specific special measures taken under section 311 of the Patriot Act are not static; they can be issued or rescinded over time as the Secretary of the Treasury determines that a subject jurisdiction, institution, class of transactions, or type of account is no longer of primary money laundering concern. In addition, special measures imposed against one jurisdiction, institution, class of transactions, or type of account may vary from those imposed in other situations. Examiners should also note that an order or rule imposing a special measure may establish a standard of due diligence that banks must apply to comply with the particular special measure.

Accordingly, this manual does not detail specific final special measures, since any such listing could quickly become dated. Examiners reviewing compliance with this section should visit FinCEN's web site at www.fincen.gov for current information on final special measures. Examiners should only examine for those special measures that are final, and should not review banks for special measures that are proposed.

Examination Procedures

Special Measures

Objective. *Assess the bank's compliance with statutory and regulatory requirements for special measures issued under section 311 of the Patriot Act.*

1. Determine the extent of the bank's international banking activities and the foreign jurisdictions in which the bank conducts transactions and activities, with particular emphasis on foreign correspondent banking and payable through accounts.
2. As applicable, determine whether the bank has established policies, procedures, and processes to respond to specific special measures imposed by FinCEN that are applicable to its operations. Evaluate the adequacy of the policies, procedures, and processes for detecting accounts or transactions with jurisdictions, financial institutions, or transactions subject to final special measures.
3. Determine, through discussions with management and review of the bank's documentation, whether the bank has taken action in response to final special measures.

Transaction Testing

4. Determine all final special measures issued by FinCEN under section 311 that are applicable to the bank (refer to www.fincen.gov).
5. For any of the first four types of special measures, determine whether the bank obtained, recorded, or reported the information required by each particular special measure.
6. For the fifth special measure (prohibition), determine whether the bank complied with the prohibitions or restrictions required by each particular special measure, and complied with any other actions required by the special measures.
7. As necessary, search the bank's management information systems (MIS) and other appropriate records for accounts or transactions with jurisdictions, financial institutions, or transactions subject to final special measures.
8. On the basis of examination procedures completed, including transaction testing, form a conclusion about the ability of policies, procedures, and processes to meet regulatory requirements associated with special measures.

Foreign Bank and Financial Accounts Reporting — Overview

Objective. *Assess the bank's compliance with statutory and regulatory requirements for the reporting of foreign bank and financial accounts.*

Each person[75] (including a bank) subject to U.S. jurisdiction with a financial interest in, or signature authority over, a bank, a securities, or any other financial account in a foreign country must file a Report of Foreign Bank and Financial Accounts (FBAR) with the Internal Revenue Service (IRS) (TD F 90-22.1) if the aggregate value of these financial accounts exceeds $10,000 at any time during the calendar year. A bank must file this form on its own accounts that meet this definition; the bank may be obligated to file these forms for customer accounts in which the bank has a financial interest or over which it has signature authority.

An FBAR must be filed with the commissioner of the IRS on or before June 30 of each calendar year for foreign financial accounts exceeding $10,000 maintained at any time during the previous calendar year.

EXAMINATION PROCEDURES

Foreign Bank and Financial Accounts Reporting

Objective. *Assess the bank's compliance with statutory and regulatory requirements for the reporting of foreign bank and financial accounts.*

1. Determine whether the bank has a financial interest in, or signature authority over, bank, securities, or other financial accounts in a foreign country, or whether the bank is otherwise required to file a Report of Foreign Bank and Financial Accounts (FBAR) (TD F 90-22.1) form for trust customers.
2. If applicable, review the bank's policies, procedures, and processes for filing annual reports.

Transaction Testing

3. On the basis of a risk assessment, prior examination reports, and a review of the bank's audit findings, select a sample of accounts to determine whether the bank has appropriately completed, submitted, and retained copies of the FBAR forms.
4. On the basis of examination procedures completed, including transaction testing, form a conclusion about the ability of policies, procedures, and processes to meet regulatory requirements associated with FBARs.

INTERNATIONAL TRANSPORTATION OF CURRENCY OR MONETARY INSTRUMENTS REPORTING — OVERVIEW

Objective. *Assess the bank's compliance with statutory and regulatory requirements for the reporting of international shipments of currency or monetary instruments.*

Each person[76] (including a bank) who physically transports, mails, or ships currency or monetary instruments in excess of $10,000 at one time out of or into the United States (and each person who causes such transportation, mailing, or shipment), must file a Report of International Transportation of Currency or Monetary Instruments (CMIR) (FinCEN Form 105).[77] A CMIR must be filed with the appropriate Bureau of Customs and Border Protection officer or with the commissioner of Customs at the time of entry into or departure from the United States. When a person receives currency or monetary instruments in an amount exceeding $10,000 at one time that have been shipped from any place outside the United States, a CMIR must be filed with the appropriate Bureau of Customs and Border Protection officer or with the commissioner of Customs within 15 days of receipt of the instruments (unless a report has already been filed). The report is to be completed by or on behalf of the person requesting transfer of the currency or monetary instruments. However, banks are not required to report these items if they are mailed or shipped through the postal service or by common carrier.[78] In addition, a commercial bank or trust company organized under the laws of any state or of the United States is not required to report overland shipments of currency or monetary instruments if they are shipped to or received from an established customer maintaining a deposit relationship with the bank and if the bank reasonably concludes the amounts do not exceed what is commensurate with the customary conduct of the business, industry, or profession of the customer concerned.

Management should implement applicable policies, procedures, and processes for CMIR filing. Management should review the international transportation of currency and monetary instruments and determine whether a customer's activity is usual and customary for the type of business. If not, a Suspicious Activity Report should be considered.

EXAMINATION PROCEDURES

International Transportation of Currency or Monetary Instruments Reporting

Objective. *Assess the bank's compliance with statutory and regulatory requirements for the reporting of international shipments of currency or monetary instruments.*

1. Determine whether the bank has (or has caused to be) physically transported, mailed, or shipped currency or other monetary instruments in excess of $10,000, at one time, out of the United States, or whether the bank has received currency or other monetary instruments in excess of $10,000, at one time, that has been physically transported, mailed, or shipped into the United States.
2. If applicable, review the bank's policies, procedures, and processes for filing a Report of International Transportation of Currency or Monetary Instruments (CMIR) (FinCEN Form 105) for each shipment of currency or other monetary instruments in excess of $10,000 out of or into the United States (except for shipments sent through the postal service, common carrier, or to which another exception from CMIR reporting applies).

Transaction Testing

3. On the basis of a risk assessment, prior examination reports, and a review of the bank's audit findings, select a sample of transactions conducted after the previous examination to determine whether the bank has appropriately completed, submitted, and retained copies of the CMIR forms.
4. On the basis of examination procedures completed, including transaction testing, form a conclusion about the ability of policies, procedures, and processes to meet regulatory requirements associated with CMIRs.
5. On the basis of the previous conclusion and the risks associated with the bank's activity in this area, proceed to expanded examination procedures, if necessary.

OFFICE OF FOREIGN ASSETS CONTROL — OVERVIEW

Objective. *Assess the bank's risk-based Office of Foreign Assets Control (OFAC) program to evaluate whether it is appropriate for the bank's OFAC risk, taking into consideration its products, services, customers, transactions, and geographic locations.*

OFAC is an office of the U.S. Treasury that administers and enforces economic and trade sanctions based on U.S. foreign policy and national security goals against entities such as targeted foreign countries, terrorists, international narcotics traffickers, and those engaged in activities related to the proliferation of weapons of mass destruction.

OFAC acts under Presidential wartime and national emergency powers, as well as authority granted by specific legislation, to impose controls on transactions and to freeze assets under U.S. jurisdiction. Many of the sanctions are based on United Nations and other international mandates, therefore, they are multilateral in scope, and involve close cooperation with allied governments. Other sanctions are specific to the interests of the United States. OFAC has been delegated responsibility by the Secretary of the Treasury for developing, promulgating, and administering U.S. sanctions programs.[79]

All U.S. persons,[80] including U.S. banks, bank holding companies, and non-bank subsidiaries, must comply with OFAC's regulations.[81] The federal banking agencies evaluate OFAC compliance systems to ensure that all banks subject to their supervision comply with the sanctions.[82] Unlike the BSA, the laws and OFAC-issued regulations apply not only to U.S. banks, their domestic branches, agencies, and international banking facilities, but also to their foreign branches, and often overseas offices and subsidiaries. In general, the regulations require the following:

- Block accounts and other property of specified countries, entities, and individuals.
- Prohibit or reject unlicensed trade and financial transactions with specified countries, entities, and individuals.

Blocked Transactions

U.S. law requires that assets and accounts of an OFAC-specified country, entity, or individual be blocked when such property is located in the United States, is held by U.S. individuals or entities, or comes into the possession or control of U.S. individuals or entities. For example, if a funds transfer comes from offshore and is being routed through a U.S. bank to an offshore bank, and there is an OFAC-designated party on the transaction, it must be blocked. The definition of assets and property is broad and is specifically defined within each sanction program. Assets and property includes anything of direct, indirect, present, future, or contingent value (including all types of bank transactions). Banks must block transactions that:

- Are by or on behalf of a blocked individual or entity;
- Are to or go through a blocked entity; or
- Are in connection with a transaction in which a blocked individual or entity has an interest.

For example, if a U.S. bank receives instructions to make a funds transfer payment that falls into one of these categories, it must execute the payment order and place the funds into a blocked account.[83] A payment order cannot be canceled or amended after it is received by a U.S. bank in the absence of an authorization from OFAC.

Prohibited Transactions

In some cases, an underlying transaction may be prohibited, but there is no blockable interest in the transaction (i.e., the transaction should not be accepted, but there is no OFAC requirement to block the assets). In these cases, the transaction is simply rejected, (i.e., not processed). For example, the Sudanese Sanctions Regulations prohibit transactions in support of commercial activities in Sudan. Therefore, a U.S. bank would have to reject a funds transfer between two companies, which are not Specially Designated Nationals or Blocked Persons (SDNs), involving an export to a company in Sudan that also is not an SDN. Because Sudanese Sanctions would only require blocking transactions with the Government of Sudan or SDNs, there would be no blockable interest in the funds between the two companies. However, because the transactions would constitute support of Sudanese commercial activity, which is prohibited, the U.S. bank can not process the transaction and would simply reject the transaction.

It is important to note that the OFAC regime specifying prohibitions against certain countries, entities, and individuals is separate and distinct from the provision within the BSA's Customer Identification Program (CIP) regulation (31 CFR 103.121) that requires banks to compare new accounts against government lists of known or suspected terrorists or terrorist organizations within a reasonable period of time after the account is opened. OFAC lists have not been designated government lists for purposes of the CIP rule. Refer to the core overview section, "Customer Identification Program," page 45, for further guidance.

However, OFAC's requirements stem from other statutes not limited to terrorism, and OFAC sanctions apply to transactions, in addition to account relationships.

OFAC Licenses

OFAC has the authority, through a licensing process, to permit certain transactions that would otherwise be prohibited under its regulations. OFAC can issue a license to engage in an otherwise prohibited transaction when it determines that the transaction does not undermine the U.S. policy objectives of the particular sanctions program, or is otherwise justified by U.S. national security or foreign policy objectives. OFAC can also promulgate general licenses, which authorize categories of transactions, such as allowing reasonable service charges on blocked accounts, without the need for case-by-case authorization from OFAC. These licenses can be found in the regulations for each sanctions program (31 CFR, Chapter V (Regulations)) and may be accessed from OFAC's web site. Before processing transactions that may be covered under a general license, banks should verify that such transactions meet the relevant criteria of the general license.[84]

Specific licenses are issued on a case-by-case basis.[85] A specific license is a written document issued by OFAC authorizing a particular transaction or set of transactions. To receive a specific license, the person or entity who would like to undertake the transaction must submit an application to OFAC. If the transaction conforms with U.S. foreign policy under a particular program, the license will be issued. If a bank's customer claims to have a specific license, the bank should verify that the transaction conforms to the terms of the license and obtain and retain a copy of the authorizing license.

OFAC Reporting

Banks must report all blockings to OFAC within ten days of the occurrence and annually by September 30 concerning those assets blocked (as of June 30).[86] Once assets or funds are blocked, they should be placed in a blocked account. Prohibited transactions that are rejected must also be reported to OFAC within ten days of the occurrence.

Banks must keep a full and accurate record of each rejected transaction for at least five years after the date of the transaction. For blocked property (including blocked transactions), records must be maintained for the period the property is blocked and for five years after the date the property is unblocked.

Additional information concerning OFAC regulations, such as Sanctions Program and Country Summaries brochures; the SDN list, including both entities and individuals; recent OFAC actions; and "Frequently Asked Questions," can be found on OFAC's web site.[87]

OFAC Program

While not required by specific regulation, but as a matter of sound banking practice and in order to ensure compliance, banks should establish and maintain an effective, written

OFAC program commensurate with their OFAC risk profile (based on products, services, customers, and geographic locations). The program should identify high-risk areas, provide for appropriate internal controls for screening and reporting, establish independent testing for compliance, designate a bank employee or employees as responsible for OFAC compliance, and create training programs for appropriate personnel in all relevant areas of the bank. A bank's OFAC program should be commensurate with its respective OFAC risk profile.

OFAC Risk Assessment

A fundamental element of a sound OFAC program is the bank's assessment of its specific product lines, customer base, and nature of transactions and identification of the high-risk areas for OFAC transactions. The initial identification of high-risk customers for purposes of OFAC may be performed as part of the bank's CIP and CDD procedures. As OFAC sanctions can reach into virtually all areas of its operations, banks should consider all types of transactions, products, and services when conducting their risk assessment and establishing appropriate policies, procedures, and processes. An effective risk assessment should be a composite of multiple factors (as described in more detail below), and depending upon the circumstances, certain factors may be weighed more heavily than others.

Another consideration for the risk assessment is account and transaction parties. New accounts should be compared with OFAC lists prior to being opened or shortly thereafter. However, the extent to which the bank includes account parties other than accountholders (e.g., beneficiaries, guarantors, principals, beneficial owners, nominee shareholders, directors, signatories, and powers of attorney) in the initial OFAC review during the account opening process, and during subsequent database reviews of existing accounts, will depend on the bank's risk profile and available technology.

Based on the bank's OFAC risk profile for each area and available technology, the bank should establish policies, procedures, and processes for reviewing transactions and transaction parties (e.g., issuing bank, payee, endorser, or jurisdiction). Currently, OFAC provides guidance on transactions parties on checks. The guidance states if a bank knows or has reason to know that a transaction party on a check is an OFAC target, the bank's processing of the transaction would expose the bank to liability, especially personally handled transactions in a high-risk area. For example, if a bank knows or has a reason to know that a check transaction involves an OFAC-prohibited party or country, OFAC would expect timely identification and appropriate action.

In evaluating the level of risk, a bank should exercise judgment and take into account all indicators of risk. Although not an exhaustive list, examples of products, services, customers, and geographic locations that may carry a higher level of OFAC risk include:

- International funds transfers.
- Nonresident alien accounts.
- Foreign customer accounts.
- Cross-border automated clearing house (ACH) transactions.
- Commercial letters of credit.
- Transactional electronic banking.
- Foreign correspondent bank accounts.
- Payable through accounts.

- International private banking.
- Overseas branches or subsidiaries.

Appendix M ("Quantity of Risk — OFAC Procedures") provides guidance to examiners on assessing OFAC risks facing a bank. The risk assessment can be used to assist the examiner in determining the scope of the OFAC examination. Additional information on compliance risk is posted by OFAC on its web site under "Frequently Asked Questions."[88]

Once the bank has identified its areas with high OFAC risk, it should develop appropriate policies, procedures, and processes to address the associated risks. Banks may tailor these policies, procedures, and processes to the specific nature of a business line or product. Furthermore, banks are encouraged to periodically reassess their OFAC risks.

Internal Controls

An effective OFAC program should include internal controls for identifying suspect accounts and transactions and reporting to OFAC. Internal controls should include the following elements:

Identifying and reviewing suspect transactions

The bank's policies, procedures, and processes should address how the bank will identify and review transactions and accounts for possible OFAC violations, whether conducted manually, through interdiction software, or a combination of both. For screening purposes, the bank should clearly define its criteria for comparing names provided on the OFAC list with the names in the bank's files or on transactions and for identifying transactions or accounts involving sanctioned countries. The bank's policies, procedures, and processes should also address how it will determine whether an initial OFAC hit is a valid match or a false hit.[89] A high volume of false hits may indicate a need to review the bank's interdiction program.

The screening criteria used by banks to identify name variations and misspellings should be based on the level of OFAC risk associated with the particular product or type of transaction. For example, in a high-risk area with a high-volume of transactions, the bank's interdiction software should be able to identify close name derivations for review. The SDN list attempts to provide name derivations; however, the list may not include all derivations. More sophisticated interdiction software may be able to catch variations of an SDN's name not included on the SDN list. Low-risk banks or areas and those with low volumes of transactions may decide to manually filter for OFAC compliance. Decisions to use interdiction software and the degree of sensitivity of that software should be based on a bank's assessment of its risk and the volume of its transactions. In determining the frequency of OFAC checks and the filtering criteria used (e.g., name derivations), banks should consider the likelihood of incurring a violation and available technology. In addition, banks should periodically reassess their OFAC filtering system. For example, if a bank identifies a name derivation of an OFAC target, then OFAC suggests that the bank add the name to its filtering process.

New accounts should be compared with the OFAC lists prior to being opened or shortly thereafter (e.g., during nightly processing). Banks that perform OFAC checks after account opening should have procedures in place to prevent transactions, other than initial deposits, from occurring until the OFAC check is completed. Prohibited transactions conducted prior to completing an OFAC check may be subject to possible penalty action. In addition, banks should have policies, procedures, and processes in place to check existing customers when there are additions or changes to the OFAC list. The frequency of the review should be based on the bank's OFAC risk. For example, banks with a low OFAC risk level may periodically (e.g., monthly or quarterly) compare the customer base against the OFAC list. Transactions such as funds transfers, letters of credit, and noncustomer transactions should be checked against OFAC lists prior to being executed. When developing OFAC policies, procedures, and processes, the bank should keep in mind that OFAC considers the continued operation of an account or the processing of transactions post-designation, along with the adequacy of their OFAC compliance program, to be a factor in determining penalty actions. [90] The bank should maintain documentation of its OFAC checks on new accounts, the existing customer base and specific transactions.

If a bank uses a third party, such as an agent or service provider, to perform OFAC checks on its behalf, as with any other responsibility performed by a third party, the bank is ultimately responsible for that third party's compliance with the OFAC requirements. As a result, banks should establish adequate controls and review procedures for such relationships.

Updating OFAC lists

A bank's OFAC program should include policies, procedures, and processes for timely updating of the lists of blocked countries, entities, and individuals and disseminating such information throughout the bank's domestic operations and its offshore offices, branches and, in the case of Cuba and North Korea, foreign subsidiaries. This would include ensuring that any manual updates of interdiction software are completed in a timely manner.

Screening ACH transactions

All parties to an ACH transaction are subject to the requirements of OFAC. Refer to the expanded overview section, "Automated Clearing House Transactions," page 196, for additional guidance. OFAC has clarified the application of its rules for domestic and cross-border ACH transactions and is working with industry to provide more detailed guidance on cross-border ACH.[91]

With respect to domestic ACH transactions, the Originating Depository Financial Institution (ODFI) is responsible for verifying that the Originator is not a blocked party and making a good faith effort to determine that the Originator is not transmitting blocked funds. The Receiving Depository Financial Institution (RDFI) similarly is responsible for verifying that the Receiver is not a blocked party. In this way, the ODFI and the RDFI are relying on each other for compliance with OFAC policies. ODFIs are not responsible for unbatching transactions and ensuring that they do not process transactions in violation of OFAC's regulations if they receive those transactions already batched from their customers. If the ODFI unbatches the transactions it received from its customers, then the ODFI is responsible for screening as though it had done the initial batching.

With respect to OFAC screening, these same obligations hold for cross-border ACH transactions. For outbound cross-border ACH transactions, however, the ODFI cannot rely on OFAC screening by the RDFI outside of the United States. In the case of inbound ACH transactions, the RDFI is responsible for compliance with OFAC requirements.

Additional information on the types of retail payment systems (ACH payment systems) is available in the FFIEC *Information Technology Examination Handbook*.[92]

Reporting

An OFAC program should also include policies, procedures, and processes for handling items that are valid blocked or rejected items under the various sanctions programs. In the case of interdictions related to narcotics trafficking or terrorism, banks should notify OFAC as soon as possible by phone or e-hotline about potential hits with a follow-up in writing within ten days. Most other items should be reported through usual channels within ten days of the occurrence. The policies, procedures, and processes should also address the management of blocked accounts. Banks are responsible for tracking the amount of blocked funds, the ownership of those funds, and interest paid on those funds. Total amounts blocked, including interest, must be reported to OFAC by September 30 of each year (information as of June 30). When a bank acquires or merges with another bank, both banks should take into consideration the need to review and maintain such records and information.

Banks no longer need to file Suspicious Activity Reports (SARs) based solely on blocked narcotics- or terrorism-related transactions, as long as the bank files the required blocking report with OFAC. However, because blocking reports require only limited information, if the bank is in possession of additional information not included on the blocking report filed with OFAC, a separate SAR should be filed with FinCEN including that information. In addition, the bank should file a SAR if the transaction itself would be considered suspicious in the absence of a valid OFAC match.[93]

Maintaining license information

OFAC recommends that banks consider maintaining copies of customers' OFAC licenses on file. This will allow the bank to verify whether a customer is initiating a legal transaction. Banks should also be aware of the expiration date on the license. If it is unclear whether a particular transaction is authorized by a license, the bank should confirm with OFAC. Maintaining copies of licenses will also be useful if another bank in the payment chain requests verification of a license's validity. Copies of licenses should be maintained for five years, following the most recent transaction conducted in accordance with the license.

Independent Testing

Every bank should conduct an independent test of its OFAC program that is performed by the internal audit department, outside auditors, consultants, or other qualified independent parties. For large banks, the frequency and area of the independent test should be based on the known or perceived risk of specific business areas. For smaller banks, the audit should be consistent with the bank's OFAC risk profile or be based on a perceived risk. The person(s) responsible for testing should conduct an objective, comprehensive evaluation of OFAC policies, procedures, and processes. The audit scope should be comprehensive enough to assess OFAC compliance risks and evaluate the adequacy of the OFAC program.

Responsible Individual

It is recommended that every bank designate a qualified individual(s) to be responsible for the day-to-day compliance of the OFAC program, including the reporting of blocked or rejected transactions to OFAC and the oversight of blocked funds. This individual should have an appropriate level of knowledge about OFAC regulations commensurate with the bank's OFAC risk profile.

Training

The bank should provide adequate training for all appropriate employees. The scope and frequency of the training should be consistent with the bank's OFAC risk profile and appropriate to employee responsibilities.

EXAMINATION PROCEDURES

Office of Foreign Assets Control

Objective. *Assess the bank's risk-based Office of Foreign Assets Control (OFAC) program to evaluate whether it is appropriate for the bank's OFAC risk, taking into consideration its products, services, customers, transactions, and geographic locations.*

1. Determine whether the board of directors and senior management of the bank have developed policies, procedures, and processes based on their risk assessment to ensure compliance with OFAC laws and regulations.
2. Regarding the risk assessment, review the bank's OFAC program. Consider the following:
   - The extent of, and method for, conducting OFAC searches of each relevant department or business line (e.g., automated clearing house (ACH) transactions, monetary instrument sales, check cashing, trusts, loans, deposits, and investments) as the process may vary from one department or business line to another.
   - The extent of, and method for, conducting OFAC searches of account parties other than accountholders, which may include beneficiaries, guarantors, principals, beneficial owners, nominee shareholders, directors, signatories, and powers of attorney.
   - How responsibility for OFAC is assigned.
   - Timeliness of obtaining and updating OFAC lists or filtering criteria.
   - The appropriateness of the filtering criteria used by the bank to reasonably identify OFAC matches (e.g., the extent to which the filtering or search criteria includes misspellings and name derivations).
   - The process used to investigate potential matches.
   - The process used to block and reject transactions.
   - The process used to inform management of blocked or rejected transactions.
   - The adequacy and timeliness of reports to OFAC.
   - The process to manage blocked accounts (such accounts are reported to OFAC and pay a commercially reasonable rate of interest).

- The record retention requirements (i.e., five-year requirement to retain relevant OFAC records; for blocked property, record retention for as long as blocked; once unblocked, records must be maintained for five years).

3. Determine the adequacy of independent testing (audit) and follow-up procedures.
4. Review the adequacy of the bank's OFAC training program based on the bank's OFAC risk assessment.
5. Determine whether the bank has adequately addressed weaknesses or deficiencies identified by OFAC, auditors, or regulators.

Transaction Testing

6. On the basis of a bank's risk assessment, prior examination reports, and a review of the bank's audit findings, select the following samples to test the bank's OFAC program for adequacy, as follows:
   - Sample new accounts (e.g., deposit, loan, trust, safe deposit, investments, credit cards, and foreign office accounts,) and evaluate the filtering process used to search the OFAC database (e.g., the timing of the search), and documentation maintained evidencing the searches.
   - Sample appropriate transactions that may not be related to an account (e.g., funds transfers, monetary instrument sales, and check-cashing transactions), and evaluate the filtering criteria used to search the OFAC database, the timing of the search, and documentation maintained evidencing the searches.
   - If the bank uses an automated system to conduct searches, assess the timing of when updates are made to the system, and when the most recent OFAC changes were made to the system. Also, evaluate whether all of the bank's databases are run against the automated system, and the frequency upon which searches are made. If there is any doubt regarding the effectiveness of the OFAC filter, then run tests of the system by entering test account names that are the same as or similar to those recently added to the OFAC list to determine whether the system identifies a potential hit.
   - If the bank does not use an automated system, evaluate the process used to check the existing customer base against the OFAC list and the frequency of such checks.
   - Review a sample of potential OFAC matches and evaluate the bank's resolution for blocking and rejecting processes.
   - Review a sample of reports to OFAC and evaluate their completeness and timeliness.
   - If the bank is required to maintain blocked accounts, select a sample and evaluate that the bank maintains adequate records of amounts blocked and ownership of blocked funds, that the bank is paying a commercially reasonable rate of interest on all blocked accounts, and that it is accurately reporting required information annually (by September 3 0th) to OFAC. Test the controls in place to verify that the account is blocked.

- Pull a sample of false hits (potential matches) to check their handling; the resolution of a false hit should take place outside of the business line.

7. Identify any potential matches that were not reported to OFAC, discuss with bank management, advise bank management to immediately notify OFAC of unreported transactions, and immediately notify supervisory personnel at your regulatory agency.
8. Determine the origin of deficiencies (e.g., training, audit, risk assessment, internal controls, management oversight), and conclude on the adequacy of the bank's OFAC program.
9. Discuss OFAC related examination findings with bank management.
10. Include OFAC conclusions within the report of examination, as appropriate.

End Notes

[1] See 12 CFR 208.63(b), 211.5(m), 211.24(j) (Board of Governors of the Federal Reserve System); 12 CFR 326.8(b) (Federal Deposit Insurance Corporation); 12 CFR 748.2(b) (National Credit Union Administration); 12 CFR 21.21 (Office of the Comptroller of the Currency); 12 CFR 563.177(b) (Office of Thrift Supervision); and 31 CFR 103.121 (FinCEN).

[2] As of the publication date of this manual, non-federally regulated private banks, trust companies, and credit unions do not have BSA/AML compliance program requirements; however, the bank's board must still approve the CIP.

[3] "Frequently Asked Questions Related to Customer Identification Program Rules" issued by FinCEN, Board of Governors of the Federal Reserve System, Federal Deposit Insurance Corporation, National Credit Union Administration, Office of the Comptroller of the Currency and Office of Thrift Supervision, April 28, 2005.

[4] When the account is a loan, the account is considered to be "opened" when the bank enters into an enforceable agreement to provide a loan to the customer.

[5] The bank may demonstrate that it knows an existing customer's true identity by showing that before the issuance of the final CIP rule, it had comparable procedures in place to verify the identity of persons who had accounts with the bank as of October 1, 2003, though the bank may not have gathered the very same information about such persons as required by the final CIP rule. Alternative means include showing that the bank has had an active and longstanding relationship with a particular person, as evidenced by such things as a history of account statements sent to the person, information sent to the Internal Revenue Service (IRS) about the person's accounts without issue, loans made and repaid, or other services performed for the person over a period of time. However, the comparable procedures used to verify the identity detailed above might not suffice for persons that the bank has deemed to be high risk.

[6] When an individual opens a new account for an entity that is not a legal person or for another individual who lacks legal capacity, the identifying information for the individual opening the account must be obtained. By contrast, when an account is opened by an agent on behalf of another person, the bank must obtain the identifying information of the person on whose behalf the account is being opened.

[7] For credit card customers, the bank may obtain identifying information from a third-party source before extending credit.

[8] For an individual: a residential or business street address, or if the individual does not have such an address, an Army Post Office (APO) or Fleet Post Office (FPO) box number, the residential or business street address of next of kin or of another contact individual, or a description of the customer's physical location. For a "person" other than an individual (such as a corporation, partnership, or trust): a principal place of business, local office, or other physical location.

[9] An identification number for a U.S. person is a taxpayer identification number (TIN) (or evidence of an application for one), and an identification number for a non-U.S. person is one or more of the following: a TIN; a passport number and country of issuance; an alien identification card number; or a number and country of issuance of any other unexpired government-issued document evidencing nationality or residence and bearing a photograph or similar safeguard. TIN is defined by section 6109 of the Internal Revenue Code of 1986 (26 USC 6109) and the IRS regulations implementing that section (e.g., Social Security number, individual taxpayer identification number, or employer identification number).

[10] A bank may keep photocopies of identifying documents that it uses to verify a customer's identity; however, the CIP regulation does not require it. A bank's verification procedures should be risk-based and, in certain

situations, keeping copies of identifying documents may be warranted. In addition, a bank may have procedures to keep copies of the documents for other purposes, for example, to facilitate investigating potential fraud. However, if a bank does choose to retain photocopies of identifying documents, it should ensure that these photocopies are physically secured to adequately protect against possible identity theft. (These documents should be retained in accordance with the general recordkeeping requirements in 31 CFR 103.38.) Nonetheless, a bank should be mindful that it must not improperly use any documents containing a picture of an individual, such as a driver's license, in connection with any aspect of a credit transaction. See "Frequently Asked Questions Related to Customer Identification Program Rules" issued by FinCEN, Board of Governors of the Federal Reserve System, Federal Deposit Insurance Corporation, National Credit Union Administration, Office of the Comptroller of the Currency, and Office of Thrift Supervision, April 28, 2005.

[11] As of the publication date of this manual, there are no designated government lists to verify specifically for CIP purposes. Customer comparisons to lists required by OFAC and 31 CFR 103.100 requests remain separate and distinct requirements.

[12] Federal functional regulator means: Board of Governors of the Federal Reserve System; Federal Deposit Insurance Corporation; National Credit Union Administration; Office of the Comptroller of the Currency; Office of Thrift Supervision; Securities and Exchange Commission; or Commodity Futures Trading Commission.

[13] High-risk accounts, for CIP purposes, include accounts in which identification verification is typically more difficult (e.g., foreign private banking and trust accounts, accounts of senior foreign political figures, offshore accounts, and out-of-area and non-face-to-face accounts).

[14] See 12 CFR 208.62, 211.5(k), 211.24(f), and 225.4(f) (Board of Governors of the Federal Reserve System); 12 CFR 353 (Federal Deposit Insurance Corporation); 12 CFR 748 (National Credit Union Administration); 12 CFR 21.11 (Office of the Comptroller of the Currency); 12 CFR 563.180 (Office of Thrift Supervision) (does not apply to Savings and Loan Holding Companies); and 31 CFR 103.18 (FinCEN).

[15] Refer to Appendix G ("Structuring") for additional guidance.

[16] If a bank knows, suspects, or has reason to suspect that a customer may be linked to terrorist activity against the United States, the bank should immediately call FinCEN's Financial Institutions Terrorist Hotline at the toll-free number: 866-556-3974. Similarly, if any other suspected violation — such as an ongoing money laundering scheme — requires immediate attention, the bank should notify the appropriate federal banking and law enforcement agencies. In either case, the bank must also file a SAR.

[17] Refer to core overview section, "Information Sharing," page 86, for a discussion on section 314(a) requests.

[18] Bank Secrecy Act Advisory Group, "Section 5 — Issues and Guidance" *The SAR Activity Review – Trends, Tips & Issues*, Issue 10, May 2006, pages 42 – 44, at www.fincen.gov.

[19] Electronic Communications Privacy Act, 18 USC 2709.

[20] Fair Credit Reporting Act, 15 USC 168 1u.

[21] Right to Financial Privacy Act of 1978, 12 USC 3401 *et seq.*

[22] Refer to the Bank Secrecy Act Advisory Group, *The SAR Activity Review — Trends, Tips and Issues*, Issue 8, April 2005 for further information on NSLs which is available at www.fincen.gov.

[23] Bank Secrecy Act Advisory Group, "Section 4 — Tips on SAR Form Preparation & Filing," *The SAR Activity Review — Trends, Tips & Issues*, Issue 10, May 2006, page 38, at www.fincen .gov.

[24] Bank Secrecy Act Advisory Group, "Section 5 — Issues and Guidance," *The SAR Activity Review – Trends, Tips & Issues*, Issue 1, October 2000, page 27, at www.fincen.gov.

[25] Bank Secrecy Act Advisory Group, "Section 5 — Issues and Guidance," *The SAR Activity Review – Trends, Tips & Issues*, Issue 10, May 2006, page 44, at www.fincen.gov.

[26] *Id.*

[27] For suspicious activity related to terrorist activity, institutions may also call FinCEN's Financial Institution's terrorist hotline at the toll free number 866-556-3974 (7 days a week, 24 hours a day) to further facilitate the immediate transmittal of relevant information to the appropriate authorities.

[28] Credit unions do not have a regulatory requirement to notify the board of directors of SAR filings, although many take this action as a matter of a sound practice. On June 22, 2006, the NCUA Board issued a proposed revision to 12 CFR 748 to require such action (71 *Federal Register* 36720).

[29] As noted in the Bank Secrecy Act Advisory Group's *The SAR Activity Review – Trends, Tips & Issues*, Issue 2, June 2001, "In the rare instance when suspicious activity is related to an individual in the organization, such as the president or one of the members of the board of directors, the established policy that would require notification of a SAR filing to such an individual should not be followed. Deviations to established policies and procedures so as to avoid notification of a SAR filing to a subject of the SAR should be documented and appropriate uninvolved senior organizational personnel should be so advised." See www.fincen.gov.

[30] "Interagency Guidance on Sharing Suspicious Activity Reports with Head Offices and Controlling Companies," issued by Financial Crimes Enforcement Network, Board of Governors of the Federal Reserve System, Federal Deposit Insurance Corporation, Office of the Comptroller of the Currency, and Office of Thrift Supervision, January 20, 2006.

[31] Bank Secrecy Act Advisory Group, "Section 5 — Issues and Guidance," *The SAR Activity Review*, Issue 1, October 2000, page 27 at www.fincen.gov.

[32] The IRS Detroit Computing Center is a central repository for the BSA reports that banks must file.

[33] Currency is defined as coin and paper money of the United States or any other country as long as it is customarily accepted as money in the country of issue.

[34] The IRS Detroit Computing Center is a central repository for the BSA reports that banks must file. The IRS Detroit Computing Center can be contacted at 800-800-2877.

[35] FinCEN has issued a directive ("Guidance on Interpreting 'Frequently' Found in the Criteria for Exempting a 'Non-Listed Business' under 31 CFR 103.22(d)(2)(vi)(B)," November 2002, www.fincen.gov) which states, "In general, a customer that is being considered for exemption as a non- listed business should be conducting at least eight large currency transactions throughout the year. In essence, this means the customer conducts a large currency transaction approximately every six weeks. The fact a customer conducts fewer than eight large currency transactions annually would generally indicate that any large currency transactions conducted do not relate to a recurring or routine need."

[36] Questions often arise in determining the "gross revenue" of gaming activities, such as lottery sales. FinCEN has ruled that for the purpose of determining if a business derives more than 50 percent of its gross revenue from gaming, the term gross revenue is intended to encompass the amount of money that a business actually earns from a particular activity, rather than the sales volume of such activity conducted by the business. For example, if a business engages in lottery sales, the "gross revenue" from this activity would be the amount of money that the business actually earns from lottery sales, rather than the amount of money that the business takes in on behalf of the state lottery system. See FinCEN Ruling 2002-1, www.fincen.gov.

[37] The IRS Detroit Computing Center is a central repository for the BSA reports that banks must file. The IRS Detroit Computing Center can be contacted at 800-800-2877.

[38] FinCEN has issued a directive ("Guidance on Interpreting 'Frequently' Found in the Criteria for Exempting a 'Non-Listed Business' under 31 CFR 103.22(d)(2)(vi)(B)," November 2002, www.fincen.gov) which states, "In general, a customer that is being considered for exemption as a non- listed business should be conducting at least eight large currency transactions throughout the year. In essence, this means the customer conducts a large currency transaction approximately every six weeks. The fact that a customer conducts fewer than eight large currency transactions annually would generally indicate that any large currency transactions conducted do not relate to a recurring or routine need."

[39] If the request contains multiple suspects, it is often referred to as a "314(a) list."

[40] The positive matches can be faxed to FinCEN at 703-905-3660.

[41] For example, regarding funds transfers, the "General Instructions" state that, unless the instructions to a specific 314(a) request state otherwise, banks are required to search funds transfer records maintained pursuant to 31 CFR 103.33, to determine whether the named subject was an originator/transmittor of a funds transfer for which the bank was the originator/transmittor's financial institution, or a beneficiary/recipient of a funds transfer for which the bank was the beneficiary/recipient's financial institution.

[42] The General Instructions and FAQs can be obtained by contacting FinCEN at 800-949-2732.

[43] This list, titled "Law Enforcement Information Sharing with the Financial Industry," is available on the "Section 314(a)" page of FinCEN's web site www.fincen.gov. The list contains information on each search request transmitted since January 4, 2005, and is updated after each transmission.

[44] Refer to the FinCEN web site www.fincen.gov, for section 314(a) contacts for each primary regulator.

[45] Instructions on submitting a notification form (initial or renewal) are available on FinCEN's web site: www.fincen.gov.

[46] FinCEN's "Guidance on Interpreting Financial Institution Policies in Relation to Recordkeeping Requirements under 31 CFR 103.29," November 2002, www.fincen.gov.

[47] The bank must verify that the person is a deposit accountholder or must verify the person's identity. Verification may be either through a signature card or other file or record at the bank, provided the deposit accountholder's name and address were verified previously and that information was recorded on the signature card or other file or record, or by examination of a document that is normally acceptable within the banking community and that contains the name and address of the purchaser. If the deposit accountholder's identity has not been verified previously, the bank shall record the specific identifying information (e.g., state of issuance and number of driver's license) of the document examined.

[48] 31 CFR 103.33(e) is the recordkeeping rule for banks, and 31 CFR 103.33(f) imposes similar requirements for non-bank financial institutions that engage in funds transfers. The procedures in this core overview section address only the rules for banks in 31 CFR 103.33(e).

[49] Funds transfer is defined under 31 CFR 103.11. Funds transfers governed by the Electronic Fund Transfer Act of 1978, as well as any other funds transfers that are made through an automated clearing house, an automated teller machine, or a point-of-sale system, are excluded from this definition and exempt from the requirements of 31 CFR 103.33(e), (f) and (g).

[50] 31 CFR 103.33(e)(6) provides exceptions to the funds transfer requirements. Funds transfers where both the originator and the beneficiary are the same person and the originator's bank and the beneficiary's bank are the

same bank are not subject to the recordkeeping requirements for funds transfers. Additionally, exceptions are provided from the recordkeeping requirements for funds transfers where the originator and beneficiary are: a bank; a wholly owned domestic subsidiary of a bank chartered in the United States; a broker or dealer in securities; a wholly owned domestic subsidiary of a broker or dealer in securities; the United States; a state or local government; or a federal, state or local government agency or instrumentality.

[51] These terms are defined under 31 CFR 103.11.

[52] The rule applies to both banks and non-banks (31 CFR 103.33(g)). Because it is broader in scope, the Travel Rule uses more expansive terms, such as "transmittal order" instead of "payment order" and "transmittor's financial institution" instead of "originating bank." The broader terms include the bank- specific terms.

[53] 68 *Federal Register* 66708.

[54] Consistent with 31 CFR 103.121, an "address" for purposes of the Travel Rule is as follows: for an individual, "address" is a residential or business street address, an Army Post Office Box or a Fleet Post Office Box, or the residential or business street address of next of kin or another contact person for persons who do not have a residential or business address. For a person other than an individual (such as a corporation, partnership, or trust), "address" is a principal place of business, local office, or other physical location. However, while 31 CFR 103.121 applies only to new customers opening accounts on or after October 1, 2003, and while the rule exempt funds transfers from the definition of "account," for banks, the Travel Rule applies to all transmittals of funds of $3,000 or more, whether or not the transmittor is a customer for purposes of 31 CFR 103.121.

[55] "Correspondent Banking: A Gateway for Money Laundering." See Senate Hearing 107-84. The report appears on p. 273 of volume 1 of the hearing records entitled "Role of U.S. Correspondent Banking in International Money Laundering," held on March 1, 2, and 6, 2001.

[56] 71 *Federal Register* 499.

[57] "Physical presence" means a place of business that:

- Is maintained by a foreign bank.
- Is located at a fixed address (other than solely an electronic address or a post office box) in a country in which the foreign financial institution is authorized to conduct banking activities, at which location the foreign financial institution:
  - Employs one or more persons on a full-time basis.
  - Maintains operating records related to its banking activities.
- Is subject to inspection by the banking authority that licensed the foreign financial institution to conduct banking activities.

[58] A "regulated affiliate" is a shell bank that is affiliated with a depository institution, credit union, or foreign bank that maintains a physical presence in the United States or in another jurisdiction. The regulated affiliate shell bank must also be subject to supervision by the banking authority that regulates the affiliated entity.

[59] To minimize the recordkeeping burdens, ownership information is not required for foreign financial institutions that file a form FR Y-7 ("Annual Report of Foreign Banking Organizations") with the Federal Reserve or for those foreign financial institutions that are publicly traded. "Publicly traded" refers to shares that are traded on an exchange or an organized over-the-counter market that is regulated by a foreign securities authority as defined in section 3(a)(50) of the Securities Exchange Act of 1934.

[60] "Service of legal process" means that the agent is willing to accept legal documents, such as subpoenas, on behalf of the foreign bank.

[61] Refer to FinCEN Guidance FIN-2006-G003, "Frequently Asked Questions, Foreign Bank Recertifications under 31 CFR 103.177," February 3, 2006, at www.fincen.gov.

[62] The term "foreign financial institution" as defined in 31 CFR 103.175(h) includes:

- A foreign bank.
- A foreign branch, or office of a U.S. bank, broker/dealer in securities, futures commission merchant, introducing broker, or mutual fund.
- Any other person organized under foreign law that, if located in the United States, would be a broker/dealer in securities, futures commission merchant, introducing broker, or mutual fund.
- Any person organized under foreign law that is engaged in the business of, and is readily identifiable as, a currency dealer or exchanger or a money transmitter.

[63] The Patriot Act defines an offshore banking license as a license to conduct banking activities that, as a condition of the license, prohibits the licensed entity from conducting banking activities with the citizens of, or with the local currency of, the country that issued the license (31 USC 531 8(i)(4)(A)).

[64] The preamble to the *Federal Register* notice that accompanied the interim final rule (67 *Federal Register* 48348) published on July 23, 2002, stated that for purposes of subsection 531 8(i)(2)(B)(i), an owner is deemed to be any person who directly or indirectly owns, controls, or has voting power over five percent or more of any class of securities of a foreign bank, the shares of which are not publicly traded. However, a second Notice of Proposed Rulemaking implementing section 531 8(i)(2) dated January 4, 2006, proposed a ten percent ownership threshold. "Publicly traded" means shares that are traded on an exchange or an organized over-the-counter market that is regulated by a foreign securities authority, as defined in section 3(a)(50) of the Securities Exchange Act of 1934 (15 USC 78c(a)(50)).

[65] Official notifications to close a foreign financial institution's account must be signed by either the Secretary of the Treasury or the U.S. Attorney General (31 CFR 103.185(d)).
[66] "Beneficial owner" of an account means an individual who has a level of control over, or entitlement to, the funds or assets in the account that, as a practical matter, enables the individual, directly or indirectly, to control, manage, or direct the account. The ability to fund the account or the entitlement to the funds of the account alone, however, without any corresponding authority to control, manage, or direct the account (such as in the case of a minor child beneficiary), does not cause the individual to be a beneficial owner (31 CFR 103.175(b)).
[67] For purposes of this definition, the terms "senior official" or "senior executive" mean an individual with substantial authority over policy, operations, or the use of government-owned resources.
[68] Additional red flags regarding transactions that may be related to the proceeds of foreign corruption are listed in "Guidance on Enhanced Scrutiny for Transactions That May Involve the Proceeds of Foreign Official Corruption," issued by the U.S. Treasury, Board of Governors of the Federal Reserve System, Federal Deposit Insurance Corporation, Office of the Comptroller of the Currency, Office of Thrift Supervision, and the Department of State, January 2001.
[69] Refer to the expanded examination procedures, "Private Banking" and "Politically Exposed Persons" (PEPs), pages 249 and 265, respectively, for additional guidance.
[70] The term "proceeds of foreign corruption" means any assets or property that is acquired by, through, or on behalf of a senior foreign political figure through misappropriation, theft, or embezzlement of public funds, the unlawful conversion of property of a foreign government, or through acts of bribery or extortion, and shall include any other property into which any such assets have been transformed or converted (31 CFR 103.178(c)(2)).
[71] The final rule defines a senior foreign political figure as: a current or former senior official in the executive, legislative, administrative, military, or judicial branches of a foreign government, whether or not they are or were elected officials; a senior official of a major foreign political party; and a senior executive of a foreign government-owned commercial enterprise. The definition also includes a corporation, business, or other entity formed by or for the benefit of such an individual. Senior executives are individuals with substantial authority over policy, operations, or the use of government-owned resources. Also included in the definition of a senior foreign political official are immediate family members of such individuals and persons who are widely and publicly known (or actually known) close associates of a senior foreign political figure.
[72] Notices of proposed rulemaking and final rules accompanying the determination "of primary money laundering concern," and imposition of a special measure(s) pursuant to section 311 of the Patriot Act are available on the FinCEN web site: www.fincen.gov.
[73] Refer to expanded overview section, "Payable Through Accounts," page 176, for additional guidance.
[74] Refer to core overview section, "Foreign Correspondent Account Recordkeeping and Due Diligence," page 105, and expanded overview section, "Correspondent Accounts (Foreign)," page 168, for additional guidance.
[75] As defined in 31 CFR 103.11(z), the term "person" means an individual, a corporation, a partnership, a trust or estate, a joint stock company, an association, a syndicate, joint venture or other unincorporated organization or group, an Indian Tribe (as that term is defined in the Indian Gaming Regulatory Act), and all entities cognizable as legal personalities.
[76] As defined in 31 CFR 103.11(z), the term "person" means an individual, a corporation, a partnership, a trust or estate, a joint stock company, an association, a syndicate, joint venture or other unincorporated organization or group, an Indian Tribe (as that term is defined in the Indian Gaming Regulatory Act), and all entities cognizable as legal personalities.
[77] The obligation to file the CMIR is solely on the person who transports, mails, ships or receives, or causes or attempts to transport, mail, ship, or receive. No other person is under any obligation to file a CMIR. Thus, if a customer walks into the bank and declares that he or she has received or transported currency in an aggregate amount exceeding $10,000 from a place outside the United States and wishes to deposit the currency into his or her account, the bank is under no obligation to file a CMIR on the customer's behalf (Treasury Administrative Ruling 88-2).
[78] In contrast, a bank is required to file a CMIR to report shipments of currency or monetary instruments to foreign offices when those shipments are performed directly by bank personnel, such as currency shipments handled by bank employees using bank-owned vehicles.
[79] Trading With the Enemy Act (TWEA), 50 USC App 1-44; International Emergency Economic Powers Act (IEEPA), 50 USC 1701 *et seq.*; Antiterrorism and Effective Death Penalty Act (AEDPA), 8 USC 1189, 18 USC 2339B; United Nations Participation Act (UNPA), 22 USC 287c; Cuban Democracy Act (CDA), 22 USC 6001–1 0; The Cuban Liberty and Democratic Solidarity Act (Libertad Act), 22 USC 6021–91; The Clean Diamonds Trade Act, Pub. L. No. 108-19; Foreign Narcotics Kingpin Designation Act (Kingpin Act), 21 USC 1901–1908, 8 USC 1182; Burmese Freedom and Democracy Act of 2003, Pub. L. No. 108– 61, 117 Stat. 864 (2003); The Foreign Operations, Export Financing and Related Programs Appropriations Act, Sec 570 of Pub. L. No. 104-208, 110 Stat. 3009-116 (1997); The Iraqi Sanctions Act, Pub. L. No. 101- 513, 104 Stat. 2047-55 (1990); The International Security and Development Cooperation Act, 22 USC 2349 aa8–9; The Trade Sanctions Reform and Export Enhancement Act of 2000, Title IX, Pub. L. No. 106- 387 (October 28, 2000).

[80] All U.S. persons must comply with OFAC regulations, including all U.S. citizens and permanent resident aliens regardless of where they are located, all persons and entities within the United States, all U.S. incorporated entities and their foreign branches. In the case of certain programs, such as those regarding Cuba and North Korea, foreign subsidiaries owned or controlled by U.S. companies also must comply. Certain programs also require foreign persons in possession of U.S. origin goods to comply.

[81] Additional information is provided in "Foreign Assets Control Regulations for the Financial Community," which is available on OFAC's web site www.treas.gov/ofac/.

[82] 31 CFR chapter V.

[83] A blocked account is a segregated interest-bearing account (at a commercially reasonable rate), which holds the customer's property until the target is delisted, the sanctions program is rescinded, or the customer obtains an OFAC license authorizing the release of the property.

[84] License information is available on OFAC's web site www.treas.gov/ofac, or by contacting OFAC's Licensing area at 202-622-2480.

[85] Specific licenses require an application directed to: Licensing Division, Office of Foreign Assets Control, 1500 Pennsylvania Avenue, NW, Washington, D.C. 20220.

[86] The annual report is to be filed on form TD F 90-22.50.

[87] This information is available on OFAC's web site www.treas.gov/ofac, or by contacting OFAC's Hotline at 800-540-6322.

[88] This document is available at www.treas.gov/offices/enforcement/ofac/faq/#finance

[89] Due diligence steps for determining a valid match are provided in "Using OFAC's Hotline" on OFAC's web site www.treas.gov/ofac.

[90] Interim final rule 31 CFR 501, "Economic Sanctions Enforcement Procedures for Banking Institutions," discusses that OFAC will take a bank-wide rather than a "per transaction" approach to enforcement. This methodology should consider risk-based efforts by banks to ensure OFAC compliance as well as evaluating violations. Further information is available on OFAC's web site www.treas.gov/ofac.

[91] See Interpretive Note 041214-FACRL-GN-02 at www.treas.gov/offices/enforcement/ofac/rulings/. NACHA rules further specify this compliance (see page 8 of the Quick Find section of the *2006 NACHA Operating Rules*).

[92] The FFIEC *Information Technology Examination Handbook* is available at www.ffiec.gov/ffiecinfobase/html_pages/it_01.html.

[93] See FinCEN Release Number 2004-02, "Unitary Filing of Suspicious Activity and Blocking Reports," 69 *Federal Register* 76847, December 23, 2004.

In: The Bank Secrecy Act and Anti-Money Laundering...
Editor: Anne Leuter
ISBN: 978-1-60876-162-3

Chapter 4

EXPANDED EXAMINATION OVERVIEW AND PROCEDURES FOR AN ENTERPRISE-WIDE COMPLIANCE PROGRAM AND OTHER STRUCTURES

ENTERPRISE-WIDE BSA/AML COMPLIANCE PROGRAM — OVERVIEW

Objective. *Assess the organization's enterprise-wide program for BSA/AML compliance through the holding company or lead financial institution.*[1]

Similar to the approach to consolidated credit, market, and operational risk, effective control of BSA/AML risk may call for coordinated risk management. An enterprise-wide BSA/AML compliance program coordinates the specific regulatory requirements throughout an organization inside a larger risk management framework. Such frameworks seek a consolidated understanding of the organization's risk exposure to money laundering and terrorist financing across all activities, business lines, or legal entities. For example, the holding company or lead financial institution may have a centralized function to evaluate BSA/AML risk; this may include the ability to understand world-wide exposure to a given customer, particularly those considered high- risk or suspicious, consistent with applicable laws.[2]

Many organizations, typically those that are larger or more complex and that may include international operations, implement an enterprise-wide BSA/AML compliance program that manages risks in an integrated fashion across affiliates, business lines, and risk types (e.g., reputation, compliance, or transaction). Some larger or more complex organizations may decide to manage their risks by developing enterprise-wide approaches to their BSA/AML compliance program. Such programs manage risk at both operational and strategic levels.

While there are currently no regulatory requirements for holding companies or lead financial institutions to adopt an enterprise-wide BSA/AML compliance program, many organizations view this as an effective tool in managing the BSA/AML risks associated with failure to comply with BSA laws and regulations, or the corresponding laws in foreign jurisdictions in which they operate. A sound practice for complex organizations is to establish corporate standards for BSA/AML compliance that reflect the expectations of the organization's board of directors. Senior management should ensure that these standards are implemented across the organization through effective programs tailored to the activities, business lines, or legal entities. This allows the holding company or lead financial institution to demonstrate to its board of directors that it has effective BSA/AML compliance programs in place across the consolidated organization. Each program should reflect the organization's business structure and be tailored to its size, complexity, and legal requirements that may vary due to the specific business line or host country jurisdiction.[3]

The enterprise-wide program should include a central point where BSA/AML risks throughout the organization are aggregated. Structurally, the point of consolidation could be established at either the level of the holding company or the lead financial institution. Therefore, organizations that implement an enterprise-wide program should assess risk both individually within business lines and on a consolidated basis across all activities and legal entities. Enterprise-wide systems that operate on a global basis need to consider the various jurisdictions in which they operate as well as the AML laws and requirements they are subject to, and then incorporate these into their overall compliance program. Internal audit should assess the level of compliance with the enterprise-wide BSA/AML compliance program.

Examiners should be aware that some complex, diversified banking organizations may have various subsidiaries that hold different types of licenses and banking charters or may organize business activities and BSA/AML compliance program components across their legal entities. For instance, a highly diversified banking organization may consolidate all its funds transfer functions in a national bank subsidiary, while centralizing its audit function at the holding company. This arrangement may present a challenge to the examiner reviewing a legal entity within the organization, as it may be difficult to evaluate that entity's BSA/AML compliance.

Subsidiaries, Affiliates, and Business Lines

A holding company or a lead financial institution may decide to implement an enterprise-wide BSA/AML compliance program, either comprehensively or for specific business functions (e.g., audit or suspicious activity monitoring systems). Where business specific functions are so managed, examiners must identify during an examination or inspection, which portions of the BSA/AML compliance program are part of the enterprise-wide program. This information is critical when scoping and planning a BSA/AML examination.

When evaluating the enterprise-wide BSA/AML compliance program for adequacy, the examiner should determine reporting lines and how each subsidiary fits into the overall enterprise-wide compliance structure. This should include an assessment of how clearly roles and responsibilities are communicated across the organization. The examiner should assess how effectively the holding company or lead financial institution monitors the compliance throughout the organization with the enterprise-wide BSA/AML compliance program, including how well the enterprise-wide system captures relevant data from the subsidiaries.

The evaluation of the enterprise-wide BSA/AML compliance program should take into consideration available information about the adequacy of the individual subsidiaries' BSA/AML compliance program. Regardless of the decision to implement an enterprise- wide BSA/AML compliance program in whole, or in part, the program should ensure that all affiliates meet their applicable regulatory requirements. For example, an audit program implemented solely on an enterprise-wide basis that does not conduct transaction testing at all subsidiaries subject to the BSA would not be sufficient to meet regulatory requirements for independent testing for those subsidiaries.

Holding Company or Lead Financial Institution

Holding companies or lead financial institutions that centrally manage the operations and functions of their subsidiary banks, other subsidiaries, and business lines should ensure that comprehensive risk management policies, procedures, and processes are in place across the organization to address the entire organization's spectrum of risk. An adequate holding company or lead financial institution enterprise-wide BSA/AML compliance program provides the framework for all subsidiaries, business lines, and foreign branches to meet their specific regulatory requirements (e.g., country or industry requirements). Accordingly, organizations that centrally manage an enterprise-wide BSA/AML compliance program should among other things provide appropriate structure; advise the business lines, subsidiaries, and foreign branches on the development of appropriate guidelines; and set risk limits consistent with their domestic and international activities. For additional guidance, refer to the expanded overview section, "Foreign Branches and Offices of U.S. Banks," page 154.

Organizations that implement an enterprise-wide BSA/AML compliance program should assess risk on a consolidated basis across all activities, business lines, and legal entities. Once the organization appropriately assesses its risk on an enterprise-wide basis, this process should be ongoing. Business line subsidiaries and foreign branches should provide periodic updates to the risk assessment process to the central point within the holding company or lead financial institution. The risk assessment should serve as the basis for the development of risk-based policies, procedures, and processes within the activities, business lines, and legal entities. Subsidiary entities should advise the holding company or lead financial institution on the development of risk-based policies, procedures, and processes. After the policies, procedures, and processes are complete, they should be approved by the holding company or lead financial institution. Increasingly, organizations use software or programming solutions to assist in the implementation of the BSA/AML compliance program; these solutions typically include, but are not limited to, monitoring, identifying, and reporting suspicious activity.

Suspicious Activity Reporting

A bank holding company (BHC) or any non-bank subsidiary thereof, or a foreign financial institution that is subject to the BHC Act or any non-bank subsidiary of such a foreign financial institution operating in the United States, is required to file a Suspicious Activity Report (SAR) (12 CFR 225.4(f)). Certain savings and loan holding companies, and their non-depository subsidiaries, are required to file SARs pursuant to Treasury regulations (e.g., insurance companies (31 CFR 103.16) and broker/dealers (31 CFR 103.19)). In addition, savings and loan holding companies, if not required, are strongly encouraged to file SARs in appropriate circumstances.

Interagency guidance clarifies that banking organizations may share SARs with head offices and controlling companies, whether located in the United States or abroad.[4] The guidance does not address whether a banking organization may share a SAR with an affiliate other than a controlling company or head office. Therefore, banking organizations should not share SARs with such affiliates. However, in order to manage risks across the organization, banks may disclose to entities within their organization the underlying information supporting a SAR filing. Refer to the core overview section, "Suspicious Activity Reporting," page 60, for additional guidance.

EXAMINATION PROCEDURES

Enterprise-Wide BSA/AML Compliance Program

Objective. *Assess the organization's enterprise-wide program for BSA/AML compliance through the holding company or lead financial institution.*[5]

1. Confirm the existence and review the scope of any enterprise-wide BSA/AML compliance program. Communicate with peers at other federal and state banking agencies, as necessary, to confirm their understanding of the organization's BSA/AML compliance program. This approach promotes consistent supervision and lessens regulatory burden for the holding company or lead financial institution. Determine the extent to which the enterprise-wide BSA/AML compliance program affects the organization being examined, considering the following:
   - The existence of enterprise-wide operations or functions responsible for day-to-day BSA/AML operations, including, but not limited to, the centralization of suspicious activity monitoring and reporting, currency transaction reporting, currency exemption review and reporting, and recordkeeping activities.
   - The centralization of operational units, such as financial intelligence units, dedicated to and responsible for monitoring transactions across activities, business lines, or legal entities. (Assess the variety and extent of information that data or transaction sources (e.g., banks, broker/dealers, trust companies, Edge Act and agreement corporations, insurance companies, or foreign branches) are entering into the monitoring and reporting systems.)
   - The extent to which the holding company or lead financial institution (or other corporate-level unit, such as audit or compliance) performs regular independent testing of BSA/AML activities.
   - Whether a corporate-level unit sponsors BSA/AML training.

2. Review audits for BSA/AML compliance throughout the organization and identify program deficiencies.
3. Review board minutes to determine the adequacy of management information systems (MIS) and of reports provided to the board of directors. Ensure that the board of directors of the holding company has received appropriate notification of Suspicious Activity Reports (SARs) filed by the holding company.
4. Review policies, procedures, processes, and risk assessments formulated and implemented by the holding company's or lead financial institution's board of directors, a board committee thereof, or senior management. As part of this review, assess effectiveness of the holding company's or lead financial institution's ability to perform the following responsibilities:
   - Manage the enterprise-wide BSA/AML compliance program and provide adequate oversight and structure.
   - Promptly identify and effectively measure, monitor, and control key risks throughout the consolidated organization.
   - Develop an adequate enterprise-wide risk assessment and the policies, procedures, and processes to comprehensively manage those risks.
   - Develop procedures for evaluation, approval, and oversight of risk limits, new business initiatives, and strategic changes.
   - Oversee the compliance of subsidiaries with applicable regulatory requirements (e.g., country and industry requirements).
   - Oversee the compliance of subsidiaries with the requirements of the enterprise-wide BSA/AML compliance program, as established by the holding company or lead financial institution.
   - Identify enterprise-wide program weaknesses and implement necessary and timely corrective action, at both the holding company and subsidiary levels.
5. To ensure compliance with regulatory requirements,[6] review the holding company's or the lead financial institution's procedures for monitoring and filing SARs. Refer to the core overview and examination procedures, "Suspicious Activity Reporting," pages 60 and 71, respectively.
6. Once the examiner has completed the above procedures, the examiner should discuss their findings with the following parties, as appropriate:
   - Examiner in charge.
   - Person (or persons) responsible for ongoing supervision of the organization and subsidiary banks, as appropriate.
   - Corporate management.
7. On the basis of examination procedures completed, form a conclusion about the adequacy of policies, procedures, and processes associated with an enterprise-wide BSA/AML compliance program.

FOREIGN BRANCHES AND OFFICES OF U.S. BANKS — OVERVIEW

Objective. *Assess the adequacy of the U.S. bank's systems to manage the risks associated with its foreign branches and offices, and management's ability to implement effective monitoring and reporting systems.*

U.S. banks open foreign branches and offices[7] to meet specific customer demands, to help the bank grow, or to expand products or services offered. Foreign branches and offices vary significantly in size, complexity of operations, and scope of products and services offered. Examiners must take these factors into consideration when reviewing the foreign branches and offices AML compliance program. The definitions of "financial institution" and "bank" in the BSA and its implementing regulations do not encompass foreign offices or foreign investments of U.S. banks or Edge and agreement corporations.[8] Nevertheless, banks are expected to have policies, procedures, and processes in place at all their branches and offices to protect against risks of money laundering and terrorist financing.[9] AML policies, procedures, and processes at the foreign office or branch should comply with local requirements and be consistent with the U.S. bank's standards; however, they may need to be tailored for local or business practices.[10]

Risk Factors

Examiners should understand the type of products and services offered at foreign branches and offices, as well as the customers and geographic locations served at the foreign branches and offices. Any service offered by the U.S. bank may be offered by the foreign branches and offices if not prohibited by the host country. Such products and services offered at the foreign branches and offices may have a different risk profile from that of the same product or service offered in the U.S. bank (e.g., money services businesses are regulated in the United States; however, similar entities in another country may not be regulated). Therefore, the examiner should be aware that risks associated with foreign branches and offices may differ (e.g., wholesale versus retail operations).

The examiner should understand the foreign jurisdiction's various AML requirements. Secrecy laws or their equivalent may affect the ability of the foreign branch or office to share information with the U.S. parent bank, or the ability of the examiner to examine on- site. While banking organizations with overseas branches or subsidiaries may find it necessary to tailor monitoring approaches as a result of local privacy laws, the compliance oversight mechanism should ensure it can effectively assess and monitor risks within such branches and subsidiaries. Although specific BSA requirements are not applicable at foreign branches and offices, banks are expected to have policies, procedures, and processes in place at all their branches and offices to protect against risks of money laundering and terrorist financing. In this regard, foreign branches and offices should be guided by the U.S. bank's BSA/AML policies, procedures, and processes. The foreign branches and offices must comply with OFAC requirements and all local AML- related laws, rules, and regulations.

Risk Mitigation

Branches and offices of U.S. banks located in high-risk geographic locations may be vulnerable to abuse by money launderers. To address this concern, the U.S. bank's policies, procedures, and processes for the foreign operation should be consistent with the following recommendations:

- The U.S. bank's head office and management at the foreign operation should understand the effectiveness and quality of bank supervision in the host country and understand the legal and regulatory requirements of the host country. The U.S. bank's head office should be aware of and understand any concerns that the host country supervisors may have with respect to the foreign branch or office.
- The U.S. bank's head office should understand the foreign branches' or offices' risk profile (e.g., products, services, customers, and geographic locations).
- The U.S. bank's head office and management should have access to sufficient information in order to periodically monitor the activity of their foreign branches and offices, including the offices' and branches' level of compliance with head office policies, procedures, and processes. Some of this may be achieved through management information systems reports.
- The U.S. bank's head office should develop a system for testing and verifying the integrity and effectiveness of internal controls at the foreign branches or offices by conducting in-country audits. Senior management at the head office should obtain and review copies, written in English, of audit reports and any other reports related to AML and internal control evaluations.
- The U.S. bank's head office should establish robust information-sharing practices between branches and offices, particularly regarding high-risk account relationships.
- The U.S. bank's head office should be able to provide examiners with any information deemed necessary to assess compliance with U.S. banking laws.

Foreign branch and office compliance and audit structures can vary substantially based on the scope of operations (e.g., geographic locations) and the type of products, services, and customers. Foreign branches and offices with multiple locations within a geographic region (e.g., Europe, Asia, and South America) are frequently overseen by regional compliance and audit staff. Regardless of the size or scope of operations, the compliance and audit staff and audit programs should be sufficient to oversee the AML risks.

Scoping AML Examinations

Examinations may be completed in the host country or in the United States. The factors that will be considered in deciding whether the examination work should occur in the host jurisdiction or the United States include:

- The risk profile of the foreign branch or office and whether the profile is stable or changing as a result of a reorganization, the introduction of new products or services, or other factors, including the risk profile of the jurisdiction itself.

- The effectiveness and quality of bank supervision in the host country.
- Existence of an information-sharing arrangement between the host country and the U.S. supervisor.
- The history of examination or audit concerns at the foreign branch or office.
- The size and complexity of the foreign branch's or office's operations.
- Effectiveness of internal controls, including systems for managing AML risks on a consolidated basis and internal audit.
- The capability of management at the foreign branch or office to protect the entity from money laundering or terrorist financing.
- The availability of the foreign branch or office records in the United States.

In some jurisdictions, financial secrecy and other laws may prevent or severely limit U.S. examiners or U.S. head office staff from directly evaluating customer activity or records. In cases when an on-site examination cannot be conducted effectively, examiners should consult with appropriate agency personnel. In such cases, agency personnel may contact foreign supervisors to make appropriate information sharing or examination arrangements. In low-risk situations when information is restricted, examiners may conduct U.S.-based examinations (see discussion below). In high-risk situations when adequate examinations (on-site or otherwise) cannot be effected, the agency may require the head office to take action to address the situation, which may include closing the foreign office.

U.S.-Based Examinations

U.S.-based, or off-site, examinations generally require greater confidence in the AML program at the foreign branch or office, as well as the ability to access sufficient records. Such off-site examinations should include discussions with senior bank management at the head and foreign office. These discussions are crucial to the understanding of the foreign branches' or offices' operations, AML risks, and AML programs. Also, the examination of the foreign branch or office should include a review of the U.S. bank's involvement in managing or monitoring the foreign branch's operations, internal control systems (e.g., policies, procedures, and monitoring reports), and, where available, the host country supervisors' examination findings, audit findings, and workpapers. As with all BSA/AML examinations, the extent of transaction testing and activities where it is performed is based on various factors including the examiner's judgment of risks, controls, and the adequacy of the independent testing.

Host Jurisdiction-Based Examinations

On-site work in the host jurisdiction enables examiners not only to better understand the role of the U.S. bank in relation to its foreign branch or office but also, perhaps more importantly, permit examiners to determine the extent to which the U.S. bank's global policies, procedures, and processes are being followed locally.

The standard scoping and planning process will determine the focus of the examination and the resource needs. There may be some differences in the examination process conducted abroad. The host supervisory authority may send an examiner to join the U.S. team or request attendance at meetings at the beginning and at the conclusion of the examination. AML reporting requirements also are likely to be different, as they will be adjusted to local regulatory requirements.

For both U.S.-based and host-based examinations of foreign branches and offices, the procedures used for specific products, services, and customers are those found in this manual. For example, if an examiner is looking at pouch activities at foreign branches and offices, he or she should use applicable expanded examination procedures.

EXAMINATION PROCEDURES

Foreign Branches and Offices of U.S. Banks

Objective. *Assess the adequacy of the U.S. bank's systems to manage the risks associated with its foreign branches and offices, and management's ability to implement effective monitoring and reporting systems.*

1. Review the policies, procedures, and processes related to foreign branches and offices[11] to evaluate their adequacy given the activity in relation to the bank's risk, and assess whether the controls are adequate to reasonably protect the bank from money laundering and terrorist financing.
2. On the basis of a review of management information systems (MIS) and internal risk rating factors, determine whether the U.S. bank's head office effectively identifies and monitors foreign branches and offices, particularly those conducting high-risk transactions or located in high-risk jurisdictions.
3. Determine whether the U.S. bank's head office system for monitoring foreign branches and offices and detecting unusual or suspicious activities at those branches and offices is adequate given the bank's size, complexity, location, and types of customer relationships. Determine whether the host country requires reporting of suspicious activities and, if permitted and available, review those reports. Determine whether this information is provided to the U.S. bank's head office and filtered into a bank-wide or, if appropriate, an enterprise-wide assessment of suspicious activities.
4. Review the bank's tiering or organizational structure report, which should include a list of all legal entities and the countries in which they are registered. Determine the locations of foreign branches and offices, including the foreign regulatory environment and the degree of access by U.S. regulators for on-site examinations and customer records.
5. Review any partnering or outsourcing relationships of foreign branches and offices. Determine whether the relationship is consistent with the bank's AML program.
6. Determine the type of products, services, customers, and geographic locations served by the foreign branches and offices. Review the risk assessments of the foreign branches and offices.
7. Review the management, compliance, and audit structure of the foreign branches and offices. Identify the decisions that are made at the bank's U.S. head office level versus those that are made at the foreign branch or office.

8. Determine the involvement of the U.S. bank's head office in managing and monitoring foreign branches and offices. Conduct a preliminary evaluation of the foreign branches or offices through discussions with senior management at the U.S. bank's head office (e.g., operations, customers, jurisdictions, products, services, management strategies, audit programs, anticipated product lines, management changes, branch expansions, AML risks, and AML programs). Similar discussions should occur with management of the foreign branches and offices, particularly those that may be considered higher risk.
9. Coordinate with the host country supervisor and, if applicable, U.S. federal and state regulatory agencies. Discuss their assessment of the foreign branches' and offices' compliance with local laws. Determine whether there are any restrictions on materials that may be reviewed, copied, or taken out of the country.
10. If available, review the following:
    - Previous regulatory examination reports.
    - Host country's regulatory examination report.
    - Audit reports and supporting documentation.
    - Compliance reviews and supporting documentation.
11. If appropriate, refer to the core examination procedures, "Office of Foreign Assets Control," page 144, for guidance.

Transaction Testing

12. Make a determination whether transaction testing is feasible. If feasible on the basis of the bank's risk assessment of this activity and prior examination and audit reports, select a sample of high-risk foreign branch and office activity. Complete transaction testing from appropriate expanded examination procedures sections (e.g., pouch activity).
13. On the basis of examination procedures completed, including transaction testing, form a conclusion about the adequacy of policies, procedures, and processes associated with the U.S. bank's foreign branches and offices.

Parallel Banking — Overview

Objective. *Assess the adequacy of the bank's systems to manage the risks associated with parallel banking relationships, and management's ability to implement effective due diligence, monitoring, and reporting systems.*

A parallel banking organization exists when at least one U.S. bank and one foreign financial institution are controlled either directly or indirectly by the same person or group of persons who are closely associated in their business dealings or otherwise acting together, but are not subject to consolidated supervision by a single home country supervisor. The foreign financial institution will be subject to different money laundering rules and regulations and a different supervisory oversight structure, both of which may be less stringent than in the

United States. The regulatory and supervisory differences heighten the BSA/AML risk associated with parallel banking organizations.

Risk Factors

Parallel banking organizations may have common management, share policies and procedures, cross-sell products, or generally be linked to a foreign parallel financial institution in a number of ways. The key money laundering concern regarding parallel banking organizations is that the U.S. bank may be exposed to greater risk through transactions with the foreign parallel financial institution. Transactions may be facilitated and risks heightened because of the lack of arm's-length dealing or reduced controls on transactions between banks that are linked or closely associated. For example, officers or directors may be common to both entities or may be different but nonetheless work together.[12]

Risk Mitigation

The U.S. bank's policies, procedures, and processes for parallel banking relationships should be consistent with those for other foreign correspondent bank relationships. In addition, parallel banks should:

- Provide for independent lines of decision-making authority.
- Guard against conflicts of interest.
- Ensure independent and arm's-length dealings between the related entities.

Examination Procedures

Parallel Banking

Objective. *Assess the adequacy of the bank's systems to manage the risks associated with parallel banking relationships, and management's ability to implement effective due diligence, monitoring, and reporting systems.*

1. Determine whether parallel banking relationships exist through discussions with management or by reviewing inter-party activities involving the bank and another foreign financial institution. Review the policies, procedures, and processes related to parallel banking relationships. Evaluate the adequacy of the policies, procedures, and processes given the bank's parallel banking activities and the risks they present. Assess whether the controls are adequate to reasonably protect the bank from money laundering and terrorist financing.
2. Determine whether there are any conflicts of interest or differences in policies, procedures, and processes between parallel bank relationships and other foreign

correspondent bank relationships. Particular consideration should be given to funds transfer, pouch, and payable through activities because these activities are more vulnerable to money laundering. If the bank engages in any of these activities, examiners should consider completing applicable expanded examination procedures that address each of these topics.

3. From a review of management information systems (MIS) and internal risk rating factors, determine whether the bank effectively identifies and monitors parallel banking relationships, particularly those that pose a high-risk for money laundering.
4. Determine whether the bank's system for monitoring parallel banking relationships for suspicious activities, and for reporting suspicious activities, is adequate given the bank's size, complexity, location, and types of customer relationships.
5. If appropriate, refer to the core examination procedures, "Office of Foreign Assets Control," page 144, for guidance.

Transaction Testing

6. On the basis of the bank's risk assessment of its parallel banking activities, as well as prior examination and audit reports, select a sample of high-risk activities from parallel banking relationships (e.g., foreign correspondent banking, funds transfer, payable through accounts, and pouch).
7. Consider the location of the foreign parallel financial institution. If the jurisdiction is high risk, examiners should review a larger sample of transactions between the two institutions. Banks doing business with parallel foreign banking organizations in countries not designated as high risk may still require enhanced due diligence, but that determination will be based on the size, nature, and type of the transactions between the institutions.
8. On the basis of examination procedures completed, including transaction testing, form a conclusion about the adequacy of policies, procedures, and processes associated with parallel banking organizations. Focus on whether controls exist to ensure independent and arm's-length dealings between the two entities. If significant concerns are raised about the relationship between the two entities, recommend that this information be forwarded to the appropriate supervisory authorities.

End Notes

[1] The lead financial institution is the largest financial institution in the holding company structure in terms of assets unless otherwise designated by the holding company.

[2] For additional guidance, refer to the expanded overview section, "Foreign Branches and Offices of U.S. Banks," page 154, and the Basel Committee on Bank Supervision's guidance "Consolidated Know Your Customer (KYC) Risk Management."

[3] Policies and procedures at the branch or subsidiary level should be consistent with, although not necessarily identical to, group or holding company standards.

[4] "Interagency Guidance on Sharing Suspicious Activity Reports with Head Offices and Controlling Companies," issued by Financial Crimes Enforcement Network, Board of Governors of the Federal Reserve System, Federal Deposit Insurance Corporation, Office of the Comptroller of the Currency, and Office of Thrift Supervision, January 20, 2006.

[5] The lead financial institution is the largest financial institution in the holding company structure in terms of assets unless otherwise designated by the holding company.

[6] Bank holding companies (BHCs) or any non-bank subsidiary thereof, or a foreign bank that is subject to the BHC Act or any non-bank subsidiary of such a foreign bank operating in the United States, are required to file SARs (12 CFR 225.4(f)). Certain savings and loan holding companies, and their non-depository subsidiaries, are required to file SARs pursuant to Treasury regulations (e.g., insurance companies (31 CFR 103.16) and broker/dealers (31 CFR 103.19)). In addition, savings and loan holding companies, if not required, are strongly encouraged to file SARs in appropriate circumstances. On January 20, 2006, the Financial Crimes Enforcement Network, Board of Governors of the Federal Reserve System, Federal Deposit Insurance Corporation, Office of the Comptroller of the Currency, and the Office of Thrift Supervision issued guidance authorizing banking organizations to share SARs with head offices and controlling companies, whether located in the United States or abroad. Refer to the core overview section, "Suspicious Activity Reporting," page 60, for additional information.

[7] Foreign offices include affiliates and subsidiaries.

[8] Edge and agreement corporations may be used to hold foreign investments (e.g., foreign portfolio investments, joint ventures, or subsidiaries).

[9] 71 *Federal Register* 13935.

[10] For additional information, refer to "Consolidated Know Your Customer (KYC) Risk Management," Basel Committee on Banking Supervision, 2004, at www.bis.org/publ.

[11] Foreign offices include affiliates and subsidiaries.

[12] For additional risks associated with parallel banking refer to the "Joint Agency Statement on Parallel- Owned Banking Organizations" issued by the Board of Governors of the Federal Reserve System, Federal Deposit Insurance Corporation, Office of the Comptroller of the Currency, and Office of Thrift Supervision, April 23, 2002.

In: The Bank Secrecy Act and Anti-Money Laundering... ISBN: 978-1-60876-162-3
Editor: Anne Leuter

Chapter 5

EXPANDED EXAMINATION OVERVIEW AND PROCEDURES FOR PRODUCTS AND SERVICES

CORRESPONDENT ACCOUNTS (DOMESTIC) — OVERVIEW

Objective. *Assess the adequacy of the bank's systems to manage the risks associated with offering domestic correspondent account relationships, and management's ability to implement effective monitoring and reporting systems.*

Banks maintain correspondent relationships at other domestic banks to provide certain services that can be performed more economically or efficiently because of the other bank's size, expertise in a specific line of business, or geographic location. Such services may include:

- **Deposit accounts.** Assets known as "due from bank deposits" or "correspondent bank balances" may represent the bank's primary operating account.

- **Funds transfers.** A transfer of funds between banks may result from the collection of checks or other cash items, transfer and settlement of securities transactions, transfer of participating loan funds, purchase or sale of federal funds, or processing of customer transactions.

- **Other services.** Services include processing loan participations, facilitating secondary market loan sales, performing data processing and payroll services, and exchanging foreign currency.

Bankers' Banks

A bankers' bank, which is organized and chartered to do business with other banks, is generally owned by the banks it services. Bankers' banks, which do not conduct business directly with the public, offer correspondent banking services to independent community banks, thrifts, credit unions, and real estate investment trusts. Bankers' banks provide services directly, through outsourcing arrangements, or by sponsoring or endorsing third parties. The products bankers' banks offer normally consist of traditional correspondent banking services. Bankers' banks should have risk-based policies, procedures, and processes to manage the BSA/AML risks involved in these correspondent relationships to detect and report suspicious activities.

Generally, a bankers' bank will sign a service agreement with the respondent bank[1] outlining each party's responsibilities. The service agreement may include the following:

- Products and services provided.
- Responsibility for recordkeeping (e.g., Currency Transaction Reports (CTRS) filed).
- Responsibility for task performed (e.g., OFAC filtering).
- Review of oversight documentation (e.g., audit and consultants reports).

Risk Factors

Because domestic banks must follow the same regulatory requirements, BSA/AML risks in domestic correspondent banking, including bankers' banks, are minimal in comparison to other types of financial services, especially for proprietary accounts (i.e., the domestic bank is using the correspondent account for its own transactions). Each bank, however, has its own approach for conducting its BSA/AML compliance program, including customer due diligence, management information systems, account monitoring, and reporting suspicious activities. Furthermore, while a domestic correspondent account may not be considered high risk, transactions through the account, which may be conducted on behalf of the respondent's customer, may be high risk. Money laundering risks can be heightened when a respondent bank allows its customers to direct or execute transactions through the correspondent account, especially when such transactions are directed or executed through an ostensibly proprietary account.

The correspondent bank also faces heightened risks when providing direct currency shipments for customers of respondent banks. This is not to imply that such activities necessarily entail money laundering, but these direct currency shipments should be appropriately monitored for unusual and suspicious activity. Without such a monitoring system, the correspondent bank is essentially providing these direct services to an unknown customer.

Risk Mitigation

Banks that offer correspondent bank services to respondent banks should have policies, procedures, and processes to manage the BSA/AML risks involved in these correspondent relationships and to detect and report suspicious activities. Banks should ascertain whether domestic correspondent accounts are proprietary or allow third-party transactions. When the respondent bank allows third-party customers to transact business through the correspondent account, the correspondent bank should ensure that it understands the due diligence and monitoring procedures applied by the respondent on its customers that will be utilizing the account.

The level of risk varies depending on the services provided and the types of transactions conducted through the account and the respondent bank's BSA/AML compliance program, products, services, customers, and geographic locations. Each bank should appropriately monitor transactions of domestic correspondent accounts relative to the level of assessed risk. In addition, domestic banks are independently responsible for OFAC compliance for any transactions that flow through their banks. Appropriate filtering should be in place. Refer to core overview section and examination procedures, "Office of Foreign Assets Control," pages 135 and 144, respectively.

EXAMINATION PROCEDURES

Correspondent Accounts (Domestic)

Objective. *Assess the adequacy of the bank's systems to manage the risks associated with offering domestic correspondent account relationships, and management's ability to implement effective monitoring and reporting systems.*

1. Review the policies, procedures, and processes, and any bank service agreements related to domestic correspondent banking relationships. Evaluate the adequacy of the policies, procedures, and processes given the bank's domestic correspondent accounts and the risks they present. Assess whether the controls are adequate to reasonably protect the bank from money laundering and terrorist financing.
2. From a review of management information systems (MIS) and internal risk rating factors, determine whether the bank has identified any domestic correspondent banking activities as high risk.
3. Determine whether the bank's system for monitoring domestic correspondent accounts for suspicious activities, and for reporting suspicious activities, is adequate given the bank's size, complexity, location, and types of customer relationships.
4. If appropriate, refer to the core examination procedures, "Office of Foreign Assets Control," page 144, for guidance.

Transaction Testing

5. On the basis of the bank's review of respondent accounts[2] with unusual or high-risk activity, its risk assessment, and prior examination and audit reports, select a sample of respondent accounts. From the sample selected, perform the following examination procedures:
   - Review bank statements for domestic correspondent accounts.
   - Review large or unusual transactions to determine their nature. As necessary, obtain and review copies of credit or debit advices, general ledger tickets, and other supporting documentation.
   - Note any currency shipments or deposits made on behalf of a respondent bank's customer. Based on this information determine whether:

     Currency shipments are adequately documented.

     The respondent bank has performed due diligence on customers that conduct large currency transactions.

     Currency Transaction Reports (CTRs) are properly filed and activity is commensurate with expected activity.
6. Review the bank statements for domestic correspondent account records, or telex records of accounts controlled by the same person for large deposits of cashier's checks, money orders, or similar instruments drawn on other banks in amounts under $10,000. These funds may possibly be transferred elsewhere in bulk amounts. Note whether the instruments under $10,000 are sequentially numbered.
7. On the basis of examination procedures completed, including transaction testing, form a conclusion about the adequacy of policies, procedures, and processes associated with domestic correspondent bank relationships.

CORRESPONDENT ACCOUNTS (FOREIGN) — OVERVIEW

Objective. *Assess the adequacy of the U.S. bank's systems to manage the risks associated with foreign correspondent banking and management's ability to implement effective due diligence, monitoring, and reporting systems. This section expands the earlier core review of statutory and regulatory requirements of foreign correspondent account relationships in order to provide a broader assessment of the AML risks associated with this activity.*

Foreign financial institutions maintain accounts at U.S. banks to gain access to the U.S. financial system and to take advantage of services and products that may not be available in the foreign financial institution's jurisdiction. These services may be performed more economically or efficiently by the U.S. bank or may be necessary for other reasons, such as the facilitation of international trade. Services may include:

- Cash management services, including deposit accounts.
- International funds transfers.
- Check clearing.
- Payable through accounts.

- Pouch activities.
- Foreign exchange services.
- Overnight investment accounts (sweep accounts).
- Loans and letters of credit.

Contractual Agreements

Each relationship that a U.S. bank has with a foreign correspondent financial institution should be governed by an agreement or a contract describing each party's responsibilities and other relationship details (e.g., products and services provided, acceptance of deposits, clearing of items, forms of payment, and acceptable forms of endorsement). The agreement or contract should also consider the foreign financial institution's AML regulatory requirements, customer base, due diligence procedures, and allowable third- party usage of the correspondent account.

Risk Factors

Some foreign financial institutions are not subject to the same or similar regulatory guidelines as U.S. banks; therefore, these foreign institutions may pose a higher money laundering risk to their respective U.S. bank correspondent(s). Investigations have disclosed that, in the past, foreign correspondent accounts have been used by drug traffickers and other criminal elements to launder funds. Shell companies are sometimes used in the layering process to hide the true ownership of accounts at foreign correspondent financial institutions. Because of the large amount of funds, multiple transactions, and the U.S. bank's potential lack of familiarity with the foreign correspondent financial institution's customer, criminals and terrorists can more easily conceal the source and use of illicit funds. Consequently, each U.S. bank, including all overseas branches, offices, and subsidiaries, should closely monitor transactions related to foreign correspondent accounts.

Without adequate controls, a U.S. bank may also set up a traditional correspondent account with a foreign financial institution and not be aware that the foreign financial institution is permitting some customers to conduct transactions anonymously through the U.S. bank account (e.g., payable through accounts[3] and nested accounts).

Nested Accounts

Nested accounts occur when a foreign financial institution gains access to the U.S. financial system by operating through a U.S. correspondent account belonging to another foreign financial institution. If the U.S. bank is unaware that its foreign correspondent financial institution customer is providing such access to third-party foreign financial institutions, these third-party financial institutions can effectively gain anonymous access to the U.S. financial system. Behavior indicative of nested accounts and other accounts of concern includes transactions to jurisdictions in which the foreign financial institution has no known business activities or interests and transactions in which the total volume significantly exceeds expected activity for the foreign financial institution, considering its customer base or asset size.

Risk Mitigation

U.S. banks that offer foreign correspondent financial institution services should have policies, procedures, and processes to manage the BSA/AML risks inherent with these relationships and should closely monitor transactions related to these accounts to detect and report suspicious activities. The level of risk varies depending on the foreign financial institution's products, services, customers, and geographic locations. Additional information relating to risk assessments and due diligence is contained in the core overview section, "Foreign Correspondent Account Recordkeeping and Due Diligence," page 105. The U.S. bank's policies, procedures, and processes should:

- Understand the intended use of the accounts and expected account activity (e.g., determine whether the relationship will serve as a payable through account).
- Understand the foreign correspondent financial institution's other correspondent relationships (e.g., determine whether nested accounts will be utilized).
- Assess the risks posed by the foreign correspondent financial institution relationships.
- Conduct adequate and ongoing due diligence on the foreign correspondent financial institution relationships, which may include periodic visits.
- Ensure foreign correspondent financial institution relationships are appropriately included within the U.S. bank's suspicious activity monitoring and reporting systems.
- Establish criteria for closing the foreign correspondent financial institution account.

As a sound practice, U.S. banks are encouraged to communicate their AML-related expectations to their foreign correspondent financial institution customers. Moreover, the U.S. bank should generally understand the AML controls at the foreign correspondent financial institution, including customer due diligence practices and recordkeeping documentation.

EXAMINATION PROCEDURES

Correspondent Accounts (Foreign)

Objective. *Assess the adequacy of the U.S. bank's systems to manage the risks associated with foreign correspondent banking and management's ability to implement effective due diligence, monitoring, and reporting systems. This section expands the earlier core review of statutory and regulatory requirements of foreign correspondent account relationships in order to provide a broader assessment of the AML risks associated with this activity.*

1. Review the policies, procedures, and processes related to foreign correspondent financial institution account relationships. Evaluate the adequacy of the policies, procedures, and processes. Assess whether the controls are adequate to reasonably protect the U.S. bank from money laundering and terrorist financing.
2. From a review of management information systems (MIS) and internal risk-rating factors, determine whether the U.S. bank effectively identifies and monitors foreign correspondent financial institution account relationships, particularly those that pose a higher risk for money laundering.
3. If the U.S. bank has a standardized foreign correspondent agreement, review a sample agreement to determine whether each party's responsibilities, products, and services provided, and allowable third party usage of the correspondent account, are covered under the contractual arrangement. If the U.S. bank does not have a standardized agreement, refer to the transaction testing examination procedures.
4. Determine whether the U.S. bank's system for monitoring foreign correspondent financial institution account relationships for suspicious activities, and for reporting suspicious activities, is adequate given the U.S. bank's size, complexity, location, and types of customer relationships.
5. If appropriate, refer to the core examination procedures, "Office of Foreign Assets Control," page 144, for guidance.

Transaction Testing

6. On the basis of the U.S. bank's risk assessment of its foreign correspondent activities, as well as prior examination and audit reports, select a sample of high-risk foreign correspondent financial institution account relationships. The high-risk sample should include relationships with foreign financial institutions located in jurisdictions that do not cooperate with international AML efforts and in other jurisdictions as designated by the U.S. bank, including correspondent accounts for small financial institutions. From the sample selected, perform the following examination procedures:
   - Review a foreign correspondent agreement or contract that delineates each party's responsibilities and the products and services provided.
   - Review U.S. bank statements for foreign correspondent accounts and, as necessary, specific transaction details. Compare expected transactions with actual activity.
   - Determine whether actual activity is consistent with the nature of the customer's business. Identify any unusual or suspicious activity.
   - Review large or unusual transactions to determine their nature. As necessary, obtain and review copies of credit or debit advices, general ledger tickets, and other supporting documentation.
   - Analyze transactions to identify behavior indicative of nested accounts, intermediary or clearing agent services, or other services for third-party foreign financial institutions that have not been clearly identified.

7. On the basis of examination procedures completed, including transaction testing, form a conclusion about the adequacy of policies, procedures, and processes associated with foreign correspondent financial institution relationships.

U.S. DOLLAR DRAFTS — OVERVIEW

Objective. *Assess the adequacy of the bank's systems to manage the risks associated with U.S. dollar drafts, and management's ability to implement effective monitoring and reporting systems.*

A U.S. dollar draft is a bank draft or check denominated in U.S. dollars and made available at foreign financial institutions. These drafts are drawn on a U.S. correspondent account by a foreign financial institution. Drafts are frequently purchased to pay for commercial or personal transactions and to settle overseas obligations.

Risk Factors

The majority of U.S dollar drafts are legitimate; however, drafts have proven to be vulnerable to money laundering abuse. Such schemes involving U.S. dollar drafts could involve the smuggling of U.S. currency to a foreign financial institution for the purchase of a check or draft denominated in U.S. dollars. The foreign financial institution accepts the U.S. currency and issues a U.S. dollar draft drawn against its U.S. correspondent bank account. Once the currency is in bank draft form, the money launderer can more easily conceal the source of funds. The ability to convert illicit proceeds to a bank draft at a foreign financial institution makes it easier for a money launderer to transport the instrument either back into the United States or to endorse it to a third party in a jurisdiction where money laundering laws or compliance are lax. In any case, the individual has laundered illicit proceeds; ultimately, the draft or check will be returned for processing at the U.S. correspondent bank.

Risk Mitigation

A U.S. bank's policies, procedures, and processes should include the following:

- Outline criteria for opening a U.S. dollar draft relationship with a foreign financial institution or entity (e.g., jurisdiction; products, services, target market; purpose of account and anticipated activity; or customer history).
- Detail acceptable and unacceptable transactions (e.g., structuring transactions or the purchase of multiple sequentially numbered drafts for the same payee).
- Detail the monitoring and reporting of suspicious activity associated with U.S. dollar drafts.
- Discuss criteria for closing U.S. dollar draft relationships.

EXAMINATION PROCEDURES

U.S. Dollar Drafts

Objective. *Assess the adequacy of the bank's systems to manage the risks associated with U.S. dollar drafts, and management's ability to implement effective monitoring and reporting systems.*

1. Review the policies, procedures, and processes related to U.S. dollar drafts. Evaluate the adequacy of the policies, procedures, and processes given the bank's U.S. dollar draft activities and the risks they present. Assess whether the controls are adequate to reasonably protect the bank from money laundering and terrorist financing. Determine whether policies address the following:
   - Criteria for allowing a foreign financial institution or entity to issue the U.S. bank's dollar drafts (e.g., jurisdiction; products, services, and target markets; purpose of account and anticipated activity; customer history; and other available information).
   - Identification of unusual transactions (e.g., structuring transactions or the purchase of multiple sequentially numbered U.S. dollar drafts to the same payee).
   - Criteria for ceasing U.S. dollar draft issuance through a foreign financial institution or entity.
2. From a review of management information systems (MIS) and internal risk rating factors, determine whether the bank effectively identifies and monitors high-risk U.S. dollar draft accounts.
3. Determine whether the bank's system for monitoring U.S. dollar draft accounts for suspicious activities, and for reporting suspicious activities, is adequate given the bank's size, complexity, location, and types of customer relationships.
4. Obtain a list of foreign bank correspondent accounts in which U.S. dollar drafts are offered. Review the volume, by number and dollar amount, of monthly transactions for each account. Determine whether management has appropriately assessed risk.

Transaction Testing

5. On the basis of the bank's risk assessment of its U.S. dollar draft activities, as well as prior examination and audit reports, select a sample of foreign correspondent bank accounts in which U.S. dollar drafts are processed. In the sample selected, include accounts with a high volume of U.S. dollar draft activity. From the sample selected, perform the following examination procedures:
   - Review transactions for sequentially numbered U.S. dollar drafts to the same payee or from the same remitter. Research any unusual or suspicious U.S. dollar draft transactions.

- Review the bank's contracts and agreements with foreign correspondent banks. Determine whether contracts address procedures for processing and clearing U.S. dollar drafts.
- Verify that the bank has obtained and reviewed information about the foreign financial institution's home country AML regulatory requirements (e.g., customer identification and suspicious activity reporting).

6. On the basis of examination procedures completed, including transaction testing, form a conclusion about the adequacy of policies, procedures, and processes associated with U.S. dollar drafts.

PAYABLE THROUGH ACCOUNTS — OVERVIEW

Objective. *Assess the adequacy of the bank's systems to manage the risks associated with payable through accounts (PTAs), and management's ability to implement effective monitoring and reporting systems.*

Foreign financial institutions use PTAs, also known as "pass-through" or "pass-by" accounts, to provide their customers with access to the U.S. banking system. Some U.S. banks, Edge Act and agreement corporations, and U.S. branches and agencies of foreign financial institutions (collectively referred to as U.S. banks) offer these accounts as a service to foreign financial institutions. Law enforcement authorities have stated that the risk of money laundering and other illicit activities is high in PTA accounts that are not adequately controlled.

Generally, a foreign financial institution requests a PTA for its customers that want to conduct banking transactions in the United States through the foreign financial institution's account at a U.S. bank. The foreign financial institution provides its customers, commonly referred to as "sub-accountholders," with checks that allow them to draw funds from the foreign financial institution's account at the U.S. bank.[4] The sub-accountholders, which may number several hundred or in the thousands for one PTA, all become signatories on the foreign financial institution's account at the U.S. bank. While payable through customers are able to write checks and make deposits at a bank in the United States like any other accountholder, they might not be directly subject to the bank's account opening requirements in the United States.

PTA activities should not be confused with traditional international correspondent banking relationships, in which a foreign financial institution enters into an agreement with a U.S. bank to process and complete transactions on behalf of the foreign financial institution and its customers. Under the latter correspondent arrangement, the foreign financial institution's customers do not have direct access to the correspondent account at the U.S. bank, but they do transact business through the U.S. bank. This arrangement differs significantly from a PTA with sub-accountholders who have direct access to the U.S. bank by virtue of their independent ability to conduct transactions with the U.S. bank through the PTA.

Risk Factors

PTAs may be prone to higher risk because U.S. banks do not typically implement the same due diligence requirements for PTAs that they require of domestic customers who want to open checking and other accounts. For example, some U.S. banks merely request a copy of signature cards completed by the payable through customers (the customer of the foreign financial institution). These U.S. banks then process thousands of sub- accountholder checks and other transactions, including currency deposits, through the foreign financial institution's PTA. In most cases, little or no independent effort is expended to obtain or confirm information about the individual and business sub- accountholders that use the PTAs.

Foreign financial institutions' use of PTAs, coupled with inadequate oversight by U.S. banks, may facilitate unsound banking practices, including money laundering and related criminal activities. The potential for facilitating money laundering or terrorist financing, OFAC violations, and other serious crimes increases when a U.S. bank is unable to identify and adequately understand the transactions of the ultimate users (all or most of whom are outside of the United States) of its account with a foreign correspondent. PTAs used for illegal purposes can cause banks serious financial losses in criminal and civil fines and penalties, seizure or forfeiture of collateral, and reputation damage.

Risk Mitigation

U.S. banks offering PTA services should develop and maintain adequate policies, procedures, and processes to guard against possible illicit use of these accounts. At a minimum, policies, procedures, and processes should enable each U.S. bank to identify the ultimate users of its foreign financial institution PTA and should include the bank's obtaining (or having the ability to obtain through a trusted third-party arrangement) substantially the same information on the ultimate PTA users as it obtains on its direct customers.

Policies, procedures, and processes should include a review of the foreign financial institution's processes for identifying and monitoring the transactions of sub- accountholders and for complying with any AML statutory and regulatory requirements existing in the host country and the foreign financial institution's master agreement with the U.S. bank. In addition, U.S. banks should have procedures for monitoring transactions conducted in foreign financial institutions' PTAs.

In an effort to address the risk inherent in PTAs, U.S. banks should have a signed contract (i.e., master agreement) that includes:

- Roles and responsibilities of each party.
- Limits or restrictions on transaction types and amounts (e.g., currency deposits, funds transfers, check cashing).
- Restrictions on types of sub-accountholders (e.g., casas de cambio, finance companies, funds remitters, or other non-bank financial institutions).
- Prohibitions or restrictions on multi-tier sub-accountholders.[5]
- Access to the foreign financial institution's internal documents and audits that pertain to its PTA activity.

U.S. banks should consider closing the PTA in the following circumstances:

- Insufficient information on the ultimate PTA users.
- Evidence of substantive or ongoing suspicious activity.
- Inability to ensure that the PTAs are not being used for money laundering or other illicit purposes.

Examination Procedures

Payable through Accounts

Objective. *Assess the adequacy of the bank's systems to manage the risks associated with payable through accounts (PTAs), and management's ability to implement effective monitoring and reporting systems.*

1. Review the policies, procedures, and processes related to PTAs. Evaluate the adequacy of the policies, procedures, and processes given the bank's PTA activities and the risks they present. Assess whether the controls are adequate to reasonably protect the bank from money laundering and terrorist financing. Determine whether:
   - Criteria for opening PTA relationships with a foreign financial institution are adequate. Examples of factors that may be used include: jurisdiction; bank secrecy or money laundering haven; products, services, and markets; purpose; anticipated activity; customer history; ownership; senior management; certificate of incorporation; banking license; certificate of good standing; and demonstration of the foreign financial institution's operational capability to monitor account activity.
   - Appropriate information has been obtained and validated from the foreign financial institution concerning the identity of any persons having authority to direct transactions through the PTA.
   - Information and enhanced due diligence have been obtained from the foreign financial institution concerning the source and beneficial ownership of funds of persons who have authority to direct transactions through the PTA (e.g., name, address, expected activity level, place of employment, description of business, related accounts, identification of foreign politically exposed persons, source of funds, and articles of incorporation).
   - Sub-accounts are not opened before the U.S. bank has reviewed and approved the customer information.
   - Master or sub-accounts can be closed if the information provided to the bank has been materially inaccurate or incomplete.
   - The bank can identify all signers on each sub-account.
2. From a review of management information systems (MIS) and internal risk rating factors, determine whether the bank effectively identifies and monitors PTA accounts.

3. Determine whether the bank's system for monitoring PTA accounts for suspicious activities, and reporting suspicious activities, is adequate given the bank's size, complexity, location, and types of customer relationships.
4. To assess the volume of risk and determine whether adequate resources are allocated to the oversight and monitoring activity, obtain a list of foreign correspondent bank accounts in which PTAs are offered and request MIS reports that show:
   - The number of sub-accounts within each PTA.
   - The volume and dollar amount of monthly transactions for each sub-account.
5. Verify that the bank has obtained and reviewed information concerning the foreign financial institution's home country AML regulatory requirements (e.g., customer identification requirements and suspicious activity reporting) and considered these requirements when reviewing PTAs. Determine whether the bank has ensured that sub-account agreements comply with any AML statutory and regulatory requirements existing in the foreign financial institution's home country.
6. If appropriate, refer to the core examination procedures, "Office of Foreign Assets Control," page 144, for guidance.

Transaction Testing

7. On the basis of the bank's risk assessment of its PTA activities, as well as prior examination and audit reports, select a sample of PTAs. From the sample, review the contracts or agreements with the foreign financial institution. Determine whether the contracts or agreements:
   - Clearly outline the contractual responsibilities of both the U.S. bank and the foreign financial institution.
   - Define PTA and sub-account opening procedures and require an independent review and approval process when opening the account.
   - Require the foreign financial institution to comply with its local AML requirements.
   - Restrict sub-accounts from being opened by casas de cambio, finance companies, funds remitters, or other non-bank financial institutions.
   - Prohibit multi-tier sub-accountholders.
   - Provide for proper controls over currency deposits and withdrawals by sub-accountholders and ensure that Currency Transaction Reports (CTRs) have been appropriately filed.
   - Provide for dollar limits on each sub-accountholder's transactions that are consistent with expected account activity.
   - Contain documentation requirements that are consistent with those used for opening domestic accounts at the U.S. bank.
   - Provide the U.S. bank with the ability to review information concerning the identity of sub-accountholders (e.g., directly or through a trusted third party).
   - Require the foreign financial institution to monitor sub-account activities for unusual or suspicious activity and report findings to the U.S. bank.

- Allow the U.S. bank, as permitted by local laws, to audit the foreign financial institution's PTA operations and to access PTA documents.

8. Review PTA master-account bank statements. (The examiner should determine the time period based upon the size and complexity of the bank.) The statements chosen should include frequent transactions and those of large dollar amounts. Verify the statements to the general ledger and bank reconcilements. Note any currency shipments or deposits made at the U.S. bank on behalf of an individual sub-accountholder for credit to the customer's sub-account.
9. From the sample selected, review each sub-accountholder's identifying information and related transactions for a period of time as determined by the examiner. Evaluate PTA sub-accountholders' transactions. Determine whether the transactions are consistent with expected transactions or warrant further research. (The sample should include sub-accountholders with significant dollar activity.)
10. On the basis of examination procedures completed, including transaction testing, form a conclusion about the adequacy of policies, procedures, and processes associated with PTAs.

Pouch Activities — Overview

Objective. *Assess the adequacy of the bank's systems to manage the risks associated with pouch activities, and management's ability to implement effective monitoring and reporting systems.*

Pouch activity entails the use of a carrier, courier (either independent or common), or a referral agent employed by the courier,[6] to transport currency, monetary instruments, and other documents from outside the United States to a bank in the United States.[7] Pouches can be sent by another bank or individuals. Pouch services are commonly offered in conjunction with foreign correspondent banking services. Pouches can contain loan payments, transactions for demand deposit accounts, or other types of transactions.

Risk Factors

Banks should be aware that bulk amounts of monetary instruments purchased in the United States that appear to have been structured to avoid the BSA-reporting requirements often have been found in pouches or cash letters received from foreign financial institutions. This is especially true in the case of pouches and cash letters received from jurisdictions with lax or deficient AML structures. The monetary instruments involved are frequently money orders, traveler's checks, and bank checks that usually have one or more of the following characteristics in common:

- The instruments were purchased on the same or consecutive days at different locations.
- They are numbered consecutively in amounts just under $3,000 or $10,000.

- The payee lines are left blank or made out to the same person (or to only a few people).
- They contain little or no purchaser information.
- They bear the same stamp, symbol, or initials.
- They are purchased in round denominations or repetitive amounts.
- The depositing of the instruments is followed soon after by a funds transfer out in the same dollar amount.

Risk Mitigation

Banks should have policies, procedures, and processes related to pouch activity that should:

- Outline criteria for opening a pouch relationship with an individual or a foreign financial institution (e.g., customer due diligence requirements, type of institution or person, acceptable purpose of the relationship).
- Detail acceptable and unacceptable transactions (e.g., monetary instruments with blank payees, unsigned monetary instruments, and a large number of consecutively numbered monetary instruments).
- Detail procedures for processing the pouch, including employee responsibilities, dual control, reconciliation and documentation requirements, and employee sign off.
- Detail procedures for reviewing for unusual or suspicious activity, including elevating concerns to management. (Contents of pouches may be subject to Currency Transaction Report (CTR), Report of International Transportation of Currency or Monetary Instruments (CMIR), and Suspicious Activity Report (SAR) reporting requirements.)
- Discuss criteria for closing pouch relationships.

The above factors should be included within an agreement or contract between the bank and the courier that details the services to be provided and the responsibilities of both parties.

Examination Procedures

Pouch Activities

Objective. *Assess the adequacy of the bank's systems to manage the risks associated with pouch activities, and management's ability to implement effective monitoring and reporting systems.*

1. Determine whether the bank has incoming or outgoing pouch activity and whether the activity is via carrier or courier.
2. Review the policies, procedures, and processes, and any contractual agreements related to pouch activities. Evaluate the adequacy of the policies, procedures, and

processes given the bank's pouch activities and the risks they present. Assess whether the controls are adequate to reasonably protect the bank from money laundering and terrorist financing.

3. From a review of management information systems (MIS) and internal risk rating factors, determine whether the bank effectively identifies and monitors pouch activities.
4. Determine whether the bank's system for monitoring pouch activities for suspicious activities, and for reporting suspicious activities, is adequate given the bank's size, complexity, location, and types of customer relationships.
5. Review the list of bank customers permitted to use pouch services (incoming and outgoing). Determine whether management has assessed the risk of the customers permitted to use this service.
6. If appropriate, refer to the core examination procedures, "Office of Foreign Assets Control," page 144, for guidance.

Transaction Testing

7. On the basis of the bank's risk assessment of its pouch activities, as well as prior examination and audit reports, and recent activity records, select a sample of daily pouches for review. Preferably on an unannounced basis and over a period of several days, not necessarily consecutive, observe the pouch opening and the data capture process for items contained in a sample of incoming pouches, and observe the preparation of outgoing pouches. Review the records and the pouch contents for currency, monetary instruments,[8] bearer securities, stored value cards, gems, art, illegal substances or contraband, or other items that should not ordinarily appear in a bank's pouch.
8. If the courier, or the referral agent who works for the courier, has an account with the bank, review an appropriate sample of their account activity.
9. On the basis of examination procedures completed, including transaction testing, form a conclusion about the adequacy of policies, procedures, and processes associated with pouch activity.

ELECTRONIC BANKING — OVERVIEW

Objective. *Assess the adequacy of the bank's systems to manage the risks associated with electronic banking (e-banking) customers, and management's ability to implement effective monitoring and reporting systems.*

E-banking systems, which provide electronic delivery of banking products to customers, include automated teller machine (ATM) transactions; on-line account opening; Internet banking transactions; and telephone banking. For example, credit cards, deposit accounts, mortgage loans, and funds transfers can all be initiated on-line, without face-to- face contact. Management needs to recognize this as a potentially high-risk area and develop adequate policies, procedures, and processes for customer identification and monitoring for specific areas of banking. Refer to the core examination procedures, "Customer Identification Program" (CIP), page 52, for further guidance. Additional information on e-banking is available in the FFIEC *Information Technology Examination Handbook*.[9]

Risk Factors

Banks should ensure that their monitoring systems adequately capture transactions conducted electronically. As with any account, they should be alert to anomalies in account behavior. Red flags may include the velocity of funds in the account or, in the case of ATMs, the number of debit cards associated with the account.

Accounts that are opened without face-to-face contact may be a higher risk for money laundering and terrorist financing for the following reasons:

- More difficult to positively verify the individual's identity.
- Customer may be out of the bank's targeted geographic area or country.
- Customer may perceive the transactions as less transparent.
- Transactions are instantaneous.
- May be used by a "front" company or unknown third party.

Risk Mitigation

Banks should establish BSA/AML monitoring, identification, and reporting for unusual and suspicious activities occurring through e-banking systems. Useful management information systems for detecting unusual activity in high-risk accounts include ATM activity reports, funds transfer reports, new account activity reports, change of Internet address reports, Internet Protocol (IP) address reports, and reports to identify related or linked accounts (e.g., common addresses, phone numbers, e-mail addresses, and tax identification numbers). In determining the level of monitoring required for an account, banks should include how the account was opened as a factor. Banks engaging in transactional Internet banking should have effective and reliable methods to authenticate a customer's identity when opening accounts on-line and should establish policies for when a customer should be required to open accounts on a face-to-face basis.[10] Banks may also institute other controls, such as establishing transaction dollar limits for large items that require manual intervention to exceed the preset limit.

EXAMINATION PROCEDURES

Electronic Banking

Objective. *Assess the adequacy of the bank's systems to manage the risks associated with electronic banking (e-banking) customers, and management's ability to implement effective monitoring and reporting systems.*

1. Review the policies, procedures, and processes related to e-banking. Evaluate the adequacy of the policies, procedures, and processes given the bank's e-banking activities and the risks they present. Assess whether the controls are adequate to reasonably protect the bank from money laundering and terrorist financing.
2. From a review of management information systems (MIS) and internal risk rating factors, determine whether the bank effectively identifies and monitors high-risk e-banking activities.
3. Determine whether the bank's system for monitoring e-banking for suspicious activities, and for reporting suspicious activities, is adequate given the bank's size, complexity, location, and types of customer relationships.
4. If appropriate, refer to the core examination procedures, "Office of Foreign Assets Control," page 144, for guidance.

Transaction Testing

5. On the basis of the bank's risk assessment of its e-banking activities, as well as prior examination and audit reports, select a sample of e-banking accounts. From the sample selected, perform the following procedures:
   - Review account opening documentation, including Customer Identification Program (CIP) and transaction history.
   - Compare expected activity with actual activity.
   - Determine whether the activity is consistent with the nature of the customer's business.
   - Identify any unusual or suspicious activity.
6. On the basis of examination procedures completed, including transaction testing, form a conclusion about the adequacy of policies, procedures, and processes associated with e-banking relationships.

FUNDS TRANSFERS — OVERVIEW

Objective. *Assess the adequacy of the bank's systems to manage the risks associated with funds transfers, and management's ability to implement effective monitoring and reporting systems. This section expands the core review of the statutory and regulatory requirements of funds transfers to provide a broader assessment of AML risks associated with this activity.*

Payment systems in the United States consist of numerous financial intermediaries, financial services firms, and non-bank businesses that create, process, and distribute payments. The domestic and international expansion of the banking industry and non- bank financial services has increased the importance of electronic funds transfers, including funds transfers made through the wholesale payment systems. Additional information on the types of wholesale payment systems is available in the FFIEC *Information Technology Examination Handbook.*[11]

Funds Transfer Services

A vast majority of the value of U.S. dollar payments in the United States are ultimately processed through wholesale payment systems, which generally handle large-value transactions between banks and either large financial services providers or non-bank financial institutions. For comparison, retail transfer systems include automated clearing houses (ACHs), automated teller machines (ATMs), point-of-sale (POS) systems, telephone bill paying, home banking systems, debit cards, and stored value cards, which are gaining widespread customer use. Most of these retail transactions are initiated by customers rather than by banks or corporate users. These individual transactions may then be combined into larger wholesale transfers, which are the focus of this section. In addition, banks conduct numerous wholesale transfers on their own behalf as well as for the benefit of other financial service providers and bank customers (corporate and consumer).

The two primary wholesale payment systems for interbank, or large-value, domestic funds transfer payment orders are the Fedwire Funds Service (Fedwire®) [12] and the Clearing House Interbank Payments System (CHIPS).[13] The bulk of the dollar value of these payments is processed electronically and is used to make large value, time-critical payments, such as the settlement of interbank purchases and sales of federal funds, settlement of foreign exchange transactions, disbursement or repayment of loans; settlement of real estate transactions or other financial market transactions; and purchasing, selling, or financing securities transactions. Fedwire and CHIPS participants facilitate these transactions on their behalf and for their customers, including non-bank financial institutions, commercial businesses, and correspondent banks that do not have direct access.

Structurally there are two components to funds transfers: the instruction, which contains the information on the ultimate sender and receiver of the funds, and the actual movement or transfer of funds. The instructions are sent in a variety of ways, including by electronic access to networks of Fedwire or CHIPS payment systems; by access to financial telecommunications systems, such as Society for Worldwide Interbank Financial Telecommunication (SWIFT); or e-mail, facsimile (fax), telephone, or telex. Fedwire and CHIPS are used for U.S. dollar transfers that are wholly domestic transactions and to facilitate the U.S. dollar leg of international transactions. CHIPS has been used predominantly to facilitate international transactions. SWIFT is an international messaging service that is used to transmit payment instructions for the vast majority of international interbank transactions, which can be denominated in numerous currencies.

Fedwire

Fedwire, operated by the Federal Reserve Banks, allows any bank with a Federal Reserve account to transfer funds from that account to the Federal Reserve account of any other bank. Payment to the receiving participant (receiving bank) over Fedwire is final and irrevocable when the Federal Reserve Bank either credits the amount of the payment order to the receiving bank's Federal Reserve Bank reserve account or sends notice to the receiving bank, whichever is earlier. Although there is no settlement risk to Fedwire participants, they may be exposed to risk caused by errors and omissions and fraud.

Participants[14] may access Fedwire by four methods:

- Direct mainframe-to-mainframe (computer interface).
- Off-line or telephone-based access to a Federal Reserve Bank operations site.
- Dial-up or Internet access over a virtual private network to web-based applications (FedLine Advantage).
- Dial-up access using a DOS-based terminal (FedLine DOS).[15]

CHIPS

CHIPS is a privately operated, real-time, multilateral payments system typically used for large-dollar payments. Participants submit payment messages to CHIPS, where they are stored in a central queue. Payment messages may be released from the queue individually using participants' positive balances or on a bilateral or multilateral basis by offsetting against incoming payment messages. Payments are final when released from the CHIPS queue. CHIPS is owned by banks, and any banking organization with a regulated U.S. presence may become a participant in the system. The payments transferred over CHIPS are often related to international interbank transactions, including the dollar payments resulting from foreign currency transactions (such as currency swap contracts) and euro placements and returns. Payment orders are also sent over CHIPS to adjust correspondent balances and make payments associated with commercial transactions, bank loans, and securities transactions.

SWIFT

The SWIFT network is a messaging infrastructure that provides users with a private international communications link among themselves. The actual U.S. dollar funds movements (payments) are completed through correspondent bank relationships, Fedwire, or CHIPS. Movement of payments denominated in foreign currencies occur through correspondent bank relationships or over funds transfer systems in the relevant country. In addition to customer and bank funds transfers, SWIFT is used to transmit foreign exchange confirmations, debit and credit entry confirmations, statements, collections, and documentary credits.

Informal Value Transfer Systems

An informal value transfer system (IVTS) (e.g., hawalas) is a term used to describe a currency or value transfer system that operates informally to transfer money as a business.[16] In countries lacking a stable financial sector or with large areas not served by formal banks, IVTS may be the only method for conducting financial transactions. Persons living in the United States may also use IVTS to transfer funds to their home countries.

Payable Upon Proper Identification Transactions

One type of funds transfer transaction that carries particular risk is the payable upon proper identification (PUPID) service. PUPID transactions are funds transfers for which there is no specific account to deposit the funds into and the beneficiary of the funds is not a bank customer. For example, an individual that has an account at a bank may transfer funds to a relative or an individual who does not have an account relationship with a bank at another location (e.g., city, state, or jurisdiction). In this case, the beneficiary bank may place the incoming funds into a suspense account and ultimately release the funds when the individual provides proof of identity.

Risk Factors

Funds transfers may represent a heightened degree of risk, depending on such factors as the number and dollar volume of transactions, geographic location of originators and beneficiaries, and whether the originator or beneficiary is a bank customer. The size and complexity of a bank's operation and the origin and destination of the funds being transferred will determine which type of funds transfer system the bank uses. The vast majority of funds transfer instructions are conducted electronically; however, examiners need to be mindful that physical instructions may be transmitted by other informal methods, as described earlier.

IVTS pose a heightened concern because they are able to circumvent the formal system. The lack of recordkeeping requirements coupled with the lack of identification of the IVTS participants may attract money launderers and terrorists. IVTS also pose heightened BSA/AML concerns because they can evade internal controls and monitoring oversight established in the formal banking environment. Principals that operate IVTS frequently use banks to settle accounts.

The risks of PUPID transactions to the beneficiary bank are similar to other activities in which the bank does business with noncustomers. However, the risks are heightened in PUPID transactions, because the bank allows a noncustomer to access the funds transfer system by providing minimal or no identifying information. Some banks that allow noncustomers to transfer funds using the PUPID service pose significant risk to both the originating and beneficiary banks. In these situations, both banks have minimal or no identifying information on the originator or the beneficiary.

Risk Mitigation

Funds transfers can be used in the placement, layering, and integration stages of money laundering. Funds transfers purchased with currency are an example of the placement stage. Detecting unusual activity in the layering and integration stages is more difficult for a bank; such transactions may appear legitimate. In many cases, a bank may not be involved in the placement of the funds or in the final integration, only the layering of transactions. Banks should consider all three stages of money laundering when evaluating or assessing funds transfer risks.

Banks need to have sound policies, procedures, and processes to manage the BSA/AML risks of its funds transfer activities. Such policies may encompass more than regulatory recordkeeping minimums and be expanded to cover OFAC. Funds transfer policies, procedures, and processes should address all foreign correspondent banking activities, including transactions in which U.S. branches and agencies of foreign banks are intermediaries for their head offices.

Obtaining customer due diligence (CDD) information is an important mitigant of risk in providing funds transfer services. Because of the nature of funds transfers, adequate and effective CDD policies, procedures, and processes are critical in detecting unusual and suspicious activities. An effective risk-based suspicious activity monitoring and reporting system is equally important. Whether this monitoring and reporting system is automated or manual, it should be sufficient to detect suspicious trends and patterns typically associated with money laundering.

Originating and beneficiary banks should establish effective and appropriate policies, procedures, and processes for PUPID activity including:

- Specifying the type of identification that is acceptable.
- Maintaining documentation of individuals consistent with the bank's recordkeeping policies.
- Defining which bank employees may conduct PUPID transactions.
- Establishing limits on the amount of funds that may be transferred to or from the bank for noncustomers (including type of funds accepted (i.e., currency or official check) by originating bank).
- Monitoring and reporting suspicious activities.
- Providing enhanced scrutiny for transfers to or from certain jurisdictions.
- Identifying disbursement method (i.e., by currency or official check) for proceeds from beneficiary bank.

Examination Procedures

Funds Transfers

Objective. *Assess the adequacy of the bank's systems to manage the risks associated with funds transfers, and management's ability to implement effective monitoring and reporting systems. This section expands the core review of the statutory and regulatory requirements of funds transfers to provide a broader assessment of AML risks associated with this activity.*

1. Review the policies, procedures, and processes related to funds transfers. Evaluate the adequacy of the policies, procedures, and processes given the bank's funds transfer activities and the risks they present. Assess whether the controls are adequate to reasonably protect the bank from money laundering and terrorist financing.
2. From review of management information systems (MIS) and internal risk rating factors, determine whether the bank effectively identifies and monitors high-risk funds transfer activities.

3. Evaluate the bank's risks related to funds transfer activities by analyzing the frequency and dollar volume of funds transfers in relation to the bank's size, its location, and the nature of its customer account relationships.
4. Determine whether an audit trail of funds transfer activities exists. Determine whether an adequate separation of duties or other compensating controls are in place to ensure proper authorization for sending and receiving funds transfers and for correcting postings to accounts.
5. Determine whether the bank's system for monitoring funds transfers suspicious activities, and for reporting of suspicious activities, is adequate given the bank's size, complexity, location, and types of customer relationships. Determine whether suspicious activity monitoring and reporting systems include:
   - Funds transfers purchased with currency.
   - Transactions in which the bank is acting as an intermediary.
   - Transactions in which the bank is originating or receiving funds transfers from foreign financial institutions, particularly to or from jurisdictions with strict privacy and secrecy laws or those identified as high risk.
   - Frequent currency deposits and subsequent transfers, particularly to a larger institution or out of the country.
6. Determine the bank's procedures for payable upon proper identification (PUPID) transactions.
   - Beneficiary bank — determine how the bank disburses the proceeds (i.e., by currency or official check).
   - Originating bank — determine whether the bank allows PUPID funds transfers for noncustomers. If so, determine the type of funds accepted (i.e., by currency or official check).
7. If appropriate, refer to the core examination procedures, "Office of Foreign Assets Control," page 144, for guidance.

Transaction Testing

8. On the basis of the bank's risk assessment of funds transfer activities, as well as prior examination and audit reports, select a sample of high-risk funds transfer activities, which may include the following:
   - Funds transfers purchased with currency.
   - Transactions in which the bank is acting as an intermediary.
   - Transactions in which the bank is originating or receiving funds transfers from foreign financial institutions, particularly to or from jurisdictions with strict privacy and secrecy laws or those identified as high risk.
   - PUPID transactions.
9. From the sample selected, analyze funds transfers to determine whether the amounts, frequency, and jurisdictions of origin or destination are consistent with the nature of the business or occupation of the customer. Identify any suspicious or unusual activity.

10. On the basis of examination procedures completed, including transaction testing, form a conclusion about the adequacy of policies, procedures, and processes associated with funds transfer activity.

AUTOMATED CLEARING HOUSE TRANSACTIONS — OVERVIEW

Objective. *Assess the adequacy of the bank's systems to manage the risks associated with automated clearing house (ACH) transactions, and management's ability to implement effective monitoring and reporting systems.*

The ACH system is a nationwide electronic payments system used by more than 20,000 participating financial institutions, four million corporations, and 145 million consumers.[17] Based on data compiled by The National Automated Clearing House Association — The Electronic Payments Association (NACHA), ACH payment volumes have doubled in the last five years.[18] The use of the ACH is growing rapidly due to the increased volume of electronic check conversion and one-time ACH debits, reflecting the lower cost of ACH processing relative to check processing. Check conversion transactions, as well as one-time ACH debits, are primarily low-dollar value, consumer transactions for the purchases of goods and services or the payment of consumer bills. The Federal Reserve Banks' FedACH system[19] is almost exclusively used for domestic payments, but can accommodate cross-border payments to Canada, Mexico, and some countries in Europe.

ACH Payment Systems

Traditionally, the ACH system has been used for the direct deposit of payroll and government benefit payments and for the direct payment of mortgages and loans. As noted earlier, the ACH has been expanding to include one-time debits and check conversion. ACH transactions are payment instructions to either credit or debit a deposit account. Examples of credit payment transactions include payroll direct deposit, Social Security, dividends, and interest payments. Examples of debit transactions include mortgage, loan, insurance premium, and a variety of other consumer payments initiated through merchants or businesses.

In general, an ACH transaction is a batch-processed, value-dated, electronic funds transfer between an originating and a receiving bank. An ACH credit transaction is originated by the accountholder sending funds (payer), while an ACH debit transaction is originated by the accountholder receiving funds (payee). Within the ACH system, these participants and users are known by the following terms:

- **Originator.** An organization or person that initiates an ACH transaction either as a debit or credit.

- **Originating Depository Financial Institution (ODFI).** The Originator's depository financial institution that forwards the ACH transaction into the national ACH network through an ACH Operator.

- **ACH Operator.** An ACH Operator processes all ACH transactions that flow between different depository financial institutions. An ACH Operator serves as a central clearing facility that receives entries from the ODFIs and distributes the entries to the appropriate Receiving Depository Financial Institution. There are currently two ACH Operators: FedACH and Electronic Payments Network (EPN).

- **Receiving Depository Financial Institution (RDFI).** The Receiver's depository institution that receives the ACH transaction from the ACH Operators and credits or debits funds from their receivers' accounts.

- **Receiver.** An organization or person that authorizes the Originator to initiate an ACH transaction, either as a debit or credit to an account.

Third-Party Service Providers

A third-party service provider (TPSP) is an entity other than an Originator, ODFI, or RDFI that performs any functions on behalf of the Originator, the ODFI, or the RDFI with respect to the processing of ACH entries.[20] NACHA Operating Rules define TPSPs and relevant subsets of TPSPs that include "Third-Party Senders" and "Sending Points."[21] The functions of these TPSPs can include, but are not limited to, the creation of ACH files on behalf of the Originator or ODFI, or acting as a sending point of an ODFI (or receiving point on behalf of an RDFI).

Risk Factors

The ACH system was designed to transfer a high volume of low-dollar transactions, thereby not posing significant BSA/AML risks. Nevertheless, the ability to send high- dollar transactions through the ACH may expose banks to BSA/AML risks. Banks without a robust BSA/AML monitoring system may be exposed to additional risk particularly when accounts are opened over the Internet without face-to-face contact.

ACH transactions that are originated through a TPSP (that is, where the Originator is not a direct customer of the ODFI) may increase BSA/AML risks, therefore making it difficult for an ODFI to underwrite and review Originator transactions for compliance with BSA/AML rules.[22] Risks are heightened when neither the TPSP nor the ODFI performs due diligence on the companies for whom they are originating payments.

Certain ACH transactions, such as those originated through the Internet or the telephone, may be susceptible to manipulation and fraudulent use. Certain practices associated with how the banking industry processes ACH transactions may expose banks to BSA/AML risks. These practices include:

- An ODFI authorizing a TPSP to send ACH files directly to an ACH Operator, in essence bypassing the ODFI.
- ODFIs and RDFIs relying on each other to perform adequate due diligence on their customers.

- Because ACH processing is highly efficient and more automated than individual funds transfers, there are fewer opportunities for human review of individual transactions.

Risk Mitigation

The BSA requires banks to have BSA/AML compliance programs and appropriate policies, procedures, and processes in place to monitor and identify unusual activity, including ACH transactions. Obtaining customer due diligence (CDD) information is an important mitigant of BSA/AML risk in ACH transactions. Because of the nature of ACH transactions and the reliance that ODFIs and RDFIs place on each other for OFAC reviews and other necessary due diligence information, it is essential that all parties have a strong CDD program for regular ACH customers. For relationships with TPSPs, CDD on the TPSP can be supplemented with due diligence on the principals associated with the TPSP and, as necessary, on the originators. Adequate and effective CDD policies, procedures, and processes are critical in detecting a pattern of unusual and suspicious activities because the individual ACH transactions are typically not reviewed. Equally important is an effective risk-based suspicious activity monitoring and reporting system. In cases where a bank is heavily reliant upon the TPSP, a bank may want to review the TPSP's suspicious activity monitoring and reporting program, either through its own or an independent inspection. The ODFI may establish an agreement with the TPSP, which delineates general TPSP guidelines, such as compliance with ACH operating requirements and responsibilities and meeting other applicable state and federal regulations. Banks may need to consider controls to restrict or refuse ACH services to potential originators engaged in questionable or deceptive business practices.

ACH transactions can be used in the layering and integration stages of money laundering. Detecting unusual activity in the layering and integration stages can be a difficult task, because ACH may be used to legitimize frequent and recurring transactions. Banks should consider the layering and integration stages of money laundering when evaluating or assessing the ACH transaction risks of a particular customer.

The ODFI may need to more closely scrutinize transaction details for international ACH. The ODFI, if frequently involved in international ACH, may develop a separate process for reviewing international ACH transactions that minimizes disruption to general ACH processing, reconcilement, and settlement.

OFAC Screening

All parties to an ACH transaction are subject to the requirements of OFAC. (Refer to core overview section, "Office of Foreign Assets Control," page 135, for additional guidance.) OFAC has clarified the application of its rules for domestic and cross-border ACH transactions and is working with industry to provide more detailed guidance on cross-border ACH.[23]

With respect to domestic ACH transactions, the Originating Depository Financial Institution (ODFI) is responsible for verifying that the Originator is not a blocked party and making a good faith effort to determine that the Originator is not transmitting blocked funds.

The Receiving Depository Financial Institution (RDFI) similarly is responsible for verifying that the Receiver is not a blocked party. In this way, the ODFI and the RDFI are relying on each other for compliance with OFAC policies. ODFIs are not responsible for unbatching transactions and ensuring that they do not process transactions in violation of OFAC's regulations if they receive those transactions already batched from their customers. If the ODFI unbatches the transactions it received from its customers, then the ODFI is responsible for screening as though it had done the initial batching.

With respect to OFAC screening, these same obligations hold for cross-border ACH transactions. For outbound cross-border ACH transactions, however, the ODFI cannot rely on OFAC screening by the RDFI outside of the United States. In the case of inbound ACH transactions, the RDFI is responsible for compliance with OFAC requirements.

Additional information on the types of retail payment systems (ACH payment systems) is available in the FFIEC *Information Technology Examination Handbook*.[24]

Examination Procedures

Automated Clearing House Transactions

Objective. *Assess the adequacy of the bank's systems to manage the risks associated with automated clearing house (ACH) transactions, and management's ability to implement effective monitoring and reporting systems.*

1. Review the policies, procedures, and processes related to ACH transactions. Evaluate the adequacy of the policies, procedures, and processes given the bank's ACH transactions and the risks they present. Assess whether the controls are adequate to reasonably protect the bank from money laundering and terrorist financing.
2. From review of management information systems (MIS) and internal risk rating factors, determine whether the bank effectively identifies and monitors high-risk customers using ACH transactions.
3. Evaluate the bank's risks related to ACH transactions by analyzing the frequency and dollar volume and types of ACH transactions in relation to the bank's size, its location, and the nature of its customer account relationships.
4. Determine whether the bank's system for monitoring customers, including third-party service providers (TPSP), using ACH transactions for suspicious activities, and for reporting of suspicious activities, is adequate given the bank's size, complexity, location, and types of customer relationships. Determine whether suspicious activity monitoring and reporting systems include:
   - Identifying customers with frequent and large ACH transactions.
   - Monitoring ACH detail activity when the batch-processed transactions are separated for other purposes (e.g., processing errors).
   - Applying increased due diligence for international ACH transactions, including domestic transactions when the Originator is based in a foreign country or that are initiated by an international messaging system.

- Identifying ACH transactions that the bank originates to foreign financial institutions, particularly to high-risk geographic locations.
- Using methods to track, review, and investigate customer complaints regarding fraudulent or duplicate ACH transactions.

5. If appropriate, refer to the core examination procedures, "Office of Foreign Assets Control," page 144, for guidance.

Transaction Testing

6. On the basis of the bank's risk assessment of customers with ACH transactions, as well as prior examination and audit reports, select a sample of high-risk customers, including TPSPs, with ACH transactions, which may include the following:
   - ACH transactions originating from or received by international parties.
   - ACH transactions originating from the Internet or via telephone, particularly those accounts opened on the Internet or via the telephone without face-to-face interaction.
   - Customers whose business or occupation does not warrant the volume or nature of ACH activity.
   - Customers who have been involved in the origination or receipt of duplicate or fraudulent ACH transactions.
   - Customers or originators (clients of customers) that are generating a high rate or high volume of invalid account returns, consumer unauthorized returns, or other unauthorized transactions.
7. From the sample selected, analyze ACH transactions to determine whether the amounts, frequency, and jurisdictions of origin or destination are consistent with the nature of the business or occupation of the customer. A review of the account opening documentation, including Customer Identification Program (CIP) documentation, may be necessary in making these determinations. Identify any suspicious or unusual activity.
8. On the basis of examination procedures completed, including transaction testing, form a conclusion about the adequacy of policies, procedures, and processes associated with ACH transactions.

ELECTRONIC CASH — OVERVIEW

Objective. *Assess the adequacy of the bank's systems to manage the risks associated with electronic cash (e-cash), and management's ability to implement effective monitoring and reporting systems.*

E-cash (e-money) is a digital representation of money. E-cash comes in two basic forms: stored value card e-cash and computer e-cash. Stored value card e-cash is most often downloaded through special terminals (e.g., specially equipped automated teller machines

(ATMs), computers, or cellular phones) onto electronic cards. Computer e-cash is downloaded to personal computer hard disks via a modem or stored in an on-line repository.

Stored value cards can operate in either an open or closed system.[25] Typically, open system cards may be reloaded, allowing the cardholder to add value. Closed system cards are usually limited to the initial value posted to the card, but some may allow the cardholder to add value. Additionally, funds can be prepaid on an open system card by one person, with someone else accessing the currency elsewhere through an ATM. Prepayment involves a transfer of funds to the card (e.g., telephone calling cards). Some domestic and offshore banks offer cards with currency access through ATMs internationally. Since stored value cards are easy to fund and transport without creating a paper trail, they are attractive for abuse by various illegal enterprises and money launderers. For example, drug dealers have been known to load currency onto prepaid cards and send the cards to their drug suppliers outside the country. Phone cards and other closed system prepaid cards can be purchased for currency and transferred from one person to another and resold. Often, a firm independent of a bank processes all card transactions through a "pooled" bank account held in the name of the firm managing the card program.[26]

Consumers use e-cash to access, store, and redeem funds that are maintained electronically. In addition, e-cash, in the form of payroll cards, is now offered by employers to their employees in place of a check to distribute wages. These payroll cards may also function as multi-purpose or general use reloadable cards (i.e., the cardholder can add value to the card at a variety of retail outlets using currency). The value of the funds stored on these cards can be transferred between cardholders using compatible electronic systems and networks, often without using banks.

Using ATMs, point-of-sale devices, or special readers, stored monetary value is subtracted from the card or the value allocated to the card that is held in a pooled bank account. When the monetary value is depleted, the card is either discarded (disposable) or, in some instances, value is replenished (reloadable). In the case of computer e-cash, monetary value is electronically deducted from the bank account when a purchase is made or funds are transferred to another person. Additional information on types of e- cash products is available in the FFIEC *Information Technology Examination Handbook*.[27]

Risk Factors

Transactions using e-cash may pose the following unique risks to the bank:

- Funds may be transferred to or from an unknown third party.
- Customers may be able to avoid border restrictions as the transactions can become mobile and may not be subject to jurisdictional restrictions.
- Transactions may be instantaneous.
- Specific cardholder activity may be difficult to determine by reviewing activity through a pooled account.
- The customer may perceive the transactions as less transparent.

Risk Mitigation

Banks should establish BSA/AML monitoring, identification, and reporting for unusual and suspicious activities occurring through e-cash. Useful management information systems for detecting unusual activity on high-risk accounts include ATM activity reports (focusing on foreign transactions), funds transfer reports, new account activity reports, change of Internet address reports, Internet Protocol (IP) address reports, and reports to identify related or linked accounts (e.g., common addresses, phone numbers, e-mail addresses, and tax identification numbers). Other controls, such as establishing transaction and account dollar limits that require manual intervention to exceed the preset limit, may also be instituted by the bank.

Examination Procedures

Electronic Cash

Objective. *Assess the adequacy of the bank's systems to manage the risks associated with electronic cash (e-cash), and management's ability to implement effective monitoring and reporting systems.*

1. Review the policies, procedures, and processes related to e-cash. Evaluate the adequacy of the policies, procedures, and processes given the bank's e-cash activities and the risk they present. Assess whether the controls are adequate to reasonably protect the bank from money laundering and terrorist financing.
2. From a review of management information systems (MIS) and internal risk rating factors, determine whether the bank effectively identifies and monitors high-risk e-cash transactions.
3. Determine whether the bank's system for monitoring e-cash transactions for suspicious activities, and for reporting suspicious activities, is adequate given the bank's size, complexity, location, and types of customer relationships.
4. If appropriate, refer to the core examination procedures, "Office of Foreign Assets Control," page 144, for guidance.

Transaction Testing

5. On the basis of the bank's risk assessment of its e-cash activities, as well as prior examination and audit reports, select a sample of e-cash transactions. From the sample selected perform the following examination procedures:
   - Review account opening documentation, including Customer Identification Program (CIP) and transaction history.
   - Compare expected activity with actual activity.
   - Determine whether the activity is consistent with the nature of the customer's business.

- Identify any unusual or suspicious activity.

6. On the basis of examination procedures completed, including transaction testing, form a conclusion about the adequacy of policies, procedures, and processes associated with e-cash relationships.

THIRD-PARTY PAYMENT PROCESSORS — OVERVIEW

Objective. *Assess the adequacy of the bank's systems to manage the risks associated with its relationships with third-party payment processors, and management's ability to implement effective monitoring and reporting systems.*

Non-bank or third-party payment processors (processors) are bank customers that provide payment-processing services to merchants and other business entities. Traditionally, processors contracted primarily with retailers that had physical locations in order to process the retailers' transactions. These merchant transactions primarily included credit card payments but also covered automated clearing house (ACH) transactions, remotely created checks,[28] and debit and stored value cards transactions. With the expansion of the Internet, retail borders have been eliminated. Processors may now service a variety of merchant accounts, including conventional retail and Internet-based establishments, prepaid travel, and Internet gaming enterprises.

Risk Factors

Processors generally are not subject to BSA/AML regulatory requirements. As a result, some processors may be vulnerable to money laundering, identity theft, and fraud schemes.

The bank's BSA/AML risks when dealing with a processor account are similar to risks from other activities in which the bank's customer conducts transactions through the bank on behalf of the customer's clients. When the bank is unable to identify and understand the nature and source of the transactions processed through an account, the risks to the bank and the likelihood of suspicious activity can increase. If a bank has not implemented an adequate processor-approval program that goes beyond credit risk management, it could be vulnerable to processing illicit or OFAC-sanctioned transactions.

Risk Mitigation

Banks offering account services to processors should develop and maintain adequate policies, procedures, and processes to address risks related to these relationships. At a minimum, these policies should authenticate the processor's business operations and assess their risk level. Verification and assessment of a processor can be completed by performing the following procedures:

- Reviewing the processor's promotional materials, including its web site, to determine the target clientele. (Businesses with elevated risk may include offshore companies, on-line gambling-related operations, and on-line payday lenders.) For example, a processor whose customers are primarily offshore would be inherently riskier than a processor whose customers are primarily restaurants.
- Determining whether the processor re-sells its services to a third party who may be referred to as an "agent or provider of Independent Sales Organization (ISO) opportunities" or "gateway" arrangements.[29]
- Reviewing the processor's policies, procedures, and processes to determine the adequacy of its due diligence standards for new merchants.
- Identifying the processor's major customers.
- Reviewing corporate documentation including independent reporting services and, if applicable, documentation on principal owners.
- Visiting the processor's business operations center.

Banks that provide account services should monitor their processor relationships for any significant changes in the processor's business strategies that may affect their risk profile. Banks should periodically re-verify and update the businesses' profiles to ensure the risk assessment is appropriate.

In addition to adequate and effective account opening and due diligence procedures for processor accounts, management should monitor these relationships for unusual and suspicious activities. To effectively monitor these accounts, the bank should have an understanding of the following processor information:

- Merchant base.
- Merchant activities.
- Average number of dollar volume and number of transactions.
- "Swiping" versus "keying" volume for credit card transactions.
- Charge-back history, including rates of return for ACH debit transactions and remotely created checks.

EXAMINATION PROCEDURES

Third-Party Payment Processors

Objective. *Assess the adequacy of the bank's systems to manage the risks associated with its relationships with third-party payment processors, and management's ability to implement effective monitoring and reporting systems.*

1. Review the policies, procedures, and processes related to third-party payment processors (processors). Evaluate the adequacy of the policies, procedures, and processes given the bank's processor activities and the risks they present. Assess whether the controls are adequate to reasonably protect the bank from money laundering and terrorist financing.

2. From a review of management information systems (MIS) and internal risk rating factors, determine whether the bank effectively identifies and monitors processor relationships, particularly those that pose a high risk for money laundering.
3. Determine whether the bank's system for monitoring processor accounts for suspicious activities, and for reporting suspicious activities, is adequate given the bank's size, complexity, location, and types of customer relationships.
4. If appropriate, refer to the core examination procedures, "Office of Foreign Assets Control," page 144, for guidance.

Transaction Testing

5. On the basis of the bank's risk assessment of its processor activities, as well as prior examination and audit reports, select a sample of high-risk processor accounts. From the sample selected:
   - Review account opening documentation and ongoing due diligence information.
   - Review account statements and, as necessary, specific transaction details to determine how expected transactions compare with actual activity.
   - Determine whether actual activity is consistent with the nature of the processor's stated activity.
   - Identify any unusual or suspicious activity.
6. On the basis of examination procedures completed, including transaction testing, form a conclusion about the adequacy of policies, procedures, and processes associated with processor accounts.

PURCHASE AND SALE OF MONETARY INSTRUMENTS — OVERVIEW

Objective. *Assess the adequacy of the bank's systems to manage the risks associated with monetary instruments, and management's ability to implement effective monitoring and reporting systems. This section expands the core review of statutory and regulatory requirements for purchase and sale of monetary instruments in order to provide a broader assessment of the money laundering risks associated with this activity.*

Monetary instruments are products provided by banks and include cashier's checks, traveler's checks, and money orders. Monetary instruments are typically purchased to pay for commercial or personal transactions and, in the case of traveler's checks, as a form of stored value for future purchases.

Risk Factors

The purchase or exchange of monetary instruments at the placement and layering stages of money laundering can conceal the source of illicit proceeds. As a result, banks have been major targets in laundering operations because they provide and process monetary instruments through deposits. For example, customers or noncustomers have been known to purchase monetary instruments in amounts below the $3,000 threshold to avoid having to provide adequate identification. Subsequently, monetary instruments are then placed into deposit accounts to circumvent the Currency Transaction Report (CTR) filing threshold.

Risk Mitigation

Banks selling monetary instruments should have appropriate policies, procedures, and processes in place to mitigate risk. Policies should define:

- Acceptable and unacceptable monetary instrument transactions (e.g., noncustomer transactions, monetary instruments with blank payees, unsigned monetary instruments, identification requirements for structured transactions, or the purchase of multiple sequentially numbered monetary instruments for the same payee).
- Procedures for reviewing for unusual or suspicious activity, including elevating concerns to management.
- Criteria for closing relationships or refusing to do business with noncustomers who have consistently or egregiously been involved in suspicious activity.

Examination Procedures

Purchase and Sale of Monetary Instruments

Objective. *Assess the adequacy of the bank's systems to manage the risks associated with monetary instruments, and management's ability to implement effective monitoring and reporting systems. This section expands the core review of statutory and regulatory requirements for purchase and sale of monetary instruments in order to provide a broader assessment of the money laundering risks associated with this activity.*

1. Review the policies, procedures, and processes related to the sale of monetary instruments. Evaluate the adequacy of the policies, procedures, and processes given the bank's monetary instruments activities and the risks they present. Assess whether controls are adequate to reasonably protect the bank from money laundering and terrorist financing.
2. From the volume of sales and the number of locations that monetary instruments are sold, determine whether the bank appropriately manages the risk associated with monetary instrument sales.
3. Determine whether the bank's system for monitoring monetary instruments for suspicious activities, and for reporting suspicious activities, is adequate given the bank's volume of monetary instrument sales, size, complexity, location, and types of customer relationships. Determine whether suspicious activity monitoring and reporting systems (either manual or automated) include a review of:

- Sales of sequentially numbered monetary instruments from the same or different purchasers on the same day to the same payee.
- Sales of monetary instruments to the same purchaser or sales of monetary instruments to different purchasers made payable to the same remitter.
- Monetary instrument purchases by noncustomers.
- Common purchasers, payees, addresses, sequentially numbered purchases, and unusual symbols.[30]

4. If appropriate, refer to the core examination procedures, "Office of Foreign Assets Control," page 144, for guidance.

Transaction Testing

5. On the basis of the bank's risk assessment, as well as prior examination and audit reports, select a sample of monetary instrument transactions for both customers and noncustomers from:
   - Monetary instrument sales records.
   - Copies of cleared monetary instruments purchased with currency.
6. From the sample selected, analyze transaction information to determine whether amounts, the frequency of purchases, and payees are consistent with expected activity for customers or noncustomers (e.g., payments to utilities or household purchases). Identify any suspicious or unusual activity.
7. On the basis of examination procedures completed, including transaction testing, form a conclusion about the adequacy of policies, procedures, and processes associated with monetary instruments.

BROKERED DEPOSITS — OVERVIEW

Objective. *Assess the adequacy of the bank's systems to manage the risks associated with brokered deposit relationships, and management's ability to implement effective due diligence, monitoring, and reporting systems.*

The use of brokered deposits is a common funding source for many banks. Recent technology developments allow brokers to provide bankers with increased access to a broad range of potential investors who have no relationship with the bank. Deposits can be raised over the Internet, through certificates of deposit listing services, or through other advertising methods.

Deposit brokers provide intermediary services for banks and investors. This activity is considered higher risk because each deposit broker operates under its own guidelines for obtaining deposits. The level of regulatory oversight over deposit brokers varies, as does the applicability of BSA/AML requirements directly on the deposit broker. However, the deposit broker is subject to OFAC requirements regardless of its regulatory status. Consequently, the deposit broker may not be performing adequate due diligence, OFAC screening. For additional information refer to the core overview section, "Office of Foreign Assets Control," page 135, or "Customer Identification Program" (CIP), core examination procedures, page 52.[31] The bank accepting brokered deposits depends on the deposit broker to sufficiently perform required account opening procedures and to follow applicable BSA/AML compliance program requirements.

Risk Factors

Money laundering and terrorist financing risks arise because the bank may not know the ultimate beneficial owners or the source of funds. The deposit broker could represent a range of clients that may be of high risk for money laundering and terrorist financing (e.g., nonresident or offshore customers, politically exposed persons (PEPs), or foreign shell banks).

Risk Mitigation

Banks that accept deposit broker accounts or funds should develop appropriate policies, procedures, and processes that establish minimum CDD procedures for all deposit brokers providing deposits to the bank. The level of due diligence a bank performs should be commensurate with its knowledge of the deposit broker and the deposit broker's known business practices and customer base.

In an effort to address the risk inherent in certain deposit broker relationships, banks may want to consider having a signed contract that sets out the roles and responsibilities of each party and restrictions on types of customers (e.g., nonresident or offshore customers, PEPs, or foreign shell banks). Banks should conduct sufficient due diligence on unknown, foreign, independent, or unregulated deposit brokers. To manage the BSA/AML risks associated with brokered deposits, the bank should:

- Determine whether the deposit broker is a legitimate business in all operating locations where the business is conducted.
- Review the deposit broker's business strategies, including targeted customer markets (e.g., foreign or domestic customers) and methods for soliciting clients.
- Determine whether the deposit broker is subject to regulatory oversight.
- Evaluate whether the deposit broker's BSA/AML and OFAC policies, procedures, and processes are adequate (e.g., ascertain whether the deposit broker performs sufficient CDD including CIP procedures).
- Determine whether the deposit broker screens clients for OFAC matches.
- Evaluate the adequacy of the deposit broker's BSA/AML and OFAC audits and ensure that they address compliance with applicable regulations and requirements.

Banks should take particular care in their oversight of deposit brokers who are not regulated entities and:

- Are unknown to the bank.

- Conduct business or obtain deposits primarily in other jurisdictions.
- Use unknown or hard-to-contact businesses and banks for references.
- Provide other services that may be suspect, such as creating shell companies for foreign clients.
- Refuse to provide requested audit and due diligence information or insist on placing deposits before providing this information.
- Use technology that provides anonymity to customers.

Banks should also monitor existing deposit broker relationships for any significant changes in business strategies that may influence the broker's risk profile. As such, banks should periodically re-verify and update each deposit broker's profile to ensure an appropriate risk assessment.

EXAMINATION PROCEDURES

Brokered Deposits

Objective. *Assess the adequacy of the bank's systems to manage the risks associated with brokered deposit relationships, and management's ability to implement effective due diligence, monitoring, and reporting systems.*

1. Review the policies, procedures, and processes related to deposit broker relationships. Evaluate the adequacy of the policies, procedures, and processes given the bank's deposit broker activities and the risks that they present. Assess whether the controls are adequate to reasonably protect the bank from money laundering and terrorist financing.
2. From a review of management information systems (MIS) and internal risk rating factors, determine whether the bank effectively identifies and monitors deposit broker relationships, particularly those that pose a high risk for money laundering.
3. Determine whether the bank's system for monitoring deposit broker relationships for suspicious activities, and for reporting suspicious activities, is adequate given the bank's size, complexity, location, and types of customer relationships.
4. If appropriate, refer to the core examination procedures, "Office of Foreign Assets Control," page 144, for guidance.

Transaction Testing

5. On the basis of the bank's risk assessment of its brokered deposit activities, as well as prior examination and audit reports, select a sample of high-risk deposit broker accounts. When selecting a sample, examiners should consider the following:
   - New relationships with deposit brokers.
   - The method of generating funds (e.g., Internet brokers).

- Types of customers (e.g., nonresident or offshore customers, politically exposed persons, or foreign shell banks).
- A deposit broker that has appeared in the bank's Suspicious Activity Reports (SARs).
- Subpoenas served on the bank for a particular deposit broker.
- Foreign funds providers.
- Unusual activity.

6. Review the customer due diligence information on the deposit broker. For deposit brokers who are considered high risk (e.g., they solicit foreign funds, market via the Internet, or are independent brokers), assess whether the following information is available:
   - Background and references.
   - Business and marketing methods.
   - Client-acceptance and due diligence practices.
   - The method for or basis of the broker's compensation or bonus program.
   - The broker's source of funds.
   - Anticipated activity or transaction types and levels (e.g., funds transfers).
7. On the basis of examination procedures completed, including transaction testing, form a conclusion about the adequacy of policies, procedures, and processes associated with deposit brokers.

PRIVATELY OWNED AUTOMATED TELLER MACHINES — OVERVIEW

Objective. *Assess the adequacy of the bank's systems to manage the risks associated with privately owned automated teller machines (ATMs) and Independent Sales Organization (ISO) relationships, and management's ability to implement effective due diligence, monitoring, and reporting systems.*

Privately owned ATMs are particularly susceptible to money laundering and fraud. Operators of these ATMs are often included within the definition of an ISO.[32]

Privately owned ATMs are typically found in convenience stores, bars, restaurants, grocery stores, or check cashing establishments. Some ISOs are large-scale operators, but many privately owned ATMs are owned by the proprietors of the establishments in which they are located. Most dispense currency, but some dispense only a paper receipt (scrip) that the customer exchanges for currency or goods. Fees and surcharges for withdrawals, coupled with additional business generated by customer access to an ATM, make the operation of a privately owned ATM profitable.

ISOs link their ATMs to an ATM transaction network. The ATM network routes transaction data to the customer's bank to debit the customer's account and ultimately credit the ISO's account, which could be located at a bank anywhere in the world. Payments to the ISO's account are typically made through the automated clearing house (ACH) system. Additional information on types of retail payment systems is available in the FFIEC *Information Technology Examination Handbook.*[33]

Sponsoring Bank

Some electronic funds transfers (EFTs) or point-of-sale (POS) networks require an ISO to be sponsored by a member of the network (sponsoring bank). The sponsoring bank and the ISO are subject to all network rules. The sponsoring bank is also charged with ensuring the ISO abides by all network rules. Therefore, the sponsoring bank should conduct proper due diligence on the ISO and maintain adequate documentation to ensure that the sponsored ISO complies with all network rules.

Risk Factors

Most states do not currently register, limit ownership, monitor, or examine privately owned ATMs or their ISOs. While the provider of the ATM transaction network and the sponsoring bank should be conducting adequate due diligence on the ISO, actual practices may vary. Furthermore, the provider may not be aware of ATM or ISO ownership changes after an ATM contract has already been established. As a result, many privately owned ATMs have been involved in, or are susceptible to, money laundering schemes, identity theft, outright theft of the ATM currency, and fraud. Consequently, privately owned ATMs and their ISOs pose increased risk and should be treated accordingly by banks doing business with them.

Some privately owned ATMs are managed by a vault currency servicer that provides armored car currency delivery, replenishes the ATM with currency, and arranges for insurance against theft and damage. Many ISOs, however, manage and maintain their own machines, including the replenishment of currency. Banks may also provide currency to ISOs under a lending agreement, which exposes those banks to various risks, including reputation and credit risk.

Money laundering can occur through privately owned ATMs when an ATM is replenished with illicit currency that is subsequently withdrawn by legitimate customers. This process results in ACH deposits to the ISO's account that appear as legitimate business transactions. Consequently, all three phases of money laundering (placement, layering, and integration) can occur simultaneously. Money launderers may also collude with merchants and previously legitimate ISOs to provide illicit currency to the ATMs at a discount.

Risk Mitigation

Banks should implement appropriate polices, procedures, and processes to address risks with ISO relationships. At a minimum, the policies should include:

- Verification of an ISO's legitimacy through a review of corporate documentation, licenses, permits, contracts, or references.
- Review of public databases to determine the existence of issues with the ISO or principal owners.

- Understanding the controls of the currency servicing arrangements for privately owned ATMs and whether legitimate currency generation is sufficient to service machines.
- Documentation of the locations of privately owned ATMs and determination of the ISO's target geographic market.
- Expected account activity, including currency withdrawals.

Because of these risks, due diligence on customers that are ISOs, beyond the minimum Customer Identification Program requirements is critical. Banks should also perform due diligence on ATM owners. This due diligence should:

- Verify the ATM owner's legitimacy through a review of corporate documentation, licenses, permits, contracts, or references, including the ATM transaction provider contract.
- Review public databases for information on the ATM owners.
- Obtain the addresses of all ATM locations, ascertain the types of businesses in which the ATMs are located, and identify targeted demographics.
- Determine expected ATM activity levels, including currency withdrawals.
- Ascertain the sources of currency for the ATMs by reviewing copies of armored car contracts, lending arrangements, or any other documentation, as appropriate.

Examination Procedures

Privately Owned Automated Teller Machines

Objective. *Assess the adequacy of the bank's systems to manage the risks associated with privately owned automated teller machines (ATMs) and Independent Sales Organization (ISO) relationships, and management's ability to implement effective due diligence, monitoring, and reporting systems.*

1. Review the policies, procedures, and processes related to privately owned ATM accounts. Evaluate the adequacy of the policies, procedures, and processes given the bank's privately owned ATM and ISO relationships and the risk they present. Assess whether the controls are adequate to reasonably protect the bank from money laundering and terrorist financing.
2. From a review of management information systems (MIS) and internal risk rating factors, determine whether the bank effectively identifies and monitors privately owned ATM accounts.
3. Determine whether the bank's system for monitoring privately owned ATM accounts for suspicious activities, and for reporting suspicious activities, is adequate given the bank's size, complexity, location, and types of customer relationships.
4. Determine whether the bank sponsors network membership for ISOs. If the bank is a sponsoring bank, review contractual agreements with networks and the ISOs to

determine whether due diligence procedures and controls are designed to ensure that ISOs are in compliance with network rules.

Transaction Testing

5. On the basis of the bank's risk assessment of its privately owned ATM and ISO relationships, as well as prior examination and audit reports, select a sample of privately owned ATM accounts. From the sample selected, perform the following examination procedures:
   - Review the bank's customer due diligence (CDD) information. Determine whether the information adequately verifies the ISO's identity and describes its:
     Background.
     Source of funds.
     Anticipated activity or transaction types and levels (e.g., funds transfers).
     ATMs (size and location).
     Currency delivery arrangement, if applicable.
   - Review any MIS reports the bank uses to monitor ISO accounts. Determine whether the flow of funds or expected activity is consistent with the CDD information.
6. Determine whether a sponsored ISO uses third-party providers or servicers to load currency, maintain ATM machines, or solicit merchant locations. If yes, review a sample of third-party service agreements for proper due diligence and control procedures.
7. On the basis of examination procedures completed, including transaction testing, form a conclusion about the adequacy of policies, procedures, and processes associated with ISOs.

NONDEPOSIT INVESTMENT PRODUCTS — OVERVIEW

Objective. *Assess the adequacy of the bank's systems to manage the risks associated with both networking and in-house nondeposit investment products (NDIP), and management's ability to implement effective monitoring and reporting systems.*

NDIP include a wide array of investment products (e.g., securities, bonds, and fixed or variable annuities). Sales programs may also include cash management sweep accounts to retail and commercial clients; these programs are offered by the bank directly. Banks offer these investments to increase fee income and provide customers with additional products and services. The manner in which the NDIP relationship is structured and the methods with which the products are offered substantially affect the bank's BSA/AML risks and responsibilities.

Networking Arrangements

Banks typically enter into networking arrangements with securities broker/dealers to offer NDIP on bank premises. For BSA/AML purposes, under a networking arrangement, the customer is a customer of the broker/dealer, although the customer may also be a bank customer for other financial services. Bank examiners recognize that the U.S. Securities and Exchange Commission (SEC) is the primary regulator for NDIP offerings through broker/dealers, and the agencies will observe functional supervision requirements of the Gramm–Leach–Bliley Act.[34] Federal banking agencies are responsible for supervising NDIP activity conducted directly by the bank. Different types of networking arrangements may include co-branded products, dual-employee arrangements, or third- party arrangements.

Co-Branded Products

Co-branded products are offered by another company or financial services corporation[35] in co-sponsorship with the bank. For example, a financial services corporation tailors a mutual fund product for sale at a specific bank. The product is sold exclusively at that bank and bears the name of both the bank and the financial services corporation.

Because of this co-branded relationship, responsibility for BSA/AML compliance becomes complex. As these accounts are not under the sole control of the bank or financial entity, responsibilities for completing Customer Identification Program (CIP), customer due diligence (CDD), and suspicious activity monitoring and reporting can vary. The bank should fully understand each party's contractual responsibilities and ensure adequate control by all parties.

Dual-Employee Arrangements

In a dual-employee arrangement, the bank and the financial services corporation such as an insurance agency or a registered broker/dealer have a common (shared) employee. The shared employee may conduct banking business as well as sell NDIP, or sell NDIP full-time. Because of this dual-employee arrangement, the bank retains responsibility over NDIP activities. Even if contractual agreements establish the financial services corporation as being responsible for BSA/AML, the bank remains responsible and needs to ensure proper oversight and compliance with all regulatory requirements.[36]

Under some networking arrangements, registered securities sales representatives are dual employees of the bank and the broker/dealer. When the dual employee is providing investment products and services, the broker/dealer is responsible for monitoring the registered representative's compliance with applicable securities laws and regulations. When the dual employee is providing bank products or services, the bank has the responsibility for monitoring the employee's performance and compliance with BSA/AML.

Third-Party Arrangements

Third-party arrangements may involve leasing the bank's lobby space to a financial services corporation to sell NDIPs. In this case, the third party must clearly differentiate itself from the bank. If the arrangement is appropriately implemented, third-party arrangements do not affect the BSA/AML compliance requirements of the bank. As a sound practice, the bank is encouraged to ascertain if the financial services provider has an adequate BSA/AML compliance program as part of its due diligence.

In-House Sales and Proprietary Products

Unlike networking arrangements, the bank is fully responsible for in-house NDIP transactions completed on behalf of its customers, either with or without the benefit of an internal broker/dealer employee.[37] In addition, the bank may also offer its own proprietary NDIPs, which can be created and offered by the bank, its subsidiary, or an affiliate.

With in-house sales and proprietary products, the entire customer relationship and all BSA/AML risks may need to be managed by the bank, depending on how the products are sold. Unlike a networking arrangement, in which all or some of the responsibilities may be assumed by the third-party broker/dealer with in-house sales and proprietary products, the bank should manage all of its in-house and proprietary NDIP sales not only on a department-wide basis, but on an enterprise-wide basis.

Risk Factors

BSA/AML risks arise because NDIP can involve complex legal arrangements, large dollar amounts, and the rapid movement of funds. NDIP portfolios managed and controlled directly by clients pose a greater money laundering risk than those managed by the bank or by the financial services provider. Sophisticated clients may create ownership structures to obscure the ultimate control and ownership of these investments. For example, customers can retain a certain level of anonymity by creating Private Investment Companies (PICs),[38] offshore trusts, or other investment entities that hide the customer's ownership or beneficial interest.

Risk Mitigation

Management should develop risk-based policies, procedures, and processes that enable the bank to identify unusual account relationships and circumstances, questionable assets and sources of funds, and other potential areas of risk (e.g., offshore accounts, agency accounts, and unidentified beneficiaries). Management should be alert to situations that need additional review or research.

Networking Arrangements

Before entering into a networking arrangement, banks should conduct an appropriate review of the broker/dealer. The review should include an assessment of the broker/dealer's financial status, management experience, National Association of Securities Dealers (NASD) status, reputation, and ability to fulfill its BSA/AML compliance responsibilities in regards to the bank's retail customers. Appropriate due diligence would include a determination that the broker/dealer has adequate policies, procedures, and processes in place to enable the broker/dealer to meet its legal obligations.

The bank should maintain documentation on its due diligence of the broker/dealer. Furthermore, detailed written contracts should address all facets of the networking arrangement, including the responsibilities of the broker/dealer and its registered representatives. The contract should specifically cover each party's responsibilities for compliance with BSA/AML regulations and laws and for suspicious activity monitoring and reporting.

A bank may also want to mitigate risk exposure by limiting certain investment products offered to its retail customers. Investment products such as PICs, offshore trusts, or offshore hedge funds may involve international funds transfers or offer customers ways to obscure ownership interests.

Bank management should make reasonable efforts to update due diligence information on the broker/dealer. Such efforts may include a periodic review of information on the broker/dealer's compliance with its BSA/AML responsibilities, verification of the broker/dealer's record in meeting testing requirements, and a review of consumer complaints. Bank management is also encouraged, when possible, to review BSA/AML reports generated by the broker/dealer. This review could include information on account openings, transactions, investment products sold, and suspicious activity monitoring and reporting.

In-House Sales and Proprietary Products

Bank management should assess risk on the basis of a variety of factors such as:

- The type of NDIP purchased and the size of the transactions.
- The types and frequency of transactions.
- The country of residence of the principals or beneficiaries, or the country of incorporation, or the source of funds.
- Accounts and transactions that are not usual and customary for the customer or for the bank.

For customers that management considers high risk for money laundering and terrorist financing, more stringent documentation, verification, and transaction monitoring procedures should be established. Enhanced due diligence may be appropriate in the following situations:

- The bank is entering into a relationship with a new customer.
- Nondiscretionary accounts have a large asset size or frequent transactions.
- The customer resides in a foreign jurisdiction.
- The customer is a PIC or other corporate structure established in a higher risk jurisdiction.
- Assets or transactions are atypical for the customer.
- Investment type, size, assets, or transactions are atypical for the bank.
- International funds transfers are conducted, particularly from offshore funding sources.
- The identities of the principals or beneficiaries in investments or relationships are unknown or cannot be easily determined.

- Politically exposed persons (PEPs) are parties to any investments or transactions.

Examination Procedures

Nondeposit Investment Products

Objective. *Assess the adequacy of the bank's systems to manage the risks associated with both networking and in-house nondeposit investment products (NDIP), and management's ability to implement effective monitoring and reporting systems.*

1. Review the policies, procedures, and processes related to NDIP. Evaluate the adequacy of the policies, procedures, and processes given the bank's NDIP activities and the risks they present. Assess whether the controls are adequate to reasonably protect the bank from money laundering and terrorist financing.
2. If applicable, review contractual arrangements with financial service providers. Determine the BSA/AML compliance responsibility of each party. Determine whether these arrangements provide for adequate BSA/AML oversight.
3. From a review of management information systems (MIS) reports (e.g., exception reports, funds transfer reports, and activity monitoring reports) and internal risk rating factors, determine whether the bank effectively identifies and monitors NDIP, particularly those that pose a high risk for money laundering.
4. Determine how the bank includes NDIP sales activities in its bank-wide or, if applicable, enterprise-wide BSA/AML aggregation systems.
5. Determine whether the bank's system for monitoring NDIP and for reporting suspicious activities is adequate given the bank's size, complexity, location, and types of customer relationships.
6. If appropriate, refer to the core examination procedures, "Office of Foreign Assets Control," page 144, for guidance.

Transaction Testing

If the bank or its majority-owned subsidiary is responsible for the sale or direct monitoring of NDIP, then examiners should perform the following transaction testing procedures on customer accounts established by the bank:

7. On the basis of the bank's risk assessment of its NDIP activities, as well as prior examination and audit reports, select a sample of high risk NDIP. From the sample selected, perform the following examination procedures:
   - Review appropriate documentation, including CIP, to ensure that adequate due diligence has been performed and appropriate records are maintained.
   - Review account statements and, as necessary, specific transaction details for:
     Expected transactions with actual activity.
     Holdings in excess of the customer's net worth.

Irregular trading patterns (e.g., incoming funds transfers to purchase securities followed by delivery of securities to another custodian shortly thereafter).

- Determine whether actual activity is consistent with the nature of the customer's business and the stated purpose of the account. Identify any unusual or suspicious activity.

8. On the basis of examination procedures completed, including transaction testing, form a conclusion about the adequacy of policies, procedures, and processes associated with NDIP sales activities.

INSURANCE — OVERVIEW

Objective. *Assess the adequacy of the bank's systems to manage the risks associated with the sale of covered insurance products, and management's ability to implement effective monitoring and reporting systems.*

Banks engage in insurance sales to increase their profitability, mainly through expanding and diversifying fee-based income. Insurance products are typically sold to bank customers through networking arrangements with an affiliate, an operating subsidiary, or other third-party insurance providers. Banks are also interested in providing cross-selling opportunities for customers by expanding the insurance products they offer. Typically, banks take a role as a third-party agent selling covered insurance products. The types of insurance products sold may include life, health, property and casualty, and fixed or variable annuities.

AML Compliance Programs and Suspicious Activity Reporting Requirements for Insurance Companies

On November 3, 2005, FinCEN issued two final rules imposing AML obligations on insurance companies.[39] The new rules impose AML compliance program requirements and Suspicious Activity Report (SAR) obligations on insurance companies similar to those that apply to banks. The insurance regulations apply only to insurance companies; there are no independent obligations for brokers and agents. However, the insurance company is responsible for the conduct and effectiveness of its AML compliance program, which includes agent and broker activities. The insurance regulations only apply to a limited range of products that may pose a high risk of abuse by money launderers and terrorist financiers. A covered product, for the purposes of an AML compliance program, includes:

- A permanent life insurance policy, other than a group life insurance policy.
- Any annuity contract, other than a group annuity contract.
- Any other insurance product with features of cash value or investment.

When an insurance agent or broker already is required to establish a BSA/AML program under a separate requirement of the BSA regulations (e.g., bank or securities broker requirements), the insurance company generally may rely on that program to address issues at the time of sale of the covered product.[40] However, the bank may need to establish specific policies, procedures, and processes for its insurance sales in order to submit information to the insurance company for the insurance company's AML compliance.

Likewise, if a bank, as an agent of the insurance company, detects unusual or suspicious activity relating to insurance sales, it can file a joint SAR on the common activity with the insurance company.[41]

Risk Factors

Insurance products can be used to facilitate money laundering. For example, currency can be used to purchase one or more life insurance policies, which may subsequently be quickly canceled by a policyholder (also known as "early surrender") for a penalty. The insurance company refunds the money to the purchaser in the form of a check. Insurance policies without cash value or investment features are lower risk, but can be used to launder money or finance terrorism through the submission by a policyholder of inflated or false claims to its insurance carrier, which if paid, would enable the insured to recover a part or all of the originally invested payments. Other ways insurance products can be used to launder money include:

- Borrowing against the cash surrender value of permanent life insurance policies.
- Selling units in investment-linked products (such as annuities).
- Using insurance proceeds from an early policy surrender to purchase other financial assets.
- Buying policies that allow the transfer of beneficial interests without the knowledge and consent of the issuer (e.g., secondhand endowment and bearer insurance policies).[42]
- Purchasing insurance products through unusual methods such as currency or currency equivalents.
- Buying products with insurance termination features without concern for the product's investment performance.

Risk Mitigation

To mitigate money laundering risks, the bank should adopt policies, procedures, and processes that include:

- The identification of high-risk accounts.
- Customer due diligence, including enhanced due diligence for higher risk accounts.
- Product design and use, types of services offered, and unique aspects or risks of target markets.
- Employee compensation and bonus arrangements that are related to sales.
- Monitoring, including the review of early policy terminations and the reporting of unusual and suspicious transactions (e.g., a single, large premium payment, a

customer's purchase of a product that appears to fall outside the customer's normal range of financial transactions, early redemptions, multiple transactions, payments to apparently unrelated third parties, and collateralized loans).
- Recordkeeping requirements.

EXAMINATION PROCEDURES

Insurance

Objective. *Assess the adequacy of the bank's systems to manage the risks associated with the sale of covered insurance products, and management's ability to implement effective monitoring and reporting systems.*

1. Review the policies, procedures, and processes related to insurance sales. Evaluate the adequacy of the policies, procedures, and processes given the bank's insurance sales activities, its role in insurance sales, and the risks the insurance sales present. Assess whether the controls are adequate to reasonably protect the bank from money laundering and terrorist financing.
2. Review the contracts and agreements for the bank's networking arrangements with affiliates, operating subsidiaries, or other third-party insurance providers conducting sales activities on bank premises on behalf of the bank.
3. Depending on the bank's responsibilities as set forth in the contracts and agreements, review management information systems (MIS) reports (e.g., large transaction reports, single premium payments, early policy cancellation records, premium overpayments, and assignments of claims) and internal risk rating factors. Determine whether the bank effectively identifies and monitors covered insurance product sales.
4. Depending on the bank's responsibilities as set forth in the contracts and agreements, determine whether the bank's system for monitoring covered insurance products for suspicious activities, and for reporting suspicious activities, is adequate given the bank's size, complexity, location, and types of customer relationships.
5. If appropriate, refer to the core examination procedures, "Office of Foreign Assets Control," page 144, for guidance.

Transaction Testing

If the bank or its majority-owned subsidiary is responsible for the sale or direct monitoring of insurance, then examiners should perform the following transaction testing procedures.

6. On the basis of the bank's risk assessment of its insurance sales activities, as well as prior examination and audit reports, select a sample of covered insurance products. From the sample selected, perform the following examination procedures:
   - Review account opening documentation and ongoing due diligence information.

- Review account activity. Compare anticipated transactions with actual transactions.
- Determine whether activity is unusual or suspicious.

7. On the basis of examination procedures completed, including transaction testing, form a conclusion about the adequacy of policies, procedures, and processes associated with insurance sales.

CONCENTRATION ACCOUNTS — OVERVIEW

Objective. *Assess the adequacy of the bank's systems to manage the risks associated with concentration accounts, and management's ability to implement effective monitoring and reporting systems.*

Concentration accounts are internal accounts established to facilitate the processing and settlement of multiple or individual customer transactions within the bank, usually on the same day. These accounts may also be known as special-use, omnibus, suspense, settlement, intraday, sweep, or collection accounts. Concentration accounts are frequently used to facilitate transactions for private banking, trust and custody accounts, funds transfers, and international affiliates.

Risk Factors

Money laundering risk can arise in concentration accounts if the customer-identifying information, such as name, transaction amount, and account number, is separated from the financial transaction. If separation occurs, the audit trail is lost, and accounts may be misused or administered improperly. Banks that use concentration accounts should implement adequate policies, procedures, and processes covering the operation and recordkeeping for these accounts. Policies should establish guidelines to identify, measure, monitor, and control the risks.

Risk Mitigation

Because of the risks involved, management should be familiar with the nature of their customers' business and with the transactions flowing through the bank's concentration accounts. Additionally, the monitoring of concentration account transactions is necessary to identify and report unusual or suspicious transactions.

Internal controls are necessary to ensure that processed transactions include the identifying customer information. Retaining complete information is crucial for compliance with regulatory requirements as well as ensuring adequate transaction monitoring. Adequate internal controls may include:

- Maintaining a comprehensive system that identifies, bank-wide, the general ledger accounts used as concentration accounts, as well as the departments and individuals authorized to use those accounts.
- Requiring dual signatures on general ledger tickets.
- Prohibiting direct customer access to concentration accounts.
- Capturing customer transactions in the customer's account statements.
- Prohibiting customer's knowledge of concentration accounts or their ability to direct employees to conduct transactions through the accounts.
- Retaining appropriate transaction and customer identifying information.
- Frequent reconciling of the accounts by an individual who is independent from the transactions.
- Establishing timely discrepancy resolution process.
- Identifying recurring customer names.

EXAMINATION PROCEDURES

Concentration Accounts

Objective. *Assess the adequacy of the bank's systems to manage the risks associated with concentration accounts, and management's ability to implement effective monitoring and reporting systems.*

1. Review the policies, procedures, and processes related to concentration accounts. Evaluate the adequacy of the policies, procedures, and processes in relation to the bank's concentration account activities and the risks they represent. Assess whether the controls are adequate to reasonably protect the bank from money laundering and terrorist financing.
2. From a review of management information systems (MIS) and internal risk rating factors, determine whether the bank effectively identifies and monitors concentration accounts.
3. Review the general ledger and identify any concentration accounts. After discussing concentration accounts with management and conducting any additional research needed, obtain and review a list of all concentration accounts and the bank's most recent reconcilements.
4. Determine whether the bank's system for monitoring concentration accounts for suspicious activities, and for reporting of suspicious activities, is adequate given the bank's size, complexity, location, and types of customer relationships.
5. If appropriate, refer to the core examination procedures, "Office of Foreign Assets Control," page 144, for guidance.

Transaction Testing

6. On the basis of the bank's risk assessment of its concentration accounts, as well as prior examination and audit reports, select a sample of concentration accounts. From the sample selected, perform the following examination procedures:
   - Obtain account activity reports for selected concentration accounts.
   - Evaluate the activity and select a sample of transactions passing through different concentration accounts for further review.
   - Focus on high-risk activity (e.g., funds transfers or monetary instruments purchases) and transactions from high-risk jurisdictions.
7. On the basis of examination procedures completed, including transaction testing, form a conclusion about the adequacy of policies, procedures, and processes associated with concentration accounts.

LENDING ACTIVITIES — OVERVIEW

Objective. *Assess the adequacy of the bank's systems to manage the risks associated with lending activities, and management's ability to implement effective due diligence, monitoring, and reporting systems.*

Lending activities include, but are not limited to, real estate, trade finance,[43] cash-secured, credit card, consumer, commercial, and agricultural. Lending activities can include multiple parties (e.g., guarantors, signatories, principals, or loan participants).

Risk Factors

The involvement of multiple parties may increase the risk of money laundering or terrorist financing when the source and use of the funds are not transparent. This lack of transparency can create opportunities in any of the three stages of money laundering or terrorist financing schemes. These schemes could include the following:

- To secure a loan, an individual purchases a certificate of deposit with illicit funds.
- Loans are made for an ambiguous or illegitimate purpose.
- Loans are made for, or are paid for, a third party.
- The bank or the customer attempts to sever the paper trail between the borrower and the illicit funds.
- Loans are extended to persons located outside the United States, particularly to those in high-risk jurisdictions and geographic locations. Loans may also involve collateral located outside the United States.

Risk Mitigation

All loans are considered to be accounts for purposes of the Customer Identification Program (CIP) regulations. For loans that may pose a higher risk for money laundering and terrorist financing, including the loans listed above, the bank should complete due diligence on related account parties (i.e., guarantors, signatories, or principals). Due diligence beyond what is required for a particular lending activity will vary according to the BSA/AML risks present, but could include performing reference checks, obtaining credit references, verifying the source of collateral, and obtaining tax or financial statements on the borrower and any or all of the various parties involved in the loan.

The bank should have policies, procedures, and processes to monitor, identify, and report unusual and suspicious activities. The sophistication of the systems used to monitor lending account activity should conform to the size and complexity of the bank's lending business. For example, the bank can review loan reports such as early payoffs, past dues, fraud, or cash-secured.

EXAMINATION PROCEDURES

Lending Activities

Objective. *Assess the adequacy of the bank's systems to manage the risks associated with lending activities, and management's ability to implement effective due diligence, monitoring, and reporting systems.*

1. Review the policies, procedures, and processes related to lending activities. Evaluate the adequacy of the policies, procedures, and processes given the bank's lending activities and the risks they represent. Assess whether the controls are adequate to reasonably protect the bank from money laundering and terrorist financing.
2. From a review of management information systems (MIS) and internal risk rating factors, determine whether the bank effectively identifies and monitors high-risk loan accounts.
3. Determine whether the bank's system for monitoring loan accounts for suspicious activities and for reporting of suspicious activities, is adequate given the bank's size, complexity, location, and types of customer relationships.
4. If appropriate, refer to the core examination procedures, "Office of Foreign Assets Control," page 144, for guidance.

Transaction Testing

5. On the basis of the bank's risk assessment of its lending activities, as well as prior examination and audit reports, select a sample of high-risk loan accounts. From the sample selected, perform the following examination procedures:

- Review account opening documentation, including CIP, to ensure that adequate due diligence has been performed and that appropriate records are maintained.
- Review, as necessary, loan history.
- Compare expected transactions with actual activity.
- Determine whether actual activity is consistent with the nature of the customer's business and the stated purpose of the loan. Identify any unusual or suspicious activity.

6. On the basis of examination procedures completed, including transaction testing, form a conclusion about the adequacy of policies, procedures, and processes associated with lending relationships.

TRADE FINANCE ACTIVITIES — OVERVIEW

Objective. *Assess the adequacy of the bank's systems to manage the risks associated with trade finance activities, and management's ability to implement effective due diligence, monitoring, and reporting systems.*

Trade finance typically involves short-term financing to facilitate the import and export of goods. These operations can involve payment if documentary requirements are met (e.g., letter of credit), or may instead involve payment if the original obligor defaults on the commercial terms of the transactions (e.g., guarantees or standby letters of credit). In both cases, a bank's involvement in trade finance minimizes payment risk to importers and exporters. The nature of trade finance activities, however, requires the active involvement of multiple parties on both sides of the transaction. In addition to the basic exporter or importer relationship at the center of any particular trade activity, relationships may exist between the exporter and its suppliers and between the importer and its customers. Both the exporter and importer may also have other banking relationships. Furthermore, many other intermediary financial and nonfinancial institutions may provide conduits and services to expedite the underlying documents and payment flows associated with trade transactions.

In transactions that are covered by letters of credit, participants can take the following roles:

- **Applicant.** The buyer or party who requests the issuance of a letter of credit.

- **Issuing Bank.** Issues the letter of credit on behalf of the Applicant and forwards it to the Advising Bank for notification to the Beneficiary. The Applicant is the Issuing Bank's customer.

- **Confirming Bank.** Typically in the country of the Beneficiary, at the request of the Issuing Bank, joins the Issuing Bank in honoring draws made by the Beneficiary, provided the terms and conditions of the letter of credit are met.

- **Advising Bank.** Branch or correspondent bank near the Beneficiary's domicile, to which the Issuing Bank sends the letter of credit or notification of its issuance, with instructions to notify the Beneficiary. The Advising Bank advises the Beneficiary without taking other active engagement in the letter of credit.

- **Beneficiary (Drawer).** The seller or party to whom the letter of credit is addressed.
- **Negotiating Bank.** Usually the Beneficiary's bank. Agrees to purchase the draft and pay the Beneficiary after satisfying itself that documentary requirements have been met.
- **Accepting Bank.** Incurs a legal obligation to pay the draft at maturity. Drafts are drawn on the Accepting Bank that dates and signs the instrument.
- **Discounting Bank.** Discounts a draft for the Beneficiary after it has been accepted by an Accepting Bank.
- **Reimbursing Bank.** Authorized by the Issuing Bank to reimburse the Drawee Bank submitting claims under the letter credit.
- **Paying (Drawee) Bank.** As named in the letter of credit, the bank where drafts are to be paid. The Paying Bank is typically the Issuing Bank, but is often a branch or correspondent of the Issuing Bank. Once paid or accepted by the Paying or Drawee Bank, there is no recourse to the drawers.

As an example, in a letter of credit arrangement, a bank can serve as the Issuing Bank, allowing its customer (the buyer) to purchase goods locally or internationally, or the bank can act as an Advising Bank, enabling its customer (the exporter) to sell its goods locally or internationally. The relationship between any two banks may vary and could include any of the roles listed above.

Risk Factors

The involvement of multiple parties can make the process of due diligence more difficult. Also, since trade finance can be more document-based than other banking activities, it can be susceptible to documentary fraud, which can be linked to money laundering, terrorist financing, or the circumvention of OFAC sanctions or other prohibitions.

While banks should be alert to transactions involving higher risk goods (e.g., trade in weapons or nuclear equipment), they need to be aware that goods may be over- or under-valued in an effort to evade AML or customs regulations. For example, an importer may pay a large sum of money from the proceeds of an illegal activity for goods that are essentially worthless and are subsequently discarded. Alternatively, trade documents, such as invoices, may be fraudulently altered to hide the scheme. Variations on this theme include double invoicing, partial shipment of goods, and the use of fictitious goods. Illegal proceeds transferred in such transactions thereby appear sanitized and enter the realm of legitimate commerce.

The Applicant may substitute third-party nominees, such as shell companies, to disguise the Applicant's role in a trade finance agreement. This substitution results in a lack of transparency, effectively hiding the identity of the purchasing party, thus increasing the risk of money laundering activity.

Risk Mitigation

Sound customer due diligence (CDD) procedures are needed to gain a thorough understanding of the customer's underlying business and locations served. The banks in the letter of credit process need to undertake varying degrees of due diligence depending upon their role in the transaction. For example, Issuing Banks should conduct sufficient due diligence on prospective import or export customers before establishing the letter of credit. The due diligence should include gathering sufficient information on Applicants and Beneficiaries, including their identities, nature of business, and sources of funding.

This may require the use of background checks or investigations, particularly in higher risk jurisdictions. As such, banks should conduct a thorough review and reasonably know their customers prior to facilitating trade-related activity and should have a thorough understanding of trade finance documentation. Refer to the core overview section, "Customer Due Diligence," page 56, for additional guidance.

Banks taking other roles in the letter of credit process should complete due diligence that is commensurate with their roles in each transaction. Banks need to be aware that because of the frequency of transactions in which multiple banks are involved, Issuing Banks may not always have correspondent relationships with the Advising or Confirming Bank.

Documentation should be reviewed, not only for compliance with the terms of the letter of credit, but also for anomalies or red flags that could indicate unusual or suspicious activity. These anomalies could appear in shipping documentation, obvious under- or over-invoicing, government licenses (when required), or discrepancies in the description of goods on various documents. Identification of these elements may not, in itself, require the filing of a Suspicious Activity Report (SAR), but may suggest the need for further research and verification. In circumstances where a SAR is warranted, the bank is not expected to stop trade or discontinue processing the transaction. However, stopping the trade may be required to avoid a potential violation of an OFAC sanction.

Issuing Banks maintain foreign correspondent relationships to facilitate international trade. Trade finance transactions frequently use Society for Worldwide Interbank Financial Telecommunication (SWIFT) messages. U.S. banks must comply with OFAC regulations, and when necessary, licensing in advance of funding. Banks should monitor the names of the parties contained in these messages and compare the names against OFAC lists. Refer to overview section, "Office of Foreign Assets Control," page 135, for guidance. Banks with a high volume of SWIFT messages should determine whether their monitoring efforts are adequate to detect suspicious activity, particularly if the monitoring mechanism is not automated. Refer to expanded overview section, "Funds Transfers," page 189, for additional guidance.

Policies, procedures, and processes should also require a thorough review of all applicable trade documentation to enable the bank to monitor and report unusual and suspicious activity, based on the role played by the bank in the letter of credit process. The sophistication of the documentation review process and management information systems should be commensurate with the size and complexity of the bank's trade finance portfolio and its role in the letter of credit process. In addition to OFAC filtering, the monitoring process should give greater scrutiny to:

- Items shipped that are inconsistent with the nature of the customer's business (e.g., a steel company that starts dealing in paper products, or an information technology company that starts dealing in bulk pharmaceuticals).
- Customers conducting business in high-risk jurisdictions.
- Customers shipping items through high-risk jurisdictions, including transit through non-cooperative countries.
- Customers involved in potentially high-risk activities (e.g., dealers in weapons, nuclear materials, chemicals, precious gems; or certain natural resources such as metals, ore, and crude oil).
- Obvious over- or under-pricing of goods and services (e.g., importer pays $400 an item for one shipment and $750 for an identical item in the next shipment; exporter charges one customer $100 per item and another customer $400 for an identical item in the same week).
- Excessively amended letters of credit without reasonable justification.
- Transactions evidently designed to evade legal restrictions, including evasion of necessary government licensing requirements.

Unless customer behavior or transaction documentation appears unusual, the bank should not be expected to spend undue time or effort reviewing all information. The examples above, particularly for an Issuing Bank, may be included as part of its routine CDD process. Banks with robust CDD programs may find that less focus is needed on individual transactions as a result of their comprehensive knowledge of the customer's activities.

Examination Procedures

Trade Finance Activities

Objective. *Assess the adequacy of the bank's systems to manage the risks associated with trade finance activities, and management's ability to implement effective due diligence, monitoring, and reporting systems.*

1. Review the policies, procedures, and processes related to trade finance activities. Evaluate the adequacy of the policies, procedures, and processes governing trade finance-related activities and the risks they represent. Assess whether the controls are adequate to reasonably protect the bank from money laundering and terrorist financing.
2. Evaluate the adequacy of the due diligence information the bank obtains for the customer's files. Determine whether the bank has processes in place for obtaining

information at account opening, in addition to ensuring current customer information is maintained.

3. From a review of management information systems (MIS) and internal risk rating factors, determine whether the bank effectively identifies and monitors the trade finance portfolio for suspicious or unusual activities, particularly those that pose a higher risk for money laundering.
4. Determine whether the bank's system for monitoring trade finance activities for suspicious activities, and for reporting of suspicious activities, is adequate, given the bank's size, complexity, location, and types of customer relationships.
5. If appropriate, refer to the core examination procedures, "Office of Foreign Assets Control," page 144, for guidance.

Transaction Testing

6. On the basis of the bank's risk assessment of its trade finance portfolio, as well as prior examination and audit reports, select a sample of trade finance accounts. From the sample selected, review customer due diligence documentation to determine whether the information is commensurate with the customer's risk. Identify any unusual or suspicious activities.
7. Verify whether the bank monitors the trade finance portfolio for potential OFAC violations and unusual transactional patterns and conducts and records the results of any due diligence.
8. On the basis of examination procedures completed, including transaction testing, form a conclusion about the adequacy of policies, procedures, and processes associated with trade finance activities.

PRIVATE BANKING — OVERVIEW

Objective. *Assess the adequacy of the bank's systems to manage the risks associated with private banking activities, and management's ability to implement effective due diligence, monitoring, and reporting systems. This section expands the core review of the statutory and regulatory requirements of private banking in order to provide a broader assessment of the AML risks associated with this activity.*

Private banking activities are generally defined as providing personalized services to high net worth customers (e.g., estate planning, financial advice, lending, investment management, bill paying, mail forwarding, and maintenance of a residence). Private banking has become an increasingly important business line for large and diverse banking organizations and a source of enhanced fee income.

U.S. banks may manage private banking relationships for both domestic and international customers. Typically, thresholds of private banking service are based on the amount of assets under management and on the need for specific products or services (e.g., real estate management, closely held company oversight, money management). The fees charged are ordinarily based on asset thresholds and the use of specific products and services.

Private banking arrangements are typically structured to have a central point of contact (i.e., relationship manager) that acts as a liaison between the client and the bank and facilitates the client's use of the bank's financial services and products. Appendix N ("Private Banking — Common Structure") provides an example of a typical private banking structure and illustrates the relationship between the client and the relationship manager. Typical products and services offered in a private banking relationship include:

- Cash management (e.g., checking accounts, overdraft privileges, cash sweeps, and bill-paying services).
- Funds transfers.
- Asset management (e.g., trust, investment advisory, investment management, and custodial and brokerage services).[44]
- The facilitation of offshore entities (e.g., Private Investment Companies (PICs), international business corporations (IBCs), and trusts).[45]
- Lending services (e.g., mortgage loans, credit cards, personal loans, and letters of credit).
- Financial planning services including tax and estate planning.
- Custody services.
- Other services as requested (e.g., mail services).

Privacy and confidentiality are important elements of private banking relationships. Although customers may choose private banking services simply to manage their assets, they may also seek a confidential, safe, and legal haven for their capital. When acting as a fiduciary, banks have statutory, contractual, and ethical obligations to uphold.

Risk Factors

Private banking services can be vulnerable to money laundering schemes, and past money laundering prosecutions have demonstrated that vulnerability. The 1999 Permanent Subcommittee on Investigations' "Private Banking and Money Laundering: A Case Study of Opportunities and Vulnerabilities"[46] outlined, in part, the following vulnerabilities to money laundering:

- Private bankers as client advocates.
- Powerful clients including politically exposed persons, industrialists, and entertainers.
- A culture of confidentiality and the use of secrecy jurisdictions or shell companies.[47]
- A private banking culture of lax internal controls.
- The competitive nature of the business.
- Significant profit potential for the bank.

Risk of Shell Companies

A shell company exists on paper but transacts either no business or minimal business. They are typically used for legitimate investment purposes and can be incorporated in the United States (e.g., Delaware) or offshore as IBCs. The risks associated with shell companies include poor or nonexistent records (e.g., ownership documentation), inadequate government oversight, the lack of public disclosures, and the large range of permissible activities that may be allowed in the incorporating jurisdiction. Some shell companies issue bearer shares (i.e., ownership is vested via bearer shares, which allows conveying ownership of the corporation by simply transferring physical possession of the shares). Because of the high degree of money laundering and terrorist financing risks associated with shell companies, especially those vesting ownership using bearer shares, banks should identify their exposure to these entities. Because many shell companies allow an individual to be shielded by the shell company's legal identity, due diligence may be difficult.

Risk Mitigation

Effective policies, procedures, and processes can help protect banks from becoming conduits for or victims of money laundering, terrorist financing, and other financial crimes that are perpetrated through private banking relationships. Additional information relating to risk assessments and due diligence is contained in the core overview section, "Private Banking Due Diligence Program (Non-U.S. Persons)," page 118. Ultimately, illicit activities through the private banking unit could result in significant financial costs and reputational risk to the bank if management oversight is lax. Financial impacts could include regulatory sanctions and fines, litigation expenses, the loss of business, reduced liquidity, asset seizures and freezes, loan losses, and remediation expenses.

Customer Risk Assessment

Banks should assess the risks its private banking activities pose on the basis of the scope of operations and the complexity of the bank's customer relationships. Management should establish a risk profile for each customer to be used in prioritizing oversight resources and for ongoing monitoring of relationship activities. The following factors should be considered when identifying risk characteristics of private banking customers:

- **Nature of the customer and the customer's business.** The source of the customer's wealth, the nature of the customer's business, and the extent to which the customer's business history presents an increased risk for money laundering and terrorist financing. This factor should be considered for private banking accounts opened for politically exposed persons (PEPs).[48]

- **Purpose and activity.** The size, purpose, types of accounts, products, and services involved in the relationship, and the anticipated activity of the account.

- **Relationship.** The nature and duration of the bank's relationship (including relationships with affiliates) with the private banking customer.

- **Customer's corporate structure.** Type of corporate structure (e.g., IBCs, shell companies (domestic or foreign), or PICs).

- **Location and jurisdiction.** The location of the private banking customer's domicile and business (domestic or foreign). The review should consider the extent to which the relevant jurisdiction is internationally recognized as presenting a greater risk for money laundering or, conversely, is considered to have robust AML standards.

- **Public information.** Information known or reasonably available to the bank about the private banking customer. The scope and depth of this review should depend on the nature of this relationship and the risks involved.

Customer Due Diligence

Customer due diligence (CDD) is essential when establishing any customer relationship and it is critical for private banking clients.[49] Banks should take reasonable steps to establish the identity of their private banking clients and, as appropriate, the beneficial owners of accounts. Adequate due diligence should vary based on the risk factors identified previously. Policies, procedures, and processes should define acceptable CDD for different types of products (e.g., PICs), services, and accountholders. As due diligence is an ongoing process, a bank should take measures to ensure account profiles are current and monitoring should be risk-based. Banks should consider whether risk profiles should be adjusted or suspicious activity reported when the activity is inconsistent with the profile.

Under the Customer Identification Program (CIP), banks must verify customer information for private banking accounts; this minimum requirement, however, does not extend to beneficiaries of those accounts. For purposes of the CIP, a bank is not required to look through accounts maintained for non-individuals (e.g., private banking accounts opened for a PIC) to verify the identities of beneficiaries. Instead, the bank is only required to verify the identity of the named accountholder. A bank may, however, need to take additional steps to verify the identity of a customer that is not an individual (e.g., a PIC) by obtaining information about individuals with ownership or control over the account in order to verify the customer's identity[50] and to determine whether the account is maintained for non-U.S. persons.[51]

Before opening accounts, banks should collect the following information from the private banking clients:

- The purpose of the account.
- The type of products and services to be used.
- Anticipated account activity.
- A description and history of the source of the client's wealth.
- The client's estimated net worth, including financial statements.
- The current source of funds for the account.
- The references or other information to confirm the reputation of the client.

Shell Company Risk Mitigation

Risk mitigation of shell companies may include maintaining control of bearer shares, entrusting the shares with a reliable independent third party, or requiring periodic certification of ownership. Banks should assess the risks these relationships pose and determine the appropriate controls. For example, banks may choose to maintain (or have an independent third party maintain) bearer shares for new clients, or those without well-established relationships with the institution. For well-known, long-time customers, banks may find that periodically re-certifying beneficial ownership is effective. The best underlying control associated with these types of structures is a strong CDD program through which banks determine the nature, purpose, and expected use of shell companies and apply appropriate monitoring and documentation standards.

Board of Directors and Senior Management Oversight

The board of directors' and senior management's active oversight of private banking activities and the creation of an appropriate corporate oversight culture are crucial elements of a sound risk management and control environment. The purpose and objectives of the organization's private banking activities should be clearly identified and communicated by the board and senior management. Well-developed goals and objectives should describe the target client base in terms of minimum net worth, investable assets, and types of products and services sought. Goals and objectives should also specifically describe the types of clients the bank will and will not accept and should establish appropriate levels of authorization for new-client acceptance. Board and senior management should also be actively involved in establishing control and risk management goals for private banking activities, including effective audit and compliance reviews. Each bank should ensure that its policies, procedures, and processes for conducting private banking activities are evaluated and updated regularly and ensure that roles, responsibilities, and accountability are clearly delineated.

Employee compensation plans are often based on the number of new accounts established or on an increase in managed assets. Board and senior management should ensure that compensation plans do not create incentives for employees to ignore appropriate due diligence and account opening procedures, or possible suspicious activity relating to the account. Procedures that require various levels of approval for accepting new private banking accounts can minimize such opportunities.

Given the sensitive nature of private banking and the potential liability associated with it, banks should thoroughly investigate the background of newly hired private banking relationship managers and should establish ongoing monitoring of their personal financial condition to detect any indications of inappropriate activities. However, when private banking relationship managers change employers, their customers often move with them. Banks bear the same potential liability for the existing customers of newly hired officers as they do for any new, private banking relationship. Therefore, those accounts should be promptly reviewed using the bank's procedures for establishing new account relationships.

Management information systems (MIS) and reports are also important in effectively supervising and managing private banking relationships and risks. Board and senior management should review relationship manager compensation reports, budget or target comparison reports, and applicable risk management reports. Private banker MIS reports should enable the relationship manager to view and manage the whole client and any related client relationships.

EXAMINATION PROCEDURES

Private Banking

Objective. *Assess the adequacy of the bank's systems to manage the risks associated with private banking activities, and management's ability to implement effective due diligence, monitoring, and reporting systems. This section expands the core review of the statutory and regulatory requirements of private banking in order to provide a broader assessment of the AML risks associated with this activity.*

1. Review the policies, procedures, and processes related to private banking activities. Evaluate the adequacy of the policies, procedures, and processes given the bank's private banking activities and the risks they represent. Assess whether the controls are adequate to reasonably protect the bank from money laundering and terrorist financing.
2. From a review of management information systems (MIS) reports (e.g., customer aggregation, policy exception and missing documentation, customer risk classification, unusual accounts activity, and client concentrations) and internal risk rating factors, determine whether the bank effectively identifies and monitors private banking relationships, particularly those that pose a higher risk for money laundering.
3. Determine whether the bank's system for monitoring private banking relationships for suspicious activities, and for reporting of suspicious activities, is adequate given the bank's size, complexity, location, and types of customer relationships.
4. Review the private banking compensation program. Determine whether it includes qualitative measures that are provided to employees to comply with account opening and suspicious activity monitoring and reporting requirements.
5. Review the monitoring program the bank uses to oversee the private banking relationship manager's personal financial condition and to detect any inappropriate activities.
6. If appropriate, refer to the core examination procedures, "Office of Foreign Assets Control," page 144, for guidance.

Transaction Testing

7. On the basis of the bank's risk assessment of its private banking activities, as well as prior examination and audit reports, select a sample of private banking accounts. The sample should include the following types of accounts:

   - Politically exposed persons (PEPs).

- Private Investment Companies (PICs), international business corporations (IBCs), and shell companies.
- Offshore entities.
- Cash-intensive businesses.
- Import or export companies.
- Customers from or doing business in a high-risk geographic location.
- Customers listed on unusual activity monitoring reports.
- Customers who have large dollar transactions and frequent funds transfers.

8. From the sample selected, perform the following examination procedures:
    - Review account opening documentation and ongoing due diligence information.
    - Review account statements and, as necessary, specific transaction details.
    - Compare expected transactions with actual activity.
    - Determine whether actual activity is consistent with the nature of the customer's business.
    - Identify any unusual or suspicious activity.
9. On the basis of examination procedures completed, including transaction testing, form a conclusion about the adequacy of policies, procedures, and processes associated with private banking relationships.

TRUST AND ASSET MANAGEMENT SERVICES — OVERVIEW

Objective. *Assess the adequacy of the bank's policies, procedures, processes, and systems to manage the risks associated with trust and asset management*[52] *services, and management's ability to implement effective due diligence, monitoring, and reporting systems.*

Trust[53] accounts are generally defined as a legal arrangement in which one party (the trustor or grantor) transfers ownership of assets to a person or bank (the trustee) to be held or used for the benefit of others. These arrangements include the broad categories of court-supervised accounts (i.e., executorships and guardianships), personal trusts (i.e., living trusts, trusts established under a will, and charitable trusts), and corporate trusts (i.e., bond trusteeships).

Unlike trust arrangements, agency accounts are established by contract and governed by contract law. Assets are held under the terms of the contract, and legal title or ownership does not transfer to the bank as agent. Agency accounts include custody, escrow, investment management,[54] and safekeeping relationships. Agency products and services may be offered in a traditional trust department or through other bank departments.

Customer Identification Program

Customer Identification Program (CIP) rules, which became effective October 1, 2003, apply to substantially all bank accounts opened after that date. The CIP rule defines an "account" to include cash management, safekeeping, custodian, and trust relationships.

However, the CIP rule excludes employee benefit accounts established pursuant to the Employee Retirement Income Security Act of 1974 (ERISA).

For purposes of the CIP, the bank is not required to search the trust, escrow, or similar accounts to verify the identities of beneficiaries, but instead is only required to verify the identity of the named accountholder (the trust). In the case of a trust account, the customer is the trust whether or not the bank is the trustee for the trust. However, the CIP rule also provides that, based on the bank's risk assessment of a new account opened by a customer that is not an individual, the bank may need "to obtain information about" individuals with authority or control over such an account, including signatories, in order to verify the customer's identity.[55] For example, in certain circumstances involving revocable trusts, the bank may need to gather information about the settlor, grantor, trustee, or other persons with the authority to direct the trustee, and who thus have authority or control over the account, in order to establish the true identity of the customer.

In the case of an escrow account, if a bank establishes an account in the name of a third party, such as a real estate agent, who is acting as escrow agent, then the bank's customer is the escrow agent. If the bank is the escrow agent, then the person who establishes the account is the bank's customer. For example, if the purchaser of real estate directly opens an escrow account and deposits funds to be paid to the seller upon satisfaction of specified conditions, the bank's customer will be the purchaser. Further, if a company in formation establishes an escrow account for investors to deposit their subscriptions pending receipt of a required minimum amount, the bank's customer will be the company in formation (or if not yet a legal entity, the person opening the account on its behalf). However, the CIP rule also provides that, based on the bank's risk assessment of a new account opened by a customer that is not an individual, the bank may need "to obtain information about" individuals with authority or control over such an account, including signatories, in order to verify the customer's identity.[56]

Risk Factors

Trust and asset management accounts, including agency relationships, present BSA/AML concerns similar to those of deposit taking, lending, and other traditional banking activities. Concerns are primarily due to the unique relationship structures involved when the bank handles trust and agency activities, such as:

- Personal and court-supervised accounts.
- Trust accounts formed in the private banking department.
- Asset management and investment advisory accounts.
- Global and domestic custody accounts.
- Securities lending.
- Employee benefit and retirement accounts.
- Corporate trust accounts.
- Transfer agent accounts.
- Other related business lines.

As in any account relationship, money laundering risk may arise from trust and asset management activities. When misused, trust and asset management accounts can conceal the sources and uses of funds, as well as the identity of beneficial and legal owners. Customers and account beneficiaries may try to remain anonymous in order to move illicit funds or avoid scrutiny. For example, customers may seek a certain level of anonymity by creating Private Investment Companies (PICs),[57] offshore trusts, or other investment entities that hide the true ownership or beneficial interest of the trust.

Risk Mitigation

Management should develop policies, procedures, and processes that enable the bank to identify unusual account relationships and circumstances, questionable assets and sources of assets, and other potential areas of risk (e.g., offshore accounts, PICs, asset protection trusts (APTs),[58] agency accounts, and unidentified beneficiaries). While the majority of traditional trust and asset management accounts will not need enhanced due diligence, management should be alert to those situations that need additional review or research.

Customer Comparison against Lists

The bank must maintain required CIP information and complete the required one-time check of trust account names against section 314(a) search requests. The bank should also be able to identify customers who may be politically exposed persons (PEPs), doing business with or located in a jurisdiction designated as "primary money laundering concern" under section 311 of the Patriot Act, or match OFAC lists.[59] As a sound practice, the bank should also determine the identity of other parties that may have control over the account, such as grantors or co-trustees. Refer to the core overview section, "Information Sharing," page 86, and expanded overview section, "Politically Exposed Persons," page 261, for additional guidance.

Circumstances Warranting Enhanced Due Diligence

Management should assess account risk on the basis of a variety of factors, which may include:

- The type of trust or agency account and its size.
- The types and frequency of transactions.
- The country of residence of the principals or beneficiaries, or the country where established, or source of funds.
- Accounts and transactions that are not usual and customary for the customer or for the bank.

Stringent documentation, verification, and transaction monitoring procedures should be established for accounts that management considers as high risk. Typically, employee benefit accounts and court-supervised accounts are among the lowest BSA/AML risks.

The following are examples of situations in which enhanced due diligence may be appropriate:

- The bank is entering into a relationship with a new customer.
- The account principals or beneficiaries reside in a foreign jurisdiction, or the trust or its funding mechanisms are established offshore.
- Assets or transactions are atypical for the type and character of the customer.
- The account type, size, assets, or transactions are atypical for the bank.
- International funds transfers are conducted, particularly through offshore funding sources.
- Accounts are funded with easily transportable assets such as gemstones, precious metals, coins, artwork, rare stamps, or negotiable instruments.
- Accounts or relationships are maintained in which the identities of the principals, or beneficiaries, or sources of funds are unknown or cannot easily be determined.
- Accounts benefit charitable organizations or other non-governmental organizations (NGOs) that may be used as a conduit for illegal activities.[60]
- Interest on lawyers' trust accounts (IOLTA) holding and processing significant dollar amounts.
- Account assets that include PICs.
- PEPs are parties to any accounts or transactions.

EXAMINATION PROCEDURES

Trust and Asset Management Services

Objective. *Assess the adequacy of the bank's policies, procedures, processes, and systems to manage the risks associated with trust and asset management*[61] *services, and management's ability to implement effective due diligence, monitoring, and reporting systems.*

If this is a standalone trust examination, refer to the core examination procedures, "Scoping and Planning," page 15, for comprehensive guidance on the BSA/AML examination scope. In such instances, the trust examination may need to cover additional areas, including training, the BSA compliance officer, independent review, and follow-up items.

1. Review the policies, procedures, and processes related to trust and asset management services. Evaluate the adequacy of the policies, procedures, and processes given the bank's trust and asset management activities and the risks they represent. Assess whether the controls are adequate to reasonably protect the bank from money laundering and terrorist financing.
2. Review the bank's procedures for gathering additional identification information, when necessary, about the settlor, grantor, trustee, or other persons with authority to direct a trustee, and who thus have authority or control over the account, in order to establish a true identity of the customer.
3. From a review of management information systems (MIS) and internal risk rating factors, determine whether the bank effectively identifies and monitors trust and asset

management relationships, particularly those that pose a high risk for money laundering.

4. Determine how the bank includes trust and asset management relationships in a bank- wide or, if appropriate, enterprise-wide BSA/AML aggregation systems.
5. Determine whether the bank's system for monitoring trust and asset management relationships for suspicious activities, and for reporting of suspicious activities, is adequate given the bank's size, complexity, location, and types of customer relationships.
6. If appropriate, refer to the core examination procedures, "Office of Foreign Assets Control," page 144, for guidance.

Transaction Testing

7. On the basis of the bank's risk assessment of its trust and asset management relationships, as well as prior examination and audit reports, select a sample of high-risk trust and asset management services relationships. Include relationships with grantors and co-trustees, if they have authority or control, as well as any high-risk assets such as Private Investment Companies (PICs) or asset protection trusts. From the sample selected, perform the following examination procedures:

    - Review account opening documentation, including the Customer Identification Program (CIP), to ensure that adequate due diligence has been performed and that appropriate records are maintained.
    - Review account statements and, as necessary, specific transaction details. Compare expected transactions with actual activity.
    - Determine whether actual activity is consistent with the nature of the customer's business and the stated purpose of the account.
    - Identify any unusual or suspicious activity.

8. On the basis of examination procedures completed, including transaction testing, form a conclusion about the adequacy of policies, procedures, and processes associated with trust and asset management relationships.

End Notes

[1] A respondent bank is any bank for which another bank establishes, maintains, administers, or manages a correspondent account relationship.

[2] A respondent bank is any bank for which another bank establishes, maintains, administers, or manages a correspondent account relationship.

[3] Refer to the expanded overview section, "Payable Through Accounts," page 176, for additional information.

[4] In this type of relationship, the foreign financial institution is commonly referred to as the "master accountholder."

[5] It is possible for a sub-account to be subdivided into further sub-accounts for separate persons.

[6] Referral agents are foreign individuals or corporations, contractually obligated to the U.S. bank. They provide representative-type services to the bank's clients abroad for a fee. Services can range from referring new customers to the bank, to special mail handling, obtaining and pouching documents, distributing the bank's brochures and applications or forms, notarizing documents for customers, and mailing customers' funds to the bank in the United States for deposit.

[7] For additional guidance, refer to core overview section, "International Transportation of Currency or Monetary Instruments Reporting," page 132.

[8] Refer to the core examination procedures, "International Transportation of Currency or Monetary Instruments Reporting," page 134, for additional guidance.

[9] The FFIEC *Information Technology Examination Handbook* is available at www.ffiec.gov/ffiecinfobase/html_pages/it_01.html

[10] Refer to "Authentication in an Internet Banking Environment" issued by the FFIEC, October 13, 2005, for additional information.

[11] The FFIEC *Information Technology Examination Handbook* is available at www.ffiec.gov/ffiecinfobase/html_pages/it_01.html.

[12] Fedwire® is a registered service mark of the Federal Reserve Banks. See www.frbservices.org/Wholesale/fedwirefunds.html for further information.

[13] CHIPS is a private multilateral settlement system owned and operated by The Clearing House Payments Company.

[14] Fedwire participants are any entities that maintain an account with a Federal Reserve Bank in the entity's name. Subject to the Federal Reserve Banks' and the Board of Governors of the Federal Reserve System's Payment System Risk policies, when applicable, entities authorized by law, regulation, policy, or agreement to be participants include:

- Depository institutions.
- Agencies and branches of foreign banks.
- Member banks of the Federal Reserve System.
- The U.S. Treasury and any entity specifically authorized by federal statute to use the Federal Reserve Banks as fiscal agents or depositories, including entities designated by the Secretary of the Treasury.
- Foreign central banks, foreign monetary authorities, foreign governments, and certain international organizations.
- Any other entities authorized by a Federal Reserve Bank to use the Fedwire Securities Service.

[15] In 2006, the Federal Reserve Banks plan to complete migration of Fedwire participants from the FedLine DOS method of access to FedLine Advantage.

[16] Sources of information on IVTS include:

- FinCEN Advisory 33, "Informal Value Transfer Systems," March 2003.
- U.S. Treasury "Informal Value Transfer Systems Report to the Congress in Accordance with Section 359 of the Patriot Act," November 2002.
- Financial Action Task Force on Money Laundering (FATF), "Interpretative Note to Special Recommendation VI: Alternative Remittance," June 2003.
- FATF, "Combating the Abuse of Alternative Remittance Systems, International Best Practices," October 2002.

[17] "*The Next Generation ACH Task Force: Future Vision of the ACH Network*," February 2002, page 1. www.nacha.org.

[18] See www.nacha.org. NACHA's figures include both government and commercial interbank ACH credit and debit transactions. Based upon the most recent Federal Reserve non-cash retail payments study, "onus" government and commercial inter-bank ACH credit and debit transactions may add up to 20 percent more in total volume for a total of more than 13 billion transactions.

[19] The Federal Reserve Banks operate FedACH, a central clearing facility for transmitting and receiving ACH payments.

[20] Refer to the expanded overview section, "Third-Party Payment Processors," page 205, for additional guidance.

[21] When independent TPSPs contract with independent sales organizations or other third-party processors, there may be two or more layers between the ODFI and the Originator.

[22] A bank's underwriting policy should define what information each application should contain. The depth of the review of an originator's application should match the level of risk posed by the originator. The underwriting policy should require a background check of each originator to support the validity of the business.

[23] See Interpretive Note 041214-FACRL-GN-02 at www.treas.gov/offices/enforcement/ofac/rulings/. NACHA rules further specify this compliance (see page 8 of the Quick Find section of the *2006 NACHA Operating Rules*).

[24] The FFIEC *Information Technology Examination Handbook* is available at www.ffiec.gov/ffiecinfobase/html_pages/it_01.html.

[25] "Open" system cards can be used to connect to global debit and ATM networks; the cards can be used for purchases at any merchant or to access currency at any ATM that connects to global payment networks. "Closed" system cards are limited in that they can only be used to buy goods or services from the merchant issuing the card or a select group of merchants or service providers that participate in a network that is limited geographically or otherwise (e.g., retail gift cards and mass transit system cards).

[26] Refer to the Money Laundering Threat Assessment Working Group, *U.S. Money Laundering Threat Assessment*, December 2005.

[27] The FFIEC *Information Technology Examination Handbook* is available at www.ffiec.gov/ffiecinfobase/html_pages/it_01.html.

[28] A remotely created check (sometimes called a "demand draft") is a check, often created by a payee or its service provider, drawn on a customer's bank account. The check often is authorized by the customer remotely, by telephone or on-line, and therefore does not bear the customer's handwritten signature.

[29] Gateway arrangements are similar to an Internet service provider with excess computer storage capacity who sells its capacity to a third party, who would then distribute computer service to various other individuals unknown to the provider. The third party would be making decisions about who would be receiving the service, although the provider would be providing the ultimate storage capacity. Thus, the provider bears all of the risks while receiving a smaller profit.

[30] Money launderers are known to identify the ownership or source of illegal funds through the use of unique and unusual stamps.

[31] For the purpose of the CIP rule, in the case of brokered deposits, the "customer" will be the broker that opens the account. A bank will not need to look through the deposit broker's account to determine the identity of each individual sub-accountholder, it need only verify the identity of the named accountholder.

[32] An ISO typically acts as an agent for merchants, including ATM owners, to process electronic transactions. In some cases, an ATM owner may act as its own ISO processor. Banks may engage the services of an ISO to solicit merchants and privately owned ATMs; however, in many situations, ISOs contract with merchants and ATM owners without the review and approval of the clearing bank.

[33] The FFIEC *Information Technology Examination Handbook* is available at www.ffiec.gov/ffiecinfobase/html_pages/it_01.html.

[34] Functional regulation limits the circumstances in which the federal banking agencies can directly examine or require reports from a bank affiliate or subsidiary whose primary regulator is the SEC, the Commodity Futures Trading Commission, or state issuance authorities. Federal banking agencies are generally limited from examining such an entity unless further information is needed to determine whether the banking affiliate or subsidiary poses a material risk to the bank, to determine compliance with a legal requirement under the federal banking agencies' jurisdiction, or to assess the bank's risk management system covering the functionally regulated activities. These standards require greater reliance on the functional regulator and better cooperation among regulators.

[35] A financial services corporation includes those entities offering NDIP, which may include investment firms, financial institutions, securities brokers/dealers, and insurance companies.

[36] If the bank uses the reliance provision under the CIP, responsibility for CIP shifts to the third-party provider. Refer to core overview section, "Customer Identification Program," page 45, for additional information.

[37] A bank shall not be considered to be a broker, nor need an employee registered as a broker/dealer, because the bank engages in any one or more of the activities under the conditions described:

- The bank effects customer transactions in municipal securities.
- The bank effects not more than 500 transactions in securities for its customers in any calendar year, and such transactions are not affected by an employee of the bank who is also an employee of a broker or dealer.
- The bank deals in commercial paper, banker's acceptances, commercial bills, or exempted securities.
- The bank effects customer transactions in identified banking products as defined in section 206 of the Gramm–Leach–Bliley Act.
- The bank effects customer transactions in certain stock purchase plans such as employee benefit plans, dividend reinvestment plans, and issuer plans.

[38] Refer to expanded overview section, "Business Entities (Domestic and Foreign)," page 284, for additional guidance on PICs.

[39] 31 CFR 103.137 and 31 CFR 103.16.

[40] 70 *Federal Register* 66758.

[41] FinCEN has issued a Frequently Asked Questions document, "Anti-Money Laundering Program and Suspicious Activity Reporting Requirements for Insurance Companies" (www.fincen.gov). Unless the SAR form accommodates multiple filers, only one institution is identified as the filer in the "Filer Identification" section of the SAR form. In these cases, the narrative must include the words "joint filing" and identify the other institutions on whose behalf the report is filed.

[42] Refer to the International Association of Insurance Supervisors' "Guidance Paper on Anti-Money Laundering and Combating the Financing of Terrorism," October 2004, available at www.iaisweb.org.

[43] Refer to the expanded overview section, "Trade Finance Activities," page 238, for additional guidance.

[44] Refer to the expanded examination procedures, "Trust and Asset Management Services," page 255, for additional guidance.

[45] Refer to the expanded examination procedures, "Business Entities (Domestic and Foreign)," page 290, for additional guidance.

[46] Refer to frwebgate.access.gpo.gov/cgi-bin/getdoc.cgi?dbname=1 06_senate_hearings&docid=f:61 699.wais.

[47] A shell company is a business entity without a physical presence in any country.

[48] Refer to the core overview section, "Private Banking Due Diligence Program (Non-U.S. Persons)," page 118, and to the expanded overview section, "Politically Exposed Persons," page 261, for additional guidance.

[49] Due diligence policies, procedures, and processes are required for private banking accounts for non-U.S. persons by section 312 of the Patriot Act. Refer to the core overview section, "Private Banking Due Diligence Program (Non-U.S. Persons)," page 118, for additional guidance.

[50] 31 CFR 103.121 (b)(2)(ii)(C).

[51] Refer to the core examination procedures, "Private Banking Due Diligence Program (Non-U.S. Persons)," page 123, for additional guidance.

[52] Asset management accounts can be trust or agency accounts and are managed by the bank.

[53] The OCC and OTS use the broader term "fiduciary capacity" instead of "trust." Fiduciary capacity includes a trustee, an executor, an administrator, a registrar of stocks and bonds, a transfer agent, a guardian, an assignee, a receiver, or a custodian under a uniform gifts to minors act; an investment adviser, if the bank receives a fee for its investment advice; and any capacity in which the bank possesses investment discretion on behalf of another (12 CFR 9.2(e) and 12 CFR 550.30).

[54] For purposes of national banks and OTS-regulated savings associations, certain investment management activities, such as providing investment advice for a fee, are "fiduciary" in nature.

[55] Refer to 31 CFR 103.121 (b)(2)(ii)(C).

[56] *Id.*

[57] Refer to expanded overview section, "Business Entities (Domestic and Foreign)," page 284, for additional guidance on PICs.

[58] APTs are a special form of irrevocable trust, usually created (settled) offshore for the principal purposes of preserving and protecting part of one's wealth against creditors. Title to the asset is transferred to a person named as the trustee. APTs are generally tax neutral with the ultimate function of providing for the beneficiaries.

[59] Management and examiners should be aware that OFAC list-matching is not a BSA requirement. However, since trust systems are typically separate and distinct from bank systems, verification of these checks on the bank system is not sufficient to ensure that these checks are also completed in the trust and asset management department. Refer to the core overview section, "Office of Foreign Assets Control," page 135, for additional guidance.

[60] Refer to the expanded overview section, "Non-Governmental Organizations and Charities," page 281, for further guidance.

[61] Asset management accounts can be trust or agency accounts and are managed by the bank.

In: The Bank Secrecy Act and Anti-Money Laundering... ISBN: 978-1-60876-162-3
Editor: Anne Leuter

Chapter 6

EXPANDED EXAMINATION OVERVIEW AND PROCEDURES FOR PERSONS AND ENTITIES

NONRESIDENT ALIENS AND FOREIGN INDIVIDUALS — OVERVIEW

Objective. *Assess the adequacy of the bank's systems to manage the risks associated with transactions involving accounts held by nonresident aliens (NRAs) and foreign individuals, and management's ability to implement effective due diligence, monitoring, and reporting systems.*

Foreign individuals maintaining relationships with U.S. banks can be divided into two categories: resident aliens and nonresident aliens. For definitional purposes, an NRA is a non-U.S. citizen who: (i) is not a lawful permanent resident of the United States during the calendar year and who does not meet the substantial presence test,[1] or (ii) has not been issued an alien registration receipt card, also known as a green card. The Internal Revenue Service determines the tax liabilities of a foreign person and officially defines the person as a "resident" or "nonresident."

Although NRAs are not permanent residents, they may have a legitimate need to establish an account relationship with a U.S. bank. NRAs use bank products and services for asset preservation (e.g., mitigating losses due to exchange rates), business expansion, and investments. The amount of NRA deposits in the U.S. banking system has been estimated to range from hundreds of billions of dollars to about $1 trillion. Even at the low end of the range, the magnitude is substantial, both in terms of the U.S. banking system and the economy.

Risk Factors

Banks may find it more difficult to verify and authenticate an NRA accountholder's identification, source of funds, and source of wealth, which may result in BSA/AML risks. The NRA's home country may also heighten the account risk, depending on the secrecy laws of that country. Since the NRA is expected to reside outside of the United States, funds transfers or the use of foreign automated teller machines (ATMs) may be more frequent. The BSA/AML risk may be further heightened if the NRA is a politically exposed person (PEP). Refer to the expanded examination procedures, "Politically Exposed Persons," page 265, for further information.

Risk Mitigation

Banks should establish policies, procedures, and processes that provide for sound due diligence and verification practices, adequate risk assessment of NRA accounts, and ongoing monitoring and reporting of unusual or suspicious activities. The following factors are to be considered when determining the risk level of an NRA account:

- The accountholder's home country.
- The types of products and services used.
- Forms of identification.
- The source of wealth and funds.
- Unusual account activity.

NRA customers may request W-8 status for U.S. tax withholding. In such cases, the NRA customer completes a W-8 form, which attests to the customer's foreign and U.S. tax-exempt status. While it is an Internal Revenue Service (IRS) form, a W-8 is not sent to the IRS, but is maintained on file at the bank to support the lack of any tax withholding from earnings.[2]

The bank's Customer Identification Program (CIP) should detail the identification requirements for opening an account for an NRA. The program should include the use of documentary and nondocumentary methods to verify a customer. In addition, the Patriot Act amended the BSA to require special due diligence for private banking accounts for non-U.S. persons, including those held for PEPs or senior foreign political figures.

Examination Procedures

Nonresident Aliens and Foreign Individuals

Objective. *Assess the adequacy of the bank's systems to manage the risks associated with transactions involving accounts held by nonresident aliens (NRAs) and foreign individuals, and management's ability to implement effective due diligence, monitoring, and reporting systems.*

1. Review the bank's policies, procedures, and processes related to NRA and foreign individual accounts. Evaluate the adequacy of the policies, procedures, and processes given the bank's nonresident alien and foreign individual activities and the risks they represent. Assess whether the controls are adequate to reasonably protect the bank from money laundering and terrorist financing.
2. From a review of management information systems (MIS) and internal risk rating factors, determine whether the bank effectively identifies and monitors high-risk NRA and foreign individual accounts.
3. Determine whether the bank's system of monitoring NRA and foreign individual accounts for suspicious activities, and for reporting of suspicious activities, is adequate based on the complexity of the bank's NRA and foreign individual relationships, the types of products used by NRAs and foreign individuals, the home countries of the NRAs, and the source of funds and wealth for NRAs and foreign individuals.
4. If appropriate, refer to core examination procedures, "Office of Foreign Assets Control," page 144, for further guidance.

Transaction Testing

5. On the basis of the bank's risk assessment of its NRA and foreign individual accounts, as well as prior examination and audit reports, select a sample of high-risk NRA accounts. Include the following risk factors:
   - An account for resident or citizen of a high-risk jurisdiction.
   - Account activity is substantially currency based.
   - An NRA or foreign individual who uses a wide range of bank services, particularly correspondent services.
   - An NRA or foreign individual for whom the bank has filed a Suspicious Activity Report (SAR).
6. From the sample selected, perform the following examination procedures:
   - Review the customer due diligence information, including Customer Identification Program information, if applicable.
   - Review account statements and, as necessary, transaction details to determine whether actual account activity is consistent with expected activity. Assess whether transactions appear unusual or suspicious.
   - For W-8 accounts, verify that appropriate forms have been completed and updated, as necessary. Review transaction activity and identify patterns that indicate U.S. resident status or indicate other unusual and suspicious activity.
7. On the basis of examination procedures completed, including transaction testing, form a conclusion about the adequacy of policies, procedures, and processes associated with NRA accounts.

POLITICALLY EXPOSED PERSONS — OVERVIEW

Objective. *Assess the adequacy of the bank's systems to manage the risks associated with senior foreign political figures, often referred to as "politically exposed persons" (PEPs), and management's ability to implement effective risk-based due diligence, monitoring, and reporting systems. If the relationship is a private banking account*[3] *refer to core overview section, "Private Banking Due Diligence Program (Non-U.S. Persons)," page 118, for guidance.*

Banks should take all reasonable steps to ensure that they do not knowingly or unwittingly assist in hiding or moving the proceeds of corruption by senior foreign political figures and their associates. Because the risks presented by PEPs will vary, controls and monitoring related to these accounts and transactions should be risk-based.

The term "politically exposed person" generally includes a current or former senior foreign political figure, their immediate family, and their close associates. Interagency guidance issued in January 2001 offers banks resources that can help them to determine whether an individual is a PEP.[4] More specifically:

- A "senior foreign political figure" is a senior official in the executive, legislative, administrative, military or judicial branches of a foreign government (whether elected or not), a senior official of a major foreign political party, or a senior executive of a foreign government-owned corporation.[5] In addition, a senior foreign political figure includes any corporation, business, or other entity that has been formed by, or for the benefit of, a senior foreign political figure.
- The "immediate family" of a senior foreign political figure typically includes the figure's parents, siblings, spouse, children, and in-laws.
- A "close associate" of a senior foreign political figure is a person who is widely and publicly known to maintain an unusually close relationship with the senior foreign political figure, and includes a person who is in a position to conduct substantial domestic and international financial transactions on behalf of the senior foreign political figure.

The definition of senior official or executive must remain sufficiently flexible to capture the range of individuals who, by virtue of their office or position, potentially pose a risk that their funds may be the proceeds of foreign corruption.[6] Titles alone may not provide sufficient information to determine if an individual is a PEP, since governments are organized differently from jurisdiction to jurisdiction.

Banks should establish risk-based controls and procedures that include reasonable steps to ascertain the status of an individual as a PEP and to conduct risk-based scrutiny of accounts held by these individuals. Banks should consider various factors when determining if an individual is a PEP including:

- Official responsibilities of the individual's office.
- The nature of the title (e.g., honorary or salaried).
- Level of authority over government activities or other officials.

- Access to significant government assets or funds.

In determining the acceptability of high-dollar or high-risk accounts, a bank should be able to obtain sufficient information to determine whether an individual is or is not a PEP. For example, when conducting due diligence on a high-dollar or high-risk account, it would be usual for a bank to review a customer's income sources, financial information, and professional background. These factors would likely require some review of past and present employment as well as general references that may identify a client's status as a PEP.

Ascertaining whether a customer has a close association with a senior foreign political figure can be difficult, although focusing on those relationships that are "widely and publicly known" provides a reasonable limitation on expectations to identify close associates as PEPs. However, banks that have actual knowledge of a close association should consider their customer a PEP, even if such association is not otherwise widely or publicly known. Banks are expected to follow reasonable steps to ascertain the status of an individual, and the federal banking agencies and FinCEN recognize that these steps may not uncover all close associations.

Risk Factors

In high-profile cases over the past few years, PEPs have used banks as conduits for their illegal activities, including corruption, bribery, and money laundering. However, not all PEPs present the same level of risk. This risk will vary depending on numerous factors, including the geographic locations involved and the individual's position or authority. Risk will also vary depending on other factors including products and services used, or size or complexity of the account relationship. As a result of these factors, some PEPs may be lower risk and some may be higher risk for foreign corruption or money laundering. Banks that conduct business with dishonest PEPs face substantial reputation risk, additional regulatory scrutiny, and possible supervisory action. Red flags regarding transactions that may be related to the proceeds of foreign corruption are listed in the January 2001 interagency guidance. Banks also should be alert to a PEP's control or influence over state-owned government or corporate accounts.

Risk Mitigation

Banks should exercise reasonable judgment in designing and implementing policies, procedures, and processes regarding PEPs. Banks should obtain risk-based due diligence information on PEPs and establish policies, procedures, and processes that provide for appropriate scrutiny and monitoring. Having appropriate risk-based account opening procedures for large-dollar or high-risk products and services are critical, as this is the prime opportunity for the bank to gather information for all customers, including PEPs. Refer to core overview section, "Private Banking Due Diligence Program (Non-U.S. Persons)," page 118, for expectations regarding private banking relationships with PEPs. Due diligence procedures should include, but should not be limited to, the following:

- Identify the accountholder and beneficial owner.
- Seek information directly from the individual regarding possible PEP status.
- Identify the accountholder's country of residence.
- Obtain information regarding employment or other sources of funds.
- Check references, as appropriate, to determine whether the individual is or has been a PEP.
- Identify the source of wealth.
- Obtain information on immediate family members or close associates having transaction authority over the account.
- Determine the purpose of the account and the expected volume and nature of account activity.
- Make reasonable efforts to review public sources of information. These sources will vary depending upon each situation; however, banks should check the accountholder against reasonably accessible public databases (e.g., government databases, major news publications, free commercial databases available on the Internet, and fee-based databases, as appropriate).

PEP accounts are not limited to large or internationally focused banks. A PEP can open an account at any bank, regardless of its size or location. Banks should specifically identify PEP accounts and assess the degree of risks involved, which will vary. Management should be involved in the decision to accept a PEP account. If management determines after-the-fact that an account is a PEP account, it should evaluate the risks and take appropriate steps. The bank should exercise additional, reasonable due diligence with regard to such accounts. For example, the bank may increase reference inquiries, obtain additional background information on the PEP from branches or correspondents operating in the client's home country, and make reasonable efforts to consult publicly available information sources. Ongoing risk-based monitoring of PEP accounts is critical to ensuring that the accounts are being used as anticipated.

EXAMINATION PROCEDURES

Politically Exposed Persons

Objective. *Assess the adequacy of the bank's systems to manage the risks associated with senior foreign political figures, often referred to as "politically exposed persons" (PEPs), and management's ability to implement effective risk-based due diligence, monitoring, and reporting systems. If the relationship is a private banking account*[7] *refer to core overview section, "Private Banking Due Diligence Program (Non-U.S. Persons)," page 118, for guidance.*

1. Review the risk-based policies, procedures, and processes related to PEPs. Evaluate the adequacy of the policies, procedures, and processes given the bank's PEP accounts and the risks they present. Assess whether the risk-based controls are

adequate to reasonably protect the bank from money laundering and terrorist financing.

2. Review the procedures for opening PEP accounts. Identify management's role in the approval and ongoing risk-based monitoring of PEP accounts.
3. From a review of management information systems (MIS) and internal risk rating factors, determine whether the bank effectively identifies and monitors PEP relationships, particularly those that pose a high risk for money laundering.
4. Determine whether the bank's system for monitoring PEPs for suspicious activities, and for reporting of suspicious activities, is adequate given the bank's size, complexity, location, and types of customer relationships.
5. If appropriate, refer to the core examination procedures, "Office of Foreign Assets Control," page 144, for guidance.

Transaction Testing

6. On the basis of the bank's risk assessment of its PEP relationships, as well as prior examination and audit reports, select a sample of PEP accounts. From the sample selected, perform the following examination procedures:
   - Determine compliance with regulatory requirements and with the bank's established policies, procedures, and processes.
   - Review transaction activity for accounts selected. If necessary, request and review specific transactions.
   - If the analysis of activity and customer due diligence information raises concerns, hold discussions with bank management.
7. On the basis of examination procedures completed, including transaction testing, form a conclusion about the adequacy of policies, procedures, and processes associated with PEPs.

Embassy and Foreign Consulate Accounts — Overview

Objective. *Assess the adequacy of the bank's systems to manage the risks associated with transactions involving embassy and foreign consulate accounts, and management's ability to implement effective due diligence, monitoring, and reporting systems.*

Embassies contain the offices of the foreign ambassador, the diplomatic representative, and their staff. The embassy, led by the ambassador, is a foreign government's official representation in the United States (or other country). Foreign consulate offices act as branches of the embassy and perform various administrative and governmental functions (e.g., issuing visas and handling immigration matters). Foreign consulate offices are typically located in major metropolitan areas. In addition, foreign ambassadors' diplomatic representatives, their families, and their associates may be considered politically exposed persons (PEPs) in certain circumstances.[8]

Embassies and foreign consulates in the United States require access to the banking system to meet many of their day-to-day financial responsibilities. Such services can range from account relationships for operational expenses (e.g., payroll, rent, and utilities) to inter- and intragovernmental transactions (e.g., commercial and military purchases). In addition to official embassy accounts, some banks provide ancillary services or accounts to embassy staff, families, and current or prior foreign government officials. Each of these relationships poses different levels of risk to the bank.

Embassy accounts, including those accounts for a specific embassy office such as a cultural or education ministry, a defense attaché or ministry, or any other account, should have a specific operating purpose stating the official function of the foreign government office. Consistent with established practices for business relationships, these embassy accounts should have written authorization by the foreign government.

Risk Factors

To provide embassy and foreign consulate services, a U.S. bank may need to maintain a foreign correspondent relationship with the embassy's or foreign consulate's bank. Banks conducting business with foreign embassies or consulates should assess and understand the potential risks of these accounts and should develop appropriate policies, procedures, and processes. Embassy or foreign consulate accounts may pose a higher risk in the following circumstances:

- Accounts are from countries that have been designated as high risk.
- Substantial currency transactions take place in the accounts.
- Account activity is not consistent with the purpose of the account (e.g., pouch activity or payable upon proper identification transactions).
- Accounts directly fund personal expenses of foreign nationals, including but not limited to expenses for college students.
- Official embassy business is conducted through personal accounts.

Risk Mitigation

Banks should obtain comprehensive due diligence information on embassy and foreign consulate account relationships. For private banking accounts for non-U.S. persons specifically, banks must obtain due diligence information as required by 31 CFR 103.178.[9] The bank's due diligence related to embassy and foreign consulate account relationships should be commensurate with the risk levels presented. In addition, banks are expected to establish policies, procedures, and processes that provide for greater scrutiny and monitoring of all embassy and foreign consulate account relationships. Management should fully understand the purpose of the account and the expected volume and nature of account activity. Ongoing monitoring of embassy and foreign consulate account relationships is critical to ensuring that the account relationships are being used as anticipated.

Examination Procedures

Embassy and Foreign Consulate Accounts

Objective. *Assess the adequacy of the bank's systems to manage the risks associated with transactions involving embassy and foreign consulate accounts, and management's ability to implement effective due diligence, monitoring, and reporting systems.*

1. Review the policies, procedures, and processes related to embassy and foreign consulate accounts. Evaluate the adequacy of the policies, procedures, and processes given the bank's embassy and foreign consulate accounts and the risks they present (e.g., number of accounts, volume of activity, and geographic locations). Assess whether the controls are adequate to reasonably protect the bank from money laundering and terrorist financing.
2. Identify senior management's role in the approval and ongoing monitoring of embassy and foreign consulate accounts. Determine whether the board is aware of embassy banking activities and whether it receives periodic reports on these activities.
3. From a review of management information systems (MIS) and internal risk rating factors, determine whether the bank effectively identifies and monitors embassy and foreign consulate accounts, particularly those that pose a high risk for money laundering.
4. Determine whether the bank's system for monitoring embassy and foreign consulate accounts for suspicious activities, and for reporting of suspicious activities, is adequate given the bank's size, complexity, location, and types of customer relationships.
5. If appropriate, refer to the core examination procedures, "Office of Foreign Assets Control," page 144, for guidance.

Transaction Testing

6. On the basis of the bank's risk assessment of its embassy and foreign consulate accounts, as well as prior examination and audit reports, select a sample of embassy and foreign consulate accounts. From the sample selected, perform the following examination procedures:
   - Determine compliance with regulatory requirements and with the bank's established policies, procedures, and processes.
   - Review the documentation authorizing the ambassador or the foreign consulate to conduct banking in the United States.
   - Review transaction activity for accounts selected. If necessary, request and review specific transactions.

7. On the basis of examination procedures completed, including transaction testing, form a conclusion about the adequacy of policies, procedures, and processes associated with embassy and foreign consulate accounts.

NON-BANK FINANCIAL INSTITUTIONS — OVERVIEW

Objective. *Assess the adequacy of the bank's systems to manage the risks associated with accounts of non-bank financial institutions (NBFIs), and management's ability to implement effective monitoring and reporting systems.*

NBFIs are broadly defined as institutions that offer financial services. The Patriot Act has defined a variety of entities as financial institutions.[10] Common examples of NBFIs include, but are not limited to:

- Casinos and card clubs.
- Securities and commodities firms (e.g., brokers/dealers, investment advisers, mutual funds, hedge funds, or commodity traders).
- Money services businesses (MSBs).[11]
- Insurance companies.
- Other financial institutions (e.g., dealers in precious metals, stones, or jewels; pawnbrokers; loan or finance companies).

Some NBFIs are currently required to develop an AML program, comply with the reporting and recordkeeping requirements of the BSA, and report suspicious activity, as are banks. NBFIs typically require a bank account in order to operate. Although NBFIs maintain operating accounts at banks, the BSA does not require, and neither FinCEN nor the federal banking agencies expect, banks to serve as the *de facto* regulator of any NBFI industry or individual NBFI customer. Furthermore, while banks are expected to manage risk associated with all accounts, including NBFI accounts, banks will not be held responsible for their customers' compliance with the BSA and other applicable federal and state laws and regulations.

Guidance on Providing Banking Services to MSBs

FinCEN and the federal banking agencies issued interpretive guidance on April 26, 2005, to clarify the BSA requirements and supervisory expectations as applied to accounts opened or maintained for MSBs.[12] The guidance sets forth the following minimum due diligence expectations for banks when opening or maintaining accounts for MSBs:

- Confirm FinCEN registration, if required.[13] (Note: registration must be renewed every two years.)
- Confirm state licensing, if applicable.
- Confirm agent status, if applicable.

- Conduct a risk assessment to determine the level of risk associated with each account and whether further due diligence is required.

While several specific components of the guidance are unique to MSBs (such as expectations to confirm registration with FinCEN), the fundamental core of the guidance — that banks should apply the requirements of the BSA on a risk-assessed basis — is applicable to accounts held for all NBFI customers, as described in the risk mitigation section below.[14]

Risk Factors

NBFI industries are extremely diverse, ranging from large multi-national corporations to small, independent businesses that offer financial services only as an ancillary component to its primary business (e.g., grocery store that offers check cashing). The range of products and services offered, and the customer bases served by NBFIs, are equally diverse. As a result of this diversity, some NBFIs may be lower risk and some may be higher risk for money laundering.

Banks that maintain account relationships with NBFIs may be exposed to a higher risk for potential money laundering activities because many NBFIs:

- Lack ongoing customer relationships and require minimal or no identification by customers.
- Maintain limited or inconsistent recordkeeping on customers and transactions.
- Engage in frequent currency transactions.
- Are subject to varying levels of regulatory requirements and oversight.
- Can quickly change their product mix or location and quickly enter or exit an operation.
- Sometimes operate without proper registration or licensing.

Risk Mitigation

Banks that maintain account relationships with NBFIs should develop policies, procedures, and processes to:

- Identify NBFIs relationships.
- Assess the potential risks posed by the NBFI relationships.
- Conduct adequate and ongoing due diligence on the NBFI relationships when necessary.
- Ensure NBFI relationships are appropriately considered within the bank's suspicious activity monitoring and reporting systems.

Risk Assessment Factors

Banks should assess the risks posed by their NBFI customers and direct their resources most appropriately to those accounts that pose a more significant money laundering risk. The following factors may be used to help identify the relative risks within the NBFI portfolio. Nevertheless, management should weigh and evaluate each risk assessment factor to arrive at a risk determination for each customer and to prioritize oversight resources. Relevant risk factors include:

- Types of products and services offered by the NBFI.
- Locations and markets served by the NBFI.
- Anticipated account activity.
- Purpose of the account.

A bank's due diligence should be commensurate with the level of risk of the NBFI customer identified through its risk assessment. If a bank's risk assessment indicates potential for a heightened risk of money laundering or terrorist financing, it will be expected to conduct further due diligence in a manner commensurate with the heightened risk.

EXAMINATION PROCEDURES

Non-Bank Financial Institutions

Objective. *Assess the adequacy of the bank's systems to manage the risks associated with accounts of non-bank financial institutions (NBFIs), and management's ability to implement effective monitoring and reporting systems.*

1. Determine the extent of the bank's relationships with NBFIs and, for banks with significant relationships with NBFIs, review the bank's risk assessment of this activity.
2. Review the policies, procedures, and processes related to NBFI accounts. Evaluate the adequacy of the policies, procedures, and processes given the bank's NBFI activities and the risks they represent. Assess whether the controls are adequate to reasonably protect the bank from money laundering and terrorist financing.
3. From review of management information systems (MIS) and internal risk rating factors, determine whether the bank effectively identifies and monitors NBFI accounts.
4. Determine whether the bank's system for monitoring NBFI accounts for suspicious activities, and for reporting of suspicious activities, is adequate given the nature of the bank's customer relationships.

Money Services Businesses

5. Consistent with the interagency guidance released on April 26, 2005, determine whether the bank has policies, procedures, and processes in place for accounts opened or maintained for money services businesses (MSBs) to:

- Confirm FinCEN registration, if required. Note: registration must be renewed every two years.
- Confirm state licensing, if applicable.
- Confirm agent status, if applicable.
- Conduct a risk assessment to determine the level of risk associated with each account and whether further due diligence is required.

6. Determine whether the bank's policies, procedures, and processes to assess risks posed by MSB customers effectively identify higher risk accounts and the amount of further due diligence necessary.

Transaction Testing

7. On a basis of the bank's risk assessment of its NBFI accounts, as well as prior examination and audit reports, select a sample of high-risk NBFI accounts. From the sample selected, perform the following examination procedures:
   - Review account opening documentation and ongoing due diligence information.
   - Review account statements and, as necessary, specific transaction details. Compare expected transactions with actual activity.
   - Determine whether actual activity is consistent with the nature of the customer's business and identify any unusual or suspicious activity.
8. On a basis of examination procedures completed, including transaction testing, form a conclusion about the adequacy of policies, procedures, and processes associated with NBFI relationships.

PROFESSIONAL SERVICE PROVIDERS — OVERVIEW

Objective. *Assess the adequacy of the bank's systems to manage the risks associated with professional service provider relationships, and management's ability to implement effective due diligence, monitoring, and reporting systems.*

A professional service provider acts as an intermediary between its client and the bank. Professional service providers include lawyers, accountants, investment brokers, and other third parties that act as financial liaisons for their clients. These providers may conduct financial dealings for their clients. For example, an attorney may perform services for a client, or arrange for services to be performed on the client's behalf, such as settlement of real estate transactions, asset transfers, management of client monies, investment services, and trust arrangements.

A typical example is interest on lawyers' trust accounts (IOLTA). These accounts contain funds for a lawyer's various clients, and act as a standard bank account with one unique feature: The interest earned on the account is ceded to the state bar association or another entity for public interest and pro bono purposes.

Risk Factors

In contrast to escrow accounts that are set up to serve individual clients, professional service provider accounts allow for ongoing business transactions with multiple clients. Generally, a bank has no direct relationship with or knowledge of the beneficial owners of these accounts, who may be a constantly changing group of individuals and legal entities.

As with any account that presents third-party risk, the bank could be more vulnerable to potential money laundering abuse. Some potential examples of abuse could include:

- Laundering illicit currency.
- Structuring currency deposits and withdrawals.
- Opening any third-party account for the primary purpose of masking the underlying client's identity.

As such, the bank should establish an effective due diligence program for the professional service provider as summarized below.

Risk Mitigation

When establishing and maintaining relationships with professional service providers, banks should adequately assess account risk and monitor the relationship for suspicious or unusual activity. At account opening, the bank should have an understanding of the intended use of the account, including anticipated transaction volume, products and services used, and geographic locations involved in the relationship. As indicated in the core overview section, "Currency Transaction Reporting Exemptions," page 80, professional service providers cannot be exempted from currency transaction reporting requirements.

EXAMINATION PROCEDURES

Professional Service Providers

Objective. *Assess the adequacy of the bank's systems to manage the risks associated with professional service provider relationships, and management's ability to implement effective due diligence, monitoring, and reporting systems.*

1. Review the policies, procedures, and processes related to professional service provider relationships. Evaluate the adequacy of the policies, procedures, and processes given the bank's relationships with professional service providers and the risks these relationships represent. Assess whether the controls are adequate to reasonably protect the bank from money laundering and terrorist financing.
2. From a review of management information systems (MIS) and internal risk rating factors, determine whether the bank effectively identifies and monitors professional service provider relationships. (MIS reports should include information about an

entire relationship. For example, an interest on lawyers' trust account (IOLTA) may be in the name of the law firm instead of an individual. However, the bank's relationship report should include the law firm's account *and* the names and accounts of lawyers associated with the IOLTA.)

3. Determine whether the bank's system for monitoring professional service provider relationship's suspicious activities, and for reporting of suspicious activities, is adequate given the bank's size, complexity, location, and types of customer relationships.
4. If appropriate, refer to the core examination procedures, "Office of Foreign Assets Control," page 144, for guidance.

Transaction Testing

5. On the basis of the bank's risk assessment of its relationships with professional service providers, as well as prior examination and audit reports, select a sample of high-risk relationships. From the sample selected, perform the following examination procedures:
   - Review account opening documentation and a sample of transaction activity.
   - Determine whether actual account activity is consistent with anticipated (as documented) account activity. Look for trends in the nature, size, or scope of the transactions, paying particular attention to currency transactions.
   - Determine whether ongoing monitoring is sufficient to identify potentially suspicious activity.
6. On the basis of examination procedures completed, including transaction testing, form a conclusion about the adequacy of policies, procedures, and processes associated with professional service provider relationships.

NON-GOVERNMENTAL ORGANIZATIONS AND CHARITIES — OVERVIEW

Objective. *Assess the adequacy of the bank's systems to manage the risks associated with accounts of non-governmental organizations (NGOs) and charities, and management's ability to implement effective due diligence, monitoring, and reporting systems.*

NGOs are private nonprofit organizations that pursue activities intended to serve the public good. NGOs may provide basic social services, work to relieve suffering, promote the interests of the poor, bring citizen concerns to governments, encourage political participation, protect the environment, or undertake community development to serve the needs of citizens, organizations, or groups in one or more of the communities that the NGO operates. An NGO can be any nonprofit organization that is independent from government.

NGOs can range from large regional, national, or international charities to community-based self-help groups. NGOs also include research institutes, churches, professional associations, and lobby groups. NGOs typically depend, in whole or in part, on charitable donations and voluntary service for support.

Risk Factors

Since NGOs can be used to obtain funds for charitable organizations, the flow of funds both into and out of the NGO can be complex, making them susceptible to abuse by money launderers and terrorists. Consequently, law enforcement has increased their scrutiny of NGOs.

Risk Mitigation

To assess the risk of NGO customers, a bank should conduct adequate due diligence on the organization. In addition to required Customer Identification Program (CIP) information, due diligence for NGOs should focus on other aspects of the organization, such as the following:

- Purpose and objectives of their stated activities.
- The geographic locations served (including headquarters and operational areas).
- The organizational structure.
- The donor and volunteer base.
- Funding and disbursement criteria (including basic beneficiary information).
- Recordkeeping requirements.
- Its affiliation with other NGOs, governments, or groups.
- Internal controls and audits.

For accounts that bank management considers to be high risk, stringent documentation, verification, and transaction monitoring procedures should be established. NGO accounts that are at higher risk for BSA/AML concerns include those operating or providing services internationally, conducting unusual or suspicious activities, or lacking proper documentation. Enhanced due diligence for these accounts should include:

- Evaluating the principals.
- Obtaining and reviewing the financial statements and audits.
- Verifying the source and use of funds.
- Evaluating large contributors or grantors of the NGO.
- Conducting reference checks.

Examination Procedures

Non-Governmental Organizations and Charities

Objective. *Assess the adequacy of the bank's systems to manage the risks associated with accounts of non-governmental organizations (NGOs) and charities, and management's ability to implement effective due diligence, monitoring, and reporting systems.*

1. Review the policies, procedures, and processes related to NGOs. Evaluate the adequacy of the policies, procedures, and processes given the bank's NGO accounts and the risks they represent. Assess whether the controls are adequate to reasonably protect the bank from money laundering and terrorist financing.
2. From a review of management information systems (MIS) and internal risk rating factors, determine whether the bank effectively identifies and monitors high-risk NGO accounts.
3. Determine whether the bank's system for monitoring NGO accounts for suspicious activities, and for reporting of suspicious activities, is adequate given the bank's size, complexity, location, and types of customer relationships.
4. If appropriate, refer to the core examination procedures, "Office of Foreign Assets Control," page 144, for guidance.

Transaction Testing

5. On the basis of the bank's risk assessment, its NGO and charity accounts, as well as prior examination and audit reports, select a sample of high-risk NGO accounts. From the sample selected, perform the following examination procedures:
   - Review account opening documentation and ongoing due diligence information.
   - Review account statements and, as necessary, specific transaction details.
   - Compare expected transactions with actual activity.
   - Determine whether actual activity is consistent with the nature of the customer's business.
   - Identify any unusual or suspicious activity.
6. On the basis of examination procedures completed, including transaction testing, form a conclusion about the adequacy of policies, procedures, and processes associated with NGO accounts.

Business Entities (Domestic and Foreign) — Overview

Objective. *Assess the adequacy of the bank's systems to manage the risks associated with transactions involving domestic and foreign business entities, and management's ability to implement effective due diligence, monitoring, and reporting systems.*

The term "business entities" refers to a variety of company formations that may be used for many purposes, such as tax and estate planning. Business entities are relatively easy to establish. Individuals, partnerships, and existing corporations establish business entities for legitimate reasons, but the entities may be abused for money laundering and terrorist financing.

Domestic Business Entities

All states have statutes governing the organization and operation of business entities, including limited liability companies, corporations, general partnerships, limited partnerships, and trusts. Shell companies registered in the United States are a type of domestic business entity that may pose heightened risks.[15] Shell companies can be used for money laundering and other crimes because they are easy and inexpensive to form and operate. In addition, ownership and transactional information can be concealed from regulatory agencies and law enforcement, in large part because most state laws require minimal disclosures of such information during the formation process. According to a report by the U.S. Government Accountability Office (GAO), law enforcement officials are concerned that criminals are increasingly using U.S. shell companies to conceal their identity and illicit activities.[16]

Shell companies can be publicly traded or privately held. Although publicly traded shell companies can be used for illicit purposes, the vulnerability of the shell company is compounded when it is privately held and beneficial ownership can more easily be obscured or hidden. Lack of transparency of beneficial ownership can be a desirable characteristic for some legitimate uses of shell companies, but it is also a serious vulnerability that can make some shell companies ideal vehicles for money laundering and other illicit financial activity. In some state jurisdictions, only minimal information is required to register articles of incorporation and maintain "good standing" for business entities — increasing the potential for their abuse by criminal and terrorist organizations.

Foreign Business Entities

Frequently used foreign entities include trusts, investment funds, and insurance companies. Two foreign entities that can pose particular money laundering risk are international business corporations (IBCs) and Private Investment Companies (PICs) opened in offshore financial centers (OFCs).[17] Many OFCs have limited organizational disclosure and recordkeeping requirements for establishing foreign business entities, creating an opportune environment for money laundering.

International Business Corporations

IBCs are entities formed outside of a person's country of residence which can be used to maintain confidentially or hide assets. IBC ownership can, based on jurisdiction, be conveyed through registered or bearer shares. There are a variety of advantages to using an IBC which include, but are not limited to, the following:

- Asset protection.
- Estate planning.
- Privacy and confidentiality.
- Reduction of tax liability.

Through an IBC, an individual is able to conduct the following:

- Open and hold bank accounts.
- Hold and transfer funds.
- Engage in international business and other related transactions.
- Hold and manage offshore investments (e.g., stocks, bonds, mutual funds, and certificates of deposit), many of which may not be available to "individuals" depending on their location of residence.
- Hold corporate debit and credit cards, thereby allowing convenient access to funds.

Private Investment Companies

PICs are separate legal entities. They are essentially subsets of IBCs. Determining whether a foreign corporation is a PIC is based on identifying the purpose and use of the legal vehicle. PICs are typically used to hold individual funds and investments, and ownership can be vested through bearer shares or registered shares. Like other IBCs, PICs can offer confidentiality of ownership, hold assets centrally, and may provide intermediaries between private banking customers and the potential beneficiaries of the PICs. Shares of a PIC may be held by a trust, which further obscures beneficial ownership of the underlying assets. IBCs, including PICs, are incorporated frequently in countries that impose low or no taxes on company assets and operations or are bank secrecy havens.

Nominee Incorporation Services

Intermediaries, called nominee incorporation services (NIS), establish U.S. shell companies and bank accounts on behalf of foreign clients. NIS may be located in the United States or offshore. Corporate lawyers in the United States often use NIS to organize companies on behalf of their domestic and foreign clients because such services can efficiently organize legal entities in any state. NIS must comply with applicable state and federal procedures as well as any specific bank requirements. Those laws and procedures dictate what information NIS must share about the owners of a legal entity. Money launderers have also utilized NIS to hide their identities. By hiring a firm to serve as an intermediary between themselves, the licensing jurisdiction, and the bank, a company's beneficial owners may avoid disclosing their identities in state corporate filings and in corporate bank account opening documentation.

An NIS has the capability to form business entities, open full-service bank accounts for those entities, and act as the registered agent to accept service of legal process on behalf of those entities in a jurisdiction in which the entities have no physical presence. Furthermore, an NIS can perform these services without ever having to identify beneficial ownership on company formation, registration, or bank account documents.

Several international NIS firms have formed partnerships or marketing alliances with U.S. banks to offer financial services such as Internet banking and funds transfer capabilities to shell companies and non-U.S. citizens. U.S. banks participating in these marketing alliances by opening accounts through intermediaries without requiring the actual accountholder's physical presence, accepting by mail copies of passport photos, utility bills, and other identifying information may be assuming increased levels of BSA/AML risk.[18]

Risk Factors

Money laundering and terrorist financing risks arise because business entities can hide the true owner of assets or property derived from or associated with criminal activity. The privacy and confidentiality surrounding some business entities may be exploited by criminals, money launderers, and terrorists. Verifying the grantors and beneficial owner(s) of some business entities may be extremely difficult, as the characteristics of these entities shield the legal identity of the owner. Few public records will disclose true ownership. Overall, the lack of ownership transparency; minimal or no recordkeeping requirements, financial disclosures, and supervision; and the range of permissible activities all increase money laundering risk.

While business entities can be established in most international jurisdictions, the majority are incorporated in OFCs that provide ownership privacy and impose few or no tax obligations. To maintain anonymity, many business entities are formed with nominee directors, officeholders, and shareholders. In certain jurisdictions, business entities can also be established using bearer shares; ownership records are not maintained, rather ownership is based on physical possession of the stock certificates. Revocable trusts are another method used to insulate the grantor and beneficial owner and can be designed to own and manage the business entity, presenting significant barriers to law enforcement.

While the majority of U.S.-based shell companies serve legitimate purposes, some shell companies have been used as conduits for money laundering, to hide overseas transactions, or to layer domestic or foreign business entity structures. For example, regulators have identified shell companies registered in the United States conducting suspicious transactions with foreign-based counterparties. These transactions, primarily funds transfers circling in and out of the U.S. banking system, evidenced no apparent business purpose. Domestic business entities with bank-like names, but without regulatory authority to conduct banking, should be particularly suspect.[19]

The following indicators of potentially suspicious activity may be commonly associated with shell company activity:

- Insufficient or no information available to positively identify originators or beneficiaries of funds transfers (using Internet, commercial database searches, or direct inquiries to a respondent bank).
- Payments have no stated purpose, do not reference goods or services, or identify only a contract or invoice number.
- Goods or services, if identified, do not match profile of company provided by respondent bank or character of the financial activity; a company references remarkably dissimilar goods and services in related funds transfers; explanation

given by foreign respondent bank is inconsistent with observed funds transfer activity.
- Transacting businesses share the same address, provide only a registered agent's address, or other address inconsistencies.
- Many or all of the funds transfers are sent in large, round dollar, hundred dollar, or thousand dollar amounts.
- Unusually large number and variety of beneficiaries receiving funds transfers from one company.
- Frequent involvement of multiple jurisdictions or beneficiaries located in high-risk offshore financial centers.
- Use of nested correspondent banking situations.

Risk Mitigation

Management should develop policies, procedures, and processes that enable the bank to identify account relationships, in particular deposit accounts, and monitor the risks associated with these accounts in all the bank's departments. Business entity customers may open accounts within the private banking department, within the trust department, or at local branches. Management should establish appropriate due diligence at account opening and during the life of the relationship to manage risk in these accounts. The bank should gather sufficient information on the business entities and their beneficial owners to understand and assess the risks of the account relationship. Important information for determining the valid use of these entities includes the type of business, the purpose of the account, the source of funds, and the source of wealth of the owner or beneficial owner.

The bank's Customer Identification Program (CIP) should detail the identification requirements for opening an account for a business entity. When opening an account for a customer that is not an individual, banks are permitted by 31 CFR 103.121 to obtain information about the individuals who have authority and control over such accounts in order to verify the customer's identity (the customer being the business entity). Required account opening information may include articles of incorporation, a corporate resolution by the directors authorizing the opening of the account, or the appointment of a person to act as a signatory for the entity on the account. Particular attention should be paid to articles of association that allow for nominee shareholders, board members, and bearer shares.

If the bank, through its trust or private banking departments, is facilitating the establishment of a business entity for a new or existing customer, the money laundering risk to the bank is typically mitigated. Since the bank is aware of the parties (e.g., grantors, beneficiaries, and shareholders) involved in the business entity, initial due diligence and verification is easier to obtain. Furthermore, in such cases, the bank frequently has ongoing relationships with the customers initiating the establishment of a business entity.

Risk assessments may include a review of the domestic or international jurisdiction where the business entity was established, the type of account (or accounts) and expected versus actual transaction activities, the types of products that will be used, and whether the business entity was created in-house or externally. If ownership is held in bearer share form, banks should assess the risks these relationships pose and determine the appropriate controls.

For example, banks may choose to maintain (or have an independent third party maintain) bearer shares for new clients, or those without well- established relationships with the institution. For well-known, established customers, banks may find that periodically recertifying beneficial ownership is effective. The bank's risk assessment of a business entity customer becomes more important in complex corporate formations. For example, a foreign IBC may establish a layered series of business entities, with each entity naming its parent as its beneficiary.

Ongoing account monitoring is critical to ensure that the accounts are reviewed for unusual and suspicious activity. The bank should be aware of high-risk transactions in these accounts, such as activity that has no business or apparent lawful purpose, funds transfer activity to and from high-risk jurisdictions, currency intensive transactions, and frequent changes in the ownership or control of the nonpublic business entity.

Examination Procedures

Business Entities (Domestic and Foreign)

Objective. *Assess the adequacy of the bank's systems to manage the risks associated with transactions involving domestic and foreign business entities, and management's ability to implement effective due diligence, monitoring, and reporting systems.*

1. Review the bank's policies, procedures, and processes related to business entities. Evaluate the adequacy of the policies, procedures, and processes given the bank's transactions with business entities and the risks they present. Assess whether the controls are adequate to reasonably protect the bank from money laundering and terrorist financing.
2. Review the policies and processes for opening and monitoring accounts with business entities. Determine whether the policies adequately assess the risk between different account types. For example, determine whether policies differentiate between U.S. shell companies and foreign business entities.
3. Determine how the bank identifies and, as necessary, completes additional due diligence on business entities. Assess the level of due diligence the bank performs when conducting its risk assessment.
4. From a review of management information systems (MIS) and internal risk rating factors, determine whether the bank effectively identifies and monitors high-risk business entity accounts.
5. Determine whether the bank's system for monitoring business entities for suspicious activities, and for reporting of suspicious activities, is adequate given the activities associated with business entities.
6. If appropriate, refer to the core examination procedures, "Office of Foreign Assets Control," page 144, for guidance.

Transaction Testing

7. On the basis of the bank's risk assessment of its accounts with business entities, as well as prior examination and audit reports, select a sample of these accounts. Include the following risk factors:
   - An entity organized in a high-risk jurisdiction.
   - Account activity that is substantially currency based.
   - An entity whose account activity consists primarily of circular-patterned funds transfers.
   - A business entity whose bearer shares are not under bank or trusted third-party control.
   - An entity that uses a wide range of bank services, particularly trust and correspondent services.
   - An entity owned or controlled by other nonpublic business entities.
   - Business entities for which the bank has filed SARs.
8. From the sample selected, obtain a relationship report for each selected account. It is critical that the full relationship, rather than only an individual account, be reviewed.
9. Review the due diligence information on the business entity. Assess the adequacy of that information.
10. Review account statements and, as necessary, specific transaction details. Compare expected transactions with actual activity. Determine whether actual activity is consistent with the nature and stated purpose of the account and whether transactions appear unusual or suspicious. Areas that may pose a high risk, such as funds transfers, private banking, trust, and monetary instruments, should be a primary focus of the transaction review.
11. On the basis of examination procedures completed, including transaction testing, form a conclusion about the adequacy of policies, procedures, and processes associated with business entity relationships.

CASH-INTENSIVE BUSINESSES — OVERVIEW

Objective. *Assess the adequacy of the bank's systems to manage the risks associated with cash-intensive businesses and entities, and management's ability to implement effective due diligence, monitoring, and reporting systems.*

Cash-intensive businesses and entities cover various industry sectors. Most of these businesses are conducting legitimate business; however, some aspects of these businesses may be susceptible to money laundering or terrorist financing. Common examples include, but are not limited to, the following:

- Convenience stores.
- Restaurants.
- Retail stores.
- Liquor stores.

- Cigarette distributors.
- Privately owned automated teller machines (ATMs).
- Vending machine operators.
- Parking garages.

Risk Factors

Some businesses and entities may be misused by money launderers to legitimize their illicit proceeds. For example, a criminal may own a cash-intensive business, such as a restaurant, and use it to launder currency from illicit criminal activities. The restaurant's currency deposits with its bank do not, on the surface, appear unusual since the business is legitimately a cash-generating entity. However, the volume of currency in a restaurant used to launder money will most likely be higher in comparison with similar restaurants in the area. The nature of cash-intensive businesses and the difficulty in identifying unusual activity may cause these businesses to be considered high risk.

Risk Mitigation

When establishing and maintaining relationships with cash-intensive businesses, banks should establish policies, procedures, and processes to identify high-risk relationships; assess AML risks; complete due diligence at account opening and periodically throughout the relationship; and include such relationships in appropriate monitoring for unusual or suspicious activity. At the time of account opening, the bank should have an understanding of the customer's business operations; the intended use of the account; including anticipated transaction volume, products, and services used; and the geographic locations involved in the relationship.

When conducting a risk assessment of cash-intensive businesses, banks should direct their resources to those accounts that pose the greatest risk of money laundering or terrorist financing. The following factors may be used to identify the risks:

- The purpose of the account.
- The volume, frequency, and nature of currency transactions.
- Customer history (e.g., length of relationship, Currency Transaction Report (CTR) filings,[20] and Suspicious Activity Report (SAR) filings).
- The primary business activity, products, and services offered.
- The business or business structure.
- Geographic locations and jurisdictions of operations.
- The availability of information and cooperation of the business in providing information.

For those customers deemed to be particularly high risk, bank management may consider implementing sound practices, such as periodic on-site visits, interviews with the business's management, or closer reviews of transactional activity.

EXAMINATION PROCEDURES

Cash-Intensive Businesses

Objective. *Assess the adequacy of the bank's systems to manage the risks associated with cash-intensive businesses and entities, and management's ability to implement effective due diligence, monitoring, and reporting systems.*

1. Review the policies, procedures, and processes related to cash-intensive businesses. Evaluate the adequacy of policies, procedures, and processes given the bank's cash-intensive business activities in relation to the bank's cash-intensive business customers and the risks that they represent. Assess whether the controls are adequate to reasonably protect the bank from money laundering and terrorist financing.
2. From a review of management information systems (MIS) and internal risk rating factors, determine whether the bank effectively identifies and monitors cash-intensive businesses and entities.
3. Determine whether the bank's system for monitoring cash-intensive businesses for suspicious activities, and for reporting of suspicious activities, is adequate given the bank's size, complexity, location, and types of customer relationships.
4. If appropriate, refer to the core examination procedures, "Office of Foreign Assets Control," page 144, for guidance.

Transaction Testing

5. On the basis of the bank's risk assessment of its cash-intensive business and entity relationships, as well as prior examination and audit reports, select a sample of cash-intensive businesses. From the sample selected, perform the following examination procedures:
   - Review account opening documentation including Customer Identification Program (CIP) information, if applicable, and a sample of transaction activity.
   - Determine whether actual account activity is consistent with anticipated account activity.
   - Look for trends in the nature, size, or scope of the transactions, paying particular attention to currency transactions.
   - Determine whether ongoing monitoring is sufficient to identify potentially suspicious activity.
6. On the basis of examination procedures completed, including transaction testing, form a conclusion about the adequacy of policies, procedures, and processes associated with cash-intensive businesses and entities.

End Notes

[1] A foreign national is a resident alien if the individual is physically present in the United States for at least 31 days in the current calendar year and present 183 days or more based on counting: all days present during the current year, plus 1/3 of the days present in the preceding year, plus 1/6 of the days present in the second preceding year. Certain days of presence are disregarded, such as (i) days spent in the United States for a medical condition that developed while the foreign national was present in the United States and unable to leave, (ii) days regular commuters spend traveling to or from Canada or Mexico, (iii) a day of less than 24 hours spent while in transit between two locations outside the United States., and (iv) days when the foreign national was an exempt individual. The individual is considered a resident alien for federal income and employment tax purposes from the first day of physical presence in the United States in the year that the test is satisfied. Refer to the Internal Revenue Service web site: www.irs.gov.

[2] Additional information can be found at www.irs.gov/formspubs. See also IRS Bulletin 515 "Withholding of Tax on Nonresident Aliens and Foreign Entities."

[3] For purposes of 31 CFR 103.178, a "private banking account" is an account (or any combination of accounts) maintained at a bank that satisfies all three of the following criteria:

- Requires a minimum aggregate deposit of funds or other assets of not less than $1,000,000;
- Is established on behalf of or for the benefit of one or more non-U.S. persons who are direct or beneficial owners of the account; and
- Is assigned to, or is administered by, in whole or in part, an officer, employee, or agent of a bank acting as a liaison between the covered financial institution and the direct or beneficial owner of the account.

[4] "Guidance on Enhanced Scrutiny for Transactions that may Involve the Proceeds for Foreign Official Corruption" issued by the U.S. Treasury, Board of Governors of the Federal Reserve System, Federal Deposit Insurance Corporation, Office of the Comptroller of the Currency, Office of Thrift Supervision, and the Department of State, January 2001.

[5] It is important to note that while government-owned corporations may present risks of their own, the government-owned corporations themselves are not within the definition of a "senior foreign political figure."

[6] 71 *Federal Register* 495–515.

[7] For purposes of 31 CFR 103.178, a "private banking account" is an account (or any combination of accounts) maintained at a bank that satisfies all three of the following criteria:

- Requires a minimum aggregate deposit of funds or other assets of not less than $1,000,000;
- Is established on behalf of or for the benefit of one or more non-U.S. persons who are direct or beneficial owners of the account; and
- Is assigned to, or is administered by, in whole or in part, an officer, employee, or agent of a bank acting as a liaison between the covered financial institution and the direct or beneficial owner of the account.

[8] Refer to the expanded overview section, "Politically Exposed Persons," for additional information, page 261.

[9] Refer to core section overview, "Private Banking Due Diligence Program (Non-U.S. Persons)," page 118, for additional guidance.

[10] Refer to Appendix D ("Statutory Definition of Financial Institution") for guidance.

[11] MSBs include five distinct types of financial services providers and the U.S. Postal Service: (1) currency dealers or exchangers; (2) check cashers; (3) issuers of traveler's checks, money orders, or stored value; (4) sellers or redeemers of traveler's checks, money orders, or stored value; and (5) money transmitters. There is a threshold requirement for businesses in the first four categories — a business that engages in such transactions will not be considered a MSB if it does not engage in such transactions in an amount greater than $1,000 for any person on any day in one or more transactions (31 CFR 103.11 (uu)). FinCEN has issued guidance stating that certain businesses that cash their own checks do not meet the definition of a "check casher." See FIN-2006-G005, "Frequently Asked Questions — Businesses Cashing Their Own Checks," March 31, 2006, at www.fincen.gov.

[12] Refer to "Interagency Interpretive Guidance on Providing Banking Services to Money Services Businesses Operating in the United States," April 26, 2005, available at www.fincen.gov.

[13] Certain MSBs are not required to register with FinCEN: (1) Solely an agent. — A person that is an MSB solely because that person serves as an agent of another MSB is not required to register. However, a person that is an MSB both because it engages in MSB activities on its own behalf and as an agent of another MSB, must register; (2) Stored value. — A person that is an MSB solely as an issuer, seller, or redeemer of stored value is not required to register. However, a person that is an MSB as an issuer, seller, or redeemer of stored value and engages in MSB activities (of a nature and value that cause the person to be an MSB on a basis other than stored value) must register; (3) U.S. Postal Service; and (4) Government Agencies. Agencies of the United States, of any State, or of any political subdivision of any State. A person that is not an MSB is not required to register (31 CFR 103.41 (a)(1) and (2)). FinCEN has issued guidance on questions related to MSB registration and de-registration. See FIN-2006-G006, "Money Services Business Guidance on Registration and De-Registration," February 3, 2006, at www.fincen.gov.

[14] On March 8, 2006, FinCEN issued an Advance Notice of Proposed Rulemaking (ANPR) seeking comments from both the MSB industry and the banking industry on the issue of MSBs obtaining appropriate access to banking services. FinCEN issued this ANPR to solicit updated facts concerning this issue as well as recommendations regarding the extent to which additional guidance or regulatory action under the BSA might address these concerns. The comment period closed on July 10, 2006. As of the release of the manual, FinCEN was reviewing the comments received and has not reached a determination on whether additional guidance or regulatory action is warranted.

[15] The term "shell company" generally refers to an entity without a physical presence in any country.

[16] See GAO, *Company Formations — Minimal Ownership Information is Collected and Available*, GAO- 06-375, April 2006, at www.gao.gov.

[17] While some OFCs are well regulated, the primary attraction of the offshore sector remains the frequent existence of legal frameworks designed to obscure the identity of beneficial owners, to promote regulatory and supervisory arbitrage, and to provide mitigation or evasion of home-country tax regimes.

[18] Money Laundering Threat Assessment Working Group, *U.S. Money Laundering Threat Assessment*, December 2005.

[19] The federal banking agencies notify banks and the public about entities engaged in unauthorized banking activities, both offshore and domestic. These notifications can be found on the federal banking agency's web sites.

[20] As discussed in the core overview section, "Currency Transaction Reporting Exemptions," page 80, certain entities are ineligible for currency transaction reporting exemptions as a non-listed business.

APPENDICES

APPENDIX A. BSA LAWS AND REGULATIONS

Statutes

12 USC 1 829b, 12 USC 1951–1959, and 31 USC 5311, *et seq.* — "The Bank Secrecy Act"

12 USC 1818(s) — "Compliance with Monetary Recordkeeping and Report Requirements"

Requires that the appropriate federal banking agencies shall prescribe regulations requiring insured depository institutions to establish and maintain procedures reasonably designed to assure and monitor the compliance of such depository institutions with the requirements of the BSA. In addition, this section requires that each examination of an insured depository institution by the appropriate federal banking agency shall include a review of the procedures, and that the report of examination shall describe any problem with the procedures maintained by the insured depository institution. Finally, if the appropriate federal banking agency determines that an insured depository institution has either 1) failed to establish and maintain procedures that are reasonably designed to assure and monitor the institution's compliance with the BSA; or 2) failed to correct any problem with the procedures which was previously reported to the depository institution in a report of examination, the agency shall issue an order requiring such depository institution to cease and desist from the violation of the statute and the regulations prescribed thereunder. Sections 181 8(b)(3) and (b)(4) of Title 12 of the USC extend section 1818(s) beyond insured depository institutions.

12 USC 1786(q) — "Compliance with Monetary Recordkeeping and Report Requirements"

Requires that the NCUA Board prescribe regulations requiring insured credit unions to establish and maintain procedures reasonably designed to assure and monitor the compliance of such credit unions with the requirements of the BSA. In addition, this section requires the NCUA Board to examine and enforce BSA requirements.

Regulations

U.S. Treasury/FinCEN

31 CFR 103 — "Financial Recordkeeping and Reporting of Currency and Foreign Transactions"

Sets forth FinCEN regulations that promulgate the BSA. Select provisions are described below.

31 CFR 103.11 — "Meaning of Terms"

Sets forth the definitions used throughout 31 CFR Part 103.

31 CFR 103.16 — "Reports by Insurance Companies of Suspicious Transactions"

Sets forth the requirements for insurance companies to report suspicious transactions of $5,000 or more.

31 CFR 103.18 — "Reports by Banks of Suspicious Transactions"

Sets forth the requirements for banks to report suspicious transactions of $5,000 or more.

31 CFR 103.22 — "Reports of Transactions in Currency"

Sets forth the requirements for financial institutions to report currency transactions in excess of $10,000. Includes 31 CFR 103.22(d) — "Transactions of Exempt Persons," which sets forth the requirements for financial institutions to exempt transactions of certain persons from currency transaction reporting requirements.

31 CFR 103.23 — "Reports of Transportation of Currency or Monetary Instruments" Sets forth the requirements for filing a Currency and Monetary Instruments Report.

31 CFR 103.24 — "Reports of Foreign Financial Accounts"

Sets forth the requirement that each person having a financial account in a foreign country must file a report with the Internal Revenue Service annually.

31 CFR 103.27 — "Filing of Reports"

Filing and recordkeeping requirements for Currency Transaction Reports (CTRs), Report of International Transportation of Currency or Monetary Instruments (CMIRs), and Report of Foreign Bank and Financial Accounts (FBARs).

31 CFR 103.28 — "Identification Required"

Sets forth the requirement that financial institutions verify the identity of persons conducting currency transactions in excess of $10,000.

31 CFR 103.29 — "Purchases of Bank Checks and Drafts, Cashier's Checks, Money Orders, and Traveler's Checks"

Sets forth the requirements that financial institutions maintain records relating to purchases of monetary instruments with currency in amounts between $3,000 and $10,000.

31 CFR 103.32 — "Records to Be Made and Retained by Persons Having Financial Interests in Foreign Financial Accounts"

Sets forth the requirement that persons having a financial account in a foreign country maintain records relating to foreign financial bank accounts reported on an FBAR.

31 CFR 103.33 — "Records to Be Made and Retained by Financial Institutions"

Sets forth recordkeeping and retrieval requirements for financial institutions, including funds transfer recordkeeping and transmittal requirements.

31 CFR 103.34 — "Additional Records to Be Made and Retained by Banks" Sets forth additional recordkeeping requirements for banks.

31 CFR 103.38 — "Nature of Records and Retention Period"

Sets forth acceptable forms of records required to be kept and establishes a five-year record-retention requirement.

31 CFR 103.41 — "Registration of Money Services Businesses"

Requirements for money services businesses to register with the U.S. Treasury/FinCEN.

31 CFR 103.57 — "Civil Penalty"

Sets forth potential civil penalties for willful or negligent violations of 31 CFR Part 103.

31 CFR 103.59 — "Criminal Penalty"

Sets forth potential criminal penalties for willful violations of 31 CFR Part 103.

31 CFR 103.63 — "Structured Transactions"

Prohibits the structuring of transactions to avoid the currency reporting requirement.

31 CFR 103.100 — "Information Sharing Between Federal Law Enforcement Agencies and Financial Institutions"

Establishes procedures and information sharing between federal law enforcement and financial institutions to deter money laundering and terrorist activity.

31 CFR 103.110 — "Voluntary Information Sharing Among Financial Institutions" Establishes procedures for voluntary information sharing among financial institutions to deter money laundering and terrorist activity.

31 CFR 103.120 — "Anti-Money Laundering Program Requirements for Financial Institutions Regulated by a Federal Functional Regulator or a Self-Regulatory Organization, and Casinos"

Establishes, in part, the standard that a financial institution regulated only by a federal functional regulator satisfies statutory requirements to establish an AML program if the financial institution complies with the regulations of its federal functional regulator governing such programs.

31 CFR 103.121 — "Customer Identification Programs for Banks, Savings Associations, Credit Unions, and Certain Non-Federally Regulated Banks"

Sets forth the requirement for banks, savings associations, credit unions, and certain non-federally regulated banks to implement a written Customer Identification Program.

31 CFR 103.137 — "Anti-Money Laundering Programs for Insurance Companies" Sets forth the requirement for insurance companies that issue or underwrite "covered products" to develop and implement a written AML program that is reasonably designed to prevent the insurance company from being used to facilitate money laundering or financing of terrorist activities.

31 CFR 103.176 — "Due Diligence Programs for Correspondent Accounts for Foreign Financial Institutions"

Sets forth the requirement for certain financial institutions to establish and apply a due diligence program that includes appropriate, specific, risk-based, and, where necessary, enhanced policies and procedures that are reasonably designed to enable the institution to detect and report known or suspected money laundering activity involving any correspondent account for a foreign financial institution.

31 CFR 103.177 — "Prohibition on Correspondent Accounts for Foreign Shell Banks; Records Concerning Owners of Foreign Banks and Agents for Service of Legal Process" Prohibits a covered financial institution from establishing a correspondent account with a foreign shell bank and requires the financial institution to maintain records identifying the owners of foreign financial institutions.

31 CFR 103.178 — "Due Diligence Programs for Private Banking Accounts"

Sets forth the requirement for certain financial institutions to establish and maintain a due diligence program that includes policies, procedures, and controls that are reasonably designed to detect and report any known or suspected money laundering or suspicious activity conducted through or involving any private banking account that is established, maintained, administered, or managed in the United States for a non-U.S. person.

31 CFR 103.185 — "Summons or Subpoena of Foreign Bank Records; Termination of Correspondent Relationship"

Requires a financial institution to provide foreign financial institution records upon the request of an appropriate law enforcement official and to terminate a correspondent relationship with a foreign financial institution.

31 CFR 103, Subpart I, Appendix A — "Certification Regarding Correspondent Accounts for Foreign Banks"

Voluntary certification forms to be completed by a foreign bank that maintains a correspondent account with a U.S. bank.

31 CFR 103, Subpart I, Appendix B — "Recertification Regarding Correspondent Accounts for Foreign Banks"

A voluntary re-certification form to be completed by a foreign bank.

Board of Governors of the Federal Reserve System

Regulation H — 12 CFR 208.62 — "Suspicious Activity Reports"

Sets forth the requirements for state member banks for filing a SAR with the appropriate federal law enforcement agencies and the U.S. Treasury.

Regulation H — 12 CFR 208.63 — "Procedures for Monitoring Bank Secrecy Act Compliance"

Sets forth the requirements for state member banks to establish and maintain procedures to ensure and monitor their compliance with the BSA.

Regulation K — 12 CFR 211.5(k) — "Reports by Edge and Agreement Corporations of Crimes and Suspected Crimes"

Sets forth the requirements for an Edge and agreement corporation, or any branch or subsidiary thereof, to file a SAR with the appropriate federal law enforcement agencies and the U.S. Treasury.

Regulation K — 12 CFR 211.5(m) — "Procedures for Monitoring Bank Secrecy Act Compliance"

Sets forth the requirements for an Edge and agreement corporation to establish and maintain procedures reasonably designed to ensure and monitor compliance with the BSA and related regulations.

Regulation K — 12 CFR 211.24(f) — "Reports of Crimes and Suspected Crimes"

Sets forth the requirements for an uninsured branch, an agency, or a representative office of a foreign financial institution operating in the United States to file a SAR with the appropriate federal law enforcement agencies and the U.S. Treasury.

Regulation K — 12 CFR 211.24(j) — "Procedures for Monitoring Bank Secrecy Act Compliance"

Sets forth the requirements for an uninsured branch, an agency, or a representative office of a foreign financial institution operating in the United States to establish and maintain procedures reasonably designed to ensure and monitor compliance with the BSA and related regulations.

Regulation Y — 12 CFR 225.4(f) — "Suspicious Activity Report"

Sets forth the requirements for a bank holding company or any non-bank subsidiary thereof, or a foreign bank that is subject to the Bank Holding Company Act or any non- bank subsidiary of such a foreign financial institution operating in the United States to file a SAR with the appropriate federal law enforcement agencies and the U.S. Treasury.

Federal Deposit Insurance Corporation

12 CFR 326 Subpart B — "Procedures for Monitoring Bank Secrecy Act Compliance" Sets forth requirements for state nonmember banks to establish and maintain procedures to ensure and monitor their compliance with the BSA.

12 CFR 353 — "Suspicious Activity Reports"

Establishes requirements for state nonmember banks to file a SAR when they detect a known or suspected violation of federal law, a suspicious transaction relating to a money laundering activity, or a violation of the BSA.

National Credit Union Administration

12 CFR 748 — "Security Program, Report of Crime and Catastrophic Act and Bank Secrecy Act Compliance"

Requires federally insured credit unions to maintain security programs and comply with the BSA.

12 CFR 748.1 — "Filing of Reports"

Requires federally insured credit unions to file compliance and Suspicious Activity Reports.

12 CFR 748.2 — "Procedures for Monitoring Bank Secrecy Act (BSA) Compliance" Ensures that all federally insured credit unions establish and maintain procedures reasonably designed to assure and monitor compliance with the recordkeeping and reporting requirements in the BSA.

Office of the Comptroller of the Currency

12 CFR 21.11 — "Suspicious Activity Report"

Ensures that national banks file a Suspicious Activity Report when they detect a known or suspected violation of federal law or a suspicious transaction relating to a money laundering activity or a violation of the BSA. This section applies to all national banks as well as any federal branches and agencies of foreign financial institutions licensed or chartered by the OCC.

12 CFR 21.21 — "Procedures for Monitoring Bank Secrecy Act (BSA) Compliance" Requires all national banks to establish and maintain procedures to ensure and monitor their compliance with the BSA.

Office of Thrift Supervision

12 CFR 563.177 — "Procedures for Monitoring Bank Secrecy Act (BSA) Compliance" Requires savings associations to implement a program to comply with the recordkeeping and reporting requirements in the BSA.

12 CFR 563.180 — "Suspicious Activity Reports and Other Reports and Statements" Sets forth the rules for savings associations or service corporations for filing a SAR with the appropriate federal law enforcement agencies and the U.S. Treasury.

APPENDIX B. BSA/AML DIRECTIVES

Board of Governors of the Federal Reserve System

Supervision and Regulation Letters, commonly known as SR Letters, address significant policy and procedural matters related to the Federal Reserve System's supervisory responsibilities. Issued by the Board of Governors' Division of Banking Supervision and Regulation, SR Letters are an important means of disseminating information to banking supervision staff at the Board of Governors and the Reserve Banks and, in some instances, to supervised banking organizations. The applicable BSA/AML SR Letters are available at the following web site: www.federalreserve.gov/boarddocs/srletters/.

Federal Deposit Insurance Corporation

Financial Institution Letters (FILs) are addressed to the chief executive officers of the financial institutions on the FIL distribution list — generally, FDIC-supervised banks. FILs may announce new regulations and policies, new FDIC publications, and a variety of other matters of principal interest to those responsible for operating a bank or savings association. The applicable FILs are available at the following web site: www.fdic.gov/news /news/financial/2006/index.html.

National Credit Union Administration

NCUA publishes Letters to Credit Unions (LCU) and Regulatory Alerts (RA) addressed to credit union boards of directors. LCUs and RAs are used to share information, announce new policies, and provide guidance for credit unions and credit union examination staff. The NCUA's *Examiner's Guide* provides overall guidance for the risk-focused examination and supervision of federally insured credit unions. NCUA's risk-focused program evaluates the degree to which credit union management identifies, measures, monitors, and controls (i.e., manages) existing and potential risks in their operations, including risk associated with AML programs. Applicable sections of the *Examiner's Guide* are available on the following web site: www.ncua.gov.

Office of the Comptroller of the Currency

OCC Alerts are issuances published with special urgency to notify bankers and examiners of matters of pressing concern, often suspicious or illegal banking practices. OCC Bulletins and Advisory Letters contain information of continuing importance to bankers and examiners. Bulletins and Advisory Letters remain in effect until revised or rescinded. Specific BSA/AML OCC Alerts, Bulletins, and Advisory Letters are available at the following web site: www.occ.treas.gov.

Office of Thrift Supervision

The Office of Thrift Supervision issues Regulatory Bulletins and CEO Letters to clarify regulations and to specify guidelines and procedures. These directives are an important means to keep examiners as well as savings associations continuously updated on BSA/AML issues. Specific BSA/AML Regulatory Bulletins and CEO Letters are available at the following web site: www.ots.treas.gov.

Appendix C. BSA/AML References

Web Sites

Board of Governors of the Federal Reserve System
www.federalreserve.gov
Federal Deposit Insurance Corporation
www.fdic.gov
National Credit Union Administration
www.ncua.gov
Office of the Comptroller of the Currency
www.occ.treas.gov
Office of Thrift Supervision
www.ots.treas.gov
Financial Crimes Enforcement Network
www.fincen.gov
Office of Foreign Assets Control
www.treasury.gov/ofac
Federal Financial Institutions Examination Council
www.ffiec.gov

Manuals or Handbooks

Federal Reserve Commercial Bank Examination Manual
Federal Reserve Bank Holding Company Supervision Manual
Federal Reserve Examination Manual for U.S. Branches and Agencies of Foreign Banking Organizations
Federal Reserve Guidelines and Instructions for Examinations of Edge Corporations
FDIC Manual of Examination Policies
NCUA Compliance Self-Assessment Manual
NCUA Examiner's Guide
OCC Comptroller's Handbook — Asset Management
OCC Comptroller's Handbook — Community Bank Supervision
OCC Comptroller's Handbook — Compliance
OCC Comptroller's Handbook — Large Bank Supervision
OCC Money Laundering: A Banker's Guide to Avoiding Problems
OTS Examination Handbook
OTS Compliance Activities Handbook

Other Materials

Federal Financial Institutions Examination Council (FFIEC)

The FFIEC's web site (www.ffiec.gov) includes the following information:

- BSA/AML Examination Manual InfoBase.
- Information Technology Handbooks.

U.S. Government

Interagency U.S. Money Laundering Threat Assessment (MLTA) (December 2005)

The MLTA is a government-wide analysis of money laundering in the United States. The MLTA offers a detailed analysis of money laundering methods, ranging from well-established techniques for integrating dirty money into the financial system to modern innovations that exploit global payment networks as well as the Internet. (www.treas.gov/press/releases/reports/js3077_01112005_MLTA.pdf)

FinCEN

FinCEN's web site (www.fincen.gov) includes the following information:

- BSA Forms — Links to BSA reporting forms, and instructions for magnetic and electronic filing.
- SAR Activity Reviews — Meaningful information about the preparation, use, and value of Suspicious Activity Reports (SARs) filed by financial institutions.
- BSA Guidance — Frequently Asked Questions, FinCEN rulings, guidance on preparing a complete and accurate SAR narrative, and country advisories.

- Reports — Links to FinCEN Reports to Congress, the U.S. Treasury's National Money Laundering Strategy, and the U.S. State Department's International Narcotics Control Strategy Report.
- *Federal Register* notices.
- Enforcement actions.

Basel Committee on Banking Supervision (BCBS)

The BCBS web site (on the Bank of International Settlements' web site, www.bis.org) includes the following publications:

- Consolidated Know Your Customer Risk Management
- Initiatives by the BCBS, International Association of Insurance Supervisors (IAIS) and International Organization of Securities Commissions (IOSCO) to Combat Money Laundering and the Financing of Terrorism
- Sharing of Financial Records Between Jurisdictions in Connection with the Fight Against Terrorist Financing
- Customer Due Diligence for Banks
- Prevention of Criminal Use of the Banking System for the Purpose of Money-Laundering
- Banking Secrecy and International Cooperation in Banking Supervision

Financial Action Task Force on Money Laundering (FATF)

FATF's web site (www.fatf-gafi.org) includes the following publications:

- Forty Recommendations to Combat Money Laundering and Terrorism
- Special Recommendations Against Terrorist Financing
- Interpretive Notes to FATF Recommendations
- Non-Cooperative Countries or Territories
- Typologies on Money Laundering Risk

New York Clearing House Association, LLC (NYCH)

The NYCH's web site (www.theclearinghouse.org) includes this publication:

- Guidelines for Counter Money Laundering Policies and Procedures in Correspondent Banking

National Automated Clearing House Association — The Electronic Payments Association (NACHA)

NACHA's web site (www.nacha.org) includes the following:

- "The Next Generation ACH Task Force: Future Vision of the ACH Network"
- NACHA Operating Rules

The Wolfsberg Group

The Wolfsberg Group's web site (www.wolfsberg-principles.com) includes the following:

- Wolfsberg AML Principles on Private Banking
- Wolfsberg Statement on the Suppression of the Financing of Terrorism
- Wolfsberg AML Principles for Correspondent Banking
- Wolfsberg Statement on Monitoring, Screening, and Searching
- Wolfsberg Guidance on Risk Based Approach for Managing Money Laundering Risks
- Wolfsberg FAQs on Correspondent Banking

APPENDIX D. STATUTORY DEFINITION OF FINANCIAL INSTITUTION

As defined in the BSA 31 USC 5312(a)(2) the term "financial institution" includes the following:

- An insured bank (as defined in section 3(h) of the FDI Act (12 USC 1813(h))).
- A commercial bank or trust company.
- A private banker.
- An agency or branch of a foreign bank in the United States.
- Any credit union.
- A thrift institution.
- A broker or dealer registered with the Securities and Exchange Commission under the Securities Exchange Act of 1934 (15 USC 78a *et seq.).*
- A broker or dealer in securities or commodities.
- An investment banker or investment company.
- A currency exchange.
- An issuer, redeemer, or cashier of traveler's checks, checks, money orders, or similar instruments.
- An operator of a credit card system.
- An insurance company.
- A dealer in precious metals, stones, or jewels.
- A pawnbroker.
- A loan or finance company.
- A travel agency.
- A licensed sender of money or any other person who engages as a business in the transmission of funds, including any person who engages as a business in an informal money transfer system or any network of people who engage as a business in facilitating the transfer of money domestically or internationally outside of the conventional financial institutions system.
- A telegraph company.
- A business engaged in vehicle sales, including automobile, airplane, and boat sales.

- Persons involved in real estate closings and settlements.
- The United States Postal Service.
- An agency of the United States government or of a state or local government carrying out a duty or power of a business described in this paragraph.
- A casino, gambling casino, or gaming establishment with an annual gaming revenue of more than $1,000,000 which —
  - Is licensed as a casino, gambling casino, or gaming establishment under the laws of any state or any political subdivision of any state; or
  - Is an Indian gaming operation conducted under or pursuant to the Indian Gaming Regulatory Act other than an operation which is limited to class I gaming (as defined in section 4(6) of such act).
- Any business or agency which engages in any activity which the Secretary of the Treasury determines, by regulation, to be an activity which is similar to, related to, or a substitute for any activity in which any business described in this paragraph is authorized to engage.
- Any other business designated by the Secretary whose cash transactions have a high degree of usefulness in criminal, tax, or regulatory matters.
- Any futures commission merchant, commodity trading advisor, or commodity pool operator registered, or required to register, under the Commodity Exchange Act (7 USC 1, *et seq.*).

APPENDIX E. INTERNATIONAL ORGANIZATIONS

Money laundering and terrorist financing can have a widespread international impact. Money launderers have been found to transfer funds and maintain assets on a global level, which makes tracing funds through various countries a complex and challenging process. Most countries support the fight against money laundering and terrorist funding; however, because of the challenges in creating consistent laws or regulations between countries, international groups have developed model recommendations for governments and financial institutions. Two key international bodies in this area follow:

- **The Financial Action Task Force on Money Laundering (FATF)** is an intergovernmental body established for the development and promotion of policies to combat money laundering and terrorist financing. The FATF has developed recommendations on various money laundering and terrorist financing issues published in the "FATF Forty Recommendations" and the "Special Recommendations on Terrorist Financing."[1]
- **The Basel Committee on Banking Supervision** is a committee of central banks and bank supervisors and regulators from major industrialized countries that meets at the Bank for International Settlements (BIS) in Basel, Switzerland, to discuss issues related to prudential banking supervision. The Basel Committee formulates broad standards and guidelines and makes recommendations regarding sound practices, including those on customer due diligence.

In addition, other global organizations are becoming increasingly involved in combating money laundering. The International Monetary Fund (IMF) and the World Bank have stressed the importance of integrating AML and counter-terrorist financing issues into their financial sector assessments, surveillance, and diagnostic activities. Furthermore, various FATF-style regional bodies exist. These groups participate as observers in FATF meetings; assess their members against the FATF standards; and, like FATF members, frequently assist in the IMF and World Bank assessment program.

End Notes

[1] Another well-known FATF initiative is its non-cooperative countries and territories (NCCT) exercise, wherein jurisdictions have been identified as NCCT. A current list of countries designated by FATF as non-cooperating countries or territories is available on the FATF web site (www.fatf-gafi.org).

Appendix F. Money Laundering and Terrorist Financing "Red Flags"

The following are examples of potentially suspicious activities, or "red flags" for both money laundering and terrorist financing. Although these lists are not all-inclusive, they may help banks and examiners recognize possible money laundering and terrorist financing schemes. Management's primary focus should be on reporting suspicious activities, rather than on determining whether the transactions are in fact linked to money laundering, terrorist financing, or a particular crime.

The following examples are red flags that, when encountered, may warrant additional scrutiny. The mere presence of a red flag is not by itself evidence of criminal activity. Closer scrutiny should help to determine whether the activity is suspicious or one for which there does not appear to be a reasonable business or legal purpose.

Potentially Suspicious Activity that May Indicate Money Laundering

Customers Who Provide Insufficient or Suspicious Information

- A customer uses unusual or suspicious identification documents that cannot be readily verified.
- A business is reluctant, when establishing a new account, to provide complete information about the nature and purpose of its business, anticipated account activity, prior banking relationships, the names of its officers and directors, or information on its business location.
- A customer's home or business telephone is disconnected.
- The customer's background differs from that which would be expected on the basis of his or her business activities.

- A customer makes frequent or large transactions and has no record of past or present employment experience.
- A customer is a trust, shell company, or Private Investment Company that is reluctant to provide information on controlling parties and underlying beneficiaries. Beneficial owners may hire nominee incorporation services to establish shell companies and open bank accounts for those shell companies while shielding the owner's identity.

Efforts to Avoid Reporting or Recordkeeping Requirement

- A customer or group tries to persuade a bank employee not to file required reports or maintain required records.
- A customer is reluctant to provide information needed to file a mandatory report, to have the report filed, or to proceed with a transaction after being informed that the report must be filed.
- A customer is reluctant to furnish identification when purchasing negotiable instruments in recordable amounts.
- A business or customer asks to be exempted from reporting or recordkeeping requirements.
- A person customarily uses the automated teller machine to make several bank deposits below a specified threshold.
- A customer deposits funds into several accounts, usually in amounts of less than $3,000, which are subsequently consolidated into a master account and transferred outside of the country, particularly to or through a location of specific concern (e.g., countries designated by national authorities and Financial Action Task Force on Money Laundering (FATF) as non-cooperative countries and territories).
- A customer accesses a safe deposit box after completing a transaction involving a large withdrawal of currency, or accesses a safe deposit box before making currency deposits structured at or just under $10,000, to evade Currency Transaction Report (CTR) filing requirements.

Funds Transfers

- Many funds transfers are sent in large, round dollar, hundred dollar, or thousand dollar amounts.
- Funds transfer activity occurs to or from a financial secrecy haven, or to or from a high-risk geographic location without an apparent business reason or when the activity is inconsistent with the customer's business or history.
- Many small, incoming transfers of funds are received, or deposits are made using checks and money orders. Almost immediately, all or most of the transfers or deposits are wired to another city or country in a manner inconsistent with the customer's business or history.
- Large, incoming funds transfers are received on behalf of a foreign client, with little or no explicit reason.
- Funds transfer activity is unexplained, repetitive, or shows unusual patterns.
- Payments or receipts with no apparent links to legitimate contracts, goods, or services are received.

- Funds transfers are sent or received from the same person to or from different accounts.
- Funds transfers contain limited content and lack related party information.

Automated Clearing House Transactions

- Large-value, automated clearing house (ACH) transactions are frequently initiated through third-party service providers (TPSP) by originators that are not bank customers and for which the bank has no or insufficient due diligence.
- TPSPs have a history of violating ACH network rules or generating illegal transactions, or processing manipulated or fraudulent transactions on behalf of their customers.

Activity Inconsistent with the Customer's Business

- The currency transaction patterns of a business show a sudden change inconsistent with normal activities.
- A large volume of cashier's checks, money orders, or funds transfers is deposited into, or purchased through, an account when the nature of the accountholder's business would not appear to justify such activity.
- A retail business has dramatically different patterns of currency deposits from similar businesses in the same general location.
- Unusual transfers of funds occur among related accounts or among accounts that involve the same or related principals.
- The owner of both a retail business and a check-cashing service does not ask for currency when depositing checks, possibly indicating the availability of another source of currency.
- Goods or services purchased by the business do not match the customer's stated line of business.

Other Suspicious Customer Activity

- A customer frequently exchanges small-dollar denominations for large-dollar denominations.
- A customer frequently deposits currency wrapped in currency straps or currency wrapped in rubber bands that is disorganized and does not balance when counted.
- A customer purchases a number of cashier's checks, money orders, or traveler's checks for large amounts under a specified threshold.
- A customer purchases a number of open-end stored value cards for large amounts. Purchases of stored value cards are not commensurate with normal business activities.
- A customer receives large and frequent deposits from on-line payments systems yet has no apparent on-line or auction business.
- Monetary instruments deposited by mail are numbered sequentially or have unusual symbols or stamps on them.
- Suspicious movements of funds occur from one bank to another, and then funds are moved back to the first bank.

- Deposits are structured through multiple branches of the same bank or by groups of people who enter a single branch at the same time.
- Currency is deposited or withdrawn in amounts just below identification or reporting thresholds.
- The customer may visit a safe deposit box or use a safe custody account on an unusually frequent basis.
- Safe deposit boxes or safe custody accounts may be opened by individuals who do not reside or work in the institution's service area despite the availability of such services at an institution closer to them.
- Unusual traffic patterns in the safe deposit box area or unusual use of safe custody accounts. For example, more individuals may enter, enter more frequently, or carry bags or other containers that could conceal large amounts of currency, monetary instruments, or small valuable items.
- A customer rents multiple safe deposit boxes to park large amounts of currency, monetary instruments, or high-value assets awaiting conversion to currency, for placement into the banking system. Similarly, a customer establishes multiple safe custody accounts to park large amounts of securities awaiting sale and conversion into currency, monetary instruments, outgoing funds transfers, or a combination thereof, for placement into the banking system.
- Loans are made for, or are paid on behalf of, a third party with no reasonable explanation.
- To secure a loan, the customer purchases a certificate of deposit using an unknown source of funds, particularly when funds are provided via currency or multiple monetary instruments.

Changes in Bank-to-Bank Transactions

- The size and frequency of currency deposits increases rapidly with no corresponding increase in noncurrency deposits.
- A bank is unable to track the true accountholder of correspondent or concentration account transactions.
- The turnover in large-denomination bills is significant and appears uncharacteristic, given the bank's location.
- Changes in currency-shipment patterns between correspondent banks are significant.

Cross-Border Financial Institution Transactions[1]

- U.S. bank increases sales or exchanges of large denomination U.S. bank notes to Mexican financial institution(s).
- Large volumes of small denomination U.S. banknotes being sent from Mexican casas de cambio to their U.S. accounts via armored transport or sold directly to U.S. banks. These sales or exchanges may involve jurisdictions outside of Mexico.
- Casas de cambio direct the remittance of funds via multiple funds transfers to jurisdictions outside of Mexico that bear no apparent business relationship with the casas de cambio. Funds transfer recipients may include individuals, businesses, and other entities in free trade zones.

- Casas de cambio deposit numerous third-party items, including sequentially numbered monetary instruments, to their accounts at U.S. banks.
- Casas de cambio direct the remittance of funds transfers from their accounts at Mexican financial institutions to accounts at U.S. banks. These funds transfers follow the deposit of currency and third-party items by the casas de cambio into their Mexican financial institution.

Trade Finance

- Transport documents do not match letter of credit documents and evidence an over-shipment or under-shipment not covered by the letter of credit agreement.
- Shipment locations of the goods, shipping terms, or descriptions of the goods are inconsistent with the letter of credit. This may include changes in shipment locations to high-risk countries or changes in the quality of the goods shipped.
- Sudden and unexplained increases in a customer's normal trade transactions.
- The letter of credit is issued as a bearer instrument or contains unusual clauses or terminology.
- Customers are conducting business in high-risk jurisdictions or geographic locations, particularly when shipping items through high-risk or non-cooperative countries.
- Customers involved in potentially high-risk activities (e.g., dealers in weapons, nuclear materials, chemicals, precious gems; or certain natural resources such as metals, ore, and crude oil).
- Obvious over- or under-pricing of goods and services (e.g., importer pays $400 an item for one shipment and $750 for an identical item in the next shipment; exporter charges one customer $100 per item and another customer $400 for an identical item in the same week).
- Excessively amended letters of credit without reasonable justification.
- Transactions evidently designed to evade legal restrictions, including evasion of necessary government licensing requirements.

Privately Owned Automated Teller Machines

- Automated teller machine (ATM) activity levels are high in comparison with other privately owned or bank-owned ATMs in comparable geographic and demographic locations.
- Sources of currency for the ATM cannot be identified or confirmed through withdrawals from account, armored car contracts, lending arrangements, or other appropriate documentation.

Insurance

- A customer purchases products with termination features without concern for the product's investment performance.
- A customer purchases insurance products using a single, large premium payment, particularly when payment is made through unusual methods such as currency or currency equivalents.
- A customer purchases product that appears outside the customer's normal range of financial wealth or estate planning needs.

- A customer borrows against the cash surrender value of permanent life insurance policies, particularly when payments are made to apparently unrelated third parties.
- Policies are purchased that allow for the transfer of beneficial ownership interests without the knowledge and consent of the insurance issuer. This would include secondhand endowment and bearer insurance policies.
- A customer is known to purchase several insurance products and uses the proceeds from an early policy surrender to purchase other financial assets.

Shell Company Activity

- A bank is unable to obtain sufficient information or information is unavailable to positively identify originators or beneficiaries of accounts or other banking activity (using Internet, commercial database searches, or direct inquiries to a respondent bank).
- Payments have no stated purpose, do not reference goods or services, or identify only a contract or invoice number.
- Goods or services, if identified, do not match profile of company provided by respondent bank or character of the financial activity; a company references remarkably dissimilar goods and services in related funds transfers; explanation given by foreign respondent bank is inconsistent with observed funds transfer activity.
- Transacting businesses share the same address, provide only a registered agent's address, or have other address inconsistencies.
- Unusually large number and variety of beneficiaries are receiving funds transfers from one company.
- Frequent involvement of multiple jurisdictions or beneficiaries located in high-risk offshore financial centers.
- Use of nested correspondent banking relationships.

Embassy and Foreign Consulate Accounts

- Official embassy business is conducted through personal accounts.
- Account activity is not consistent with the purpose of the account, such as pouch activity or payable upon proper identification transactions.
- Accounts are funded through substantial currency transactions.
- Accounts directly fund personal expenses of foreign nationals without appropriate controls, including, but not limited to, expenses for college students.

Employees

- An employee has lavish lifestyle that cannot be supported by his or her salary.
- An employee fails to conform to recognized policies, procedures, and processes, particularly in private banking.
- An employee is reluctant to take a vacation.

Potentially Suspicious Activity that May Indicate Terrorist Financing

The following examples of potentially suspicious activity that may indicate terrorist financing are primarily based on guidance "Guidance for Financial Institutions in Detecting Terrorist Financing" provided by the FATF.[2] FATF is an intergovernmental body whose purpose is the development and promotion of policies, both at national and international levels, to combat money laundering and terrorist financing.

Activity Inconsistent with the Customer's Business

- Funds are generated by a business owned by persons of the same origin or by a business that involves persons of the same origin from high-risk countries (e.g., countries designated by national authorities and FATF as non-cooperative countries and territories).
- The stated occupation of the customer is not commensurate with the type or level of activity.
- Persons involved in currency transactions share an address or phone number, particularly when the address is also a business location or does not seem to correspond to the stated occupation (e.g., student, unemployed, or self-employed).
- Regarding nonprofit or charitable organizations, financial transactions occur for which there appears to be no logical economic purpose or in which there appears to be no link between the stated activity of the organization and the other parties in the transaction.
- A safe deposit box opened on behalf of a commercial entity when the business activity of the customer is unknown or such activity does not appear to justify the use of a safe deposit box.

Funds Transfers

- A large number of incoming or outgoing funds transfers take place through a business account, and there appears to be no logical business or other economic purpose for the transfers, particularly when this activity involves high-risk locations.
- Funds transfers are ordered in small amounts in an apparent effort to avoid triggering identification or reporting requirements.
- Funds transfers do not include information on the originator, or the person on whose behalf the transaction is conducted, when the inclusion of such information would be expected.
- Multiple personal and business accounts or the accounts of nonprofit organizations or charities are used to collect and funnel funds to a small number of foreign beneficiaries.
- Foreign exchange transactions are performed on behalf of a customer by a third party, followed by funds transfers to locations having no apparent business connection with the customer or to high-risk countries.

Other Transactions That Appear Unusual or Suspicious

- Transactions involving foreign currency exchanges are followed within a short time by funds transfers to high-risk locations.

- Multiple accounts are used to collect and funnel funds to a small number of foreign beneficiaries, both persons and businesses, particularly in high-risk locations.
- A customer obtains a credit instrument or engages in commercial financial transactions involving the movement of funds to or from high-risk locations when there appear to be no logical business reasons for dealing with those locations.
- Banks from high-risk locations open accounts.
- Funds are sent or received via international transfers from or to high-risk locations.
- Insurance policy loans or policy surrender values that are subject to a substantial surrender charge.

End Notes

[1] FinCEN Advisory FIN-2006-A003, "Guidance to Financial Institutions on the Repatriation of Currency Smuggled into Mexico from the United States," April 28, 2006.

[2] "Guidance for Financial Institutions in Detecting Terrorist Financing," April 24, 2002, is available at www.fatf-gafi.org.

Appendix G. Structuring

Structuring transactions to evade BSA reporting and certain recordkeeping requirements can result in civil and criminal penalties under the BSA. Under the BSA (31 USC 5324), no person shall, for the purpose of evading the Currency Transaction Report (CTR) or a geographic targeting order reporting requirement, or certain BSA recordkeeping requirements:

- Cause or attempt to cause a bank to fail to file a CTR or a report required under a geographic targeting order or to maintain a record required under BSA regulations.
- Cause or attempt to cause a bank to file a CTR or report required under a geographic targeting order, or to maintain a BSA record that contain a material omission or misstatement of fact.
- Structure, as defined above, or attempt to structure or assist in structuring, any transaction with one or more banks.

The definition of structuring, as set forth in 31 CFR 103.11 (gg) (which was implemented before a Patriot Act provision extended the prohibition on structuring to geographic targeting orders and BSA recordkeeping requirements) states, "a person structures a transaction if that person, acting alone, or in conjunction with, or on behalf of, other persons, conducts or attempts to conduct one or more transactions in currency in any amount, at one or more financial institutions, on one or more days, in any manner, for the purpose of evading the [CTR filing requirements]." "In any manner" includes, but is not limited to, breaking down a single currency sum exceeding $10,000 into smaller amounts that may be conducted as a series of transactions at or less than $10,000. The transactions need not exceed the $10,000 CTR filing threshold at any one bank on any single day in order to constitute structuring.

Money launderers and criminals have developed many ways to structure large amounts of currency to evade the CTR filing requirements. Unless currency is smuggled out of the United States or commingled with the deposits of an otherwise legitimate business, any money laundering scheme that begins with a need to convert the currency proceeds of criminal activity into more legitimate-looking forms of financial instruments, accounts, or investments, will likely involve some form of structuring. Structuring remains one of the most commonly reported suspected crimes on Suspicious Activity Reports (SARs).

Bank employees should be aware of and alert to structuring schemes. For example, a customer may structure currency deposit or withdrawal transactions, so that each is less than the $10,000 CTR filing threshold; use currency to purchase official bank checks, money orders, or traveler's checks with currency in amounts less than $10,000 (and possibly in amounts less than the $3,000 recordkeeping threshold for the currency purchase of monetary instruments to avoid having to produce identification in the process); or exchange small bank notes for large ones in amounts less than $10,000.

However, two transactions slightly under the $10,000 threshold conducted days or weeks apart may not necessarily be structuring. For example, if a customer deposits $9,900 in currency on Monday and deposits $9,900 in currency on Wednesday, it should not be assumed that structuring has occurred. Instead, further review and research may be necessary to determine the nature of the transactions, prior account history, and other relevant customer information to assess whether the activity is suspicious. Even if structuring has not occurred, the bank should review the transactions for suspicious activity.

In addition, structuring may occur before a customer brings the funds to a bank. In these instances, a bank may be able to identify the aftermath of structuring. Deposits of monetary instruments that may have been purchased elsewhere might be structured to evade the CTR filing requirements or the recordkeeping requirements for the currency purchase of monetary instruments. These instruments are often numbered sequentially in groups totaling less than $10,000 or $3,000; bear the same handwriting (for the most part) and often the same small mark, stamp, or initials; or appear to have been purchased at numerous places on the same or different days.

APPENDIX H. REQUEST LETTER ITEMS

Core Examination Procedures[1]

As part of the examination planning process, the examiner should prepare a request letter. The list below includes materials that examiners *may* request or request access to for a bank BSA/AML examination. This list should be tailored for the specific bank's risk profile and the planned examination scope. Additional materials may be requested as needed.

BSA/AML Compliance Program

- Name and title of the designated BSA compliance officer and, if different, the name and title of the person responsible for monitoring BSA/AML compliance.

    - Organization charts showing direct and indirect reporting lines.
    - Copies of resumés and qualifications of person(s) new to the bank serving in BSA/AML compliance program oversight capacities.
- Make available copies of the most recent written BSA/AML compliance program approved by board of directors (or the statutory equivalent of such a program for foreign financial institutions operating in the United States), including Customer Identification Program (CIP) requirements, with date of approval noted in the minutes.
- Make available copies of the policy and procedures relating to all reporting and recordkeeping requirements, including suspicious activity reporting.
- Completed Officer's Questionnaire (BSA), if required by the bank's federal banking agency.
- Correspondence addressed between the bank, its personnel or agents, and its federal and state banking agencies, the U.S. Treasury (Office of the Secretary and Department of the Treasury, Internal Revenue Service, FinCEN, Detroit Computing Center, and OFAC) or law enforcement authorities since the previous BSA/AML examination.

Independent Testing

- Make available copies of the results of any internally or externally sourced independent audits or tests performed since the previous examination for BSA/AML, including the scope or engagement letter, management's responses, and access to the workpapers.
- Make available access to the auditor's risk assessment, audit plan (schedule), and program used for the audits or tests.

Training

- Training documentation (e.g., materials used for training since the previous BSA/AML examination).
- BSA/AML training schedule with dates, attendees, and topics. A list of persons in positions for which the bank typically requires BSA/AML training but who did not participate in the training.

Risk Assessment

- Make available copies of management's BSA/AML risk assessment of products, services, customers, and geographic locations.
- List of bank identified high-risk accounts.

Customer Identification Program

- List of accounts without taxpayer identification numbers (TINs).
- File of correspondence requesting TINs for bank customers.
- Written description of the bank's rationale for CIP exemptions for existing customers who open new accounts.
- List of new accounts covering all product lines (including accounts opened by third parties) and segregating existing customer accounts from new customers, for

________. *(Examiner to insert a period of time appropriate for the size and complexity of the bank.)*

- List of any accounts opened for a customer that provides an application for a TIN.
- List of any accounts opened in which verification has not been completed or any accounts opened with exceptions to the CIP.
- List of customers or potential customers for whom the bank took adverse action,[2] on the basis of its CIP.
- List of all documentary and nondocumentary methods the bank uses to verify a customer's identity.
- Make available customer notices and a description of their timing and delivery, by product.
- List of the financial institutions on which the bank is relying, if the bank is using the "reliance provision." The list should note if the relied-upon financial institutions are subject to a rule implementing the BSA/AML compliance program requirements of 31 USC 5318(h) and are regulated by a federal functional regulator.
- Provide the following:
  - Copies of any contracts signed between the parties.
  - Copies of the CIP or procedures used by the other party.
  - Any certifications made by the other party.
- Copies of contracts with financial institutions and with third parties that perform all or any part of the bank's CIP.

Suspicious Activity Reporting

- Access to Suspicious Activity Reports (SARs) filed with FinCEN during the review period and the supporting documentation. Include copies of any filed SARs that were related to section 314(a) requests for information or to section 314(b) information sharing requests.
- Any analyses or documentation of any activity for which a SAR was considered but not filed, or for which the bank is actively considering filing a SAR.
- Description of expanded monitoring procedures applied to high-risk accounts.
- Determination of whether the bank uses a manual or an automated account monitoring system, or a combination of the two. If an automated system is used, determine whether the system is proprietary or vendor supplied. If the system was provided by an outside vendor, request (i) a list that includes the vendor, (ii) application names, and (iii) installation dates of any automated account monitoring system provided by an outside vendor. Request a list of the algorithms or rules used by the systems and copies of the independent validation of the software against these rules.
- Make available copies of reports used for identification of and monitoring for suspicious transactions. These reports include, but are not limited to, suspected kiting reports, cash activity reports, monetary instrument records, and funds transfer reports. These reports can be generated from specialized BSA/AML software, the bank's general data processing systems, or both.

- If not already provided, copies of other reports that can pinpoint unusual transactions warranting further review. Examples include nonsufficient funds (NSF) reports, account analysis fee income reports, and large item reports.
- Provide name, purpose, parameters, and frequency of each report.
- Correspondence filed with federal law enforcement authorities concerning the disposition of accounts reported for suspicious activity.
- Make available copies of criminal subpoenas received by the bank since the previous examination or inspection.
- Make available copies of policies, procedures, and processes used to comply with all criminal subpoenas, including National Security Letters (NSLs), related to BSA.

Currency Transaction Reporting

- Access to filed Currency Transaction Reports (CTRs) (FinCEN Form 104) for the review period.
- Access to internal reports used to identify reportable currency transactions for the review period.
- List of products or services that may involve currency transactions.

Currency Transaction Reporting Exemptions

- Access to filed Designation of Exempt Person form(s) for current exemptions (FinCEN Form 110).
- List of customers exempted from CTR filing and the documentation to support the exemption (e.g., currency transaction history).
- Access to documentation of required annual reviews for CTR exemptions.

Information Sharing

- Documentation of any positive match for a section 314(a) request.
- Make available any vendor-confidentiality agreements regarding section 314(a) services, if applicable.
- Make available copies of policies, procedures, and processes for complying with 31 CFR 103.100 (Information Sharing Between Federal Law Enforcement Agencies and Financial Institutions).
- If applicable, a copy of the bank's most recent notification form to voluntarily share information with other financial institutions under 31 CFR 103.110 (Voluntary Information Sharing Among Financial Institutions), or a copy of the most recent correspondence received from FinCEN that acknowledges FinCEN's receipt of the bank's notice to voluntarily share information with other financial institutions.
- If applicable, make available copies of policies, procedures, and processes for complying with 31 CFR 103.110.

Purchase and Sale of Monetary Instruments

- Access to records of sales of monetary instruments in amounts between $3,000 and $10,000 (if maintained with individual transactions, provide samples of the record made in connection with the sale of each type of monetary instrument).

Funds Transfers Recordkeeping

- Access to records of funds transfers, including incoming, intermediary, and outgoing transfers of $3,000 or more.

Foreign Correspondent Account Recordkeeping and Due Diligence

- List of all foreign correspondent bank accounts, including a list of foreign financial institutions, for which the bank provides or provided regular services, and the date on which the required information was received (either by completion of a certification or by other means).
- If applicable, documentation to evidence compliance with 31 CFR 103.177 (Prohibition on Correspondent Accounts for Foreign Shell Banks; Records Concerning Owners of Foreign Banks and Agents for Service of Legal Process) and 31 CFR 103.185 (Summons or Subpoena of Foreign Bank Records; Termination of Correspondent Relationship) (for foreign correspondent bank accounts and shell banks).
- List of all payable through relationships with foreign financial institutions as defined in 31 CFR 103.175.
- Access to contracts or agreements with foreign financial institutions that have payable through accounts.
- List of the bank's foreign branches and the steps the bank has taken to determine whether the accounts with its branches are not used to indirectly provide services to foreign shell banks.
- List of all foreign correspondent bank accounts and relationships with foreign financial institutions that have been closed or terminated in compliance with the conditions in 31 CFR 103.177 (i.e., service to foreign shell banks, records of owners and agents).
- List of foreign correspondent bank accounts that have been the subject of a 31 CFR 103.100 (Information Sharing Between Federal Law Enforcement Agencies and Financial Institutions) or any other information request from a federal law enforcement officer for information regarding foreign correspondent bank accounts and evidence of compliance.
- Any notice to close foreign correspondent bank accounts from the Secretary of the Treasury or the U.S. Attorney General and evidence of compliance.
- Make available copies of policies, procedures, and processes for complying with 31 CFR 103.177.
- List of all the bank's embassy or consulate accounts, or other accounts maintained by a foreign government, foreign embassy, or foreign political figure.
- List of all accountholders and borrowers domiciled outside the United States, including those with U.S. power of attorney.

Currency-Shipment Activity

- Make available records reflecting currency shipped to and received from the Federal Reserve Bank or correspondent banks, or reflecting currency shipped between branches and their banks' central currency vaults for the previous _____ months.

(Examiner to insert a period of time appropriate for the size and complexity of the bank.)

Other BSA Reporting and Recordkeeping Requirements

- Record retention schedule and procedural guidelines.
- File of Reports of International Transportation of Currency or Monetary Instruments (CMIR) (FinCEN Form 105, formerly Customs Form 4790).
- Records of Report of Foreign Bank and Financial Accounts (FBARs) (TD F 90-22.1).

OFAC

- Name and title of the designated OFAC compliance officer and, if different, the name and title of the person responsible for monitoring OFAC compliance.
  - Organization charts showing direct and indirect reporting lines.
  - Copies of resumés and qualifications of person (or persons) new to the bank serving in OFAC compliance program oversight capacities.
- OFAC training schedule with dates, attendees, and topics. A list of persons in positions for which the bank typically requires OFAC training but who did not participate in the training.
- Make available copies of the results of any internally or externally sourced independent audits or tests performed since the previous examination for OFAC, including the scope or engagement letter, management's responses, and access to the workpapers.
- Make available copies of management's OFAC risk assessment of products, services, customers, and geographic locations.
- Make available copies of OFAC policies and procedures.
- Make available a list of blocked or rejected transactions with individuals or entities on the OFAC list and reported to OFAC. *(Banks must report all blockings within ten days by filing a Report of Blocked Transactions.)*
- If maintained, make available logs or other documentation related to reviewing potential OFAC matches, including the method for reviewing and clearing those determined not to be matches.
- Provide a list of any OFAC licenses issued to the bank. *(OFAC has the authority, through a licensing process, to permit certain transactions that would otherwise be prohibited under its regulations. If a bank's customer claims to have a specific license, the bank should verify that the transaction conforms to the terms of the license and obtain a copy of the authorizing license.)*
- If applicable, provide a copy of the records verifying that the most recent updates to OFAC software have been installed.
- Provide a copy of the Annual Report of Blocked Property submitted to OFAC (TD F 90-22.50). *(Banks must report all blocked assets to OFAC annually by September 30.)*

Expanded Examination Procedures

As part of the examination planning process, the examiner should prepare a request letter. The listing below includes materials that *may* be requested for a bank BSA/AML examination. This list should be tailored for the specific institution profile and the planned examination scope. Additional materials may be requested as needed.

Correspondent Accounts (Domestic)

- Make available copies of policies, procedures, and processes specifically for correspondent bank accounts, including procedures for monitoring for suspicious activity.
- Make available a list of domestic correspondent bank accounts.
- List of SARs filed relating to domestic correspondent bank accounts.

Correspondent Accounts (Foreign)

- Make available copies of policies, procedures, and processes specifically for foreign correspondent financial institution accounts, including procedures for monitoring for suspicious activity.
- Make available a list of foreign correspondent financial institution accounts.
- Risk assessments covering foreign correspondent financial institution account relationships.
- List of SARs filed relating to foreign correspondent financial institution accounts.

U.S. Dollar Drafts

- Make available copies of policies, procedures, and processes specifically for U.S. dollar drafts, including procedures for monitoring for suspicious activity.
- Make available a list of foreign correspondent bank accounts that offer U.S. dollar drafts. If possible, include the volume, by number and dollar amount, of monthly transactions for each account.
- List of SARs filed relating to U.S. dollar drafts.

Payable through Accounts

- Make available copies of policies, procedures, and processes specifically for payable through accounts (PTAs), including procedures for monitoring for suspicious activity.
- Make available a list of foreign correspondent bank accounts with PTAs. Include a detailed summary (number and monthly dollar volume) of sub-accountholders for each PTA.
- List of SARs filed relating to PTAs.

Pouch Activities

- Make available copies of pouch activity policies, procedures, and processes, including procedures for monitoring for suspicious activity.
- List of customer accounts permitted to use pouch services.
- List of CTRs, CMIRs, or SARs filed relating to pouch activity.

- As needed, a copy of pouch logs.

Foreign Branches and Offices of U.S. Banks

- Make available copies of policies, procedures, and processes specific to the foreign branch or office, if different from the parent's policies, procedures, and processes.
- Most recent management reports received on foreign branches and offices.
- Make available copies of the bank's tiering or organizational structure report.
- AML audit reports, compliance reports, and supporting documentation for the foreign branches and offices.
- List of the types of products and services offered at the foreign branches and offices and information on new products or services offered by the foreign branch, including those that are not already offered by the parent bank.
- A description of the method for aggregating each customer relationship across business units and geographic locations throughout the organization.
- Code of ethics for foreign branches or offices, if it is different from the bank's standard policy.
- When testing will be performed, a list of accounts originated or serviced in the foreign branch or office. Examiners should try to limit this request and focus on accounts for specific products or services, high-risk accounts only, or accounts for which exceptions or audit concerns have been noted.
- List of the locations of foreign branches and offices, including, if possible, the host country regulatory agency and contact information.
- Organizational structure of the foreign branches and offices, including reporting lines to the U.S. bank level.

Parallel Banking

- List any parallel banking relationships.
- Make available copies of policies, procedures, and processes specifically for parallel banking relationships, including procedures relating to high-risk money laundering activities. Such policies and procedures should include those that are specific to the relationship with the parallel entity.
- List of SARs filed relating to parallel banking relationships.
- Documents that specify limits or procedures that should be followed when dealing with the parallel entity.
- A list of directors or officers of the bank who are also associated with the foreign parallel bank.

Electronic Banking

- Make available copies of any policies and procedures related directly to electronic banking (e-banking) that are not already included in the BSA/AML policies.
- Management reports that indicate the monthly volume of e-banking activity.
- A list of business customers regularly conducting e-banking transactions, including the number and dollar volume of transactions.

Funds Transfers

- Funds transfer activity logs, including transfers into and out of the bank. Include the number and dollar volume of funds transfer activity for the month.
- List of funds transfers purchased with currency over a specified time period.
- List of noncustomer transactions over a specified time period.
- If not already included in the BSA/AML policies, make available copies of any policies, procedures, and processes related to funds transfers or payable upon proper identification (PUPID).
- List of suspense accounts used for PUPID proceeds.
- List of PUPID transactions completed by the bank, either as the beneficiary bank or as the originating bank.

Automated Clearing House Transactions

- Make available copies of any policies and procedures related directly to automated clearing house (ACH) transactions that are not already included in the BSA/AML policies.
- Make available copies of management reports that indicate the monthly volume of ACH activity.
- Make available a list of large or frequent ACH transactions.
- Make available a list of international ACH transactions (both those originated from or received by the bank).
- Make available a list of customer complaints regarding ACH transactions.

Electronic Cash

- Make available copies of any policies and procedures related directly to electronic cash (e-cash) that are not already included in the BSA/AML policies.
- Management reports that indicate the monthly volume of e-cash activity.
- A list of business customers regularly conducting e-cash transactions, including the number and dollar volume of transactions.

Third-Party Payment Processors

- If not already included in the BSA/AML policies, make available copies of any policies, procedures, and processes related to third-party payment processors.
- A list of third-party payment processor relationships. Include the number and dollar volume of payments processed per relationship.
- List of SARs filed on third-party payment processor relationships.

Purchase and Sale of Monetary Instruments

- If not already included in the BSA/AML policies, make available copies of any policies, procedures, and processes related to the sale of monetary instruments for currency. In particular, include policies, procedures, and processes related to the monitoring sales of monetary instruments in order to detect unusual activities.
- Monetary instrument logs or other management information systems reports used for the monitoring and detection of unusual or suspicious activities relating to the sales of monetary instruments.

- List of noncustomer transactions over a specified period of time.
- List of monetary instruments purchased with currency over a specified time period.
- List of SARs filed related to the purchase or sale of monetary instruments.

Brokered Deposits

- Make available copies of specific policies and procedures specifically for brokered deposits, including procedures for monitoring for suspicious activity.
- Risk assessment covering brokered deposits.
- Internal audits covering brokered deposits.
- List of approved deposit brokers.
- Management reports covering nonrelationship funding programs (including reports on balances, concentrations, performance, or fees paid).
- SARs and subpoenas related to brokered deposit relationships.
- Copy of account documentation or agreements for deposit broker arrangements.

Privately Owned Automated Teller Machines

- Risk assessment covering privately owned automated teller machines (ATMs) and Independent Sales Organizations (ISOs), including a list of high-risk privately owned ATM relationships.
- Make available copies of policies, procedures, and processes for privately owned ATM and ISO account acceptance, due diligence, and ongoing monitoring.
- List of ISO clients and balances.
- SARs and subpoenas related to privately owned ATMs and ISOs.

Nondeposit Investment Products

- Make available copies of policies, procedures, and processes relating to nondeposit investment products (NDIPs) and relationships with any independent NDIP providers.
- Internal audits covering NDIP sales and provider relationships.
- Risk assessment covering NDIP customers and transactions.
- If available, list of NDIP clients and balances.
- List of suspense, concentration, or omnibus accounts used for NDIP. Describe the purpose for and controls surrounding each account.
- Management reports covering 25 to 50 of the largest, most active, and most profitable NDIP customers.
- SARs and subpoenas related to NDIP customers.
- Copy of account opening documentation or agreements for NDIP.
- Copy of contracts or agreements between the bank and third-party NDIP providers for the completion of CIP, due diligence, and ongoing monitoring of NDIP customers.

Insurance

- Make available copies of BSA/AML policies and procedures related to the sale of insurance.
- Risk assessment covering insurance products.

- Management information systems reports related to the sales of insurance products. Reports may include large transaction reports, single premium payments, early cancellation, premium overpayments, and assignments of claims.
- Copy of contracts or agreements between the bank and insurance providers for the completion of CIP, due diligence, and ongoing monitoring of insurance customers.
- List of insurance products approved for sale at the bank.
- Management reports covering insurance products (including large transactions, funds transfers, single premium payments, and early cancellations).
- SARs or subpoenas related to insurance clients.
- Copy of account documentation requirements and applications for insurance products.

Concentration Accounts

- Make available copies of BSA/AML policies, procedures, and processes that are specific to concentration accounts (also known as special-use, omnibus, suspense, settlement, intraday, sweep, or collection accounts).
- List of all concentration accounts and each account's most recent reconcilement.
- Account activity reports for concentration accounts for __________. (*Examiner to insert a period of time appropriate for the size and complexity of the bank.)*

Lending Activities

- Make available copies of BSA/AML policies and procedures specific to lending.
- Risk assessment relating to the lending function, including a list of any high-risk lending relationships identified by the bank.
- For loans secured by cash collateral, marketable securities, or cash surrender value of life insurance products:
    - A list of all loans that have defaulted since the previous BSA/AML examination, including those that were charged off.
    - A list of all loans that have been extended since the previous BSA/AML examination.

Trade Finance Activities

- Make available copies of BSA/AML policies and procedures specific to trade finance activities.
- Risk assessment relating to trade finance activities, including a list of any high-risk trade finance transactions, accounts, or relationships identified by the bank.
- List of customers involved in transactions with high-risk geographic locations or for whom the bank facilitates trade finance activities with high-risk geographic locations.

Private Banking

- Make available copies of policies, procedures, and controls used to manage BSA/AML risks in the private banking department.
- Business or strategic plans for the private banking department.

- The most recent version of management reports on private banking activity, such as customer aggregation reports, policy exception reports, client concentrations, customer risk classification reports, and unusual account activity.
- Recent private banking reports from compliance, internal audit, risk management, and external auditors or consultants that cover BSA/AML.
- List of products and services offered to private banking clients. Information on new products and services offered to private banking clients and the bank's process for approving new activities.
- A description of the method for aggregating customer holdings and activities across business units throughout the organization.
- A description of account officer and manager positions, and the compensation, recruitment, and training program for these positions.
- Code of ethics policy for private banking officers.
- Risk assessment covering private banking customers and transactions.
- List of suspense, concentration, or omnibus accounts used for private banking transactions. Describe the purpose for each account and the controls governing it.
- Management reports covering 25 to 50 of the largest, most active, or most profitable private banking customers.
- A list of the bank's private banking accountholders who meet the following criteria:
    - Politically exposed persons (PEPs), export or import business owners, money transmitters, Private Investment Companies (PICs), financial advisers, offshore entities, or money managers (when an intermediary is acting on behalf of customers).
    - Customers who were introduced to the bank by individuals previously employed by other financial institutions.
    - Customers who were introduced to the bank by a third-party investment adviser.
    - Customers who use nominee names.
    - Customers who are from, or do business with, a high-risk geographic location.
    - Customers who are involved in cash-intensive businesses.
    - Customers who were granted exceptions to policies, procedures, and controls.
    - Customers who frequently appear on unusual activity monitoring reports.
- SARs and subpoenas related to private banking customers.
- Copy of account-opening documentation or agreements for private banking customers.

Trust and Asset Management Services

- Make available copies of BSA/AML policies, procedures, and processes for trust and asset management services.
- Trust and asset management procedures and guidelines used to determine when enhanced due diligence is appropriate for higher risk accounts and parties to the relationship. These should include methods for identifying account-interested parties (i.e., individual grantors, co-trustees, or outside investment managers).
- A list of the bank's trust and asset management accountholders who meet the following criteria:

- Politically exposed persons (PEPs), export or import business owners, money transmitters, Private Investment Companies (PICs), financial advisers, offshore entities, or money managers (when an intermediary is acting on behalf of customers).
- Customers who were introduced to the bank by individuals previously employed by other financial institutions.
- Customers who were introduced to the bank by a third-party investment adviser.
- Customers who use nominee names.
- Customers who are from, or do business with, a high-risk geographic location.
- Customers who are involved in cash-intensive businesses.
- Customers who were granted exceptions to policies, procedures, and controls.
- Customers who frequently appear on unusual activity monitoring reports.

- Reports and minutes submitted to the board of directors or its designated committee relating to BSA/AML matters pertaining to trust and asset management business lines and activities.
- An organizational chart for the BSA/AML compliance function as it relates to the trust and asset management services.
- A risk assessment of trust and asset management services that identifies those customers, prospective customers, or products the bank has determined to be high risk.
- Management reports covering 25 to 50 of the largest, most active, or most profitable trust and asset management customers.
- BSA/AML independent review or audit of trust and asset management services. Make workpapers available upon request.
- Make available a copy of the BSA/AML training materials for management and employees involved in trust and asset management activities.
- Identify the trust accounting systems used. Briefly explain how they accommodate and assist compliance with BSA/AML regulations and guidelines.
- List of newly opened trust and asset management accounts since _______*(Examiner to insert a period of time appropriate for the size and complexity of the bank.)*
- Procedures for checking section 314(a) requests relating to trust and asset management services.
- List of all trust and asset management accounts designated as high risk, and a list of all accounts whose assets consist of PICs and asset protection trusts.
- Copies of SARs associated with trust and asset management services.
- List of subpoenas, particularly BSA/AML-related, relating to trust and asset management activities.

Nonresident Aliens and Foreign Individuals

- Make available copies of policies, procedures, and processes specific to nonresident alien (NRA) accounts, including guidelines and systems for establishing and updating W-8 exempt status.
- A list of NRA and foreign individual accounts held by the bank, particularly those accounts the bank has designated as high risk.

- A list of NRA and foreign individual accounts without a TIN, passport number, or other appropriate identification number.
- A list of SARs and subpoenas related to NRA and foreign individual accounts.

Politically Exposed Persons

- Make available copies of policies, procedures, and processes specific to politically exposed persons (PEPs). Policies should include the bank's definition of a PEP as well as procedures for opening PEP accounts and senior management's role in the approval process for opening PEP accounts.
- List of accounts in the name of or for the benefit of a PEP. List should include the country of residence of the PEP, the account balances, and the average number and dollar volume of transactions per month.
- List of the information systems or other methods used to identify PEP accounts.
- Management reports used to monitor PEP accounts, including reports for identifying unusual and suspicious activity.

Embassy and Foreign Consulate Accounts

- Make available copies of policies, procedures, and processes specific to embassy and foreign consulate account relationships.
- List of embassy and foreign consulate accounts held by the bank, including the average account balances and the average number and dollar volume of transactions per month.
- List of accounts that are in the name of individuals who work for the embassy or foreign consulate.

Non-Bank Financial Institutions

- Make available copies of policies, procedures, and processes related to non-bank financial institutions.
- A list of non-bank financial institution accounts, including all related accounts.
- A risk assessment of non-bank financial institution accounts, identifying those accounts the bank has designated as high risk. This list should include products and services offered by the non-bank financial institution; the average account balance; and the average number, type, and dollar volume of transactions per month.
- A list of foreign non-bank financial institution accounts, including the products and services offered; the average account balance; and the average, number, type, and dollar volume of transactions per month.
- A sample of account opening documentation for high-risk non-bank financial institutions.
- A list of SARs and subpoenas related to non-bank financial institutions.

Professional Service Providers

- Make available copies of policies, procedures, and processes related to professional service provider accounts.

- List of professional service provider accounts, including all related accounts (such as interest on lawyers' trust accounts (IOLTA) which should include the name of the attorney on each account).
- List of any professional service provider accounts that the bank has designated as high risk.

Non-Governmental Organizations and Charities

- Make available copies of policies, procedures, and processes related to non-governmental organizations and charities.
- List of non-governmental organizations and charities, particularly those that the bank the bank has designated as high risk. This list should include average account balances and the average number and dollar volume of transactions.
- List of non-governmental organizations involved in high-risk geographic locations.

Business Entities (Domestic and Foreign)

- Make available copies of policies, procedures, and processes specifically related to domestic and international business entities.
- List of accounts opened by business entities. If this list is unreasonably long, amend the request to look at those entities incorporated in high-risk jurisdictions or those accounts the bank has designated as high risk.
- List of loans to business entities collateralized by bearer shares.

Cash-Intensive Businesses

- Make available copies of policies, procedures, and processes related to other businesses and entities.
- Risk assessment of other businesses and entities, list those other businesses and entities that the bank has designated as high risk. The listing should include average account balances and the average number and dollar volume of transactions.

End Notes

[1] For Expanded Examination Procedures Request Letter Items, see page H-8.
[2] As defined by 12 CFR 202.2(c).

APPENDIX I. RISK ASSESSMENT LINK TO THE BSA/AML COMPLIANCE PROGRAM

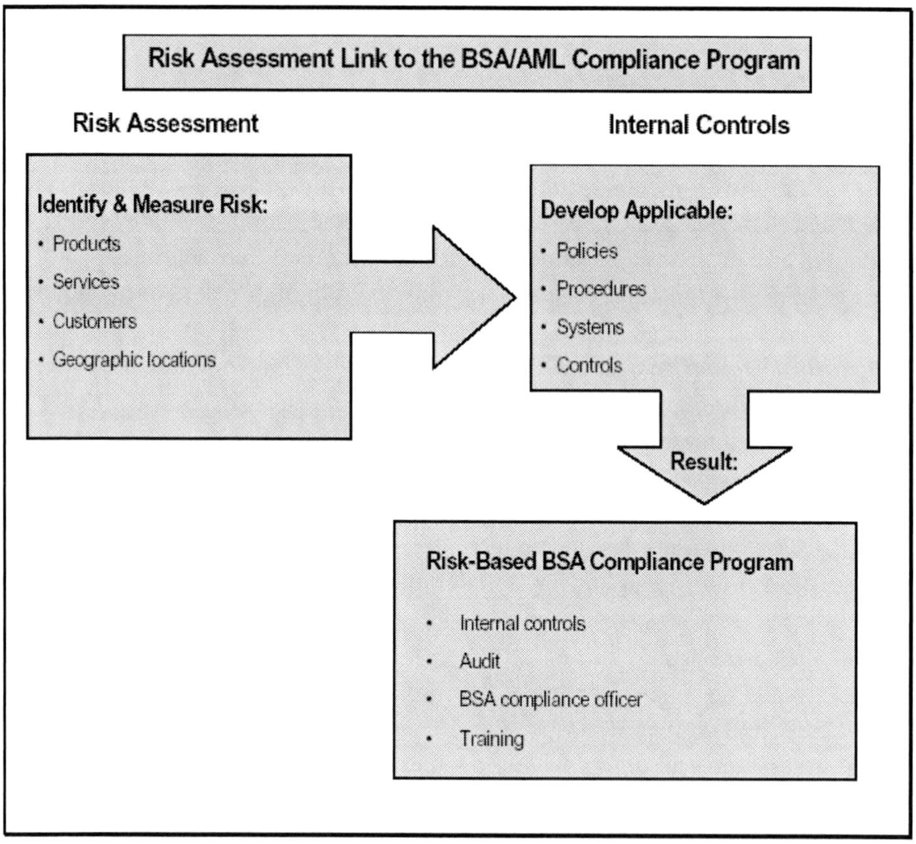

APPENDIX J. QUANTITY OF RISK MATRIX

Examiners should use the following matrix, as appropriate, when assessing the quantity of BSA/AML risks.

Low	Moderate	High
Stable, known customer base.	Customer base increasing due to branching, merger, or acquisition.	A large and growing customer base in a wide and diverse geographic area.
No electronic banking (e-banking) or the web site is informational or non-transactional.	The bank is beginning e- banking and offers limited products and services.	The bank offers a wide array of e-banking products and services (i.e., account transfers, e-bill payment, or accounts opened via the Internet).

On the basis of inform-ation received from the BSA- reporting datab-ase, there are few or no large currency or struct-ured transactions.	On the basis of information received from the BSA-reporting database, there is a moderate volume of large currency or structured transactions.	On the basis of information received from the BSA-repor-ting database, there is a signif-icant volume of large currency or structured transactions.
Identified a few high-risk customers and businesses.	Identified a moderate number of high-risk customers and businesses. These may include check cashers, convenience stores, money transmitters, casas de cambio, import or export companies, offshore corporations, politically expo-sed persons (PEPs), nonres-ident aliens (NRAs), and foreign individuals.	Identified a large number of high-risk customers and busin-esses. These may include check cashers, convenience stores, money transmitters, casas de cambio, import or export com-panies, offshore corporations, PEPs, NRAs, and foreign individuals.
Low	**Moderate**	**High**
No foreign correspondent financial institution acc-ounts. The bank does not engage in pouch activities, offer specialuse accounts, or offer paya-ble through accounts (PTAs), or provide U.S. dollar draft services.	The bank has a few foreign correspondent financial institution accounts, but typically with financial institute-ions with adequate AML policies and procedures from low-risk countries, and minimal pouch activities, special-use accounts, PTAs, or U.S. dollar draft services.	The bank maintains a large number of foreign correspondent financial instit-ution accounts with financial institutions with inadequate AML policies and procedures, particularly those located in high-risk jurisdictions, or offers substantial pouch activities, special-use accounts, PTAs, or U.S. dollar draft services.
The bank offers limited or no private banking services or trust and asset management products or services.	The bank offers limited domestic private banking services or trust and asset management products or services over which the bank has investment discretion. Strategic plan may be to increase trust business.	The bank offers significant domestic and international private banking or trust and asset management products or services. Private banking or trust and asset management services are growing. Products offered include investment management services, and trust accounts are predominantly nondiscretionary versus where the bank has full investment discretion.
Few international accounts or very low volume of currency activity in the accounts.	Moderate level of internat-ional accounts with unexpla-ined currency activity.	Large number of international accounts with unexplained currency activity.
A limited number of funds transfers for cust-omers, noncustomers, limited third-party transactions, and no foreign funds transfers.	A moderate number of funds transfers. A few international funds transfers from personal or business accounts with typically low-risk countries.	A large number of noncustomer funds transfer transactions and payable upon proper identific-ation (PUPID) transactions. Frequent funds from personal or business accounts to or from high-risk jurisdictions, and financial secrecy havens or jurisdictions.

Appendix J (Continued)		
The bank is not located in a High Intensity Drug Trafficking Area (HIDTA)[1] or High Intensity Financial Crime Area (HIFCA). No fund transfers or account relationships involve HIDTAs or HIFCAs.	The bank is located in an HIDTA or an HIFCA. Bank has some fund transfers or account relationships that involve HIDTAs or HIFCAs.	Bank is located in an HIDTA and an HIFCA. A large number of fund transfers or account relationships involve HIDTAs or HIFCAs.
Low	**Moderate**	**High**
No transactions with high-risk geographic locations.	Minimal transactions with high-risk geographic locations.	Significant volume of transa-ctions with high-risk geographic locations.
Low turnover of key personnel or frontline personnel (i.e., customer service representatives, tellers, or other branch personnel).	Low turnover of key person-nel, but frontline personnel in branches may have changed.	High turnover, especially in key personnel positions.

APPENDIX K. CUSTOMER RISK VERSUS DUE DILIGENCE AND SUSPICIOUS ACTIVITY MONITORING

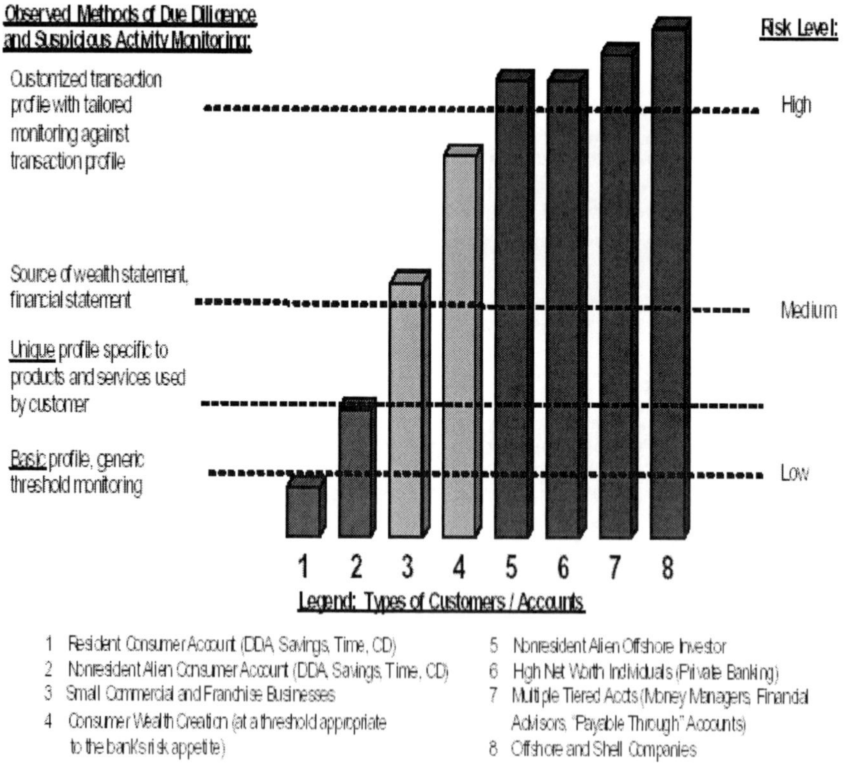

Customer Risk versus Due Diligence and Suspicious Activity Monitoring

Certain customer relationships may pose a higher risk than others. This chart provides an example of how a bank may stratify the risk profile of its customers (see legend and risk levels). Because the nature of the customer is only one variable in assessing risk, this simplified chart is for illustration purposes only. The chart also illustrates the progressive methods of due diligence and suspicious activvity monitoring systems that banks may deploy as the risk level rises. (See Observed Methods, below.)

Appendix L. SAR Quality Guidance

The following information is provided as guidance. Refer to FinCEN's "Guidance on Preparing a Complete & Sufficient Suspicious Activity Report Narrative" (November 2003) for original text, which can be found at www.fincen.gov.

Often Suspicious Activity Reports (SARs) have been instrumental in enabling law enforcement to initiate or supplement major money laundering or terrorist financing investigations and other criminal cases. Information provided in SAR forms also allows FinCEN and the federal banking agencies to identify emerging trends and patterns associated with financial crimes. The information about those trends and patterns is vital to law enforcement agencies and provides valuable feedback to financial institutions.

Banks must file SAR forms that are complete, sufficient, and timely. Unfortunately, some banks file SAR forms that contain incomplete, incorrect, or disorganized narratives, making further analysis difficult, if not impossible. Some SAR forms are submitted with blank narratives. Because the SAR narrative serves as the only free text area for summarizing suspicious activity, the narrative section is "critical." The care with which the narrative is written may make the difference in whether or not the described conduct and its possible criminal nature are clearly understood by law enforcement, and thus a failure to adequately describe the factors making a transaction or activity suspicious undermines the purpose of the SAR.

The SAR form should include any information readily available to the filing bank obtained through the account opening process and due diligence efforts. In general, a SAR narrative should identify the five essential elements of information (who? what? when? where? and why?) for the suspicious activity being reported. The method of operation (or how?) is also important and should be included in the narrative.

Who Is Conducting the Suspicious Activity?

While one section of the SAR form calls for specific suspect information, the narrative should be used to further describe the suspect or suspects, including occupation, position or title within the business, the nature of the suspect's business (or businesses), and any other information and identification numbers associated with the suspects.

What Instruments or Mechanisms Are being Used to Facilitate the Suspect Transactions?

A list of instruments or mechanisms that may be used in suspicious activity includes, but is not limited to, funds transfers, letters of credit and other trade instruments, correspondent accounts, casinos, structuring, shell companies, bonds or notes, stocks, mutual funds, insurance policies, traveler's checks, bank drafts, money orders, credit or debit cards, stored value cards, and digital currency business services. The SAR narrative should list the instruments or mechanisms used in the reported suspicious activity. If a SAR narrative summarizes the flow of funds, the narrative should always include the source of the funds (origination) and the use, destination, or beneficiary of the funds.

When Did the suspicious Activity Take Place?

If the activity takes place over a period of time, indicate the date when the suspicious activity was first noticed and describe the duration of the activity. When possible, in order to better track the flow of funds, individual dates and amounts of transactions should be included in the narrative rather than only the aggregated amount.

Where Did the Suspicious Activity Take Place?

The narrative should indicate if multiple offices of a single bank were involved in the suspicious activity and provide the addresses of those locations. The narrative should also specify if the suspected activity or transactions involves a foreign jurisdiction.

Why Does the Filer Think the Activity Is Suspicious?

The SAR should describe, as fully as possible, why the activity or transaction is unusual for the customer, considering the types of products and services offered by the filing bank's industry, and drawing any applicable contrasts with the nature and normally expected activities of similar customers.

How Did the Suspicious Activity Occur?

The narrative should describe the "modus operandi" or the method of operation of the subject conducting the suspicious activity. In a concise, accurate, and logical manner, the narrative should describe how the suspect transaction or pattern of transactions was committed. For example, if what appears to be structuring of currency deposits is matched with outgoing funds transfers from the accounts, the SAR narrative should include information about both the structuring and outbound transfers (including dates, destinations, amounts, accounts, frequency, and beneficiaries of the funds transfers).

A Bank Should Not Include Any Supporting Documentation with a Filed SAR Nor Use the Terms "See Attached" in the SAR narrative

When SAR forms are received at the IRS Detroit Computing Center, only information that is in an explicit, narrative format is keypunched; thus tables, spreadsheets, or other attachments are not entered into the BSA-reporting database. Banks should keep any supporting documentation in their records for five years so that this information is available to law enforcement upon request.

APPENDIX M. QUANTITY OF RISK MATRIX —OFAC PROCEDURES

Examiners should use the following matrix, as appropriate, when assessing a bank's risk of encountering an OFAC issue.

Low	Moderate	High
Stable, well-known custom-mer base in a localized environment.	Customer base changing due to branching, merger, or acquisition in the domestic market.	A large, fluctuating client base in an international environment.
Few high-risk customers; these may include nonresident aliens, foreign individuals (including accounts with U.S. powers of attorney), and foreign commercial customers.	A moderate number of high- risk customers.	A large number of high-risk customers.
No overseas branches and no correspondent accounts with foreign banks.	Overseas branches or correspondent accounts with foreign banks.	Overseas branches or multiple correspondent accounts with foreign banks.
No electronic banking (e-banking) services offered, or products available are purely informational or non-transactional.	The bank offers limited e-banking products and services.	The bank offers a wide array of e-banking products and services (i.e., account trans-fers, e-bill payment, or acco-unts opened via the Internet).
Limited number of funds tran-sfers for customers and nonc-ustomers, limited third- party transactions, and no interna-tional funds transfers.	A moderate number of funds transfers, mostly for customers. Possibly, a few international funds transfers from personal or business accounts.	A high number of customer and noncustomer funds tran-sfers, including international funds transfers.
Low	**Moderate**	**High**
No other types of international transactions, such as trade finance, cross- border ACH, and management of sovereign debt.	Limited other types of international transactions.	A high number of other types of international transactions.

Appendix M (continued)		
No history of OFAC actions. No evidence of apparent violation or circumstances that might lead to a violation.	A small number of recent actions (i.e., actions within the last five years) by OFAC, including not-ice letters, or civil money penalties, with evidence that the bank addressed the issues and is not at risk of similar violations in the future.	Multiple recent actions by OFAC, where the bank has not addressed the issues, thus leading to an increased risk of the bank undertaking similar violations in the future.

APPENDIX N. PRIVATE BANKING — COMMONSTRUCTURE

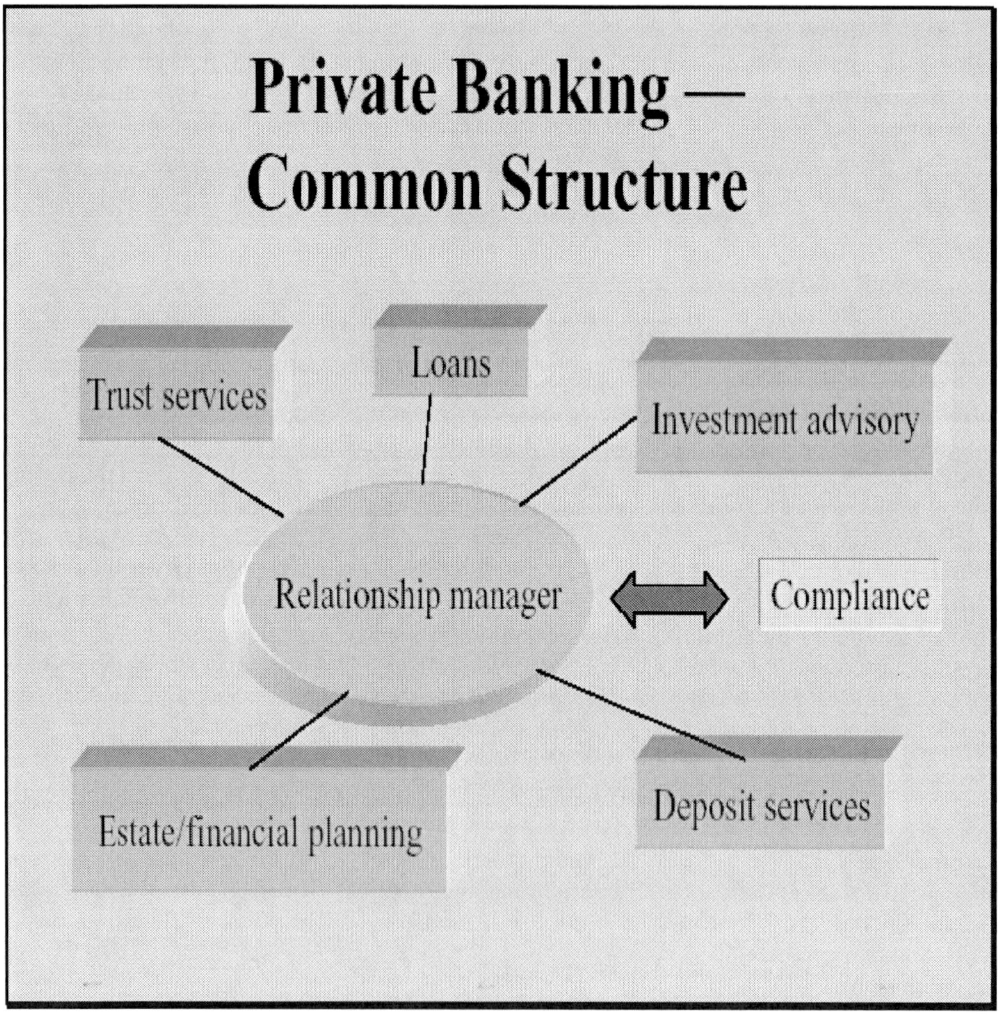

APPENDIX O. EXAMINER TOOLS FOR TRANSACTION TESTING

Currency Transaction Reporting and Suspicious Activity Reporting

If the bank does not have preset filtering reports for currency transaction reporting and the identification of suspicious currency transactions, the examiner should consider requesting a custom report. For example, a report could be generated with the following criteria: currency transactions of $7,000 or higher (in and out) for the preceding period (*to be determined by the examiner*) before the date of examination. The time period covered and the transaction amounts may be adjusted as determined by the examiner. The report should also capture:

- The customer information file (CIF) number, if available, or Social Security number (SSN)/taxpayer identification number (TIN).
- The date, amount, and account number of each transaction.
- The teller and branch or other applicable identifying information.

This data should be prepared in an electronic spreadsheet or database format to facilitate the sorting of the data. The data can be sorted in a number of different criteria (e.g., by branch, by teller, by SSN/TIN, or CIF number, if available). Analysis of this information should enable the examiner to determine whether Currency Transaction Reports (CTRs) and Suspicious Activity Reports (SARs) have been appropriately filed.

Funds Transfer Monitoring

If the bank does not have preset filtering reports for funds transfer recordkeeping and the identification of suspicious transactions, the examiner should consider requesting a custom report. The examiner may consider requesting that the bank provide a report from its funds transfer systems that identifies all funds transfers (in and out) for a time period determined by the examiner. The report should also capture:

- The customer's full name, country of residence, SSN/TIN, and BSA/AML risk rating, if applicable.
- The date, amount, transaction type, and account number of each transaction.
- The originator's name, country, financial institution, and account number.
- The beneficiary's name, country, financial institution, and account number.

The bank should provide a list of bank internal codes necessary to fully identify the account type, BSA/AML risk rating, country, transaction type, bank number, account number, and any other codes on the electronic reports. The list should be sorted to identify those accounts that do not contain sufficient originator or beneficiary information. Missing information may indicate funds transfer monitoring deficiencies. A large number of transfers or those of high-dollar amounts to and from high-risk jurisdictions or involving parties that do not appear likely to be involved in such transactions may indicate the need for additional scrutiny.

Adequacy of Deposit Account Information and Trust and Asset Management Account Information

This test is designed to ensure that the bank is in compliance with the Customer Identification Program (CIP) regulatory requirements and to test the adequacy of the bank's customer due diligence (CDD) policies, procedures, and processes.

The examiner should request an electronic list (spreadsheet or database) of all deposit accounts and trust/asset management accounts as of the date of examination. The balances should be reconciled to the general ledger. The report should also capture:

- The customer's full name, date of birth, address, country of residence, SSN/TIN, and BSA/AML risk rating, if applicable.
- The date the account was opened.
- The average daily balance (during the review period) and balance of the account as of the examination date.

The bank should provide a list of bank internal codes necessary to fully identify the account type, BSA/AML risk rating, country, transaction type, branch number, teller number, and any other codes found on the electronic reports. The list should be sorted to identify those accounts that do not contain sufficient information.

Testing of Currency-Shipment Logs for Unusual Activity

Review all, or a sample, of the bank's currency-shipment logs for significant aberrations or unusual patterns of currency-shipment activity. Examiners may also consider reviewing the FDIC Summary of Deposits (SOD) data for unusual trends in branch deposit growth.

Assess whether shipment levels and the frequency of shipments appear commensurate with the expected bank and branch activity levels. This assessment should include transactions to and from the central currency vault and the branches. Unusual activity warranting further research may include significant exchanges of small-denomination bills for large-denomination bills and significant requests for large bills.

Nonresident Aliens and Foreign Individuals

An effective method to identify and review the level of the bank's nonresident aliens (NRAs), foreign individuals, and offshore corporations is by obtaining management information systems (MIS) reports that provide no TINs or accountholders with individual taxpayer identification numbers (ITINs). The report should capture:

- The customer's full name, date of birth, address, country of residence, and SSN/TIN.
- The date the account was opened.
- The average daily balance and balance of the account as of the examination date.

This data should be prepared in an electronic spreadsheet or database format to facilitate the sorting of the data. The bank should provide a list of bank internal codes necessary to fully identify the information on the spreadsheet. This information can be used to assess whether the amount of NRAs and foreign individuals provide heightened risk to the bank by determining the aggregate average daily balance, the account types, and countries in which the bank is exposed.

Funds Flow Reports

Examiners can review this information to identify customers with a high velocity of funds flow and those with unusual activity. A velocity of funds report reflects the total debits and credits flowing through a particular account over a specific period (e.g., 30 days). The electronic reports should capture:

- Name of customer.
- Account number.
- The date of transaction.
- The dollar amount of payments (debits).
- The dollar amount of receipts (credits).
- The average balance of the account.
- The type of account.

This data should be prepared in an electronic spreadsheet or database format to facilitate the sorting of the data. This chapter can be used to identify customer accounts with substantial funds flow relative to other accounts.

Appendix P. BSA Record Retention Requirements

This appendix is provided as a summary listing. For comprehensive and current record retention requirements, refer to U.S. Treasury/FinCEN regulations found at 31 CFR 103.

Five-Year Retention for Records as Specified Below

The BSA establishes recordkeeping requirements related to various types of records including: customer accounts (e.g., loan, deposit, or trust), BSA filing requirements, and records that document a bank's compliance with the BSA. In general, the BSA requires that a bank maintain most records for at least five years. These records can be maintained in many forms including original, microfilm, electronic, copy, or a reproduction. A bank is not required to keep a separate system of records for each of the BSA requirements; however, a bank must maintain all records in a way that makes them accessible in a reasonable period of time.

The records related to the transactions discussed below must be retained by a bank for five years. However, as noted below, the records related to the identity of a bank customer must be maintained for five years after the account (e.g., loan, deposit, or trust) is closed. Additionally, on a case-by-case basis (e.g., U.S. Treasury Department Order, or law enforcement investigation), a bank may be ordered or requested to maintain some of these records for longer periods.

Extension of Credit in Excess of $10,000 (not secured by real property)

This record shall contain:

- Name of borrower.
- Address of borrower.
- Amount of credit extended.
- Nature or purpose of loan.
- Date of loan.

International Transactions in Excess of $10,000

A record of any request made or instructions received or given regarding a transfer of currency or other monetary instruments, checks, funds, investment securities, or credit greater than $10,000 to or from any person, account, or place outside the United States.

Signature Cards

A record of each grant of signature authority over each deposit account.

Account Statements

A statement, ledger card, or other record on each deposit account showing each transaction in, or with respect to, that account.

Checks in Excess of $100

Each check, draft, or money order drawn on the bank or issued and payable by it that is in excess of $100.

Deposits in Excess of $100

Each deposit slip or credit ticket reflecting a transaction in excess of $100 or the equivalent record for direct deposit or other funds transfer deposit transactions. The slip or ticket must record the amount of any currency involved.

Records to Reconstruct Demand Deposit Accounts

Records prepared or received by the bank in the ordinary course of business, which would be needed to reconstruct a transaction account and to trace a check in excess of $100 deposited in a demand deposit account through its domestic processing system or to supply a description of a deposited check in excess of $100.

Certificates of Deposit Purchased or Presented

This record shall contain:

- Name of customer (purchaser or presenter).
- Address of customer.
- Taxpayer identification number (TIN) of customer.
- Description of the certificate of deposit.
- Notation of the method of payment if purchased.
- Date of transaction.

Purchase of Monetary Instruments of $3,000 or More

A bank must maintain a record of each bank check or draft, cashier's check, money order, or traveler's check for $3,000 or more in currency.

If the purchaser has a deposit account with the bank, this record shall contain:

- Name of purchaser.
- Date of purchase
- Type(s) of instrument purchased.
- Amount in dollars of each of the instrument(s) purchased.
- Serial number(s) of the instrument(s) purchased.

If the purchaser does not have a deposit account with the bank, this record shall contain:

- Name of purchaser.
- Address of purchasers.
- Social security number of purchaser or alien identification number.
- Date of birth of purchaser.
- Date of purchase
- Type(s) of instrument purchased.
- Amount in dollars of each of the instrument(s) purchased.
- Serial number(s) of the instrument(s) purchased.
- Description of document or method used to verify the name and address of the purchaser (e.g., state of issuance and number driver's license).

Funds Transfers of $3,000 or More

A bank's BSA recordkeeping requirements with respect to funds transfer vary based upon the role of a bank with respect to the funds transfer.

Bank acting as an originator's bank. For each payment order that a bank accepts as the originator's bank, the bank must obtain and retain a record of the following information:

- Name and address of originator.
- Amount of the payment order.

- Execution date of the payment order.
- Any payment instruction received from the originator with the payment order.
- Identity of the beneficiary's bank.
- As many of the following items as are received with the payment order:
  - Name and address of the beneficiary.
  - Account number of the beneficiary.
  - Any other specific identifier of the beneficiary.
- For each payment order that a bank accepts for an originator that is not an established customer of the bank, in addition to the information listed above, a bank must obtain additional information as required under 31 CFR 103.33(e)(2).

Bank acting as an intermediary bank or a beneficiary's bank. For each payment order that a bank accepts as an intermediary bank, or a beneficiary's bank, the bank must retain a record of the payment order.

- For each payment order that a bank accepts for a beneficiary that is not an established customer of the bank, the bank must also obtain additional information as required under 31 CFR 103.33(e)(3).

Exceptions. The BSA does not require a bank to maintain records for the following types of funds transfers: (1) funds transfers where both the originator and beneficiary are the same person and that originator's bank and the beneficiary's bank are the same bank; and (2) transfers where the originator and beneficiary are any of the following:

- A bank.
- A wholly owned domestic subsidiary of a bank chartered in the United States.
- A broker or dealer in securities.
- A wholly owned domestic subsidiary of a broker or dealer in securities.
- The United States.
- A state or local government.
- A federal, state, or local government agency or instrumentality.

Taxpayer Identification Number

A record of the TIN of *any* customer opening an account. In cases of joint accounts, information on a person with a financial interest must be maintained. (If the person is a nonresident alien (NRA), record the passport number or a description of some other government document used to verify identity.) This information must be recorded within 30 days of the date the transaction occurs. In the event a bank is unable to secure the information, it must maintain a list containing the names, addresses, and account numbers of those members for whom it has been unable to secure the information.

Exceptions. A bank does not need to maintain TIN for accounts or transactions with the following:

- Agencies and instrumentalities of federal, state, local, or foreign governments.

- Judges, public officials, or clerks of courts of record as custodians of funds in controversy or under the control of the court.
- Certain aliens as specified in 31 CFR 103.34(a)(3)(iii-vi).
- Certain tax exempt organizations and units of tax-exempt organizations (31 CFR 103.34(a)(3)(vii)).
- A person under 18 years of age with respect to an account opened as a part of a school thrift savings program, provided the annual dividend is less than $10.
- A person opening a Christmas club, vacation club, and similar installment savings programs, provided the annual dividend is less than $10.
- NRAs who are not engaged in a trade or business in the United States.

Suspicious Activity Report and Supporting Documentation

A bank must maintain a record of any Suspicious Activity Report (SAR) filed and the original or business record equivalent of any supporting documentation for a period of five years from the date of filing.

Currency Transaction Report

A bank must maintain a record of all Currency Transaction Reports (CTRs) for a period of five years from the date of filing.

Designation of Exempt Person

A bank must maintain a record of all designation of persons exempt from CTR reporting as filed with the Treasury (i.e., FinCEN Form 110) for a period of five years from the designation date.

Customer Identification Program

A bank must maintain a record of all information it obtains under its procedures for implementing its Customer Identification Program (CIP). At a minimum, these records must include the following:

- All identifying information about a customer (e.g., name, date of birth, address, and TIN).
- A description of the document that the bank relied upon to identity of the customer.
- A description of the nondocumentary methods and results of any measures the bank took to verify the identity of the customer.
- A description of the bank's resolution of any substantive discrepancy discovered when verifying the identifying information obtained.

A bank must retain the identifying information about a customer for a period of five years after the date the account is closed, or in the case of credit card accounts, five years after the account becomes closed or dormant.

A bank must retain the information relied on, methods used to verify identity, and resolution of discrepancies for a period of five years after the record is made.

These BSA recordkeeping requirements are independent of and in addition to requirements to file reports for certain types of transactions. For the meaning of the BSA terms, see 31 CFR 103.11.

APPENDIX Q: ACRONYMS

Acronym or abbreviation	**Full name**
ACH	Automated Clearing House
AML	Anti-Money Laundering
ANPR	Advance Notice of Proposed Rulemaking
APO	Army Post Office
ATM	Automated Teller Machine
APT	Asset Protection Trust
BCBS	Basel Committee on Banking Supervision
BHC	Bank Holding Company
BIS	Bank for International Settlements
BSA	Bank Secrecy Act
CBQS	Currency and Banking Query System
CBRS	Currency and Banking Retrieval System
CDD	Customer Due Diligence
CFR	Code of Federal Regulations
CHIPS	Clearing House Interbank Payments System
CIF	Customer Information File
CIP	Customer Identification Program
CMIR	Report of International Transportation of Currency or Monetary Instruments
CTR	Currency Transaction Report
DCN	Document Control Number
E-cash	Electronic Cash
EFT	Electronic Funds Transfer
EFTA	Electronic Funds Transfer Act
EIC	Examiner in charge
EIN	Employer Identification Number
EPN	Electronic Payments Network
ERISA	Employee Retirement Income Security Act of 1974
FAQ	Frequently Asked Question
FATF	Financial Action Task Force on Money Laundering
FBAR	Report of Foreign Bank and Financial Accounts
FBI	Federal Bureau of Investigation
FDI Act	Federal Deposit Insurance Act
FDIC	Federal Deposit Insurance Corporation

FFIEC	Federal Financial Institutions Examination Council
FIL	Financial Institution Letters
FinCEN	Financial Crimes Enforcement Network
FPO	Fleet Post Office
HIDTA	High Intensity Drug Trafficking Area
HIFCA	High Intensity Financial Crime Area
IAIS	International Association of Insurance Supervisors
IBC	International Business Corporation
IMF	International Monetary Fund
INCSR	International Narcotics Control Strategy Report
IOLTA	Interest on Lawyers' Trust Accounts
IOSCO	International Organization of Securities Commissions
IP	Internet Protocol
IRA	Individual Retirement Account
IRS	Internal Revenue Service
ISO	Independent Sales Organization
ITIN	Individual Taxpayer Identification Number
IVTS	Informal Value Transfer Systems
KYC	Know Your Customer
LCU	Letters to Credit Unions
MIS	Management Information Systems
MLSA	Money Laundering Suppression Act of 1994
MLTA	Money Laundering Threat Assessment
MSB	Money Services Business
NACHA	National Automated Clearing House Association — The Electronic Payments Association
NAICS	North American Industry Classification System
NASD	National Association of Securities Dealers
NASDAQ	National Association of Securities Dealers Automated Quotation Systems
NBFI	Non-Bank Financial Institutions
NCCT	Non-Cooperative Countries and Territories
NCUA	National Credit Union Administration
NDIP	Nondeposit Investment Products
NGO	Non-Governmental Organization
NIS	Nominee Incorporation Services
NRA	Nonresident Alien
NSF	Nonsufficient Funds
NSL	National Security Letter
NYCH	New York Clearing House Association, L.L.C.
OCC	Office of the Comptroller of the Currency
ONDCP	The Office of National Drug Control Policy
ODFI	Originating Depository Financial Institution
OFAC	Office of Foreign Assets Control
OFC	Offshore Financial Center
OTS	Office of Thrift Supervision

PEP	Politically Exposed Person
PIC	Private Investment Company
POS	Point-of-Sale
PTA	Payable Through Account
PUPID	Payable Upon Proper Identification
RA	Regulatory Alerts
RDFI	Receiving Depository Financial Institution
ROE	Report of Examination
SAR	Suspicious Activity Report
SDN	Specially Designated Nationals or Blocked Persons
SEC	U.S. Securities and Exchange Commission
SOD	Summary of Deposits
SSN	Social Security Number
SWIFT	Society for Worldwide Interbank Financial Telecommunication
TD F	Treasury Department Form
TIN	Taxpayer Identification Number
TPSP	Third-Party Service Provider
UBPR	Uniform Bank Performance Report
USA PATRIOT Act (Patriot Act)	Uniting and Strengthening America by Providing Appropriate Tools Required to Intercept and Obstruct Terrorism Act of 2001
USC	United States Code

INDEX

A

B

C

K

L

M

N

O

P

Q

R

S

T

U

V

W